Vice Patrol

Vice Patrol

Cops, Courts, and the Struggle over Urban Gay Life before Stonewall

ANNA LVOVSKY

The University of Chicago Press
Chicago and London

The University of Chicago Press, Chicago 60637
The University of Chicago Press, Ltd., London
© 2021 by Anna Lvovsky
Published 2021
Printed in the United States of America

30 29 28 27 26 25 24 23 22 21   1 2 3 4 5

ISBN-13: 978-0-226-76964-6 (cloth)
ISBN-13: 978-0-226-76978-3 (paper)
ISBN-13: 978-0-226-76981-3 (e-book)
DOI: https://doi.org/10.7208/chicago/9780226769813.001.0001

Library of Congress Cataloging-in-Publication Data

Names: Lvovsky, Anna, author.
Title: Vice patrol : cops, courts, and the struggle over urban gay life before
    Stonewall / Anna Lvovsky.
Other titles: Cops, courts, and the struggle over urban gay life before Stonewall
Description: Chicago ; London : University of Chicago Press, 2021. |
    Includes bibliographical references and index.
Identifiers: LCCN 2020045745 | ISBN 9780226769646 (cloth) |
    ISBN 9780226769783 (paperback) | ISBN 9780226769813 (ebook)
Subjects: LCSH: Male homosexuality—United States—History—20th century. |
    Gays—Legal status, laws, etc.—United States. | Vice control—United States—
    History—20th century. | Law enforcement—United States—History—
    20th century.
Classification: LCC HQ76.3.U6 L96 2021 | DDC 306.76/60973—dc23
LC record available at https://lccn.loc.gov/2020045745

CONTENTS

ILLUSTRATIONS

0.1. A plainclothes decoy with the Los Angeles Police Department waiting on a street corner in 1964. Photograph by Bill Eppridge © Estate of Bill Eppridge.

Introduction

In the spring of 1957, a researcher in Detroit interviewed a judge on the Recorder's Court about the local vice squad's undercover campaigns: the practice of plainclothes officers idling in bars, parks, and bathrooms, hoping to entice suspected gay men into making sexual advances. The judge, the researcher reported, grew red in the face. The vice squad's tactics, he decried, were "atrocious," "miserable," "horrible," and "appalling."[1]

Some years later, a bar owner accused by New Jersey's Division of Alcoholic Beverage Control of catering to gay patrons in his Newark tavern found himself in a surprising disagreement with the agency. Hoping to disprove the charge that he had knowingly served gay customers, the owner called a special witness, a respected psychiatrist, to explain the difficulties of identifying anyone "diseased with the sickness of homosexuality," when the liquor board's own prosecuting attorney leaped in to object. "Counsel takes it for granted that homosexuality is a disease," Edward F. Ambrose protested. "There is not a human man that can give an [expert] opinion on that point."[2]

Meanwhile, two thousand miles away, the Los Angeles Police Department (LAPD) was struggling with a different type of special insight into queer life. Charged with the task of infiltrating an increasingly complex gay world, the department had begun to offer all new vice officers a formal course of instruction on how to dress, act, and talk in order to blend into the city's cruising culture—as well as, in theory, what *not* to do to avoid "public criticism or embarrassment." Perhaps that advice was embarrassing in its own right, because after an excerpt from the department's instructional materials leaked to the press in the summer of 1964, the LAPD promptly denied the manual's existence. The idea that vice officers received deliberate training on the customs of the gay world, it insisted, reflected a simple "misunderstanding."[3]

The law's confrontations with gay life in the twentieth century are a core part of any history of sexuality in the United States. Over the course of that century, legislatures across the country enacted and reaffirmed a host of laws aimed at suppressing queer communities, from sodomy statutes to antisolicitation laws to regulations against gay-friendly bars. Police officers and liquor investigators, in turn, developed a range of intrusive tactics to enforce those laws, spending late nights at bars watching for potential violations, flirting with men in parks to entice propositions, crouching behind peepholes and one-way mirrors in public bathrooms to catch sexual encounters in the act. All this aside from the less formal abuses and indignities, the bouts of harassment and bursts of violence that hung over the state's attempts to repress what it regarded as a deviant social practice.

This story may sound familiar. It is a part of essentially every history of gay life in the United States, a key backdrop for the many rightfully celebrated tales of community building and political empowerment unearthed by scholars over the past several decades. Most writers, however, have kept that story on the peripheries of their accounts, focusing more on the gay community's responses to legal repression than on the operation of the law itself. Scholars who have examined the regulation of gay life have looked primarily at the federal government and the military, and especially at the formulation of legal policy. Few have delved into the daily realities of urban policing—the types of interactions that most commonly defined gay individuals' encounters with state power in the mid-twentieth century.[4]

This book brings that story into the center, tracing the shifting priorities, investigative tactics, and legal disputes that shaped the gay world's confrontations with the law. And it reveals that the typical account of antihomosexual policing, as a tale of the state's painful, ultimately unsuccessful attempts to repress nonnormative social practices, is both true and incomplete. As the anecdotes offered above suggest, the project of policing gay life at midcentury was not simply a contest over the limits of permissible sexual practice in the United States, or even over acceptable social conduct in the public sphere. It was also the site of an institutional struggle over the boundaries of the criminal justice system itself: the wisdom of the criminal law, the limits of proper policing, and the power of the courts to intervene in either. At the same time, it was the site of an epistemic debate over the very meaning of sexual difference: what homosexual desire meant, who homosexual people were, and who ultimately had the authority to answer those questions. Two sets of controversies that were, it turned out, often intertwined.

Revisiting the vice squads' antihomosexual campaigns with these controversies in mind makes for a complex dive into a dark chapter of American history, one that is frequently heartbreaking and appalling but also full of resistance, of surprising alliances and remarkable legal gambits, of courage, perseverance, and humor in the shadow of the law. That story also has much to teach us about the history of sexuality and the administration of the law more broadly. At heart, this book makes three interrelated claims. First, it contends that the project of antigay policing in the United States was, far from a monolithic or universally embraced endeavor, a site of profound contestation and struggle among the different arms of the criminal justice system, reflecting a range of political, institutional, and pragmatic disputes well beyond the law's proper treatment of sexual difference. Second, it argues that, at a time when public and professional authorities espoused a range of views about the nature of same-sex practices, legal battles over antigay policing provided a powerful arena for shaping the standing and ultimate legacy of those competing accounts—both a site that brought the weight of the law to bear in choosing which bodies of knowledge were deemed authoritative and one in which the impact of those bodies of knowledge was often unexpected. Finally, it proposes that, amid these warring accounts of both the value of vice enforcement and the nature of homosexuality itself, the continuing success of the police's campaigns rested in key part on the coexistence, within the legal system, of multiple conflicting understandings of gay life, dividing how vice officers and judges understood the social practices they regulated. The rights and freedoms of gay men and women at midcentury, that is, did not simply reflect the legal system's internal disputes about the merits of antihomosexual policing. They often reflected its deeper disagreements about the very thing being policed.

The remainder of this introduction begins to develop these claims. Taken together, I hope, they may enrich our understandings of both the regulation of queer life in the twentieth century and disputes about police power that have continued to this day.

Vice Patrol and the Courts

This book centers on the mid-twentieth century, tracing an arc stretching roughly from the 1930s through the 1960s, when the regulation of gay life loomed especially large on the agendas of local police forces. It focuses on three sites of antihomosexual enforcement: liquor board proceedings against gay-friendly bars, plainclothes campaigns to entice sexual overtures, and the use of clandestine surveillance to uncover sexual acts in public bathrooms. These are not the only sites where gay communities felt the weight of the law in the United States. This book does not delve, for instance, into the censorship of homophile publications, the use of uniformed officers to patrol cruising sites, or the purge of queer employees from the federal government, though these stories hang around the edges of the narrative. It looks, instead, at licensing disputes, decoy enforcement, and clandestine surveillance as those fields that drew the most sustained use of police resources, left behind the richest records, and most commonly brought the police, and gay men themselves, into court.[5]

The policing of same-sex activities in the United States, of course, did not begin in the twentieth century. On the grandest scale, that project was just the latest chapter in a long history of repression in Anglo-American societies, grounded in a repudiation of homosexual practices as an offense to the natural order, an affront to established domestic structures, not least an outrageous rejection of the norms and privileges of proper manhood. Taking their cue from England, the American colonies typically recognized sodomy as a crime at common law: a violation of the laws of either God or nature, as the local courts preferred. By the late nineteenth century, most states had adopted statutes against sodomy, typically designated simply as the abominable "crime against nature."[6]

Enforcing those laws was a separate matter. Well through the nineteenth century, convictions under the sodomy statutes remained rare, frustrated by the innate evidentiary difficulties of prosecuting acts pursued in private between willing participants. Even when men seeking sex with other men claimed a more public presence in American cities, not least through the practice of prostitution in commercial districts, their activities rarely drew sustained police attention. By the early twentieth century, queer men—most notably the cheekily flamboyant "fairies" who advertised their difference through their effeminate clothing and demeanor—emerged as staples of working-class neighborhoods in New York, Chicago, and San Francisco. Those men certainly did not escape regulation, risking arrest when they ventured beyond their neighborhoods in drag or engaged in sexual acts in public. But they were hardly high on the police agenda.[7]

By the mid-twentieth century, the law's relationship with queer life had begun to shift. The reasons for this change were many, and they are difficult to disentangle. One catalyst traced back to the late 1930s, when a rash of publicized sex crimes spawned a panic about degeneracy in the nation's cities. The reports almost invariably involved morbid attacks on young girls, but the ensuing outcry against "sex fiends," fanned by enforcement officials like J. Edgar Hoover, often conflated gay men with a darker category of criminal. The shifting demographics of the city hardly helped. As a generation of soldiers flocked to urban centers following World War II, the country's burgeoning queer populations, with their attendant bars and cruising grounds, struck some citizens and politicians as a blight on the orderly city. Other observers discerned a more particular risk. In the winter of 1950, Senate Republicans eager to discredit the Democratic Truman administration embarked on a vocal campaign against homosexual employees in the federal government. At a time when major newspapers still typically avoided overt discussions of homosexuality, the "Lavender Scare" sparked a broad debate about the purported security risks posed by gay men and women, giving newfound significance to the police's campaigns.[8]

This rising demand for vice enforcement was accompanied by the state's growing capacity to perform it. Reflecting both the public concern with sex crimes and more incidental administrative developments, the twentieth century witnessed the rise of a host of novel enforcement agencies whose purview included the key sites of gay life. The demise of Prohibition ushered in a spate of specialized liquor boards, tasked with ensuring the orderly operation of bars and taverns. A campaign to professionalize the municipal police led most large and midsized departments by the early 1950s to form vice or morals squads focusing on sex-related offenses. Charged with suppressing the public manifestations of queer life, these units also boasted an expanding legal arsenal for doing so. The most prominent addition was a rash of "sexual psychopath" laws enacted in response to the sex-crime panic, which often subjected men accused of illicit sexual practices, from rape and child molestation to consensual sodomy, to indefinite confinement and involuntary treatment. More central to the vice squads' daily operations were a number of lower-profile developments, including liquor laws prohibiting bars from serving gay patrons, sodomy laws expanded to cover oral sex, and disorderly conduct and antisolicitation provisions that empowered policemen to arrest men who so much as sought sexual partners in public.[9]

To many of its victims, this looming police apparatus felt, not unreasonably, like a concerted encroachment on the civil liberties of queer communities. As one defense attorney in Los Angeles put it, his clients tended to see police officers, prosecutors, and courts as the component pieces of one broad edifice of state repression, part of a legal "machinery aligned against [them]." In many cases, indeed, that impression was likely true. Liquor boards, in particular, typically investigated and adjudicated charges under the auspices of a single regulatory agency, and they tended to follow a consistent agenda, minimally sympathetic to bar owners who served gay crowds.[10]

The enforcement of the criminal law, however, fell to multiple arms of the legal system, each driven by its own personalities and institutional pressures. And that project often inspired greater ambivalence, both among police officers themselves, who sometimes resented the unsavory demands of vice work, and especially among the courts. Driven by a combination of personal principle and pragmatic self-interest, trial judges lodged a range of objections against the vice squads' campaigns, from the excessiveness of statutory penalties to the waste of public resources on what they saw as petty charges to, in some cases, genuine sympathy for the men prosecuted for consensual sexual conduct—not least, the white, middle-class men whom trial courts rarely encountered in other contexts. Perhaps most crucially, judges took issue with the sordid tactics that such campaigns forced policemen to perform: the late-night flirtations in bars and parks, the intimate observations in public bathrooms. At a time when the progressive legal community increasingly questioned the limits of police discretion and investigative power, plainclothes enticement in bars and bathrooms struck some courts as yet another iteration of the official misconduct they had a moral, if not legal, duty to monitor. And those judges drew on their authority in the courtroom—their discretion with regard to both the law and the facts of each case—to push back on what they regarded as unjust prosecutions and unsavory arrests.

A closer look at the internal politics of antigay policing complicates our understanding of the law's relationship with queer life in the mid-twentieth century. Most histories of homosexuality in the United States have focused on efforts by individual defendants, activists, and liberal attorneys to resist the law's many injuries against gay men and women, portraying the justice system itself as largely adversarial to this endeavor. Certainly, historians have recognized that courts tended to shy away from imposing maximum sentences, and they have celebrated the intermittent victories against the vice squad. But the core impression has remained one of broad institutional support for the vice squads' campaigns: a shared commitment to the regulation of queer social and sexual practices from the police station through the courts.[11]

This book argues that the criminal justice system itself was the site of profound and sometimes creative contestation over the work of antihomosexual policing—a struggle over not only the law's proper treatment of same-sex practices but also the ideal character of democratic governance itself. The policing of so-called sexual deviance was part of a long tradition of morals regulations in the United States, pursued in the mid-twentieth century against a backdrop of heightened suspicions of sexual nonconformity as a threat to both public safety and national security. Yet even in that context, such regulations were not consistently embraced by the agents of the law, or even tolerated as an inevitability of the criminal system. They inspired trenchant disagreements over a variety of questions, from the propriety of punishing "victimless" crimes to the appropriate limits of police power to the authority of trial judges in shaping police practices. A closer look at the project of antihomosexual policing reveals the influence of the different arms of the justice system, and especially the courts, as not simply the soldiers of legislative policy but institutions shaped by their own moral and professional pressures. And it suggests that the states' attempts to police same-sex practices at midcentury cannot be seen apart from the era's broader disputes over policing and state power—disputes that sometimes pitted the vice squads against the courts as much as against the communities they patrolled.[12]

More than simply the courts' sometimes-surprising appetite for tempering the vice squads' campaigns, that history reveals their power to do so: the many levers of discretion that allowed judges to tailor individual cases to their liking. Precisely because of the profound tensions it inspired, the project of antihomosexual policing fueled an array of enforcement innovations by judges and vice officers alike. Trial courts handed out reduced sentences to soften the bite of individual prosecutions. They creatively construed the law to bar overzealous charges. They exercised their unreviewable discretion over the evidence to acquit or dismiss cases against sympathetic defendants. These tactics did not fully erase or even always mitigate the harms of the vice squads' arrests, but they made enough of a dent to confound prosecutors and policemen, who often resented what they saw as the courts' misguided leniency. And they pushed vice officers to shift their tactics accordingly, sometimes rethinking their commitment to antihomosexual enforcement but more typically finding ways to refine it, reworking their surveillance operations or enticements to avoid judicial scrutiny. Some of the police's most resented intrusions into gay life in these years were, in part, reactions to the pressures of the courts. The story of antihomosexual policing in the United States is in large part a story of creative intervention: a tale of how individual judges vindicated their preferred outcomes in the face of harsh criminal laws, punitive policies by police departments, and unforgiving legal doctrines imposed by the higher courts. And it is a story, too, of how police departments accommodated those pressures—rarely to the advantage of the communities they policed.[13]

Recognizing the legal system's contestations over the proper limits of antihomosexual policing does not change how gay men and women experienced the weight of police repression in these years. But it does allow us to better understand the system that repressed them, as a fractious battleground over the boundaries of not only private sexual conduct but also state power itself. Historians have ascribed the ebb and flow of the police's antihomosexual campaigns in the twentieth century to a range of political and public pressures, from popular anxieties about sex crimes to the conservative beliefs of police executives and politicians to the vagaries of electoral cycles. But the practical contours of those campaigns did not merely reflect shifting political or ideological commitments to the regulation of sexual difference. They also reflected a set of less visible disputes over the proper administration of the law, which helped determine, sometimes more and sometimes less intentionally, the rights and freedoms of gay individuals on the ground.[14]

Vice Patrol and the "Homosexual"

The legal system's disagreements over the value of antihomosexual enforcement, of course, were not simply disputes about whether and how the state should regulate queer life. They were also disputes about what exactly the state was regulating. At a time when a range of social and scientific authorities wrestled over the nature of same-sex conduct and desire, the policing of homosexual practices invariably came down to a negotiation over who precisely the homosexual was—a dispute that required parsing both the definition of sexual deviance and, as importantly, who could be trusted to define it.

That debate hardly began or ended with the justice system. To the contrary, the history of homosexuality in the United States and Europe has witnessed a long-running struggle over the nature of same-sex desire, one populated by too many competing accounts to survey but from which several trends can be discerned. That struggle began in earnest roughly in the mid-nineteenth century, when physicians on both sides of the Atlantic broke from the clergy's long-standing grip on homosexuality as a moral failing and ventured to examine it as a disease, traceable to some degeneration of the flesh. By the turn of the century, their search for the physiological roots of same-sex desire gave way to a more disembodied theory of difference. Sexologists like Havelock Ellis and Magnus Hirschfeld characterized homosexual men as benign biological variations, the products of some enigmatic misalignment between a masculine body and a female soul. By these accounts, homosexuality was defined by gender inversion as much as by sexual practice: a tendency, through either physical or psychological compulsion, toward the demeanor and desires of the other sex.[15]

That view bled into popular understandings in the early twentieth century. To the extent that urban Americans manifested some awareness of queer men in these years, their views were shaped primarily by the communities that thrived in working-class neighborhoods, and especially the so-called fairies who self-consciously adopted the mannerisms of the fairer sex. That image was popularized by the entertainment culture of the day, from vaudeville performances to local tabloids to the "pansy craze" of the early 1930s, when nightclubs in major cities enticed spectators with overtly gender-bending performers. Thriving in a period of minimal policing, these entertainments introduced much of the public to the queer underworld, teaching Americans to associate all homosexual men with an outward repudiation of masculine norms.

By the early 1950s, that popular trope—although never entirely sidelined—was facing mounting competition. For one thing, the sex-crime panics that bookended World War II cast a sinister shadow over the figure of the fairy, painting all shows of sexual difference as not simply deviant but dangerous. And soon after the war ended, a new line of professionals emerged to challenge the public's familiar presumptions about queerness. In 1948, Alfred Kinsey's report on the sexual habits of American men shocked the public with its pervasive accounts of same-sex behavior among seemingly ordinary men, a trend Kinsey tried to characterize—not entirely successfully—as a form of natural sexual experimentation. Meanwhile, buoyed by their recent collaborations with the military, psychiatrists leaped to the forefront of public debates in the early 1950s, redefining same-sex desire as neither a moral failing nor a benign variation but the symptom of some deeper psychological maladjustment. Individual doctors differed in their approaches, from conservatives who decried homosexuality as a dangerous dysfunction to more progressive therapists who worked alongside gay activists to urge greater tolerance of sexual difference. Neither camp, however, questioned the presumption that homosexuality was essentially a sickness, deserving of pity more than acceptance.[16]

The reign of psychiatrists over popular discussions of homosexuality would meet genuine resistance only in the 1960s. Partly responsible was a generation of newly vocal activists who urged queer men and women to extract themselves from the clutches of even the most liberal "experts" on sexual difference. Also to credit, however, was the rise of a new expert authority itself: a sociological view that characterized gay men and women as neither mental patients nor criminal concerns but members of a cultural minority. Closely associated with the work of the psychologist Evelyn Hooker, whose studies defended both gay men's thriving cultural life and their psychological health, the dawning recognition of gay communities as urban subcultures was instrumental in challenging the disease theory espoused by psychiatrists, culminating with the American Psychiatric Association's removal of homosexuality from its list of mental disorders in 1973. It also suffused popular understandings of queer life, as media outlets in the 1960s increasingly portrayed the "gay world" as a harmless, if bemusing, pocket of the urban landscape.[17]

The history of the American public's encounters with homosexuality in the twentieth century, in short, is a story of competing paradigms: a struggle among different understandings of the nature, origins, and social meaning of same-sex desire. Was homosexuality a type of conduct or a personal identity? A medical affliction or a moral failing? An irresistible impulse or a systematic way of life? Not least, who had the right to answer these questions—to establish authoritative truths about a subject that inspired often-intense public and professional opinion? The resolution of these debates shaped the public's shifting relationship with what would emerge in the 1960s as the gay world, affecting both popular demand for legal regulation and gay activists' own bids for civil rights.

It also shaped the less visible daily dynamics of vice enforcement. There were, in fact, few controversies over the nature of homosexuality in these years that were not debated in the courtroom. Sometimes, the impact of these discussions was straightforward. The shadow of the sexual psychopath, whispering around the vice squads' campaigns well into the 1960s, fueled public appetites for enforcement and encouraged harsher treatment of individual defendants, pushing policemen toward more aggressive tactics and judges toward more punitive sentences. The dawning recognition of gay men as a cultural minority, pervading the legal system as well as the press in the 1960s, quieted the drive toward regulation, diminishing judicial appraisals of gay world's alleged dangers and highlighting the excesses of tactics like enticement and clandestine surveillance. The work of challenging the vice squads' campaigns in court was, in large part, the work of determining which of these paradigms defined the proceedings.

Often, however, the relationship between antihomosexual policing and the era's rival accounts of sexual difference could also be more complex. Introduced into the legal system by individual lawyers, litigants, and doctors, all with their own institutional interests and ideological commitments, different paradigms of homosexuality sometimes emerged to play unexpected roles in the collective enterprise of policing gay life.

Among the most popular and most contested of those paradigms was the medicalization of homosexual desire, which gave psychiatrists such a powerful claim to public authority after the war. Psychiatry first entered the state's antihomosexual campaigns on a dark note, underwriting the draconian sexual psychopath laws that proliferated in the early 1950s. But individual doctors questioned the medical pedigree and wisdom of those campaigns, and they often used their professional standing to temper their bite. Frequently, they did so as expert witnesses for the defense—a task that revealed both the range of psychiatrists' political commitments and the elasticity of the medical model itself, bending to support any number of litigation strategies. They also intervened in less formal ways. It was the psychiatric theory of homosexuality—espoused, not least, by employees at the state clinics funded through the sexual psychopath laws, who had a direct line to the local courts—that inclined many judges toward leniency for gay offenders, not simply leading them to question the value of criminal punishment but also fueling their outrage over manipulative police tactics. Prevailing historical accounts understandably tend to portray the medical model as a source of profound social stigma, legal discrimination, and personal distress for the men and women it pathologized—what John D'Emilio has described as a "millstone around [the] neck" of the gay liberation movement. Yet in the daily legal battles over the policing of queer life, the medicalization of deviance—including, ironically, the institutional infrastructure erected by the sexual psychopath statutes—often genuinely softened the hand of the criminal system, mitigating many men's encounters with the law.[18]

If trial judges wary of aggressive police tactics embraced the doctors' input, other legal actors put up more resistance. That ambivalence sometimes emerged in the criminal courts themselves, where some judges remained wary of calling psychiatrists as expert witnesses, questioning the extent to which medical opinions on a defendant's sexuality bore on the matter of legal liability. But it appeared most clearly in the liquor boards' proceedings against gay-friendly bars. Prohibiting bar owners from knowingly serving gay patrons, liquor laws forced the states' investigators to prove that defendants had not only welcomed gay customers but also recognized them as such—a burden often met by establishing that a bar's patrons were so unmistakably homosexual that any manager or bartender could have identified them on sight. The boards' charges, that is, rested on the presumption that urban Americans possessed some reliable, *shared* insights into what queer individuals looked like—a presumption drawn, in key part, from the ostensibly liberal entertainment culture of the early twentieth century. And when, in the 1950s, that presumption came under fire from a line of self-identified experts, including psychiatrists, whom bar owners engaged to challenge the liquor boards' evidence, the boards defended the public's insights against attack. Founded on the public's purportedly commonsense authority over the hallmarks of homosexuality, the liquor boards' campaigns against gay-friendly bars created an unusual set of incentives for all parties involved. Hoping to challenge the states' evidence, owners of gay bars pathologized gay men and women as within the unique purview of medical professionals, while liquor officials themselves disdained the experts whose wisdom commonly guided the law's treatment of queer life in other spheres.

Taken together, the states' antihomosexual campaigns open a unique window into the unstable contours of both popular and scientific views of deviance in the postwar years. An unusually high-stakes arena for debating the nature of sexual difference, those campaigns encompassed a range of questions about homosexual practice and desire, from a married man's likelihood of committing homosexual acts to the sexual connotations of cocktails and polo shirts in urban bars. In doing so, they exposed and often explicitly litigated tensions that remained buried in other spheres, from the profound flexibility of the medical model to the class tensions underlying the public's ostensibly shared gender norms. Those proceedings offer a rich record of the cultural and professional frictions surrounding the delineation of permissible sexual practices in the mid-twentieth century, within and beyond the auspices of the law.[19]

At the same time, those proceedings reveal the law's own role in establishing authoritative knowledge about sexual difference. From liquor hearings to criminal trials, legal proceedings against the public manifestations of homosexuality did not simply showcase the era's competing accounts of queer life. They took sides in an ongoing dispute about the boundaries of popular and expert authority. The states' antihomosexual drives accelerated in an age when trained psychiatrists and researchers increasingly professionalized the study of sexual difference, claiming questions of sex—and sexual deviance in particular—as matters of expert opinion. Yet in the field of sexuality as in any other, professionals' claims of expertise were not self-effectuating; they depended on the public's willingness to accept such supposedly superior insights *as* expert, a process that reflected political and institutional preferences, certainly, but also a preliminary sense that those insights genuinely improved on its own commonsense understandings. Accordingly, even as lawmakers, journalists, and some private individuals elevated doctors to the forefront of public debates, compelled by the novelty of their findings and the comfort of their professional assurances, courtroom disputes walked a finer line, alternately embracing and resisting such claims in light of the precise statutory frameworks and evidence at play. The law's ambivalent relationship with expertise—its struggle to decide whether it answered to professional or lay opinion on the nature and significance of deviant sexual practices—suggests that any account of medical authority over homosexuality in the mid-twentieth century is incomplete without a history of the courts.[20]

Perhaps most crucially, a closer look at the project of antihomosexual policing complicates our understanding of certain familiar moments in the history of queer life in the United States—moments like the pansy craze or the sex-crime panic, well-known to most historians as bursts of unique public tolerance or hostility toward sexual difference. It was in the realm of law enforcement, after all, that the public's shifting views of homosexuality had the most direct impact on the lives of gay individuals, and their legacy in this sphere was sometimes unexpected. Commonly dismissed for its corrosive association of homosexuality with mental illness, the psychiatric view of deviance genuinely tempered the bite of the criminal law, fanning judicial doubts about the wisdom of criminal punishment and the ethics of decoy enforcement. Remembered for their conflation of gay men with more predatory offenders, the sexual psychopath debates of the postwar years created an institutional infrastructure that actively softened the justice system's treatment of consensual sexual activities. Celebrated as a short-lived, if condescending, moment of visibility and tolerance for queer communities, the entertainment culture of the early twentieth century directly expanded the state's regulation of gay life, fueling a legal apparatus founded on the public's supposedly shared knowledge about queer communities. Bearing down on the legal demands and daily realities of antihomosexual policing recovers the double life of these seemingly familiar cultural moments—one that does not override their more established legacy but that compels us to grapple with the full complexity of their impact, in the court of law as well as the court of public opinion.[21]

The history of shifting public understandings of homosexuality in the twentieth century, this book contends, cannot be fully understood without a history of policing. From the Supreme Court's opinions to the daily work of lower courts, historical and legal scholars have long traced the intimate link between public culture and the law. Historians, in particular, have demonstrated the value of studying legal battles as reflections of broader social and cultural debates, examining how shifting public discourse helps explain the pace and direction of legal change. This book demonstrates that the inverse is also true. The history of antihomosexual policing reveals that litigation is not necessarily a microcosm of broader social debates about policed communities or public morality. It is a process that follows its own institutional pressures and norms, which can meaningfully alter those debates as they are translated into the courts. Just as an eye toward contemporary culture can illuminate the tides of the law, so examining the inner operations of law enforcement can illuminate the ebb and flow of public culture, providing a key perspective on how popular discussions and social trends affect the lives of some of our most heavily policed populations.[22]

Vice Patrol and Police Knowledge

Ultimately, however, the history of antigay policing is not merely a tale of how the legal system navigated competing public claims about queer life in the United States. It is also a story of how that system navigated police officers' own understandings of that phenomenon—understandings that echoed but also often crucially departed from what the public, and certainly the courts, knew about the American homosexual.

As the historian Christopher Agee has documented, most policemen in the postwar years came to the force with little knowledge about gay life. Drawn from a cross section of the community and subject to the same stereotypes that shaped broader public presumptions about sexual difference, many derided all homosexual men as the effeminate creatures of the popular imagination. Some harkened, more darkly, to the lingering specter of the sexual predator, a trope commonly invoked by vice squads to justify their ongoing campaigns.[23]

As their work patrolling urban nightlife exposed them to gay cruising culture, however, vice officers also amassed a more unusual perspective. Especially as gay men in the 1950s cohered into increasingly robust communities, vice officers developed an unusual intimacy with the gay world's social and sexual practices, from its telltale clothing to its range of cruising sites to its systematic signals for identifying sexual partners. Whether enticing solicitations from wary suspects or turning to clandestine surveillance to evade cruisers' defenses in public bathrooms, vice officers relied on those cultural insights to bolster their effectiveness in the field. And they helped relay those insights to the broader public. When the American media redis-covered the homosexual in the 1960s, it was policemen whom journalists most frequently credited as the source and model for their investigations—vice officers, rather than gay men or academic researchers, who most vis-ibly introduced the American public to the modern gay world.

The vice squads' professional forays into cruising culture exemplify the sometimes-surprising intersection between the regulation of queer life and shifting understandings of same-sex practice in the United States. The dawning recognition of gay communities as urban subcultures, with their own language, group dynamics, and social customs, has long held a privi-leged place in the history of sexuality, commemorated as a valuable ally in the struggle to destigmatize queer men and women. Yet the excavation of the gay world's systematic codes and customs did not unfold solely among sociologists and academic researchers, nor did it simply push against the criminalization of sexual difference. It found some of its earliest and most effective practitioners within the police station, as a powerful tool for re-stricting the social and sexual freedoms of queer men.[24]

At the same time, the vice squads' unusual fluency in cruising culture confirms the centrality of the police to any history of public knowledge about sexual difference. More than simply negotiating among competing popular and professional accounts of same-sex practices, the project of vice enforcement was a key site for the production of new knowledge about gay life, a wellspring of often-genuine insights into a subculture that would soon capture the attention of trained sociologists and, eventually, the pop-ular press. Scholars have examined how attempts to regulate sexual differ-ence in the twentieth century, and especially to formulate antihomosexual policies, helped usher in new understandings of queer practice and iden-tity in the United States. Local police departments and vice officers, no less than high-level policy makers, played a key role in this story, presaging and ultimately shaping the public's discovery of the urban gay world.[25]

The suggestion that police officers might develop special insights into criminalized communities, of course, was hardly unique to the vice squads. As early as the mid-nineteenth century, judges credited detectives in spe-cialized fields like gambling with some unique knowledge about the crimi-nal worlds they patrolled. In the twentieth century, that view underwent a strategic expansion, as police executives reeling from a string of scandals over corruption and incompetence during the Prohibition era, as well as a growing concern with the justice system's abuse of black and poor commu-nities, embarked on a comprehensive campaign to "professionalize" the urban police force. They did so partly by rooting out bribery and streamlining the organization of local departments, but also by emphasizing police officers' training and investigative experience—by recasting the individual policeman, in essence, not as a boorish foot soldier for the state but as a trained expert in his field. In practice, those reforms were uneven at best, often paying lip service to change more than genuinely refining police practices. But they played well in court. At a time when the expanding administrative state led courts to place increasing faith in a government of experts, judges appraising the strength of state evidence or the legitimacy of an arrest commonly invoked the officer's professional insight—his expertise in his investigative domain—to avoid deeper scrutiny of controversial police tactics.[26]

In many ways, the vice squads' antihomosexual campaigns fit neatly with this trend. Officers who spent their nights patrolling bars and cruising grounds amassed new and often-unusual knowledge about queer life, and they used that knowledge to enhance their efficiency in the field. Yet here, the stories also diverge. Even as policemen in other units emphasized their intimacy with criminalized communities as a mark of professional authority and a call for deference in court, vice squads rarely advertised their similar insights into gay life. To the contrary, they often did their best to deny them. Whether disclaiming any special ability to recognize gay men, dismissing the social customs that allowed them to entice solicitations, or obscuring the cruising patterns that led them to adopt intrusive surveillance tactics, vice officers and the prosecutors who defended their arrests commonly downplayed the very cultural codes and presumptions that often greased their most effective operations.

That trend reflected a variety of factors. Sometimes, it responded to the precise legal framework at play: charged with proving that bar owners knowingly served queer patrons, liquor agents predictably denied that recognizing homosexuals required any special skill. Sometimes, it accommodated a more inchoate pressure. At a time when media debates about homosexuality often still treated the topic as one best avoided in polite society—both a matter of substantial public interest and one prone to invite skepticism of anyone who knew too much about it—the vice squads' modesty about their intimacy with gay cruising bespoke the lingering suspicions attaching to any appearance of excess entanglement with a taboo sexual culture. Often, however, that reticence reflected the ongoing tensions between the vice squads and the courts. As many judges in the postwar years continued to look askance at the police's more aggressive tactics, vice officers' budding insights into the gay world's insular social customs threatened to exacerbate those concerns, simultaneously highlighting the sly manipulations used to entice solicitations and diminishing the apparent value of antihomosexual policing to begin with. Given those institutional pressures, successful cases often depended less on publicizing the cultural codes that fueled the vice squads' arrests than on leaving judges blind to them.

Beyond a window on the moral economy of vice policing or the era's competing views of sexual difference, in this sense, the history of antihomosexual policing provides a useful case study of the politics of knowledge underlying the administration of the criminal law—what we can think of as the epistemology of law enforcement. For one thing, that story reveals the disconnect between professional knowledge and professional legitimacy in the enforcement of controversial statutes. Conventional accounts have imagined the promise of police expertise as a shortcut to judicial deference, a reliable claim to authority in a legal culture sensitive to questions of relative competence. But the history of antihomosexual policing shows that the promise of police expertise was hardly an unalloyed good. Far from automatically entitling officers to deference, the practical value of the police's professional knowledge depended on a range of legal, institutional, and social factors, including the statutory frameworks at play and the courts' baseline support for the police's enforcement methods. Depending on how those factors aligned, advertising vice officers' intimacy with the cultures they patrolled did not necessarily shore up their cases in court. It sometimes undermined their legal and ultimately even their public authority.[27]

At the same time, the history of antihomosexual policing demonstrates the sometimes-counterintuitive relationship between state knowledge about policed communities and state power over those groups: the extent to which the legal system's blind spots about policed communities, no less than its growing sophistication, can expand its regulatory power. Exposed to the intricacies of gay men's social and sexual practices, vice officers at midcentury amassed often-rarefied insights into the organization of queer life in the United States, and they used those insights to implement more robust campaigns. Yet the ultimate vitality of those campaigns did not depend simply on vice officers' own sensitivities to cruising culture, or on how efficiently they operationalized such knowledge on the ground. It depended, in key part, on the courts' continuing ignorance of that culture. In a contested arena like the states' antihomosexual campaigns—a field that inspired both often-zealous investigative tactics and lingering qualms about those techniques within the judiciary—the success of the vice squads' drives sometimes hung on a type of *epistemic gap* among the different agents of the legal system: a disconnect between what the policemen who arrested gay men knew about queer social and sexual practices and what the judges who evaluated their arrests presumed about those practices in court.

From the rise of population statistics to records tracking criminal offenders, historians and political scientists have long remarked on state actors' imperative to amass knowledge as a form of governance: how the work of accumulating and, crucially, standardizing information about subject populations expands the regulatory power of the state. The project of governing, as Nikolas Rose and Peter Miller have suggested, rests on the bedrock of particular *political rationalities*, ways of knowing that both offer "some account of the persons over which government is to be exercised" and provide "moral justifications" for its use. The history of sexuality, and the regulation of homosexuality especially, has provided a case in point. Starting with Michel Foucault's seminal studies, historians of sexuality have examined the importance of defining citizens in order to control them— the extent to which state agencies establish power over deviant groups by promulgating their own preferred understanding of those populations, facilitating and legitimating their enforcement efforts.[28]

The history of antihomosexual policing tells a different story. That history reveals how legal regimes can maintain and even expand their power over policed groups not by popularizing any one paradigm of so-called deviance, but precisely by leaving room for multiple competing views—by sustaining exploitable disagreements about the nature of the very conduct being regulated. In a legal system administered by multiple agencies, each with its own institutional pressures and policy preferences, the power of the state's antihomosexual operations rested less on the spread of novel insight about queer life through the justice system than on its selective distribution among the different arms of the law, creating gaps that weakened potential checks on police tactics on the ground. The long, painful project of policing gay life, this book ultimately argues, was not shaped simply by the legal system's divergent views of the wisdom of antihomosexual policies, or even by its disputes about the limits of ethical policing. It was also shaped by the legal system's persisting disagreements about the thing being policed: the law's many ways of understanding, and misunderstanding, the nature of gay life.

Vice Patrol and the Archive

These, then, are the book's core aims: to explore the institutional struggles and disagreements occasioned by the vice squads' campaigns against gay life in the mid-twentieth century; to illuminate how competing public and professional views of sexual difference shaped, and were in turn shaped by, legal disputes over the states' regulatory drives; and to examine how the legal system's often-divergent understandings of queer practices affected both institutional relationships among vice officers and judges and, ultimately, the rights and freedoms of gay communities themselves. With those arguments in mind, it makes sense to conclude, now, with some words on how this book intends to make them.

This book examines the machinery of antihomosexual policing, probing the legal, institutional, and epistemic frictions inspired by an effort to regulate an essentially contested social category. It does so by diving into sources that yield an unusually candid view of the motivations of and rivalries among the different agents of the law, sources that expand and sometimes meaningfully revise the incomplete accounts derived from more public records. The inherent drawback of those sources, of course, is the lesser visibility they offer into the perspectives of the individuals captured in the law's proceedings. This book does not focus on the subjective experience of policing among queer communities, a subject explored in heartbreaking detail in other work, nor does it concentrate on the shifting social and political boundaries of gay life, although that story provides an important backdrop for the history unearthed. The limited time spent on these other narratives certainly does not aim to express a judgment on their relative importance. It reflects, rather, the inevitable constraints of an attempt to delve comprehensively into a story not yet told, one that, this book hopes, will deepen our understanding of both law enforcement and the history of gay life itself.

That story proceeds in six chapters, arranged into four sections that are both thematic and loosely chronological. Chapters 1 and 2 examine the enforcement of liquor laws in New Jersey, New York, and California from the late 1930s through the 1960s, focusing on the intractable relationship between the policing of queer social spaces and the public's presumptions about queer life. Chapters 3 and 4 turn to the criminal law, and specifically to the use of plainclothes decoys to entice solicitations. Surveying enticement tactics from the late 1940s through the 1960s in a range of cities, including Los Angeles, New York, Washington, DC, and Detroit, these chapters explore the courts' and gay men's own responses to the vice squads' campaigns and how the police adapted to those pressures. Chapter 5 turns to another controversial tool of the vice squad: clandestine surveillance. Picking up in the early 1950s and tracing one high-profile legal battle through to its resolution in the early 1970s, it examines the uniquely rich records left by police surveillance operations as a window into the law's persisting moral and epistemic disagreements over vice enforcement. Finally, Chapter 6 looks beyond the courts, toward the burst of media interest in gay life and antigay policing in the mid-1960s. Media responses to the specter of sexual deviance play a key role in the story of vice enforcement, appearing intermittently throughout the foregoing chapters, but the unprecedented attention to antihomosexual policing in the mid-1960s demands a discrete account of that cultural moment.

As this survey suggests, this book tells the history of antihomosexual policing from a national perspective. In part, that scope is a matter of necessity. Police departments have never been famous for the thoroughness of their records, and few left detailed traces of their operations. Trial records, although illuminating, are limited by the vagaries of institutional record keeping and the reluctance of many men to fight their arrests in court. Reflecting those limitations, the story presented here is cobbled together from a range of sources, including court opinions, case records, and administrative dispositions; police periodicals, training manuals, and instructional materials; field reports by contemporary criminal justice researchers; interviews and notes left by defense lawyers and district attorneys; books by psychiatrists, sociologists, journalists, and gay men; homophile periodicals like *ONE* and the *Mattachine Review*; tabloids, national newspapers, and magazines ranging from *Life* to *Playboy*; and an extended correspondence with a former vice instructor with the LAPD.

Part of what these sources reveal is that the history of antihomosexual policing may best be read as a national story. This is certainly not because one story captures the operations of vice enforcement in every jurisdiction or even major city in these years, but it is because a national story sheds unique light on how that project played out and why. Throughout the twentieth century, vice policing reacted to a series of national trends, some though not all specific to the urban setting: the demise of Prohibition, the sex-crime panics of the late 1930s and early 1950s, the professionalization of municipal police forces, the shifting demographics of the city following World War II. Given the availability of published opinions and the courts' shared institutional interests, moreover, numerous judicial trends, formal and informal, reverberated across state lines. At the same time, a national perspective is useful precisely for the differences it reveals among jurisdictions: the divergent ways that considerations of class shaped vice squad arrests in different cities, for example, or the power of individual officials to determine local enforcement policies. This book tracks these broad trends, examining how different police departments and courts handled similar social and legal pressures in the same years.

Two broad trends, worth quickly noting here, relate to which parts of the gay community drew the most police attention. From the birth of the urban police department, the brunt of law enforcement in the United States has typically fallen on poor and nonwhite communities, and in many ways the vice squads were no different. Reflecting both the biases of many officers and the economic pressures structuring queer life, patrols in public cruising sites often posed a special risk to socially and economically underprivileged individuals, especially black and gender-nonconforming suspects. Following an arrest, too, "respectable" men could often expect preferential treatment, from greater courtesies at the police station to dropped charges ahead of any court appearances. At the same time, however, the vice squads' antihomosexual campaigns are notable precisely for the extent to which they complicate this familiar story. Among the rare forms of urban policing that targeted conduct prevalent among wealthier men, the vice squads' operations consistently captured white, middle-class suspects who otherwise rarely crossed paths with the police. In some cities, indeed, political pressure focused officers' attention on that demographic. This trend, in turn, was instrumental to fueling the ambivalence that often greeted homosexuality-related arrests in court, and the epistemic battles that such ambivalence frequently inspired. Tracing these institutional disputes, the story told here can be seen as a complement to the eye-opening histories of racialized policing published in recent years: a study of the very different project of enforcing a largely white-identified morals offense.[29]

The second trend is more straightforward. Whether targeting poor or wealthy suspects, white or black, the vice squads' operations consistently focused on men. Although lesbian activity never entirely avoided legal scrutiny, the lesser visibility of women's sexual practices, coupled with the greater acceptance of intimate friendships among women, mitigated criminal attention to lesbians throughout most of American history. At the same time, the specific concerns driving the vice squads' campaigns at midcentury, from fears of predatory sex crimes to anxieties about national security, were associated primarily with men. Lesbians hardly escaped the federal government's crusades, and they sometimes captured the sustained attention of the liquor boards. But the vice squads that proliferated among midcentury police departments simply did not see women as a priority. Nevertheless, police agencies were not entirely blind to lesbian life, and the special problem of surveilling queer women pops up intermittently throughout the book, from the pervasive campaigns against lesbian bars in New Jersey to the discussion of lesbians in police manuals.[30]

Finally, a note on terminology. Tracing the history of antihomosexual policing alongside shifting public and expert understandings of sexual difference, this story trades in several potentially slippery terms. These include, first and foremost, *public* and *expert*. Expertise is often seen as a deeply normative word, laden with social authority and professional respect—one that many readers might hesitate to ascribe not only to police officers but also to many so-called medical authorities at midcentury. Taking its cue from the history and the sociology of science, which have long sought to demystify *expertise* as a label emerging through a complex, deeply politicized negotiation with its intended audience, this book defines that term as neither stable nor intrinsically worthy of deference but rather contingent, relational, and socially constructed. *Expertise*, simply enough, encompasses any body of generalizable knowledge that cannot be attributed to the average person and thereby gives those who claim it some authority in determining "truth" over those who do not. At all times, the focus is less on the substance or rigor of the underlying knowledge than on the institutional and social capital it confers.[31]

By the same token, *public* is not meant to connote a specific body of information actually attributable to the American populace—something that would be impossible to pinpoint, especially in a national account. Public knowledge, rather, connotes any epistemic claims, bodies of insight, or forms of reasoning that were seen by cultural, legal, or scientific authorities in these years as characteristic of popular conceptions of sexual difference. Common stereotypes are thus public, though they are hardly universal, and strands of initially rarefied insight can become public as they suffuse popular debates. The focus, once more, is on the social, institutional, or legal value of defining something as publicly shared knowledge—sometimes despite disagreements within the public itself.

Which brings us, finally, to *homosexual*. From the pansy craze to the media's discovery of the gay world in the 1960s, contemporary understandings of the social, scientific, and even sexual dimensions of same-sex practices in the United States underwent significant changes. Beyond the realm of discourse, too, the private experiences and identities of the men targeted by the vice squads, from the patrons of gay bars to the cruisers arrested in public bathrooms, shifted throughout these years. That definitional instability is, of course, a core part of the story—but that leaves the problem of identifying individuals along the way. Throughout the following chapters, this book tries to confine itself to those terms that best capture the identities of the individuals under discussion at a given time. This means that chapters examining the 1930s and early 1940s speak primarily of *homosexuals*, while subsequent sections turn to *gay men* and *gay communities*, as these self-identified groups begin to emerge, or simply to *cruisers*, when discussing those who shirked such designations. None of these terms is always adequate, and I also use the generic *queer* to refer broadly to individuals engaging in nonnormative sexual practices. That word departs from the self-conception of many of these individuals, and it risks introducing a modern sensibility to the narrative. But it represents, to my mind, the most satisfying solution to the problem of presenting a coherent story about complex and shifting sexual identities. And it keeps a spotlight on what this story is ultimately all about: a slippery attempt to patrol a marginalized social practice, often in the absence of any precise or accepted understanding of what that practice is, whom it implicates, and why—or whether—it poses such a threat.[32]

ONE

When Anyone Can Tell

On the afternoon of December 5, 1933, following years of rampant boot-legging, overflowing criminal dockets, and criticism from civic groups, Utah became the thirty-sixth state to ratify the Twenty-First Amendment to the Constitution. Few mourned the passing of the Prohibition era. "Look-ing back over fourteen years of national prohibition," observed the edito-rial board of *The Nation* a week after the fateful vote, "it is probably not an exaggeration to say that it was the worst legislative mistake this coun-try ever made." On the ground, the effect was immediate. Long an illicit part of urban nightlife, liquor now poured freely in clubs, bars, and res-taurants across the nation. For the budding homosexual enclaves that had sprung up in America's cities, however, the Twenty-First Amendment did not just bring legal alcohol back into American bars. It also brought the police.[1]

Queer nightlife in the early twentieth century thrived in a period of minimal scrutiny by local authorities. Policemen kept an eye out for men loitering, among other activities, in public parks and bathrooms, and the effeminate fairies who openly flouted gender norms sometimes came to blows with officers on the street, but private clubs and restaurants were largely left to conduct their business as they pleased. At the height of the Prohibition era, when most nightclubs already bribed patrolmen to turn a blind eye to their stores of whiskey, the presence of a homosexual (or sev-eral) on the premises failed to register as a police priority.[2]

By the end of the 1930s, all that would begin to change. Within a few years of Repeal, each state in the nation enacted a host of laws controlling how bar owners could operate their businesses and how their customers could behave inside. While uniformed police officers continued to patrol parks for public manifestations of deviance, plainclothes officers and liquor agents were now also responsible for ensuring that bars conformed to the many pricing, service, and morals restrictions imposed by the law—not least, restrictions against catering to suspected homosexuals.

In enforcing these laws, agents visited a range of bars and relied on a diversity of evidence. But one type of evidence in particular stood out. Typically requiring some proof that a bar owner not only served queer patrons but also did so *knowingly*, proceedings against gay-friendly bars frequently came down to allegations that a bar's customers conformed to widely held assumptions about what homosexuals looked and acted like. Drawing on a long-standing association of homosexuality with certain overt signs of effeminacy—the swishing hips and limp wrists popularized by the entertainment culture of the early twentieth century—liquor boards insisted that certain visual hallmarks of sexual difference were so well-established that any manager or bartender who saw them had to have recognized them as such. The power of the liquor boards' campaigns against gay bars, in short, depended on the availability of some *shared public knowledge* about the homosexual: the presumption that urban Americans harbored some universal insights into who the homosexual was and how he differed from the ordinary man.

Recognizing the link between the liquor boards' campaigns and popular understandings of homosexuality illuminates the internal logic of the boards' operations in these years—why disciplinary proceedings against gay bars so commonly devolved into the most commonplace, simplistic tropes about queer men. More than liquor officials' own narrow conceptions of male homosexuality or even their unique antipathy to those bars that most flagrantly flouted conventional masculine norms, the use of such reductive evidence to prosecute gay bars reflected the unique demands of a regulatory framework that tied the states' enforcement power to the public's shared presumptions about deviance. The liquor boards' antihomosexual proceedings exemplify the extent to which regulatory regimes targeting knowing violations, and especially knowing interactions with marginalized groups, invite state agents to stereotype those communities as the bedrock of their enforcement campaigns.

At the same time, the boards' reliance on the public's shared understandings of homosexuality complicates the legacy of certain celebrated chapters in the history of queer life in the United States: those brief moments of visibility, like the permissive urban culture of the 1920s and especially the pansy craze of the 1930s, that helped define public understandings of homosexuality to begin with. Developments like the pansy craze are often remembered as short-lived bursts of liberality in an otherwise hostile culture, times when the public's aversion to sexual deviance gave way, however briefly, to a relatively open, even objective discourse about queer life. But in the legal realm, the legacy of such progressive moments proved to be far more complex. Familiarizing much of the urban public with the nation's queer subcultures, the permissive entertainment culture of the early twentieth century emerged as a core building block in the states' campaigns against gay life following Repeal, underwriting a regulatory regime based on a presumption of public intimacy with a marginalized community. Far from simply ushering in a more tolerant public discourse on sexual deviance, or even entrenching reductive stereotypes about queer communities, such celebrated moments of queer visibility fueled the states' most literal uses of police power against gay men and women.[3]

As the years went on, of course, the familiar hallmarks of the pansy became increasingly outdated. As gay bar culture in the postwar years grew more subdued and the liquor boards expanded their purview to new categories of establishments, investigators trying to prove that bar owners knowingly served their queer customers had to adjust their evidence. Less than relying on any established tropes of the fairy, investigators turned to what they identified as the public's shared intuitions about a proliferating set of supposedly abnormal behaviors, from patrons' leisure wear to their drink orders to their choice of nickname. In doing so, they essentially turned liquor proceedings into a battleground over who "the public" might be. From clothing fads like loafers and polo shirts to a man's preference for cocktails over beer, the liquor boards categorized as deviant a broad range of social behaviors—behaviors that often correctly identified gay patrons, but also carried very different connotations among different classes, races, and cultural groups.

Beyond illuminating the link between popular knowledge and state power in the regulation of queer life, the liquor boards' campaigns thus offer a useful window into the contested contours of popular knowledge about sexual difference itself. A uniquely high-stakes environment for charting the boundaries of normality and deviance, the boards' anti-homosexual proceedings laid bare the social and political presumptions underlying the public's purportedly shared norms of sex and gender in the mid-twentieth century—or, at the least, those norms the law was willing to recognize as public. At a time of shifting standards governing men's and women's conduct in the public sphere, fueled by a range of disruptions from the changing demographics of the city to a growing female workforce to the Cold War's politicized struggles between upper- and lower-class values, the liquor boards' attempt to identify some commonsense hallmarks of deviance did not simply stigmatize homosexuality as an unacceptable social practice. It endorsed a hierarchy of cultural and class aesthetics as the threshold of normality for all Americans. The records of the liquor boards' campaigns expose the class and cultural conflicts stirred up by any attempt to define the public's shared instincts about sexual normality, in and beyond the legal realm: the difficulties of identifying common sexual or gender norms in a pluralistic society defined by its varying intuitions about proper manhood and womanhood.

Taking a long view of the liquor boards' campaigns from the 1930s through the early 1960s, this chapter examines the intractable, often unpredictable relationship between state regulation and popular knowledge about sexual difference—a relationship that revises our understandings of both antihomosexual enforcement and popular culture in the early twentieth century. It tells this story by focusing primarily on three states: New York, New Jersey, and California. These states were hardly alone in regulating homosexual-friendly bars and restaurants, and other jurisdictions sometimes provide useful counterpoints. But these three are notable for the extensive judicial and administrative records detailing their campaigns. Together, those records open a telling window on the intersection between public culture and government power in the policing of gay life.

Repeal and the Rise of the Liquor Boards

The repeal of the Eighteenth Amendment marked the end of the nation's experiment with Prohibition, but it did not end the government's concern with alcohol in America's cities. To the contrary, with thousands of bars and restaurants now openly pouring libations, the states stepped forward to regulate a profitable new industry. Within a year of ratification, legislatures across the nation passed regulations policing the sale of liquor in both retail and service establishments. Some relied on preexisting agencies, typically taxing boards like the California State Board of Equalization (BOE), which administered the state's liquor regulations as a series of tariffs. Others created specialized agencies to issue liquor licenses, including New York's State Liquor Authority (SLA) and New Jersey's Division of Alcoholic Beverage Control (ABC). Both types of agencies were responsible for implementing a host of rules, from prohibitions against serving minors to mandatory closing times and minimum food sales. Not least, they were responsible for ensuring that bars and restaurants did not become havens for certain undesirable elements: drug addicts, gamblers, prostitutes, and, certainly, homosexuals.[4]

That the accelerating regulation of queer life began in the setting of the bar should hardly be surprising. From the advent of the nation's first police departments, law enforcement in the United States had often focused on bars and saloons as special threats to conventional—to wit, white, middle-class, Protestant—standards of morality. It should also be unsurprising because, both before and following Repeal, bars, restaurants, and taverns were among the most reliable sites of queer social life. Spaces defined by their ambiguous straddling of the public and the private, simultaneously open to strangers and shielded from the eyes of passersby, bars provided an appealing setting for social practices that might have drawn more hostility on the city streets. Beginning in the 1910s in cities like Chicago and New York, night clubs and saloons in working-class and bohemian neighbor-hoods became meccas for queer men, not least the self-consciously effeminate fairies sometimes employed there as both servers and a type of live entertainment. In the early 1930s, that once-niche culture spilled into the mainstream, as cabarets and nightclubs seeking to draw crowds with sensational floor shows embraced a short-lived passion for attractions hosted by fairies or female impersonators. But by the middle of the decade, having exhausted their popularity with more cosmopolitan crowds, these provocative entertainments were increasingly drawing the attention of urban moralists and police departments alike.[5]

It was against this backdrop that, with the repeal of the Eighteenth Amendment, liquor boards in the mid-1930s emerged. Not all these agencies saw homosexual-friendly bars—or, really, any liquor violations—as a top priority. Tax boards like California's BOE, in particular, were often more interested in maximizing revenue than patrolling the moral character of urban nightlife. But some agencies, including the liquor boards in New Jersey and New York, took the project of protecting the public order more seriously. Some of their rigor reflected the personal dispositions of the men who steered the boards in their first years: in both states, political appointees in the tradition of Progressive era moral reformers, who drew simultaneous praise and complaints of "self-righteous[ness]" for their rigid regulations. The boards also faced immediate political pressure from the temperance lobby, diminished but hardly vanquished by the Twenty-First Amendment, which made liquor commissioners aware, as one reporter in New Jersey put it, that Repeal would in some ways "have to be stricter than Prohibition." In New Jersey itself, that public pressure soon came to focus directly on the problem of the homosexual. Not yet a year into his tenure, Commissioner D. Frederick Burnett received a direct entreaty from the state's Licensed Beverage Association warning that the "evil" of bars featuring female impersonators would lead inexorably back to Prohibition, undercutting a thriving new industry. Sharing the association's concern over such "indecent, disgusting practices," Burnett promptly committed himself to a program of stricter oversight.[6]

The regulations used to police such "indecent" establishments rarely mentioned homosexuality by name. Most commonly, liquor officials relied on broader prohibitions targeting disorderly or disruptive conduct, seeing the manifestations of queer life as squarely within the realm of the public immorality those laws aimed to eliminate. In New York, the Alcoholic Beverage Control Law forbade bar owners from allowing their establishments "to become disorderly," a provision the SLA read as including owners who "permitt[ed] homosexuals, degenerates and undesirable people to congregate." In California, the Alcoholic Beverage Control Act imposed charges on any "disorderly house"—including, per the BOE, any establishment that functioned "as a meeting place" for "known homosexual[s]."[7]

New Jersey took a somewhat different approach. Personally responsible for drafting liquor regulations, Commissioner Burnett soon enacted Rule 4, which banned licensed bars from hosting "any known . . . prostitutes, female impersonators, or other persons of ill repute." Inspired largely by the cross-dressing spectacles that graced vaudeville stages and cabarets during the Prohibition years, Rule 4 was sometimes invoked against female impersonation in the classic sense: hired performers who entertained patrons with their feminine stylings and often-salacious musical numbers. But Burnett made no secret of his ambition for the provision to capture a broader scope of venues. "Everybody of mature age today," he explained, "probably knows the repulsive meaning of the colloquial term 'pansy.'" Targeting homosexual-friendly bars under the language of the rule, indeed, required no special leap of imagination. At a time when the popular press still commonly conceived of homosexuals as a *third sex*—some mix of a feminine psyche and a masculine body—liquor officials commonly conflated homosexuality and gender inversion as twin sides of the same pathology, using *fag*, *fairy*, and *female impersonator* as synonyms separated only by their varying vulgarity.[8]

With their regulations in place, the liquor boards began the labor of enforcement itself. Most disciplinary proceedings unfolded entirely under the auspices of the newly created agencies, subject to relatively little oversight from the courts or other external bodies. While the specifics varied by state, cases against wayward bar owners typically began with an appearance before a hearing officer employed by the board, where attorneys for both sides argued over the evidence, before being appealed to a board of

directors or the individual commissioner himself. Subsequently, bar owners could request an independent review by the state courts, but the cost
and delay associated with continuing appeals meant that few availed themselves of the option.[9]

Before the hearings, of course, came the matter of gathering evidence.
Almost all liquor boards had their own staff of specialized agents, paid
exclusively to investigate violations of the liquor codes. Those men were
chosen in key part for their ability to hold their liquor, but beyond that
their backgrounds differed. Some turned to law enforcement only after a
series of professional disappointments in other fields. One agent with New
Jersey's ABC, for instance, joined the division after past stints as a lineman,
a cabinetmaker, and a refrigerator repairman. William Wickes, an investigator with New York's SLA, tried to make it as an actor in Manhattan before resigning himself, like so many men before him, to a more practical
pursuit. Others came to the liquor boards from established careers in law
enforcement, from local police departments to the Bureau of Prohibition,
which had policed speakeasies and distilleries prior to Repeal. For such
officers, liquor investigation sometimes provided a respite from the more
dangerous assignments they had handled in their prior roles. Walter van
Wagner, a former investigator with the New York district attorney's office,
joined the SLA shortly after a high-profile mafia case led to multiple kid-
napping attempts against his children.[10]

These specialized investigators took the lead in the boards' cases, often staging repeated visits to suspected violators to gather evidence for a
charge. Given their limited manpower, however, liquor boards also looked
to local policing agencies for much-needed assistance. As a practical matter, uniformed officers were often the first line of defense against violations
of state and municipal liquor regulations, patrolling neighborhood bars,
warning bar owners when they began attracting questionable patrons, and
sometimes fielding complaints from businessmen trying to disperse their
own unwelcome clientele.[11]

When it came to more extended investigations, the precise terms of the
police and the liquor boards' partnerships varied. In New York City and
San Francisco, liquor agents gathering evidence against gay-friendly bars
collaborated closely with local policemen, especially members of specialized vice squads. Whether working alongside each other or taking turns
visiting offending establishments, agents and plainclothes officers spent
extensive time observing suspected bars, and they provided essentially
identical testimony at the subsequent hearings. Smaller police departments

often had fewer resources to spare, and their relationships with the liquor boards could be more complex. In New Jersey in the 1930s and 1940s, police officers often stepped in to make individual arrests and raids, but they provided the ABC with scant help in investigating liquor violations, leading the division to rely almost exclusively on its own agents. By the 1960s, policemen and ABC agents had begun to cooperate more closely in their daily duties, yet even then they continued to experience some problems of coordination. Failing to keep track of the ABC's cases, local departments sometimes investigated bars already under surveillance, or assured nervous bar owners that they were compliant with the law even as the ABC prepared charges against them. When the ABC brought charges against Club Delite in Newark, for example, the owner protested that the local police had assured him he could continue serving queer customers "so long as they didn't act up."[12]

More than a lack of communication, such conflicts reflected a deeper strategic divergence between the policemen and the liquor agents charged with surveilling queer life in these years. Unlike investigators tasked exclusively with enforcing civil regulations against wayward bar owners, police officers balanced their investigations with a host of other enforcement duties, not least patrolling other suspected sites of homosexual activity. Used to exercising significant discretion in ignoring what they saw as petty infractions, and aware that shutting down any one bar typically funneled its patrons to the next door over—or, worse yet, the streets—policemen often preferred to look the other way when bar owners managed to keep their businesses orderly. As San Francisco's Chief Thomas Cahill would later put it, ferreting out gay-friendly bars was the "ABC's problem," not his own. And in some cases, officers' relative forbearance with homosexual-friendly bars accommodated less upstanding motives. Although state liquor agents were hardly immune to corruption, local police officers integrated into the neighborhood economy often had more opportunities to extract payoffs from bar owners in exchange for official protection. It was unsurprising, in context, that policemen often adopted a more flexible interpretation of the liquor laws.[13]

Whether led by police officers or liquor agents, investigations typically followed the same pattern. Agents visited bars in groups, watching for anything that departed from their view of an orderly establishment, from drag entertainers to a handful of gay customers. Often staying late into the night, they struck up conversations with bartenders, joked with other patrons, and purchased a steady supply of alcohol. Most agents adopted the part of good-natured tourists, perplexed but unoffended by the scene they had discovered, but some let themselves be drawn into more intimate encounters with their fellow patrons. In 1939, Investigator Walter van Wagner visited the Gloria Bar and Grill in Manhattan "on the invitation of [a] 'fag'" who, having spied his guest, "proceeded to fondle [him] by rubbing his hand along the front of [the investigator's] trousers and attempting to open the fly." At a tavern run by Peter Orsi in Newark that spring, a customer with a "very effeminate voice" asked an ABC agent to buy him a drink at the bar before beginning to stroke his legs and chest. Some officers actively encouraged such encounters, dancing with male patrons or inviting new acquaintances to "take care of" them.[14]

For the most part, however, especially in the first two decades following Repeal, the liquor boards' charges did not rest primarily on evidence of overt sexual overtures. Sensitive to the risk of liquor agents looking for violations, bar owners did their best to keep any explicit erotic displays, homosexual or otherwise, in check. Bartenders and managers broke up dancing couples, prohibited patrons from visiting the bathroom together, and scolded men striking up conversations with strangers. When a patron tried to flirt with an officer seated at the counter of Hy and Sol's Bar in Newark one winter evening, for instance, the owner immediately intervened. "Drink your beer and keep quiet and don't bother anyone," he instructed. Helen Branson, the owner of a popular bar in Los Angeles, excommunicated any customer who dared so much as to introduce himself to an unvetted newcomer. "If you want to risk your liberty by speaking to someone you don't know, you do it somewhere else," she explained. "You are not going to risk *my* license."[15]

Even when a flirtation inevitably slipped past the eyes of the management, such encounters were not always helpful in establishing a violation. Prohibiting owners from "permitting" homosexual customers or harboring known female impersonators, liquor laws generally required some evidence that the bar's employees knew that they were serving a queer clientele. In the rare instance, sexual propositions on the premises might have sufficed to establish that a bar owner must have recognized his customers' proclivities—where, for example, the overtures were particularly frequent or overt, or where a proposal came from one of the bar's own employees. Yet in most cases, an intermittent solicitation in a bar's back corner, commonly consummated entirely off the premises, was hardly enough to put bartenders on notice of their customers' sexual practices. As judges and liquor commissioners alike conceded, invitations "made in secret, under circumstances which could not have come to the attention of the bartender," simply could not carry the liquor board's burden of proving a knowing violation.[16]

Instead, liquor agents hoping to build a case had to look to more circumstantial evidence to try getting inside bar owners' heads. And they adopted a variety of approaches, largely reflecting the diversity of the gay bars they prosecuted.

Some of those establishments did not intend to operate as gay bars at all. When the authorities shut down another spot nearby or when new owners bought out an older venue, queer men and women sometimes found themselves buying their drinks from owners who never would have tried to court their business. Some of these unwilling hosts shunned their new customers, evicting individuals they suspected of being homosexual and sometimes even enlisting local authorities to help. After liquor agents visiting Peter Orsi's bar in 1939 noticed a crowd of conspicuously effeminate patrons, for instance, the bartender immediately asked for their assistance getting the "fags" to leave. He "had been trying to get rid of them" for months, he insisted, "but they keep coming back every week." The owner of Times Square Garden and Grill was even more proactive. After inheriting a displaced clientele of gay patrons from a nearby bar in 1938, he went straight to the local police for aid "abat[ing] the nuisance." On their advice, he tried watering the men's beer and dropping salt in their drinks, but the tactics proved unavailing.[17]

Other bar owners resigned themselves to their unsought clientele, recognizing a reliable stream of income when they saw it, even as they denigrated their "disgusting" and "perverted" customers to anyone who asked. "I really wish they would go away," one bartender confided to an agent in Atlantic City. "It gets to be kind of a drag after a while." In some cases, owners and their employees varied in their levels of tolerance for the offbeat crowds. Hired before the influx of a queer clientele, a bartender at Club Delite in Newark pointedly distanced himself from his new customer base: "I don't like them myself, but the boss says it is all right to serve them." By contrast, the staff at Pappy's Bar in Atlantic City may have been more liberal than its owner appreciated, thanking two agents who complimented Pappy's as a "very nice gay spot" even as the owner insisted that he had been "trying to 'clean the place up'" for years.[18]

Many establishments, of course, were far less ambivalent, actively advertising themselves as havens for queer men and women. In Manhattan, the Gloria Bar and Grill styled itself as a port of call for the city's sexual underground in the 1930s, hiring a "well-known fag" from the West Village cabarets as its manager and welcoming gay men and straight tourists alike.

The owner of the Paddock Bar in New Jersey, destined for a series of fateful run-ins with the ABC in the 1950s and early 1960s, openly informed two undercover agents that she had no straight customers and "d[id]n't want any." Some of these proprietors likely saw their bars simply as shrewd business ventures, grateful for a well-paying and uniquely loyal clientele. For that reason, indeed, in cities like New York and Chicago operating gay-friendly bars would become a popular venture among criminal syndicates, happy to use their existing network of police protection to capture a profitable market. But many bar owners also developed personal relationships with their regulars, following their romantic exploits and coming to see them as a type of extended family—what some, and particularly older women like Helen Branson, referred to as "their boys."[19]

Deeply invested in their businesses, bar owners who courted gay customers often went to great lengths to hide their operations from the police: secret locks, bouncers to screen new customers, backrooms reserved for dancing, lights or other signals to alert patrons to act "in a normal, well-behaved manner" at the entry of the police. When those tactics failed and they found themselves confronted by suspicious agents, some owners stood by their customers, insisting on their right to some oasis against the outside world. "Tell me one thing," demanded Ruth Loomis, the owner of Anthony's in Paterson, of a group of agents in 1959. "These people who you call homosexuals, gays or whatever you call them—what are they supposed to do?" A 1962 visit to the Latin Quarter in Newark, popular with gay men and lesbians alike, led to an especially aggressive confrontation. Having weathered a temporary suspension just months earlier and now facing another group of liquor agents asking for his paperwork, Anthony Faliveno, the club's manager, briskly made his way through the bar dispersing his more visibly queer patrons before turning back to the agents. "Show me the lesbians," he challenged them. Intimidated by the remaining crowd, the agents were forced to leave that evening without completing their investigation.[20]

These diverse relationships between bar owners and their patrons lent themselves to different forms of evidence before the liquor boards. Ironically, bar owners who best tried to comply with the liquor code or who openly disdained their queer customers sometimes found themselves in a weaker legal position. A bartender's protests that he had attempted to eject his gay patrons or even his good-faith requests for police assistance, after all, provided incontrovertible proof that the bar's staff knew of their customers' unorthodox tendencies. By the same token, bartenders who openly complained about their "perverted" crowds could be their own worst enemies, conceding to the undercover agents that they knowingly served a queer clientele.[21]

Sloppy disclosures to plainclothes agents, however, were hardly limited to hostile bar owners. Bartenders who basked in compliments about their "gay bars," scorned heterosexual customers, or warmly gossiped about their patrons' romantic lives similarly found themselves strung up by their own words. Others knew better than to gossip but had a bad poker face: after three ABC agents identified themselves to the manager at Connie Gannitti's bar in Saddle Brook, New Jersey, she immediately slapped her forehead and swore aloud, a reaction the board took as proof that she recognized her own misdoings. (Sometimes, of course, agents who claimed that a bartender openly welcomed his queer crowd might have taken some liberties with their testimony. At a proceeding against Jessie Lloyd's bar in 1954, a group of ABC agents reenacted some particularly stilted dialogue. "See these three guys coming in now," the bartender purportedly told them. "They are all queers. . . . Look, I'm going to serve them now.")[22]

Where bars actively welcomed gay customers, liquor authorities also relied on less direct evidence. Some produced testimony that a bar enjoyed or even cultivated a reputation as "a homosexual's haven"—a type of evidence that depended especially on the cooperation of local officers attuned to the neighborhood gossip. Others pointed to decorations and other paraphernalia that might betray an owner's sympathies. At Marion Brown's Paddock Bar in 1956, agents noticed matchbooks emblazoned with the slogan "The Gayest Spot in Town"—a phrase, her employees insisted, that referred simply to the "gaiety of the establishment." At the Clock Bar in Dauphin County, investigators with the Pennsylvania Liquor Control Board confiscated a copy of the *Lavender Baedeker*, an underground guide to gay bars across North America. (A sign hanging nearby, equally incriminating, read: "Pickled eggs laid by gay roosters.") Where bars owners implemented surreptitious alarms to help keep out the agents of the state—the secret locks, the bouncers, the coded lights behind the counter—those same mechanisms ironically doubled as proof of guilt once the agents got inside.[23]

All these forms of evidence could, in their own way, establish that a bar owner had knowingly served homosexual patrons. But most commonly, liquor officials hoping to accomplish that minor flight of mind reading relied on neither an owner's statements nor the vagaries of a bar's decor. Instead, they turned to a type of evidence that was far more universal, more ubiquitous—evidence that allowed them to argue that any bartender who served queer customers must have recognized them for what they were.

Fairy Spectacles in the Public Eye

Conveniently for liquor investigators, homosexual men had, by the mid-1930s, acquired a distinct image among urban Americans. That image traced back at least to the late nineteenth century and owed its existence to many sources, but one deserved more credit than most: an urban entertainment culture, expanding in popularity in the interwar years, that assured the public of its ability to recognize queer bodies on the basis of certain reliable, often flamboyant, physical cues.

By the first decades of the twentieth century, observant Americans had at least some passing familiarity with the traces of queer life in their cities. In New York, Chicago, and San Francisco, affluent slummers appeased their appetites for vice by visiting the cities' working-class enclaves of sexual liberality, where men who sought sex with other men gathered openly and often peacefully with other locals. The figure of the "nance" or fairy, a man marked both by his effete demeanor and by some sly whispers of deviant desire, intermittently made his way into a range of popular media, from popular tabloids like *Broadway Brevities* to the novels of acclaimed writers like Ernest Hemingway.[24]

The reach of most of these early attractions was, of course, limited. Activities like slumming in the Bowery, an urban pastime with an extended pedigree, were pursued by a narrow segment of the public. Not all Americans read *Broadway Brevities* or, for that matter, Hemingway's novels, and not all who did understood the coded references. Outside the working-class neighborhoods where fairies were regularly tolerated, police officers in the 1920s cracked down on overt displays of sexual difference on the city streets, arresting men who ventured to wear women's clothing or adopted any signs of feminine grooming in public. In commercial theaters, the arbiters of public taste sidelined productions with homoerotic themes, from solemn plays like Edouard Bourdet's *The Captive* to Mae West's campier drag productions. As one critic predicted, reviewing *The Captive* in 1926, "a good percentage of the audience will fail to ascertain what it is all about."[25]

Just a few years later, most self-respecting cosmopolitans had become more familiar with the urban homosexual. As nightclub operators in entertainment strongholds like Manhattan's Times Square and Chicago's Towertown sought to protect their business against the twin misfortunes of the cratering stock market and Prohibition, the spectacle of "pansy" performers—singers, dancers, and cabaret hosts who boldly transgressed gender and sexual norms—emerged as a leading attraction.

The most prominent pansy spectacles were the drag balls held annually in cities like New York, Chicago, and Philadelphia. Beginning in the nineteenth century, queer men and women had sometimes subverted the aristocratic convention of the masquerade ball and organized their own private drag parties, but in the late 1920s that niche world erupted into a citywide pastime. In glamorous venues like the Astor Hotel and Madison Square Garden, galas featuring gender-bending participants lured thousands of spectators, eager "to see men who out-womened women, and women who out-mened men." The events commanded a broad audience in Chicago and, to a lesser extent, Philadelphia, but the unquestioned crown jewel was the Hamilton Lodge Ball in Harlem's Rockland Palace, an event that drew social luminaries from New York patricians like the Vanderbilts to the Hollywood starlet Tallulah Bankhead. Those unable to make the journey relived the evening's thrills through the next day's headlines, as local, predominantly black newspapers like the *New York Amsterdam News*, the *Baltimore Afro-American*, and the *Pittsburgh Courier*—perhaps reflecting the black working class's relative openness toward nonnormative gender performance—regaled their readers with descriptions and photographs of the gala's most memorable contestants.[26]

While drag balls typically occurred once each year, another venue offered to satisfy the public's curiosity for deviant bodies year-round. Starting in the early 1930s, mainstream nightclubs embraced a short-lived passion for floor shows hosted by self-identified fairies, sometimes appearing in drag but more typically relying on subtler shows of deviance. The fairy cabaret burst to the forefront of New York nightlife in the winter of 1930, when Jean Malin, a darling of the Greenwich Village nightlife, opened a new floor show at the Club Abbey in Times Square. Appearing each night in an immaculate tuxedo, his hair bleached and his eyebrows delicately contoured, Malin built his name less on female impersonation than on bawdy banter and double entendres. By the year's end, the Club Abbey's success had inspired six other pansy clubs in Times Square alone, as well as numerous popular attractions uptown in Harlem. Soon enough, venues featuring fairy entertainers made their way to cities from cosmopolitan Los Angeles and Chicago to the smaller Cleveland. The comedian Roy Spencer Bartlett, among Chicago's most popular entertainers, became widely recognized for his trademark red tie, among the day's more coded nods to homosexuality. The phenomenon even made its way onto the silver screen. Released in 1932, Clara Bow's star vehicle *Call Her Savage* featured a detour to a Greenwich Village cabaret where two limp-wristed waiters, each sporting a lace headdress and a maid's apron, sing a falsetto musical number before a room of rapt diners.[27]

1.1. A peek inside a Greenwich Village gay bar in *Call Her Savage*.
Call Her Savage, dir. John Francis Dillon (Fox Film Corp., 1932).

Here, once more, newspapers and magazines helped popularize the trend. Tabloids like the *Amsterdam News* and the scandal sheet *Broadway Brevities* printed cartoons of delicate men with plucked eyebrows and fastidiously styled hair, expecting readers to discern the import of those grooming choices. A 1931 issue of *Vanity Fair* singled out the Club Abbey as among the nation's most popular evening draws: an exclusive venue where, "through a lavender mist," crowds of patrons "smirk with self-conscious sophistication at the delicate antics of their host." A sketch accompanying the article captured Malin's "wilted postures" as he swished among the tables—cocked hip, limp wrists, and all.[28]

Neither the drag balls nor the pansy cabarets, of course, advertised their performers as homosexual per se. Indeed, the cross-dressing attractions of galas like the Hamilton Lodge Ball might have reminded some viewers of a more wholesome entertainment: female impersonators like the vaudeville star Julian Eltinge, who had dazzled audiences in the 1910s with his elaborate costumes and feminine affectations all while cultivating a reputation for rugged machismo offstage. Yet most spectators at drag balls and popular nightclubs understood that they were witnessing a slightly different genre. Newspaper articles often described drag balls in jargon more closely associated with sexual transgression than female impersonation, abounding in coded references to the "twilight men" and "lavender lads" who "let their hair down" at the Rockland Palace. The pansy cabarets, for their part, were even further removed from the costumed illusions of the vaudeville stage, treating their audiences to subtler displays of deviance: Malin's painted eyebrows, the singing waiters' limp wrists. "Mature" audiences, the New Jersey ABC's Commissioner Burnett confidently asserted in 1934, understood what these quirks connoted. As the showgirl Evelyn Nesbit acknowledged in an interview with the *Broadway Tattler*: "Queers are undoubtedly the heaviest drawing cards in the night clubs of today." A patron of Chicago's pansy clubs described the entertainments in similarly blunt terms. "After spending a while at these queer places you do not get a kick out of it," he complained. "I pity them, the queer people."[29]

As such remarks suggested, the public interest in drag balls and cabarets was not an entirely liberal phenomenon. Inviting the public to scrutinize

1.2. Tsuguharu Foujita, "Helen Morgan Jr. and Jean Malin at the Smart Club Abbey," in *Vanity Fair*, 1931. © Foujita Foundation / Artists Rights Society (ARS), New York 2021. Courtesy of *Vanity Fair*.

the fairy's flamboyant mannerism as an amusing visual novelty, the provocative entertainments of the early 1930s simultaneously reassured the public of its superiority to the queer bodies on view and turned those bodies into spectacles at the pleasure of the public, commodities produced on demand to satisfy patrons' appetite for entertainment. Unsurprisingly, many viewers approached such spectacles with more than a touch of condescension, visiting pansy bars, as one sociology student in the 1930s noted, just to "ridicule the homos." Years after the pansy craze died down, curious clubgoers in New York and Chicago continued to feel entitled to visit gay bars to "watch the antics and gestures of the fags"—and even to harass the regular customers—as part of their "sight-seeing tour" of the city.[30]

Crucially, however, entertainments like the pansy cabarets did not simply mark the homosexual body as available to the public eye. They also marked that body as *legible*, marked by a series of conspicuous visual codes. Popularizing a visual trope previously confined to narrower segments of the public, those spectacles soon identified all queer bodies—and especially queer men—with a set of reliable physical signals. Chief among these was the overt gender-bending displayed at drag balls and on some cabaret stages, where participants donned full-length gowns, elaborate wigs, and consummate makeup. But even performers who avoided full drag adopted some of its visual hallmarks, powdering their faces, rouging their lips, or penciling their eyebrows. Others played up the spectacular nature of the fairy's physical affectations: the limp wrists, high-pitched voice, and swaying hips that soon became identified as the telltale homosexual "swish." By the early 1930s, entertainers like Jean Malin and Roy Spencer had taught perceptive observers to recognize even more ambiguous signals, like the fairy's bleached hair or symbolic red tie, as the calling card of the pansy. When the art critic C. J. Bulliet observed that the Broadway stage was "full of chorus men, with all the symptoms of homosexuality worn on the sleeve," he was referring not only to female drag but also to red ties—an item, he noted, worn for all the "broadest hints of its acquired significance." By 1932, at least one homosexual man felt the need to rebut the association. "It is not true that queers will wear Red nec[k]ties," he protested under hypnosis.[31]

Through a combination of flamboyance and sheer repetition, in short, the permissive leisure culture of the early twentieth century, from slumming in the Bowery to the theatrical spectacles of the pansy craze, taught urban Americans to associate certain visual cues indelibly with the homosexual. Inspired by that example, some urbanites began to pride themselves on their ability to recognize queer men on sight. "[I can] [t]ell them by the walk, the eyes, the way they act," boasted one Chicagoan in the mid-1930s. "I can spot one a block away." A 1931 novel about Manhattan's homosexual underworld, Blair Niles's *Strange Brother*, featured a character explaining his method in strikingly similar language: "Oh, I can spot 'em! Can tell 'em as far as I can see 'em. Tell by the way they cock their hats . . . by their walk even . . . the way they swing their hips." In the coming years, patrons in the bars surveilled by the liquor boards—men and women alike—would commonly insist that they could "know" simply "from [their] observation . . . a person known as a homosexual male." Indeed, Niles's novel suggested that identifying fairies was hardly an imposing accomplishment for a self-respecting urbanite. After the book's female protagonist marveled at a group of effeminate men entering a nightclub, her cousin, Phil, shrugged dismissively. "They're degenerates, June," he explained of their penciled eyebrows and high-pitched laughs. "That type of thing is degenerate."[32]

All in all, then, by the time the Prohibition era wound to a close, many urban Americans—and certainly the self-consciously sophisticated ones—had developed some fluency in the signs of sexual difference. Whether encountering the fairy in the dives of the Bowery, in the spotlights of Times Square, in the pictures circulated by *Vanity Fair*, or on the silver screen, urban dwellers discovered the homosexual as a deeply conspicuous spectacle. And many left confident in their ability to recognize that curious figure, on and off the stage.

Liquor Laws and the Presumption of Public Knowledge

It was this confidence, more than anything else, that underwrote the liquor boards' enforcement efforts following Repeal. Required by the liquor codes to prove that a bar's management knowingly served its queer crowds, liquor authorities commonly met that burden by drawing on a presumed baseline of public knowledge about sexual difference: the premise that some hallmarks of homosexuality were so well-established that any cosmopolitan—certainly, any bartender—would immediately recognize them as such.

Records of liquor proceedings in these years often read like a catalog of codes and mannerisms associated with the fairy. Arriving at the Times Square Garden in 1938, Patrolman Daniel Linker noticed what he identified as a crowd of homosexuals on the basis of their "rouged" faces, "lipstick," and the "effeminate" way they "spoke . . . [and] walked." At the Gloria Bar and Grill, Investigator William Wickes reported over one hundred customers sporting blush and bleached hair, moving their hands in "a very

graceful motion," and walking with "a swaying movement of the hips."
Even where agents reported abundant evidence of overt sexual conduct
by a bar's patrons, they made a point of emphasizing the customers' high
voices, "wiggl[ing]" gaits, and feminine nicknames.[33]

In part, cataloging the patrons' effeminate conduct allowed agents to
prove that they had accurately identified a gay bar to begin with. As one SLA
investigator explained at a hearing against the Gloria in 1939, he "c[ould]
tell" that a bar's customers were homosexual through a rundown of physical clues: the "fingernails which are usually rouged," the "lips . . . rouged
and faces powdered," an effeminate "tone of voice." Like so many urban
Americans in these years, liquor agents were confident that they could spot
queer men, immediately and infallibly, on the basis of the telltale mannerisms of the fairy. Investigator Wickes, indeed, attributed his confidence
directly to the pansy craze. Clarifying the source of his visual fluency with
pansies, he emphasized that he had previously worked "in show business,"
at which time he had ample "occasion to observe the actions, conduct, and
demeanor of the parties."[34]

Some bar owners challenged this presumption, questioning what qualified the liquor boards' agents to lodge such damning accusations against
their patrons. At the proceeding against the Gloria, defense attorney Clarence Goldberg pressed Wickes and his colleague Walter van Wagner on the
scientific pedigree behind their diagnoses of sexual deviance. "Are you a
doctor?" he demanded. "Have you ever studied the psychology of homosexualism?" Pressed to explain whether all homosexuals "practice degeneracy and perversion," van Wagner equivocated that he did not "associate" enough to know. "But you would say a homosexual is identified by
a high-pitched voice?" Goldberg derided. Meanwhile, Wickes fell directly
into Goldberg's trap, mystically describing the origins of homosexuality as
"an unnatural throwback" of "misconceived seed." Given the witnesses' answers, Goldberg concluded, Wickes and van Wagner simply had not "qualified as experts" capable of judging whether "any one or anybody is a homosexual degenerate."[35]

If Goldberg expected the investigators to defend their qualifications,
however, he mistook the SLA's strategy. Beyond proving the presence of
queer patrons at a given bar, the agents' descriptions of a defendant's effeminate customers also carried a heavier burden: they sought to establish
that a bar's management *knowingly* served homosexual men, under circumstances that left no doubt about their nature. As Patrolman Dudley Hanley
concluded in his report on the Times Square Garden and Grill: "From the
above it is apparent that the proprietor of this bar and grill had knowledge

that degenerates frequent and loiter therein." Considering the prevalence of the cultural trope of the fairy, the reasoning went, anyone faced with such an unusually effeminate crowd could be presumed to understand what its characteristics implied.[36]

Bar owners, once more, rejected that assumption. At a proceeding against the Times Square Garden, one waitress flatly denied that she could recognize a homosexual "from [her] observation." At the hearing against the Gloria, the owner, Isidore Schwartz, protested that he had never taken his admittedly dainty customers for homosexuals. "How do I know which one is a degenerate[?]" he demanded. "I can't go up and ask a man if he is . . . a fairy." Like Schwartz, some bar owners tried to turn the very sordidness of the charges to their advantage, imagining the outcry that might ensue if they began accusing their paying customers of homosexuality. As Helen Palma, a part owner of the Clover Leaf Inn in Hamilton Township, protested to a liquor agent in 1959, she "c[ould]n't very well insult" her patrons by asking them to leave "because they look queer."[37]

Pushing back specifically against the trope of the fairy, defendants disputed whether any outward physical codes, however flamboyant, could provide a reliable indicator of deviance. Some admitted noticing that their customers were on the "effeminate side" or that they acted "oddly," but they denied reading any more sinister significance into that fact. Others set their sights on the subtler hallmarks of difference sometimes associated with queer men. After one SLA investigator observed that a patron at Lynch's Builders Café in Manhattan wore a red tie with his otherwise respectable suit, the bar's attorney promptly seized on the reference, challenging the agent to concede that such accessories were hardly exclusive to homosexual men. When, at the hearing for Times Square Garden in 1939, an SLA investigator testified that several patrons wore feathers on the sides of their hats, the bar's counsel scorned the leap from the men's headwear to their supposedly deviant character. "Did you ever see the hat store sell hats with small feathers in them?" William Cohen demanded. "Would you say all the people with feathers in their hats are effeminate?"[38]

Many bar owners proposed more innocent explanations for their customers' unusual appearance. Patrons who appeared to be wearing rouge or mascara, the defense team for Manhattan's Stanwood Cafeteria insisted in 1954, might have been actors stepping in from the local television studio. Men with traces of powder on their faces, proposed the attorney defending Peter Orsi's bar in 1939, might have been shedding talcum powder from a recent shave. Patrons overseen dancing, suggested Adele Kaczka and Halina Bolcato in their respective proceedings, were likely dance instructors teaching each other the latest fads. The ABC's investigation of the Wardell Hotel in Phillipsburg, New Jersey, elicited a particularly inspired campaign of deflection. Facing down a set of liquor agents on the premises, one customer insisted that the powder on his face was the residue from his acne medication. Another credited his blondined hair to regular sessions under a sunlamp. A third, aligning himself with a group only slightly less maligned than homosexuals, explained away his "swish[y]" hips as the lingering legacy of three years in art school.[39]

Emphasizing the many legitimate ways a man could accidentally stumble into deviance, the defendants' argument seized on a core danger at the heart of liquor agents' claims: the extent to which the agency's presumptions skirted a thin, often arbitrary line around what could be considered normal male conduct in any case. The liquor boards' evidence against gay bars, after all, did not simply endorse a popular stereotype of homosexual effeminacy. It narrowed the realm of permissible behavior for all men on a bar's premises. As the defense teams were well aware, nothing could derail the state's accusation like comparing the alleged homosexuals to the accusers themselves. When the SLA's counsel asked one of the Times Square Garden's loyal customers to describe the bar's patrons, for instance, she coyly characterized them as "ordinary men, like yourself." Having already compelled Wickes to admit that he himself used rouge in his theater days, Gloria's attorney reminded him that a heterosexual patron at the bar had assumed Wickes himself was "queer." "He was balmy," Wickes immediately shot back—or, at the least, "I hope he was." At a time when public understandings of sexual deviance depended as much on gender presentation as on sexual practice, liquor agents and officers who spent late nights patrolling gay bars and even flirting with the regulars still harbored some discomfort at blending in too closely with the patrons they observed. It was one thing to tolerate or even to initiate intimacies on a barroom floor. It was another to be mistaken for one of the fairies who departed so dramatically from the bounds of masculine respectability.[40]

Sometimes, bar owners' challenges to the evidence found a sympathetic ear among the liquor boards. In 1942, Burnett's successor, Commissioner Alfred Driscoll, dismissed charges that James and Edna McClyment had employed female impersonators at their bar in Gloucester City. Although the employees described "came dangerously close, in their type and by their actions, to being female impersonators," Driscoll concluded, he nevertheless retained "some doubt" about their true natures. At a 1956 proceeding against the Rutgers Cocktail Bar, a hearing officer conceded that the patrons' "swaying" hips and "effeminate" gestures "might arouse suspicion," but he, too, was not quite convinced the owner knowingly catered to homosexuals. Such holdings were few and far between, and some were reversed by less lenient directors. But they demonstrated that at least some officials, even within the liquor agencies themselves, had their doubts about what a man's feminine demeanor said about his sexual predisposition.[41]

For the most part, however, bar owners' attempts to sever the link between homosexuality and the fairy of the popular imagination did not fare well. The case against Peter Orsi's restaurant in Newark in 1939 exemplified the presumptions of the time. After Orsi denied that he had recognized his rouged, mascaraed, and falsettoed customers as homosexuals, speculating that they might have been wearing stage makeup or shaving powder, Commissioner Burnett dismissed his arguments with a passion perhaps unusual for an administrative disposition. "Possible—yes! But not at all probable!!" Burnett wrote. "Real men don't act that way, whether they are in the theatrical line or have just left a barber shop." Insisting on some clear, inviolable understanding of what "real men" act like, Burnett's outburst bespoke the ABC's commitment to preserving a bright line between ostensibly normal and deviant masculine conduct. But it also reflected the division's commitment to the belief that distinguishing homosexuals from ordinary men was a simple task, easily performed by the average person. Considering that "anyone can tell objectively and most of us know what they are," as Burnett put it, he was "not at all squeamish in imputing knowledge" that the patrons Orsi served were homosexual.[42]

Here, indeed, was the liquor boards' response to bars, like the Gloria Bar and Grill, that tried to question their agents' qualifications to identify queer customers. Even as Goldberg decried the state witnesses' meager expert credentials, the officers were happy to concede the point. "I don't consider myself an expert," van Wagner agreed, "but I consider myself sufficiently versed that [I know] when I see a pansy or a degenerate." Goldberg tried his hand again with Wickes: "But you will admit that it is sometimes difficult to tell the difference between the homosexual and a normal man?" "Hardly," Wickes replied. The reason the agents' inferences about homosexual customers were so credible, the liquor boards suggested, was not because they had any special training in the art. It was because those inferences were so very unremarkable—simple deductions that could be corroborated by any patron at the bar. As the SLA's attorney memorably objected to Goldberg's continued attempts to probe the agents' professional qualifications: "You don't have to be an expert to be able to see a homosexual."[43]

The evidence undergirding the liquor boards' campaigns against gay bars following Repeal illustrates the powerful symbiosis between the regulation of queer life and popular knowledge about sexual difference in the twentieth century. Requiring proof that bar owners knowingly welcomed queer patrons on their premises, liquor proceedings often came down to two interrelated assumptions. First, they assumed that homosexual men were identifiable through certain discrete visual codes, embodied in the popular trope of the fairy. Second, they assumed that the average bar owner or bartender *knew* those codes—that the telltale fashions and quirks of the fairy were sufficiently well-established that anyone tending a bar could be presumed to recognize them on sight. More than the boards' rigorous enforcement policies or even liquor agents' own sensitivities to the contours of queer life, the scope and success of the liquor boards' antihomosexual campaigns rested on the availability of some shared public understanding of sexual deviance: the assumption that certain visual tropes were not just reliable hallmarks of homosexuality, but also so widely recognized that their meaning could be imputed, without further evidence, to a bar's employees.

The unique incentives created by the liquor boards' regulations illuminate those agencies' pervasive reliance on broad stereotypes of homosexuality to prosecute gay-friendly bars: why investigators so frequently played up the most commonplace, more flamboyant tropes of gay men in their proceedings. To the extent that the boards relied on such superficial evidence, that reliance did not simply reveal the agents' own reductive view of gay men. Nor did it merely express, as historians have thoughtfully suggested, the boards' special antipathy to bars whose patrons most clearly transgressed conventional norms of masculinity—that most flagrantly offended the traditional ideals of public order that liquor boards saw it as their job to maintain. That reliance was also compelled by the particular legal framework in which the boards operated, which demanded proof that defendants knowingly served gay patrons and so inevitably pushed investigators to invoke the most widespread public presumptions available. Targeting only deliberate violations—and, more specifically, deliberate interactions with marginalized social groups—the boards' antihomosexual campaigns inevitably invited liquor agents to stereotype queer communities as the bedrock of their enforcement efforts.

And they invited private individuals to stereotype those communities, too, as a cost of doing business. Penalizing establishments that failed to screen their clientele on the basis of certain popular presumptions about what homosexual men look and act like, the liquor boards' antihomosexual charges did not merely conflate effeminacy and sexual deviance as a matter of law. They demanded that same inference from the bar owners and bartenders subject to their authority, requiring a bar's employees to treat certain unorthodox behaviors, fashions, and grooming choices as determinative of homosexuality in their routine interactions with their customers. Scholars have insightfully examined how licensing schemes like the states' liquor laws following Repeal conscripted private business owners into the work of policing their own customers, watching for "undesirable" patrons and ejecting them as they appeared. But the legal demands placed on the diligent bartender under the liquor codes were not solely duties to act. They were also duties to *know*: to buy into and maintain a certain level of fluency in the purported markers of homosexuality. Whatever their own views on the significance of a high-pitched voice, feathered hat, or bleached hair, bar owners hoping to protect their livelihoods had to accept—or at least to enforce—a rigid boundary between normal and deviant male conduct as the condition of holding a liquor license.[44]

More significantly than illuminating the role of stereotype in the policing of queer communities, however, the liquor boards' reliance on popular knowledge as the bedrock of their campaigns invites a deeper reevaluation of the role of public discourse in the regulation of queer life. Not least, that pattern urges us to reconsider the cultural moments that gave rise to the public's presumptively shared insights about homosexuality in the first place: those bursts of popular attention, like the urban entertainments of the 1920s and 1930s, that broke from a culture generally averse to any visible signs of homosexuality and introduced many Americans to their cities' fledgling queer subcultures. The pansy craze, especially, is often remembered as a bubble of relative tolerance in the long history of public antipathy to queer men and women in the twentieth century, a moment when the public set aside its concerns about policing the public manifestations of sexual difference and allowed itself, however briefly, to be entertained by them. Yet that flowering of public interest—that flash of relatively open, even if often condescending, discourse on the homosexual—ultimately left a far more complicated legacy. Far from simply a moment of liberal curiosity about the urban underworld, or even merely a tool of informal social regulation, assuring mainstream audiences of their superiority to a maligned minority, the pansy craze provided a direct tool of legal regulation itself, underwriting an enforcement regime predicated on the public's shared intimacy with sexual deviance. The availability of some open discourse about queer men in America's cities—and all the more so, one that genuinely reflected the social quirks and contours of that group—created a powerful foundation for the states' campaigns against urban queer life.

Disorderly Conduct and the Continuing Salience of Public Knowledge

In the first decades following Repeal, of course, the liquor boards' reliance on the outward hallmarks of the fairy to prosecute gay-friendly bars reflected a key feature of the liquor codes: that most laws prohibited bar owners from so much as permitting homosexuals on their premises. Beginning in the early 1950s, a number of legal shifts led liquor boards to adopt a different standard, focusing less on patrons' ostensibly deviant identities than on their public behavior. Read at face value, that shift might have reined in the boards' ability to charge bar owners simply on the ground that they must have recognized their homosexual customers. But agencies accustomed to relying on such inferences to support their cases were not willing to change stream so quickly.

The shift toward a conduct-based regime began in 1951 in California, a state not especially notable for its campaigns against gay bars until that point. Throughout the 1940s, the BOE, a taxing agency and a notoriously disorganized one at that, had taken few steps to enforce the liquor code against gay-friendly venues. But in 1949, on the heels of an investigation into what began as a labor dispute, the board suspended the license of the Black Cat, a popular bohemian nightspot in San Francisco, for permitting "persons of known homosexual tendencies" to gather on the premises. The Black Cat's owner, Sol Stoumen, appealed his suspension all the way to the Supreme Court of California, insisting that mere evidence of his patrons' effeminate mannerisms failed to establish any legal violation. That particular court would soon become a darling in liberal circles, famous—or infamous, given the audience—for its protection of individual liberties in matters ranging from criminal procedure to product liability to reproductive rights. And in *Stoumen v. Reilly*, it sided, once more, with the underdog. Chief Justice Phil Gibson accepted at face value the charge that the Black Cat's customers were, in fact, homosexual. But, invoking a deep-seated principle against excluding disfavored groups from places of public accommodation, he insisted that charges of a "disorderly" house required actual evidence of improper behavior on the premises. "Mere proof of patronage" by even avowedly homosexual men, absent some further "proof of the commission of illegal or immoral acts," was simply not enough to violate the statute.[45]

Stoumen was a milestone in the history of gay civil rights, the first case to defend the right of queer men and women to exist openly in the public sphere. And its rationale was soon echoed on the East Coast. In New York, the judiciary first confronted the issue in 1954, when the SLA revoked the license of Bernard's Bar and Grill on the basis of testimony that men had embraced and used "endearing terms" at the bar. Bernard's owner initially tried a familiar defense, questioning how the state's witnesses could tell "whether those present at the bar were homosexuals," but the court paid this argument little mind. It was, however, compelled by the claim that the SLA's evidence failed to establish that Bernard's was disorderly in violation of section 106. Relying less on first principles than on the statutory language, Magistrate Judge William Ringel insisted that a charge of operating a disorderly establishment required proof that the defendant's patrons had engaged in illicit or disreputable conduct, such as overt "lewd and indecent acts." Over the following years, higher courts echoed Ringel's reasoning, agreeing that the "mere congregation" of homosexuals at a bar did not suffice to violate the liquor code.[46]

In a decade when regulators at the federal level commonly broadened their antihomosexual campaigns by shifting their focus from illicit sexual acts toward identifiable homosexual "persons," the liquor laws might have seemed to move in the opposite direction. Indeed, in California, where the lower courts often shared the supreme court's liberal leanings, *Stoumen*'s demand for some proof of disorderly conduct imposed a meaningful restraint on the liquor boards' operations. In the coming years, the BOE found itself forced to produce genuine evidence that a bar's customers had, beyond gathering at a bar, done something in particular to disturb the peace. Balking at that strict standard, in 1955 the state legislature took matters into its own hands, shifting responsibility for the state's liquor laws from the tax board to a specialized, far more robust Department of Alcoholic Beverage Control. It also passed a new provision targeting bars operating as "a resort for sexual perverts," a move aimed directly at overriding *Stoumen*. Yet the California courts would not disavow the principle behind that decision so easily. Loosely interpreting the new statute, appellate courts insisted on reading it as codifying, not eliminating, *Stoumen*'s requirement of disorderly behavior. In 1959, the Supreme Court of California rejected that interpretation as against the plain text of the provision— and promptly invalidated the law as unconstitutional, under the same rationale that drove its reasoning in that earlier case. Absent a pattern of solicitation or other lewd behavior by a bar's patrons, the Department of Alcoholic Beverage Control's remedies against even the most avowedly gay-friendly venues came down to posting warnings on their windows and letting business continue as usual.[47]

In New York, however, the courts' seemingly stricter new standard made surprisingly little difference in the SLA's enforcement efforts. Unlike California's agencies, after all, the SLA had spent the previous fifteen years developing a pattern of charges against gay-friendly establishments, one that relied on the unmistakable signs of the fairy as the backbone of its campaigns, and it was unwilling to abandon such a convenient form of evidence. Well into the 1960s, it brought charges of disorderly conduct on the basis of much the same testimony it had used to establish the mere congregation of homosexuals in prior years. In 1959, for instance, investigators testified that the patrons at the Fulton Bar and Grill "wore tight fitting trousers," spoke in "effeminate tones," and walked "with a sway in their walk"—evidence that demonstrated, per the board, that the bar's customers "conducted themselves in an offensive and indecent manner." The courts, for their part, acquiesced. Having questioned the liquor law's reach on statutory grounds rather than the deeper principles animating *Stoumen*, New York judges proved less eager to pick high-profile battles with the liquor board. Even conceding that "the mere congregation of homosexuals . . . does not make the premises disorderly," as the appellate division reasoned in a proceeding against Handy's Bar and Grill on the Upper West Side, patrons who swished or dropped their wrists did not merely congregate; they "exhibited characteristics and mannerisms which evidenced homosexual propensities." As interpreted by the SLA and affirmed by the New York courts, disorderly conduct did not require any illegal or lewd behavior at a bar. It encompassed any behavior that revealed a customer's unorthodox sexual preferences: any conduct recognizable to the public as a mark of queerness. The public's presumptive ability to identify gay men, in effect, bridged the gap between a status-based and a conduct-based legal regime, turning the very presence of visibly homosexual patrons into evidence of disorderly behavior.[48]

The toothlessness of the shift from status to conduct was perhaps best illustrated by the experience of New Jersey, where the ABC switched regulations not by order of any court but by fiat of the board itself, expressly as a way to reach more gay-friendly establishments. After two decades of prosecutions brought under Rule 4, one of Commissioner Burnett's successors—newly designated as the Director of the ABC—decided in 1954 that the regulation, inspired by the overtly gender-bending spectacles of the pansy craze, failed to address the broader spectrum of queer conduct pervading New Jersey's nightlife in the 1950s. Instead, he turned to Rule 5, New Jersey's own disorderly conduct provision, which prohibited bars from operating "in such a manner as to become a nuisance." Echoing the New York appellate courts' reasoning, the ABC concluded that a bar conducted its business so "as to become a nuisance" whenever it "allowed, permitted, and suffered . . . persons who *appeared to be homosexuals*." Adopting that principle, the vast majority of proceedings against gay bars in New Jersey in the coming years did not allege that the defendants tolerated disruptive or lewd acts on the premises. They merely alleged that bar owners served "apparent homosexuals."[49]

If anything, indeed, the ABC's switch to Rule 5 heightened its dependence on public perceptions of gay men to prosecute gay bars—a point made unmistakably clear in the proceedings against the Paddock Bar in 1957. In addition to defending her patrons' peaceful conduct, the owner, Marion Brown, protested like so many before her that the ABC had failed to prove that her customers were truly homosexual. Yet the liquor board and, subsequently, the Superior Court of New Jersey rejected that entire line of defense. Conceding the absence of conclusive evidence that the bar's patrons "were in actuality homosexuals," the court noted, the Paddock Bar was not charged with catering to homosexuals. It was charged with offending public morals by serving apparent homosexuals: "persons who conspicuously displayed by speech, tone of voice, bodily movements, gestures, and other mannerisms the common characteristics [of queer men]." Even if the state had failed to prove that Brown's customers "were in fact homosexuals," the panel concluded, "it certainly proved that they had the conspicuous . . . *appearance* of such personalities." Far from limiting the division's reliance on popular assumptions about gay men, the ABC's turn to Rule 5 lowered its evidentiary burden, eliminating any requirement that agents accurately identify a gay bar to begin with. It was enough to prove that bar owners served anyone who resembled a homosexual—who conformed to public presumptions of what queer men looked like.[50]

The liquor boards' insistence that the mere presence of identifiably queer customers rendered a bar disorderly reflected their modest appraisal of the public's tolerance of any signs of sexual difference. As far as the liquor boards were concerned, a homosexual patron's most disruptive conduct did not consist of any overt sexual overtures—acts that, inconveniently enough, were often quite discreet. It consisted of any visual clues that the average bargoer could be expected to recognize as the hallmarks of sexual deviance. Back in 1941, Burnett's successor had avowed his continuing commitment to the division's antihomosexual campaigns, warning that the "mere thought of such perverts is repugnant to the normal person." The division's goal, it now emerged, was to prevent the normal person from ever having to think of them: from so much as getting an opportunity to detect a homosexual in the public sphere.[51]

At the same time, New York's and New Jersey's continuing reliance on popular presumptions about gay men as the fulcrum of their proceedings underscored the centrality of public knowledge to the liquor boards' antihomosexual operations. Even under a standard supposedly concerned with disorderly conduct rather than group identity, the breadth of the liquor boards' enforcement efforts reflected, first and foremost, their appraisal of the average bargoer's presumptive familiarity with the homosexual: his ability to recognize particular physical affects or visual cues as among the "common characteristics" of sexual difference and, therefore, as disruptive of the public order. As interpreted by the liquor boards, the disorderliness of a queer crowd was as much the product of gay men's own behavior as of the public's intimacy with the signifiers of urban gay life—the average American's currency in the signs and hallmarks of the queer body.

Public Knowledge and Politics of Common Sense

In the years following the liquor boards' uneven shift to a disorderly conduct standard, their campaigns against gay-friendly bars continued unabated. Indeed, as the end of the Second World War sent an influx of gay men and some women, fresh from military service and inspired by the friendships they had formed there, into the nation's urban centers, many American cities observed a boom in businesses catering to queer customers. Responding to those trends, the liquor boards' antihomosexual proceedings frequently expanded over the course of the 1950s, proliferating in California with the advent of its specialized Department of Alcoholic Beverage Control and roughly tripling in New Jersey with the ABC's switch to Rule 5. In California and, eventually, New York, as urban gay men grew increasingly confident in their social spaces, the boards' charges often came to focus on evidence of overt sexual conduct, though demeanor evidence remained a staple of the proceedings. In New Jersey, reflecting Rule 5's focus on "apparent homosexuals," disciplinary hearings well into the 1960s continued to hang substantially on the patrons' outward appearance. Across the board, however, the logistics of the proceedings shifted to accommodate the evolving patterns of queer life, in at least two ways.[52]

The first had to do with the types of bars that occupied the boards' attention and, in particular, the emergence of a new type of offending establishment: the lesbian bar. The liquor boards' growing attention to lesbian bars in these years largely mirrored the growth of lesbian nightlife itself. In the first decades following Repeal, businesses catering specifically to lesbians were often constrained by a broader taboo against unaccompanied women in public spaces, especially in seedier establishments like bars and taverns. Under those circumstances, lesbians, and particularly middle-class women, rarely ventured to claim a bar or restaurant as their own, more commonly socializing in private homes. By the mid-1950s, American women began stepping more confidently into their cities' professional and commercial worlds, and in that setting queer women, especially among the working class, turned to bars as a new center of social life. Sometimes they shared their gathering spots with gay men, mixing in the same establishments or at least congregating in separate corners. But some lesbian communities, eager for their own social spaces, also sustained a broad patchwork of bars aimed primarily if not exclusively at their patronage. In New Jersey alone around the late 1950s and early 1960s, lesbians hoping to spend an evening with their own could pick among a range of venues—including, at various points, the Blue Room in Elizabeth, the Speedway Inn in Waterford, Edna's Rendezvous in Paterson, Helene's Bar in Roselle, the Clover Leaf Inn in Mays Landing, the Famous Bar in Atlantic City, and the Pelican Bar, the Latin Quarter, and Club Delite in Newark.[53]

At a time when public discussions of sexual deviance made little room for women, businesses catering to lesbians tended to receive less police scrutiny than gay or even mixed bars. To be sure, they did not entirely escape the brunt of official harassment; police officers often idled outside suspected lesbian bars to intimidate prospective customers or kept an especially keen eye out for technical violations. Some bars endured intermittent raids, violent confrontations in which poor and butch women were particularly likely to face arrest. Yet, owing both to women's lesser access to the public sphere and to the relative equanimity with which male agents often greeted their relationships, lesbian bars typically failed to inspire the same indignation that attended the boards' campaigns against gay bars. Lesbianism, as one sergeant with the Los Angeles Police Department would explain in the 1960s was less innately abhorrent than male homosexuality and tended to be more discreet, posing a minor public nuisance. In San Francisco, law enforcement agents typically cracked down on lesbian bars only when their investigation implicated owners or patrons in additional criminal conduct, like prostitution or the use of narcotics. Records of liquor board proceedings in New York City show few traces of any activities against lesbian bars.[54]

Some liquor boards, however, saw the rise of female-dominated drinking spaces as precisely the type of social disorder they were charged with patrolling, and they took a more expansive approach. In New Jersey, especially, where the ABC prided itself on its rigorous enforcement efforts, charges against lesbian bars soon emerged as a staple of the state's anti-homosexual campaigns.

As in their cases against primarily male establishments, the boards' evidence against lesbian bars focused largely on their patrons' demeanor. Not unlike gay life in these years, lesbian culture by the 1950s had developed its own social customs and fashions, adopted for a combination of expressive and functional purposes. The best established of these was the convention of *butch* and *femme*: the common practice of lesbian women, and especially partners in a romantic pairing, to divide between those who self-consciously cast off the trappings of traditional femininity and those who meticulously enacted them. Unsurprisingly, femme women often escaped the liquor boards' attention, but the butch lesbian immediately came to stand at the center of their cases. Alongside reports of women dancing or kissing each other on the premises, investigators commonly recounted seeing crowds of female patrons with closely cropped hair, their faces free of makeup or bearing only "slight traces of it," wearing no jewelry except perhaps a man's watch on the wrist. They described women dressed in men's fashions, from boots to collared shirts to trousers that zipped up the front. At Jack's Star Bar in Newark, an agent took note of one woman sporting a double-breasted jacket, brown collared shirt, and prominent sideburns. At Helene's in the fall of 1960, an investigator observed a woman in dress shoes, pants, a black tie, and a "red sweater"—the latter of which, he emphasized, "he had seen worn by men."[55]

Beyond the matter of dress, liquor agents identified a broad array of behaviors that supposedly separated lesbians from other women. The patrons at the defendants' bars, they observed, used "filthy," "vile," and "indecent" language. They kept their cigarettes in the sides of their mouths, held the stubs "back-handed," and flicked the ashes with their thumbs rather than "in a daintier fashion as a girl might do it." They sipped their beer straight from the bottle, set down their glasses "roughly" at the bar, and sometimes "gulp[ed] a shot of whiskey in one drink." Few behaviors escaped being parsed as sufficiently or insufficiently feminine. The patrons at Club Tequila, one investigator recounted, held their pool cues "in much the same way as a male would."[56]

Defining a broad swath of conduct as intrinsically masculine and therefore deviant when performed by a woman, the boards' observations were not simply concerned with ferreting out nonnormative sexual practices. As the continuing reverberations of the recent war effort triggered broader anxieties about the future of conventional gender roles, they helped patrol the lines of all decorous femininity in public spaces. From bar patrons' language to their failure to wear sufficient makeup, traditional norms of female attractiveness were far more central to the ABC's conception of lesbianism than were actual erotic acts. Indeed, although by the 1960s many investigators had come to recognize that not all gay men were effeminate, agents continued to define lesbians solely in terms of their butch appearance, often erasing the category of the femme lesbian altogether. Numerous hearings featured accounts of "lesbians" buying drinks for, dancing with, and even kissing their "normal" or "straight girlfriends."[57]

As in proceedings against gay bars, the boards' evidence in these cases harkened back to a long-standing association between sexual difference and gender nonconformity. Alongside feminine emcees like Jean Malin, in fact, the pansy craze had featured its share of lesbian performers. Perhaps the preeminent act in Harlem in the 1930s was the singer Gladys Bentley, a butch black woman who appeared on stage wearing a tuxedo and proudly informed the press of her plans to marry her white female lover.[58]

Yet, perhaps owing to her lesser comic value or to the greater elasticity of women's gender norms in the early twentieth century, the lesbian never claimed as strong a grasp on the popular imagination as did her male counterpart. Certainly, she was not a social type that loomed quite as large as the fairy. In context, the liquor boards' catalogs of the incriminating behaviors observed in lesbian-friendly bars did not necessarily rely on any established stereotypes of what queer women looked or acted like. More foundationally, they expressed some instinctive sense that *any* woman who strayed too far from the proper boundaries of femininity—who rejected the familiar pleasures of the home for a seedy drinking establishment—had to have something abnormal, and specifically sexually abnormal, about her.

In that regard, the ABC's proceedings against lesbian bars reflected a broader shift confronting the liquor boards in the 1950s: the extent to which gay male life, too, increasingly diverged from the public's most familiar presumptions about queer communities. In the first two decades following Repeal, the liquor boards' campaigns depended largely on the fact that many patrons of gay bars in fact conformed, at least in part, with the flamboyant trappings of the fairy. In the coming years, some men continued to do so, especially in the working-class communities where the fairy's camp style had historically been rehearsed. But as growing numbers of white-collar gay men settled in the nation's cities in the 1950s, eager to build professional and social lives beyond the shadow of public disapproval, many eschewed the effeminate affectations that had often marked gay nightlife in prior years. Even in the safety of their own circles, they opted for a cultural code that was similarly reliable but subtler, replacing the tweezed eyebrows and painted nails with tailored slacks, sweaters, sport coats, and loafers. That cultural shift itself was a product of the gay community's ongoing struggle against state surveillance at midcentury—one that would shape the nature of antihomosexual policing well beyond the liquor boards (see chapter 4). For present purposes, it suffices to note that the gay world's new fashions were, by design, a departure from the public's long-standing assumptions about queer life. That dress code was self-consciously respectable: the type of clothing, one researcher observed, "that an average college under-graduate might wear." Heterosexuals visiting gay bars in the early 1960s would remark on how little their patrons matched popular conceptions of the fairy.[59]

None of that stopped the liquor boards from prosecuting gay bars on the basis of their patrons' supposedly telltale appearance. Having fought to harness their charges to the public's presumptively shared ability to recognize queer men—often over the protests of recalcitrant bar owners—they were not willing to change their ways so easily. They simply shifted their account of what made those patrons' appearance so very telling. Common signs of a gay crowd, police officers and liquor agents now insisted, included not only men wearing women's blouses or rouging their cheeks but also a range of arguably middle-of-the-road fashions: chinos and dress pants, sport coats and bulky sweaters, button-downs and polos, loafers and sneakers. Damning behaviors, too, expanded beyond the familiar affectations modeled by the fairy to encompass a broader array of allegedly incriminating conduct. Agents took note of men sticking out their tongues, rolling their eyes, and running their fingers through their hair. They observed men sipping through straws, lifting their drinks to toast each other, ordering cocktails "with straws and cherries," and taking too long to finish their drinks. They reported men looking directly into each other's eyes, crossing their legs while they sat, and raising their arms as they danced. If the women at Club Tequila played pool in a manly fashion, a customer at a popular gay bar in Trenton "bowl[ed] in an effeminate manner."[60]

Insisting on identifying gay men through their clothes and conduct without impugning the way many ordinary men in the 1960s tended to act and dress, investigators ended up drawing some very fine lines around the boundaries of permissible masculinity. Singling out the primarily gay crowd at the Fulton Bar and Grill from the "two or three" straight patrons there, one New York investigator described "normal male attire" as a jacket, shirt, and tie, while homosexual attire consisted of a jacket, dress shirt or sweater, and no tie. A colleague deemed deeply incriminating men wearing loafers without socks or sweaters with no undershirts. Meanwhile, agents committed to characterizing any unusual social interactions spotted in gay bars as inherently emasculating sometimes strained to fit their observations into a gendered binary. Describing several pairs of customers singing at a piano bar, one liquor agent in New Jersey observed that they "sang into each other's face . . . as a female would sing perhaps to a male."[61]

The treacherous contours of the liquor boards' evidence emerged most clearly in comparison with their testimony against lesbian-friendly bars. As a careful observer might have noticed—and some defendants did—those proceedings often attributed vastly different connotations to essentially identical behaviors. At Pauline Brakatselos's restaurant in New York's Chelsea neighborhood, male patrons who held their beer bottles by their top or drank by taking the bottle into their mouths rather than sipping from the edge were, per the state witnesses, conspicuously feminine. According to a liquor agent at Club Tequila in Newark, women who drank their beer straight from the bottle, regardless of how they sipped it, were incriminatingly masculine. Worn by men, popular items like dress shirts, sport coats, and bulky sweaters (without ties, at least) were emasculating and indicative of homosexuality. Worn by women, these same items were quintessentially masculine and indicative of lesbianism—especially since, as one California liquor agent explained after spotting a group of female patrons wearing button-downs in pink, yellow, and blue tones, "men are now wearing clothes in the pastel shades."[62]

Bar owners protested these ever-shifting markers of deviance. As defendants reminded the liquor boards, a male homosexual, and certainly an *apparent* homosexual, was a man who "st[ank] of perfume," fluttered his wrists, and "swish[ed] [his] hips when walking"—the kind of theatrical creature, as one bartender at Murphy's Tavern in Newark suggested in 1960, that might be "seen . . . in shows in New York." Men dressed in ordinary leisurewear hardly qualified, even if they did stick up their pinkies or roll their eyes as they talked. That objection was not entirely novel; in earlier decades, too, bar owners had denied that they found anything incriminating about their customers' allegedly effeminate conduct. Yet as the evidence against gay bars encompassed an increasingly diverse and complex terrain of social behaviors, that objection found ever-greater purchase. As liquor agents themselves admitted, ordinary men in the 1960s wore sweaters, preferred tailored trousers, and sometimes even went for manicures. Ordinary men bought each other drinks, patted each other on the back, and ordered cocktails topped with straws or cherries. Ordinary men sported long hair (an attribute, one agent conceded, connoting only that "a man needs a haircut"), and ordinary men crossed their legs when they sat down.[63]

Sensitive to the ambiguous nature of the charges brought against them, some defense witnesses offered themselves as evidence, daring the state's lawyers to impugn their masculinity. As the owner of Trenton's Paddock Inn—no relation to Marion Brown's beleaguered Paddock Bar in Asbury Park—testified before the ABC, he flicked his cigarettes just like his supposedly queer patrons. Did the board's attorney want to say that he was "one too"? Manuel Joseph Fernandez, a regular at Murphy's Tavern, testified that he owned a loose-knit sweater—purchased from "Bamberger's, on sale"—and that his wardrobe choices were in reputable company: President Kennedy had recently been photographed wearing a bulky Italian-weave sweater in Hyannis Port, proving that there was "nothing unusual about that." As for the delicate mannerisms spotted by the investigators, his father sometimes lifted his pinky when he drank, and, no, he did not "find anything peculiar about [his] father." These forms of testimony frequently involved a type of bluff between the witness and the court. No matter how closely a witness matched queer stereotypes, few hearing officers or judges were willing to call a stranger homosexual to his face—to have the same awkward confrontations in their courtrooms, in effect, that they demanded of bartenders on a daily basis. But that testimony also demonstrated the genuine ambiguity of at least some hallmarks of queerness identified by the liquor boards, popular among not only alleged homosexuals but also family men and elite politicians.[64]

Bar owners' efforts to defend the cultural currency of knit sweaters, long haircuts, and elaborate cocktails did not simply point to the shifting tides of urban fashion. They took aim at the cultural and class presumptions inherent in the liquor boards' attempts to chart the lines of normative manhood and womanhood. Particularly in cities with substantial recent immigrant communities, some bar owners decried the conservative, even provincial norms underlying the liquor boards' evidence. Fending off charges of salacious dancing, for instance, the owner of Pearl's Bar in Oakland claimed that the steps described by the ABC investigators—men gyrating their hips or moving their pelvises in a suggestive manner—were characteristic of Latin American dance styles that had grown popular in California in the 1950s. The department's claims that there was anything inappropriate about them revealed a lack of cosmopolitanism, cultural sensitivity, or both. (This despite the fact that most gay bars in these years—Pearl's included—themselves featured precious little ethnic and racial mixing. While investigators occasionally remarked on the presence of one or two black patrons, most crowds remained homogeneous even in cities that no longer mandated the segregation of public accommodations, and what mingling occurred was not always peaceful. When one black patron at Pearl's tried groping a white man, a form of horseplay commonly spotted in gay bars at the time, the white man responded by slapping him across the face—the sole "altercation" investigators reported witnessing in their hours there.)[65]

More commonly, bar owners pointed to economic divides to undermine the state's evidence. In numerous proceedings, defendants insisted that agents' incriminating descriptions of their patrons' unusual clothing or mannerisms were simply misinterpreting class signals. At Pearl's Bar itself, the attorney suggested, men wearing what the investigators classified as jewelry were likely just wearing their college rings. At the Rutgers Cocktail Bar in Newark, a bartender testified that the "delicate" men who gathered at his business were gentlemanly and "well-educated"—not like the "riffraff" at other establishments. After an investigator accused a patron at Murphy's Tavern of speaking with an effeminate lisp, the bar's attorney seized on the agent's qualifications to judge the man's diction. "And if I told you that this man graduated from Harvard and spoke with a Harvard accent," he demanded, "would you say that was true or untrue?" The quintessentially gay fashions invoked by investigators, in particular—polo shirts, sweaters, sport jackets—borrowed directly from the so-called Ivy League styles popular among collegiate men in the late 1950s and the 1960s, and bar owners commonly criticized such evidence as insulting all upper-class men. "I wonder what the Ivy League boys would think of [the ABC's homoerotic inferences]," sneered the attorney for Murphy's Tavern—"particularly, boys from Yale and Harvard."[66]

In some cases, no doubt, bar owners who defended their patrons' fine breeding were looking for any less incriminating explanation for the investigators' observations. In others, they also likely did so as a form of loose character evidence. Taking advantage of the legal system's habitual preferential treatment of higher-class men, defendants who lauded the elite respectability of their clientele—contrasted, implicitly, against the liquor agents' own lesser education and rougher pedigree—invited the courts to weigh the charges in light of the targets' relative social standing.[67]

Yet some bar owners' claims of mismatched class signals also had a ring of truth. For one thing, many gay bars—especially those whose patrons favored collegiate fashions—did cater to a relatively well-off crowd. For that reason among others, gay nightspots that operated in lower-class neighborhoods sometimes came into friction with the locals, who chafed at the "queers" flocking to their favorite haunts. And it was, regardless, true that the fashions identified by liquor agents as the red flags of homosexuality were hardly limited to gay men. Elite men, at Harvard and elsewhere, commonly wore such clothing—not as a subversion of traditional masculine norms but as a way of enacting their own brand of aggressive masculinity. On Ivy League campuses in the 1960s, the urbane clothing described by the agents was a ticket to manhood: a way for wealthier students to assert their sexual attractiveness and superior social status over outsiders who lacked their manners and fine dress. The same thing could be said of the many unusual behaviors reported by liquor agents. Testifying against Brakatselos's restaurant in Chelsea, for instance, one police officer emphasized the "very refined" tenor of one customer's voice, pronouncing "every word . . . just so." A colleague added, as in his mind deeply incriminating, that the patrons referred to each other by their full names: rather than Frank or Frankie, as a friend would "normally" call him, one man went by "Francis." Such rugged definitions of normal masculinity excluded not just the overt effeminacy of the fairy or even the homoerotic conduct increasingly common in gay bars in the 1960s, but also a range of aesthetic and social conventions common among the wealthier classes.[68]

In that context, bar owners' efforts to defend the class valence of their patrons' clothes and drink orders did not merely reflect a creative legal strategy, attempting to undermine the state's evidence in any way possible. They exploited the genuinely complicated class politics underlying the liquor boards' definitions of normal male and female conduct. The states' attempts to chart the boundaries of conventional masculinity—to establish, as Commissioner Burnett had years earlier, what "real men" act like—not only assumed that some recognized standard of manhood prevailed among the public, but also forced the boards to choose *whose* standard they were willing to enforce. And while liquor officials' own backgrounds likely differed, their preferred paradigm was self-consciously antielite. Far from deferring to upper-class social standards, as bar owners invoking the fashions and manners of Harvard boys might have hoped, the liquor boards' evidence commonly evinced a fundamental skepticism of the legitimacy of masculine norms espoused by the upper class. Still only some years after Senate Republicans successfully savaged the reputations of patrician Democrats like Dean Acheson as overdelicate eggheads incapable of manly leadership, the suspicions that attached to the effete patrons at gay bars—the eyebrows raised at ordering a cocktail rather than a beer, or wearing an imported sweater—reflected the precarious status of elite men among the Cold War public more broadly.[69]

Proceedings against lesbian bars waged precisely the opposite debate. If liquor agents impugning gay patrons' collegiate fashions insulted all Harvard graduates, the boards' instinctive suspicion of women wearing pants or forgoing jewelry in public, bar owners argued, displayed a striking insensitivity to lower-class women. That many lesbian bars in fact catered to working-class patrons, reflecting wealthier lesbians' continued reliance on more private gatherings, only strengthened their case. Questioned about a crowd of women wearing pants, boots, and denim jackets at Club Tequila in the spring of 1963, the bartender Frank Fernandez protested that such fashions were common among the workers at the nearby factories in Newark. Margaret Simmons, the owner of the Keyhole Cocktail Lounge, made a similar argument about the plain-faced women wearing slacks and boots at her bar in Montville. Those patrons, she explained, were "rough and tough" "working girls" from the Metal Frame plant nearby: "I can't say those girls are not women just by their actions and by the way they dress." Perhaps owing to the greater flexibility of women's gender norms at midcentury, these arguments sometimes made headway with the boards. At the hearing against the Keyhole, for example, the hearing officer recommended dismissing any charges of serving homosexuals, deeming it "common knowledge that in recent years a large segment of the female population," including factory workers, "has adopted an attire which appears to be masculine." Although such fashions might disturb "conservative stylists," calling all women who wore them lesbians "require[d] 'the courage of a lion.'"[70]

But the ABC director promptly reversed, rejecting the hearing officer's attempts to diversify the board's standards of decorous femininity. Factory workers or otherwise, William Howe Davis insisted, "it takes only common sense . . . to distinguish a so-called lesbian from a normal woman," and the hardy patrons at Simmons's bar clearly crossed the line.[71] Proceedings like those against the Keyhole confirmed the class-based assumptions that undergirded so much of the liquor boards' evidence against lesbian bars: their insistence on the luxuries and aesthetics of the leisure class as the only acceptable threshold of American womanhood. And they illustrated the divergent presumptions that governed public norms of femininity and masculinity in these years, which measured men and women against very different socioeconomic standards. Normative visions of femininity, with their greater demands of delicacy and refinement as intrinsic to the fairer sex, remained an essentially bourgeois and upper-class conceit, even as popular norms of manhood aspired toward a hardier ideal.

In that sense, the liquor boards' proceedings against gay and lesbian bars in the 1950s and the early 1960s did not simply place queer men and women's social freedoms at the mercy of the public's shifting understandings of deviance. They also laid bare—even as they attempted to paper over—the innately contested boundaries of public knowledge itself: the ongoing cultural and political tensions entailed in deciding which supposedly shared intuitions ought to define the law's understanding of sexual difference. As queer communities in the postwar years retreated further and further away from the familiar trope of the fairy, the liquor boards' proceedings against queer bars devolved into an increasingly naked struggle over what constituted the public itself—*whose* cultural and class-based priors ought to be privileged in maintaining the bounds of permissible masculinity and femininity in the public sphere. More than just the persisting role of popular knowledge in the regulation of gay life, the liquor boards' proceedings against gay-friendly bars illuminate the broader cultural battle lines undergirding the search for some intuitive hallmarks of queerness at midcentury: the extent to which the project of distinguishing homosexual from "normal" bodies was always, in key part, a struggle over the racial, class, and cultural foundations of true American manhood and womanhood, at a time when both appeared increasingly uncertain.

From the 1930s through the early 1960s, from the ban on female impersonators to the hunt for apparent homosexuals, the liquor boards' proceedings against gay-friendly bars exemplify the intimate relationship between state regulation and popular knowledge about sexual difference: the extent to which the accelerating policing of queer social spaces in the United States rested, from the very start, on the public's presumptive ability to recognize and agree about at least some aspects of queer life. The role of public knowledge in the boards' campaigns explains the centrality of stereotype in liquor charges against gay bars, not simply as a reflection of the boards' strategic priorities but as an inevitable symptom of a regime grounded on the public's shared cultural presumptions. It complicates the legacy of certain familiar moments in the history of gay life, like the pansy craze of the 1930s, that shaped popular understandings of homosexuality to begin with, demonstrating how the unique pressures of the legal realm can transform the significance of seemingly progressive cultural developments. Not least, it turns the liquor boards' proceedings into a uniquely rich case study of the cultural fault lines underlying the public's supposedly shared instincts about sexual difference at midcentury. Beginning in the first years following Repeal and increasing alongside the demographic and political shifts of the postwar era, the liquor boards' attempts to patrol the boundaries of social order in urban America expose the inevitably contested boundaries of public knowledge on a sensitive subject like sexual deviance: the difficulties of defining any commonsense standards of social and sexual normality in a diverse society marked by its conflicting intuitions about acceptable public conduct.

It may have struck some observers as fortunate, in that context, that by the mid-1950s, popular intuitions about sex and gender were far from the sole arbiters of deviance among the American public. As liquor boards continued to debate the contours of apparent homosexuality in licensed bars, the social problem of the homosexual also caught the attention of a new line of public authorities—figures that defined sexual difference not as a matter of lay knowledge, but as a field of expert training.

TWO

Expert Witnesses on Trial

When, in his 1940 hearing before New York's State Liquor Authority (SLA), an attorney for the Gloria Bar and Grill pressed Investigator William Wickes on his readings in "the psychology of homosexualism," he was not simply deriding the agent's limited insights into sexual difference. He was pointing to a deeper shadow overhanging the liquor boards' campaigns: the extent to which the core presumption at the heart of the proceedings—the common man's unparalleled ability to identify queer men through certain well-worn, well-established codes—ignored the existence of an entire class of superior experts on the subject.

On appeal, defense attorney Clarence Goldberg made that claim more explicit. His briefs to the appellate division included a statement by the psychiatrist George W. Henry, a longtime researcher in the field of homosexuality and, per Goldberg, the "outstanding authority upon this subject." Contrary to popular opinion, the good doctor reported, there is "no necessary relationship between effeminacy in a man and his type of sexual desire." The SLA's claim that Gloria's employees must have recognized their queer patrons, in context, did not merely contradict their own sworn testimony. It contradicted the leading medical wisdom on sexual difference.[1]

In 1940, that intervention left little mark on the case. But just a decade later, professional opinions like Henry's would become harder for the courts to ignore. In the years following World War II, a new generation of doctors and researchers rose to the forefront of public debates about homosexuality as established experts on sexual difference. These authorities clashed on many matters, from the origins of same-sex desire to the possibility of treatment, but they tended to agree on at least one thing. Eager to defend their professional status, they contrasted their superior insights about queer men and women with what they saw as the public's oversimplified presumptions—not least, the long-standing trope of the fairy. That claim made this new class of experts attractive allies for beleaguered bar owners. Capitalizing on their professional standing, bar owners retained psychiatrists and researchers as expert witnesses in their confrontations with the liquor boards, called to dispute the significance of a patron's unorthodox appearance or even, in some cases, the policies behind the states' antihomosexual codes. Often pushing the limits of the witnesses' authority, beyond the origins or psychology of homosexuality to the boundaries of normal masculine conduct in the public sphere, these defendants tried to turn the liquor boards' proceedings into expert debates on the nature of sexual deviance.

The partnership between bar owners and medical professionals was sometimes an uneasy alliance. For one thing, expert witnesses often had their own motives for testifying, viewing the litigation as a platform for cementing their professional status as much as helping the defense. More fundamentally, bar owners who called psychiatrists to testify on their behalf pursued a delicate legal strategy, challenging the liquor boards' antihomosexual campaigns by pathologizing homosexuality itself as a disease best left to the ministrations of medical authorities. Decades before progressive doctors moved to declassify homosexuality as a mental illness, homophile activists had frequently made the choice to embrace psychiatrists as public ambassadors for the greater social tolerance of queer communities, accepting their stigmatizing theories as, in effect, the cost of their support. In the unique legal setting of the liquor boards' proceedings, that partnership also served a more specific function: undermining a regulatory regime grounded on the validity of the public's commonsense presumptions about gay men and women.

If bar owners hoped that judges and liquor officials would defer to the wisdom of medical and scientific professionals, however, they were in for a disappointment. In the face of growing public and even legal deference to expert voices on the subject of sexual difference, both liquor boards and courts rejected the suggestion that the defendants' witnesses claimed any unique authority when it came to recognizing the outward hallmarks of the homosexual. To an extent, that resistance was likely strategic, preserving the boards' ability to rely on an especially convenient form of evidence. Yet it also appeared at least partly genuine, reflecting the limits of liquor officials' and judges' ability to recognize novel expert claims. On the basis of their own personal and professional experiences, many directors and judges simply could not believe that, for all their credentials, the defendants' witnesses could improve on the layman's commonsense ability to spot queer patrons at a bar.

More than simply a site of struggle over the contours of sexual difference, the liquor boards' campaigns against gay bars in the mid-twentieth century thus emerged as a key battleground over the nature of public authority over same-sex practices: a contest over who precisely got to define the boundaries of normality and deviance before the law. At a time when medical and scientific professionals increasingly dominated public discussions of homosexuality, the liquor boards' proceedings did not merely exploit the availability of some shared public insights into sexual difference. They defended the validity of those insights when they came under attack by a class of supposedly more knowledgeable authorities, upholding the value of common sense and popular intuition about a subject increasingly claimed as the province of trained professionals. Driven largely by their own interest in bolstering enforcement, liquor officials participated in an ongoing debate over the contours of expert and lay authority on sexual deviance, resisting psychiatrists' and researchers' efforts to claim jurisdiction over a matter the boards saw as both instrumental to their regulatory efforts and, simply enough, self-evident.

It may have been of secondary concern that the liquor boards' resistance to expert witnesses ultimately put them in a delicate position. As it turned out, professional psychiatrists were not the only surprising allies marshaled by embattled bar owners at midcentury. As police officers in the 1950s staked out a newly vocal claim to professional authority over the hallmarks of urban crime, some bar owners sought out local patrolmen as defense witnesses, calling them to testify that they themselves had never noticed gay patrons on the premises. Cooperating officers likely had a variety of personal and institutional motives for coming to the bar owners' aid, but they often left the liquor boards in an uncomfortable bind. Sensitive both to their institutional relationships with law enforcement and to the evidentiary pressures of the liquor codes, judges and liquor officials had to walk a thin line, simultaneously acknowledging the investigators' professional knowledge and denying that any such knowledge was necessary to identify a gay bar. Even as police officers in other fields commonly legitimated their tactics through their allegedly superior insights into surveilled communities, investigators enforcing the states' liquor laws found it more advantageous to downplay their often-genuine intimacy with gay life—to take care not to know too much about the queer men and women they patrolled.

Tracing the liquor boards' recurrent jousts with expert testimony in the postwar years, this chapter explores the intersection between the policing of queer social spaces and the professionalization of sexual difference at midcentury: the extent to which, at a time when the topic of homosexuality inspired increasing professional and popular interest, the states' campaigns against gay bars waded into a live debate about the relative authority of lay and expert knowledge about queer life. That story unearths the role of the law in arbitrating those epistemic struggles, examining how the boards' proceedings held the line of lay wisdom and common sense in the face of rising expert authority over questions of sexual difference. And it demonstrates how the unique internal pressures of the liquor codes transformed the value of expertise of all kinds, forging surprising alliances among medical professionals and the defenders of gay social spaces, on the one hand, while straining familiar institutional hierarchies within the legal system, on the other. From the trained psychiatrist to the veteran investigator, the liquor boards' ongoing negotiations with expertise epitomize how the law's efforts to chart the contours of authoritative knowledge about sexual difference raised inevitable and immediate questions about the nature of knowledge production and social authority themselves: who ought to have the right to establish legal, if not medical, truths about the American homosexual.

Early Scientific Overlap with the Paradigm of the Fairy

It is impossible to appreciate the role of professional experts in the liquor boards' proceedings in the postwar years—and, indeed, in popular discussions of homosexuality more broadly—without looking back some decades earlier. For the professional tensions that dominated these debates hardly originated after World War II. As far back as the late nineteenth century, warring camps of researchers embarked on what would become a lasting campaign to defend their superior insights into the subject of sexual difference—not only among themselves, but also against the less tutored presumptions of the public.

Until roughly the mid-nineteenth century, neither science nor, for that matter, public culture in the United States or Europe had much to say about the homosexual. Like any other alleged sexual vice, same-sex practices were seen largely as a moral failing, sometimes punished through the criminal law but otherwise left to the ministrations of the clergy. That account essentially imagined same-sex acts as passing indulgences, temptations capable of ensnaring anyone sufficiently disrespectful of the laws of

God or man. As the practice of medicine began making broader claims to professional status in the mid-nineteenth century, however, physicians on both sides of the Atlantic began to claim homosexuality as yet another illness subject to their purview—traceable, like any other, to some discrete physiological root. In France, Claude François Michea explained it as the presence of female organs in male bodies. In the United States, G. Frank Lydston attributed it to "the maldevelopment, or arrested development, of the sexual organs."[2]

By the turn of the century, these physiological theories of deviance began to give way to a more holistic approach. Sexologists like Magnus Hirschfeld and Havelock Ellis, who effectively captured the study of homosexuality in the late nineteenth century, theorized same-sex desire as the symptom of a deeper gender inversion—a female soul or psyche in a male body—even as they continued to betray some lingering fascination with what Ellis called the homosexual's "physical abnormalities." Meanwhile, a generation of primarily German doctors, precursors to the psychiatrists of the twentieth century, recast homosexuality as a sexual pathology rather than a physical disease. The disembodiment of perversion culminated most famously in the work of Sigmund Freud, the father of psychoanalysis, who depicted homoerotic desire as an adverse psychological reaction to any number of potential childhood traumas. Conceiving of homosexuality as part of a deep-rooted psychological profile—the province of a discrete personality type—that view continued to narrow the category of those susceptible to same-sex desire, even as it shifted the roots of that condition from the body to the mind.[3]

Far from putting the physiological approach to rest, however, the growing emphasis on the intangible aspects of homosexuality inspired its resurgence in the early twentieth century, as researchers who had had their fill of the homosexual's psychosexual history recommitted themselves to examining his "physiological factors." And not simply physiological, now, but increasingly visible, a condition evident on the surface of the body. In 1924, the German physician Arthur Weil published a study of the "anatomical foundations" of homosexuality, measuring the limbs, hips, and shoulders of 380 homosexual men. A decade later, George Henry and Hugh Galbraith, formally trained as psychiatrists, applied a similar methodology on the other side of the Atlantic, compiling measurements of bodily traits ranging from hair density to the girth of testicles, thighs, and buttocks. That investigative spirit soon led Henry to pursue a longer research project sponsored by the Committee for the Study of Sex Variants, a private research coalition helmed out of New York City. Working alongside Jan Gay, a lesbian researcher who proved instrumental in recruiting subjects, Henry compiled over two hundred case studies of homosexual men and women in New York between 1935 and 1937, consisting of personal interviews as well as physical inspections, pelvic exams, and X-rays.[4]

The project of tracing same-sex desire to some innate physical symptoms carried within it the seeds of an emancipatory project: an attempt to recast homosexuality not as a sin or a psychological disturbance, but as a natural biological variation. That was the reason someone like Jan Gay volunteered to participate in Henry's research in the first place. In practice, however, the ensuing studies often took a darker tone. Although homosexual anthropometrists followed partly in the footsteps of nineteenth-century physicians, their methodology borrowed more closely from an intervening phenomenon: criminal anthropology. Popularized by the Italian criminologist Cesare Lombroso, criminal anthropology insisted that social delinquents, from murderers to pickpockets, could be distinguished by certain stigmata—their sloping foreheads, their unusually long arms, their diminutive brains. Echoing that same ambition, homosexual anthropometrists tested the long-standing suspicion that there was "something in the physiognomy and manner of these unfortunates that [is] easily recognizable." And once more like Lombroso, whose measurements situated the criminal at a lower evolutionary stage than the ordinary man, they often pinpointed that difference in terms that confirmed the homosexual's supposedly innate inferiority. Researchers described the homosexual's purportedly atypical height and overlong limbs. They noted the apparent weakness of his build: his light bone structure, his rounded and narrow shoulders, his meager muscle mass. They emphasized the alleged unattractiveness of his body: the excess fat concentrated around his hips, his enlarged thighs, his unappealingly fleshy breasts.[5]

From the patient's soft skin to his generous fat deposits, such observations did not simply mark the homosexual body as different from the ideal male physique. Revealing the lasting impact of the gender-inversion model of same-sex desire, they were distinctly feminizing. Weil expressly compared his subjects to control groups both of heterosexual men and of women, hoping to situate the homosexual somewhere between the two. Henry's priors were less transparent, but his case studies, too, frequently emphasized the peculiar delicacy of the homosexual body. (Henry's published research went rather against the grain of his statement on behalf of the Gloria Bar and Grill, which denied any meaningful connection between homosexuality and effeminacy. But then Henry was not an apolitical man. His reductive focus on the body reflected an underlying sympathy for homosexuality as an inborn condition, deserving some measure of forbearance from the public.) Seen in this light, homosexual anthropometry effectively provided a scientific basis for the popular paradigm of the fairy, tracing the pansy's most lampooned physical traits—the wrists, the hips—to a congenital condition of the flesh. Building on the established theory of homosexuality as a form of gender inversion—what early writers imagined as a woman's psyche in a man's body—researchers now suggested that the homosexual's body was itself innately womanly.[6]

The reductive tenor of such anthropometric inquiries did not sit well with everyone, not least the psychologists and psychiatrists who prompted their resurgence. "One has only to look about at a random group of adult men in the shower room of a bath house," the psychiatrist John Wortis drily observed in 1937, to see the "feminine" patterns of pubic hair identified by Henry. The pushback against homosexual anthropometry reflected the genuinely inconclusive results of many such studies, whose authors sometimes strained to fit their results into their preconceptions of the homosexual physique. It also bespoke a more political motive, allowing psychiatrists and psychologists to shore up their professional authority over homosexuality as a psychic condition untethered from more physiological factors—to redefine the condition, in effect, not as a matter of gender deviance but as one of psychic maladjustment. The psychologist Thomas Moore, indeed, wasted little time between denouncing the myth of a homosexual physique and assuring readers that "the psychological laboratory" could nevertheless "do something to detect homosexuality."[7]

Even doctors who balked at the crudeness of homosexual anthropometry, however, found themselves agreeing on at least one point: the homosexual's characteristic effeminacy. If not through the patient's anatomical stigmata, they found their way to the same conclusion through his mannerisms and affectations, outward traces of a deeper psychological compulsion that betrayed his deviance despite his greatest efforts at concealment. That theory itself gained traction among researchers like Henry, who painstakingly reported not only the homosexual's bodily proportions but also his "more evident" feminine mannerisms: his "mincing steps," the "girlish wriggling of his body," his unusually "high-pitched voice." But it also commanded a broader consensus. Wortis himself conceded that his homosexual patients were frequently "effeminate . . . [based on] their tastes and manners"—a bearing, he surmised, "attributable on close analysis to a wish to be a woman." Moore agreed that a man's "dress, gait, and posture, or feminine 'airs' might well indicate that [he] is homosexual." Unlike the search for a telltale queer physique, the homosexual's instinctive effeminacy fit neatly with the leading psychiatric theories of the time, which characterized same-sex desire as the result of improper gender modeling: the paradigmatic overbearing mother or detached father, providing no healthy model for a son's sexual identity. Unsurprisingly, that consensus found some of its strongest proponents among psychoanalysts in the Freudian vein, who attributed the homosexual's effeminacy to his misdirected identification with his mother. As the psychoanalyst David Abrahamsen summarized in 1944: "A typical homosexual . . . behaves like a girl, walks like a girl, smiles like a girl."[8]

That these descriptions often recalled popular stereotypes of homosexual effeminacy did not mean that doctors saw their findings as confirming the public's widely held presumptions. Recognizing that their claims to professional status hung in large part on their unique insight into deviance, most doctors denounced the trope of the fairy even as their work often confirmed its most familiar features. As the psychologist Samuel Kahn warned in 1937: "Some people may have some [stereotypical effeminate] characteristics, and yet not be homosexuals." Nor were all homosexuals incapable of disguising themselves in public. A patient whose mannerisms made him "one of the gayest of the 'queens,'" Henry observed, could still "avoid being conspicuous" when he put his mind to it. The very breadth of Henry's case studies revealed the range of appearances among homosexual men, some of whom seemed at least initially to comport with conventional standards of masculinity.[9]

Far from advertising himself through any reliable, conclusive physical markers, by this view, the homosexual revealed himself only on cautious and diligent examination, requiring a trained and probing eye. As Kahn warned his readers, the risk of false positives meant that the "diagnosis of homosexuality is indeed a difficult and dangerous matter," demanding vigilance even from medical professionals. Henry, for his part, juxtaposed his expert analysis of each patient against the untutored observer's more facile conclusions. In the case of one Paul A., he seized on Paul's effeminate mouth and "feminine" attention to grooming, even though Paul's athletic build would likely seem adequate "to the layman." Rodney S.'s telltale effeminacy came through only "on closer inspection," to those who benefited from ample exposure to his movements. Although perhaps anyone might have recognized a touch of delicacy in Percival G.'s actions, only "the discerning" would identify him "as an 'aunty.'" Even as they echoed the popular trope of homosexual effeminacy, psychiatrists and physicians thus staked out the recognition of homosexual signals as an expert skill, honed through practice and specialized training. Men like Henry could take some professional pride in their fluency at ferreting out the hallmarks of sexual deviance. It was only a minor inconvenience that such claims put research- ers in an awkward position, forced to echo many of the public's most in- grained presumptions about queer men even as they insisted that their own insights were somehow different.[10]

The Postwar Expert Turn

That delicate balance, simultaneously confirming and deriding popular stereotypes, characterized much of the medical discourse on homosexual- ity through the mid-1940s. Following World War II, however, a new gener- ation of researchers shifted the terms of the debate. Like their predecessors, this new class of experts sought to establish themselves as unique authori- ties on sexual difference, and they too justified that status by distinguishing their insights from the facile assumptions of the broader public. But they were increasingly willing to dismiss the much-maligned fairy as popular whimsy rather than scientific fact.

The first major shift came during World War II, as the military's expe- riences trying to screen out homosexual recruits undermined its familiar presumptions about the nature of sexual difference. In the early twentieth century, the military had been a key subscriber to the principles of homo- sexual anthropometry. Army regulations during and following World War I instructed physical examiners to weed out recruits on the basis of much the same "anatomical stigmata of degeneration" that would subsequently be examined by Weil and Henry: narrow shoulders, broad hips, under- developed genitals, unusual distributions of hair or body fat. When the War Department released its Mobilization Instructions in 1942, it directed screening boards to filter out applicants drawing on essentially similar cri- teria. On the basis of such outward physical signals, the induction station in New York reportedly rejected twelve hundred out of one million men as "obvious and frank homosexualists."[11]

With its mobilization efforts under way, however, the military was forced to reconsider its standards. As a matter of logistics, after the United States entered the war in earnest, the military's need for manpower trumped its distaste for homosexual recruits. The Selective Service eliminated psychi- atric evaluations entirely. Examiners stopped scrutinizing recruits for the "anatomical stigmata of degeneration" and simply asked them outright about their sexual practices, accepting whatever answers often-enthusiastic enlistees chose to give. Just months after the War Department issued its standards for physical examinations, one New Yorker, nervous that his bleached hair, effeminate walk, and "sissy" voice would give him away to the induction board, found himself welcomed warmly to the army.[12]

Even before the demands of the battlefield overwhelmed its induction procedures, the military's attempts to screen out homosexual applicants taught it that classifying gay men was more easily said than done. In April 1941, the psychiatrist J. Paul de River wrote New York mayor Fiorella La-Guardia, "amazed" at the number of men arrested in the city who were "typed as homosexuals" and yet found carrying a draftee card. The military, de River insisted, should provide a lecture series to teach its examiners "how to recognize the sex pervert." LaGuardia forwarded the letter to a colonel in the army's Medical Division, who promptly assured de River that the screening boards investigated all recruits in whom "the stigmata of degeneration are evident on examination." The problem, it turned out, was that such screening mechanisms were woefully unreliable. Setting aside the embarrassing arrests of servicemen in port cities like New York and San Francisco, the military's troubles policing sexual intimacy on its own bases demonstrated that the most physically inconspicuous recruit could yet turn out to commit homosexual acts. By 1948, the chief of naval personnel had begun warning officers and sailors alike against relying on outward effeminacy to identify suspected homosexuals. Although many homosexuals "display effeminate mannerisms and characteristics," an indoctrination lecture cautioned, "sometimes there will be no outward signs at all," nor was any recruit with overly "effeminate" characteristics "necessarily a 'homo.'"[13]

The military's growing disillusionment with the physical hallmarks of sexual deviance deepened its reliance on another source of wisdom: professional psychiatry. The war effort ushered in a close alliance between the military and psychiatrists, as national officials sensitive to the epidemic of trauma and combat fatigue among deployed soldiers, remembering the recent experience of the Great War, turned to medical professionals for assistance. The result was a growing embrace of the discipline, both within and outside the medical profession, as a font of valuable insights into the science of human behavior. As William Menninger, the psychiatric consultant to the surgeon general of the army, observed in 1948, "as a result of the war" the "public interest in the problems of mental health . . . is at an all-time high."[14]

With regard to homosexuality, no less, psychiatrists proved useful allies for the military, not only helping screen out suspected homosexuals but also evaluating soldiers accused of sexual intimacies on its bases. Having long sought to redefine sexual deviance as an interior condition to be diagnosed and dissected by trained professionals, the military's psychiatrists shared the sense that unskeptical reliance on effeminate stereotypes did more harm than good in classifying recruits. Although never fully disavowing the significance of a man's outward appearance, doctors downplayed the role of visual examination, diagnosing their patients through a set of more holistic and specialized techniques, including physical examinations, slang and cultural knowledge, clinical tests like Rorschach blots, and, most importantly, comprehensive personal histories detailing each man's sexual development.

Buoyed by these collaborations, psychiatrists emerged in the 1950s as the nation's foremost public authorities on homosexuality. Whether publishing popular books on sexual neuroses, participating in radio shows on the dangers of the homosexual, or treating individual patients who hoped—or whose families hoped—to constrain their unconventional urges, medical experts dominated popular debates on same-sex desire. Psychiatrists' precise theories of homosexual development varied. Some, like the New York physician Fredric Wertham, placed the blame on violent or oversexualized entertainment. The majority followed more closely in Freud's footsteps, singling out the archetypical overbearing mother or the hostile or absent father. Beyond the matter of origins, psychiatrists diverged on their approach toward treatment. Among the most prolific authorities in the 1950s was a group of conservative psychoanalysts, including Edmund Bergler, Charles Socarides, and Irving Bieber, who insisted that anyone with homosexual tendencies could and should be reconditioned into heterosexual life. Writers like Charles Berg and the psychologist Albert Ellis adopted a humbler posture, disavowing any aspirations of curing their homosexual patients. A therapist's primary duty, they suggested, was helping his patients lead functional and fulfilling lives, regardless of their sexual maladjustment. Even the most liberal doctors, however, shared the belief that homosexuality was at heart a disease, a manifestation of an unstable personality at best and a dangerous pathology at worst—something that might, with sufficiently bad luck and environmental pressure, afflict any American man or woman. It was that pathological quality that threw the homosexual into their jurisdiction in the first place.[15]

While psychologists and psychiatrists enjoyed the flush of popularity in the postwar years, the national conversation on sexual deviance witnessed another turning point. In February 1948, the zoologist Alfred C. Kinsey ushered in a new era of debate about sexuality with the publication of his landmark *Sexual Behavior in the Human Male.* Hailed as a "revolutionary" work of "extraordinary merit," the Kinsey Report soon drew the ire of more skeptical readers for its questionable statistical methods and bloodless disregard for traditional values. Yet the work's influence was undeniable. Initially printed in a run of 5,000 copies, the report sold 185,000 copies within two weeks of publication and spent months on the *New York Times* bestseller list. Its chief author became a national icon, lending his name to late-night jokes, racy advertisements ("fictionalized Kinsey reports"), and even radio songs ("The Kinsey Boogie"). "As a subject of conversation," *Life Magazine* noted in August 1948, "the Report can be depended on to nose out [the presidential candidate Henry] Wallace, Russia, the elections and the high cost of living for the better part of an evening."[16]

Kinsey's statistics covered a range of topics, from masturbation to bestiality, but none were as widely disseminated or as shocking as his statistics about same-sex practices. On the basis of his interviews, Kinsey estimated that at least 37 percent of American men had engaged in some homosexual behavior to the point of orgasm between adolescence and old age. "This is more than one male in three of the persons that one may meet as he passes along a city street," he emphasized. If that number seemed shockingly high, it was because, popular stereotypes notwithstanding, homosexual activity was prevalent among men who never gave the slightest outward indication of sexual difference. Kinsey marshaled his findings in service of a very different conclusion than that espoused by most psychiatrists: that homosexuality was, far from a symptom of mental maladjustment, a natural and even common form of erotic experimentation. Like the leading psychiatric theories, however, his statistics undercut the stereotype of the fairy largely by shifting what it was that constituted "sexual deviance" itself. Measuring homosexuality in terms of sexual contacts rather than gender presentation, the report characterized same-sex eroticism as a private practice rather than a social identity or a medical disorder—even as it suggested that male homosexuals were far more pervasive, and more elusive, than previously imagined.[17]

Like the military's collaborations with psychiatrists, Kinsey's findings did more than disrupt popular stereotypes of sexual difference. They boosted the prestige of researchers like Kinsey himself. Reflecting a very different methodology from the leading psychiatric studies of the day, the Kinsey Report corroborated the public's growing view of sexuality as a matter of professionalized study. Bloodlessly empirical and rife with discoveries that contradicted readers' prevailing assumptions about sex, the report did not simply recast homosexuality from a deviant personality to a sexual practice; it recast human sexuality itself from a private concern to "a fit subject of scientific investigation." Few conversations surrounding homosexuality in the coming decades, from popular press coverage to legal debates

about statutes governing sexual conduct, proceeded without some significant discussion of the report.[18]

By the dawn of the Cold War, in short, the United States had entered
a new era of public discussion of sexuality: the appropriation of sexuality, and sexual difference especially, as the stuff of professional expertise.
For many law enforcement agencies, the new industry of experts could not
have come at a better time. As it turned out, the years following the war did
not simply feature growing public deference to professional experts over
matters of sexual practice. They also featured a growing interest in nonnormative sexuality as a criminal concern.

That interest traced back to the late 1930s and specifically to a series of
headlines that, on their face, had little to do with homosexuality. In the
spring of 1937, an apparent rash of violent assaults against young children,
almost exclusively young girls victimized by older men, captured the attention of newspapers and magazines across the country. It is unclear whether
the coverage reflected a genuine spike in crime or a self-perpetuating journalistic trend; as the economic dislocations of the Great Depression fueled
broader anxieties about undomesticated male sexuality, indeed, the focus
on violent predators likely displaced deeper concerns about the shifting
character of American manhood. Regardless, the headlines sparked an outcry for more stringent protections against so-called degeneracy in American
cities. In 1937, a citizens' meeting in New York City demanded increased
police attention to the problem of sex offenders. The following year, the
Los Angeles Police Department formally launched its Sex Bureau, the first
division dedicated solely to sex-related violations.[19]

Facing pressure to expand the state's arsenal against a distressing new
category of offender, legislators and law enforcement officials looked, in
turn, to the guidance of professional psychiatrists. Starting even before
World War II, some police departments had worried that the problem of
sex crimes might require some insight beyond their traditional experience.
The Sex Bureau, in fact, operated under the auspices of none other than
the psychiatrist J. Paul de River, who oversaw its investigations—and published controversial field guides to his work—until a scandal surrounding
a particularly high-profile murder case led to his ouster in 1950. But in the
postwar years, especially, the growing stature of professional psychiatrists
placed them at the center of legal debates about sex offenses. Multiple states
engaged trained psychiatrists to perform extended studies of the problem
of the sex criminal. Others consulted prominent doctors and published
sources in drafting new laws targeting such predators. As Dr. Alan Canty, a

lead figure in drafting Michigan's new sex law, surmised in 1957, the police investigator faced with the sex criminal "feels insecure and welcomes the advice and assistance of the skilled psychologist or psychiatrist."[20]

Those efforts led to the creation of a new legal category disguised as a medical one. The *sexual psychopath*, as he came to be known, was a psychological prototype characterized by severe "psycho-sexual immaturity," unable to control his basest erotic instincts. That prototype was epitomized by violent or predatory offenses, such as murder, rape, and child molestation, but the actual scope of sexual psychopath statutes varied by state, and some reached broadly enough to encompass consensual same-sex acts. Governing how the states could treat suspects detained on sex-related charges rather than staking out new criminal charges themselves, sexual psychopath laws typically authorized indefinite civil confinement and mandatory psychiatric treatment for anyone deemed to pose a high risk of recidivism, even absent a formal conviction. They also cemented a new infrastructure for delegating these difficult questions to the medical profession, funding state-run psychiatric clinics responsible for advising judges and prosecutors on which individuals to process under the law and how to treat them. Canty himself, having helped draft Michigan's statute, served for decades as the executive director of Detroit's Psychopathic Clinic. First adopted by California and a handful of midwestern legislatures, by the mid-1950s sexual psychopath laws spread to over twenty states.[21]

They spread, indeed, against the advice of medical professionals themselves. Although psychiatrists initially welcomed the chance to bring some greater scientific enlightenment to the state's treatment of sex criminals, they soon grew uncomfortable with the details of the legislation. Critics objected to the vagueness of *sexual psychopath* as a medical category. They denounced the draconianism of confining suspects without the procedural protections of a trial. Most crucially, they questioned whether psychiatry could genuinely provide an antidote to the recidivist sex offender. In practice, there was little evidence that sexual psychopath laws helped prevent the violent or predatory crimes that had inspired public outrage to begin with.[22]

Proliferating despite professional psychiatrists' own skepticism, the sexual psychopath laws were thus a distinctly popular creation: a reflection of the public's growing embrace of medical expertise as a tool with which to refine law enforcement efforts against sexual deviance. Drawing both scientific and popular legitimacy from their association with professional psychiatry, the sexual psychopath laws exemplified the public's newfound rec-

ognition of human sexuality, and sexual difference specifically, as a realm
to be illuminated by medical authorities.

Liquor Proceedings and the Expert Witness

The rise of this new class of professionals did not go unnoticed by bar
owners. After all, both the experts' assault on the trope of the fairy and
their very identity as experts, privy to unique insights into deviance, went
directly to the presumption at the heart of the liquor boards' campaigns:
that anyone, regardless of training or educational background, could reliably identify a homosexual. As psychiatrists and researchers in the postwar years called that presumption into question, bar owners invoked their
greater expertise to try dislodging the evidence against them.

They started, unsurprisingly, with the most prominent authorities available. Not long after the Kinsey Report assumed its perch on the bestseller
lists, it began to provide an attractive tool for defendants fighting charges
that they welcomed homosexual patrons on their premises. After California's Board of Equalization (BOE) initiated its proceedings against Sol
Stoumen's Black Cat bar in 1949, indeed, a core debate in the ensuing
litigation centered on the role of the report. Appending a copy of *Sexual
Behavior in the Human Male* to his briefs, Stoumen's attorney relied extensively on Kinsey's findings to challenge the BOE's evidence against his client. "On the basis of the most recent and authori[ta]tive studies of the subject," Morris Lowenthal insisted, an informed reader would question both
the existence of an "exclusively homosexual person" and "whether, even
to the most trained observer, such a person can be identified" on sight.
Lowenthal took particular issue with the testimony of several San Francisco
policemen who claimed that they immediately recognized the Black Cat's
flamboyant patrons. The officers' testimony, he derided, put them in the
naive "category of persons claiming to identify [homosexuals] by their 'effeminate' appearance, something that Kinsey says cannot be done." At a
time when sexual deviance lent itself to increasingly rigorous study, courts
should not "accept the wholly erroneous judgment of an untrained police
officer in place of scientific or actual facts on the subject."[23]

The BOE balked at the claim that the Kinsey Report had any bearing on
its disciplinary hearings. A revocation proceeding, it reminded the court,
was neither "a medical clinic, nor a sociological seminar." And in the end,
precisely owing to the Supreme Court of California's unusually progressive
character, Lowenthal's arguments had little impact on the case. Interpreting California's liquor laws to require some evidence of disorderly conduct

beyond the mere presence of queer patrons, the court in *Stoumen* avoided wading into the intellectual pedigree of the police officers' conclusion that the patrons were, in fact, homosexual. (The parties, for their part, never abandoned the debate. After the state legislature enacted a new provision against bars serving "sexual perverts" and replaced the BOE with the more aggressive Department of Alcoholic Beverage Control, the new agency brought a second set of charges against the Black Cat in 1956, prompting Lowenthal to try another shot at his defense and insist that Kinsey's findings disproved that Stoumen could have recognized his queer clientele. California's deputy attorney general disagreed. "It is our contention," he informed the press, that "anyone can tell a homosexual.")[24]

If the science of identifying homosexuals dropped out of the California courts, however, it hardly faded from liquor proceedings on the East Coast. As agencies like New Jersey's Division of Alcoholic Beverage Control (ABC) and New York's SLA continued to prosecute bar owners simply for serving apparently homosexual customers, defendants called expert witnesses to refute the suggestion that they—or, for that matter, the states' own agents—could have reliably recognized their patrons' predilections. After the ABC brought charges against the Rutgers Cocktail Bar in 1956, for instance, a professional psychiatrist took the stand to challenge the board's leap from a customer's "delicate" mannerisms to his sexual character. Conceding that some homosexuals affect the mannerisms of the other sex, the doctor insisted, the average patient had "a deceptive appearance," making it nearly impossible to recognize him on sight. The owner of Murphy's Tavern in Newark, having weathered one suspension in 1961 and facing a second round of charges in 1966, tried a similar strategy, engaging Harry F. Farb, a psychiatric consultant who served for eight years at an army induction center, to testify that "the determination of a homosexual cannot be made from appearances." Emphasizing a patient's personal history as "the most important part" of his own analysis, Farb insisted that an effeminate demeanor was simply "not enough" to reveal a man's sexuality.[25]

Bar owners who retained expert witnesses to rebut the boards' charges capitalized on the prominence of professional researchers in public discussions of sexual difference, and, unsurprisingly, their evidence often intersected with the leading debates of the day. After the ABC initiated charges against Val's Bar in Atlantic City, Val's owners, Mark and Pamela Weintrob, rested their entire defense on the testimony of Wardell B. Pomeroy, a principal researcher at the Kinsey Institute and the author of several books on homosexuality. At the hearing, Pomeroy discussed Kinsey's published studies of male and female sexual behavior, emphasizing the notorious statistic that a full 37 percent of American men had engaged in homosexual activity. Given that most of those subjects were indistinguishable from straight men, he concluded, it simply "could not be said from mere observation that any given individual was a homosexual." Others looked to a more surprising authority. When the division moved against Adele Kaczka's N.Y. Bar in 1955, citing the patrons' swishing hips, pursed lips, and high-pitched voices, a psychiatrist engaged by the defense invoked the paradigm of the sexual psychopath to rebut the board's evidence. Echoing the psychiatric studies commonly cited in support of the psychopath laws, the doctor characterized homosexuality as a case of stunted psychosexual development rather than intrinsic femininity: a failure to have "progressed to the so-called mature level of sexual adjustment in our society." As such, it simply had "no direct correlation [with] a man's . . . physical makeup."[26]

Questioning the reliability of the physical signs invoked by the liquor boards, witnesses like Farb and Pomeroy partly offered themselves as superior readers of queer bodies. But they also tried, once more, to redefine the essential measure of sexual deviance, from an outward departure from gender norms to an interior sexual instinct, diagnosable only through professional analysis. That tactic did not always fit neatly with the legal frameworks governing the boards' proceedings, which were primarily concerned with public disorder rather than private sexuality and often hung, accordingly, on public norms rather than scientific truths about sexual deviance. It also pushed psychiatrists and researchers to the limits of their professional authority, beyond the roots of sexual difference or the statistical frequency of sexual behavior, to the culturally contingent boundaries of normal and deviant conduct in the public sphere. Far from ignoring the technical directives of the law, however, bar owners who rested their hopes in expert witnesses were making a novel claim about the proper relationship between expertise and the law itself. At a time when professionals like Farb and Pomeroy dominated public debates about sexual difference, they suggested, the law, too—including the liquor boards' attempts to police the public order—should privilege their rarefied insights over the public's less tutored presumptions.

The sheer expansiveness of the bar owners' alliance with expert witnesses emerged most clearly in California. Although the supreme court's decision in *Stoumen* preempted any debates about the vagaries of identifying homosexuals, it hardly tarnished the strategic appeal of the expert witness. If not disputing whether a bar's patrons were in fact gay or lesbian, psychiatrists and researchers now took the stand to question whether those patrons' conduct qualified as disorderly—or, echoing the language of the state's continually evolving liquor laws, as a form of "sexual perversion." After the ABC's agents reported men holding hands and dancing in Pearl's Bar in Oakland, for example, the owner, Pearl Kershaw, produced a Harvard-educated psychiatrist to dispute whether her patrons' conduct could be classified as sexual in any sense. In a remarkable legal gambit, Dr. John Alden testified that the mere fact of men dancing or holding hands said little about their sexual preferences absent more rigorous evidence that those actions produced a subjective sensation of "sexual excitement." (On cross-examination, he conceded that the "usual motivation" for such conduct was an erotic one, though he noted the possibility of alternative explanations, such as improving one's dancing.)[27]

More commonly, bar owners did not question that their patrons' affectionate displays raised a reasonable inference of sexual attraction. They debated whether, even if they manifested some deeper sexual motives, such anodyne activities as dancing or embracing at a bar fell under California's statutory ban on sexual perversion. The term *perverted*, as Dr. Alden himself insisted, referred only to specific sexual acts, not to social gatherings or individuals, whose erotic practices and desires were too unstable to lend themselves to such reductive labels. After the department revoked the license of the First and Last Chance Bar in Oakland, the appellate proceedings again centered largely on the statutory definition of *perversion*. Citing Kinsey's findings that nearly all Americans engaged in some form of nonnormative sexual conduct, owners Albert Vallerga and Mary Azar insisted that "the term 'sexual pervert' has no valid meaning" in the scientific community. Fresh off his defense of the Black Cat, Morris Lowenthal filed an amicus brief in the case, citing over a dozen medical publications, and warning against stigmatizing any individual as a pervert "in the complete absence of expert medical evidence" to that effect.[28]

Challenging the California liquor board's conflation of homosexuality and perversion, bar owners essentially made two separate arguments. Most basically, they attempted to draw a distinction between sexual acts and sexual desire, insisting that public displays of affection like dancing, however indicative of same-sex affection, failed to prove that a bar's patrons also engaged in prohibited sexual conduct. Limiting their definition of *perversion* to actual erotic acts, these litigants defended their patrons' right to gather in bars, or even indulge in displays of affection, without defending homosexual sex per se.[29]

More ambitiously, however, some litigants sought to depathologize homosexual desire altogether. Defining *perversion* as a condition characterized by some measure of social and psychological dysfunction—a label reserved for violent predators and child molesters rather than consenting adults—they cast homosexuality as a benign sexual variation, distinct from the pathologies that genuinely commanded a professional's attention. Pushing against the media's frequent conflation of all sexual difference under the umbrella of the sexual psychopath, defense witnesses tried to reassert some line between *deviation* and *deviance*, conceding that homosexuality might depart from sexual convention without justifying the weighty arm of the law. In doing so, they effectively sought to recast the concept of perversion from a question of evolving cultural mores to a matter of scientific certainty—and, in the process, to extend their own claims of authority from the medical to the legal realm.[30]

Bar owners' attempts to depathologize homosexuality in California diverged from their uses of expert testimony in New Jersey, where the evidentiary demands of the liquor laws compelled litigants, inversely, to emphasize the pathological nature of homosexuality as a defensive strategy. As the psychiatrist testifying for Adele Kaczka's N.Y. Bar insisted in 1955, homosexual urges represented a patient's failure to attain a "mature level of sexual adjustment," often arising from his "abnormal upbringing" or other disruptive developmental factors. Dismissing the purported dangers of unregulated gay bars, the witness assured the board that homosexuality was "not contagious," but he did not deny that it was, at heart, a pathology. And predictably so. Given the ABC's reliance on public insight about queer bodies as the foundation of their charges, after all, the work of an effective expert witness in New Jersey was not solely to sever homosexuality from the familiar hallmarks of the fairy. It was to undercut the public's authority by situating all questions of sexual difference squarely within the jurisdiction of professionals, as a condition requiring the superior insights of medical experts. In that context, the task of defending homosexual men's relative mental health fell, ironically, to the liquor board itself. After an attorney for Murphy's Tavern invited a psychiatrist to explain how he identified persons "diseased with the sickness of homosexuality," the ABC's own Edward Ambrose—the prosecuting attorney single-handedly responsible for nearly every antihomosexual proceeding since 1948—promptly jumped in to denounce the lawyer's characterization of homosexuality as an illness. "There is not a human man," Ambrose insisted, "that can give an [expert] opinion on" such a controversial claim.[31]

Bar owners' willingness to embrace the medicalization of homosexuality reflected the mixed motives of the litigants leading the charge against the liquor boards' operations against gay bars. Although lawsuits challenging those disciplinary proceedings were often lauded by homophile activists for promoting the fair treatment of homosexual men and women, most defendants came to court to preserve their livelihoods rather than to take a stand for gay rights, and they put a higher premium on winning than on presenting an untarnished public image for their customers. Sacrificing their patrons to the medical profession's bid for institutional authority likely struck many as a small price to pay for the privilege of keeping their license—particularly if they never sought their queer crowds in the first place.

Yet the prominence of such pathologizing rhetoric in cases aimed, at heart, at vindicating the civil rights of queer men and women also reveals the sometimes-surprising intersections between the medicalization of same-sex desire and the regulation of queer communities in the United States. Well beyond the liquor boards' proceedings, of course, the psychiatric model of homosexuality at midcentury supported a range of moral and political commitments. Among conservative psychiatrists and politicians, that medical rhetoric justified more zealous crackdowns on the public spaces of queer life, portraying homosexuality as something to be cured with sufficient discipline, or at least as a contagious condition to be shunned rather than normalized. In the hands of more liberal doctors and activists, it could be more progressive: a way to nudge consenting homosexual practices beyond the purview of the criminal law, into the warmer, if still costly, embrace of the medical profession. In context of the liquor boards' regulatory campaigns, however, the medical model also offered bar owners a more specific tool for resisting the states' drives to eliminate the public manifestations of queerness. In a regulatory regime fueled by the allegedly commonsense nature of sexual difference, relegating homosexuality to the authority of medical professionals provided defendants a direct path for challenging the best evidence against them, undermining the purported public wisdom that buttressed so many charges. More than granting the mantle of scientific objectivity to the gay community's pleas for tolerance or even casting homosexuality as a medical rather than a penal concern, bar owners' alliances with medical experts allowed them to resist a regulatory regime premised on the public's supposedly shared insights about a marginalized social group.

The Rejection of Expertise

At a time when police departments, legislators, and judges actively enlisted the input of professional psychiatrists to help identify and treat sex offenders, bar owners may have hoped that liquor boards would be equally willing to place the diagnosis of sexual difference in expert hands. But defendants who anticipated a warm reception for their witnesses had, it appeared, misjudged the liquor boards and the local courts alike.

Least surprisingly, the California courts took poorly to bar owners' attempts to complicate the moral status of homosexuality. The litigants' proposals to turn the acceptability of homosexuality into an expert question, after all, contradicted the very purpose of morals legislation like the states' antihomosexual codes: to define the outer boundaries of social behavior tolerated by the community, throwing not simply deviation but deviance itself into the public's purview. As the court overseeing Pearl Kershaw's appeal concluded, whatever the term's potential ambiguities among the scientific community, "'sex pervert' ha[d] a core of meaning to the average person," and that definition easily encompassed homosexuality. For all their credentials, medical experts simply lacked the authority to weigh in on a moral judgment defined, intrinsically, by public consensus rather than professional study.[32]

Yet the resistance to expert testimony extended far beyond California's inherently democratic debates over its citizens' sexual mores. Even with regard to strictly factual disputes about the outward hallmarks of queerness, liquor boards and state judges rejected the claim that psychiatrists or researchers like Wardell Pomeroy offered any insights beyond the common sense of the average American. At the proceedings against Val's Bar in Atlantic City, for instance, the ABC's director, Joseph Lordi, had little patience for the suggestion that only medical experts could accurately recognize homosexuals. Not unlike the identification of drunk patrons, a judgment frequently exercised by bartenders and liquor agents alike, Lordi reasoned, identifying gay men was "a matter of common observation, not requiring any special knowledge or skill." Dr. Farb, appearing on behalf of Murphy's Tavern, fared no better. Lordi himself derided the claim that liquor agents need "medical or psychiatric training . . . to form an opinion" about the presence of gay patrons in a bar. On appeal, the appellate division of the Superior Court of New Jersey affirmed. Although it was not "callous to the problem of the homosexual, medically or socially," the panel disclaimed, the enforcement of the liquor laws required "neither the curative approach of the physician nor the analytical view of the sociologist." Whatever the value of professional research in illuminating the nuances of deviant psychology, the task of recognizing homosexuals in public was simply too intuitive to demand expert intervention.[33]

In part, the ABC's interpretation of Rule 5 as targeting apparent rather than actual homosexuals predetermined the outcome. As the prosecuting attorney Edward Ambrose protested, even assuming that psychiatrists or scientific researchers harbored some unique capacity to diagnose true homosexuals, surely they claimed no special talents when it came to recognizing *apparent homosexuals*—a designation defined less by the underlying truth of a man's sexual practices than by his outward performance of certain well-recognized tropes of difference.[34]

In practice, however, liquor officials did not always rely on such technicalities, defending the layman's ability to identify actual gay patrons as reliably as any self-styled expert. The ABC's proceedings against Rutgers Cocktail Bar in 1956, an apparently close case that divided the agency's own officers, captured the terms of the debate. Accused by the ABC of catering to a regular crowd of delicate men and mannish women, the bar's owners retained a psychiatrist to testify that one simply "cannot tell a homosexual merely by his appearance or actions." On the basis of the agents' accounts of men with high-pitched voices and delicately balanced cigarettes, the doctor insisted that he himself could not conclusively identify the men as homosexual. Drawing partly on that testimony, the hearing officer took the rare step of recommending a dismissal of the charges. Even if the patron's mannerisms "might arouse suspicion" of sexual deviance, he concluded, they failed to establish that the Rutgers Cocktail Bar had served homosexuals.

The ABC's latest Director, William Howe Davis, reversed. He did not question the doctor's impressive professional credentials, nor did he overlook the substance of his testimony. To the contrary, Davis made a point of acknowledging the claims of the "well qualified," "learned psychiatrist that a layman could not tell a homosexual from an ordinary individual." Nevertheless, considering the patrons' purported "manner of speech, their walk, gestures and other mannerisms," he had no trouble concluding that the patrons described "were obviously homosexuals." More than defending the layman's commonsense ability to recognize apparent homosexuals, Davis's reasoning presumed his own ability to identify genuinely gay men. And it exemplified the legal system's ability simultaneously to flatter the authority of medical professionals and to reject their claims of exclusive jurisdiction over sexual deviance, at least where the recognition of homosexuals was concerned. Granting all due respect for the doctor's professional experience, Davis simply could not believe that an ordinary person, however untrained, could have any trouble picking out a queer crowd at a bar.[35]

It did not help matters that, from a surplus of either confidence or honesty, the bars' experts often muddied the waters of their own testimony.

Despite the professional modesty shown by the Rutgers psychiatrist, most expert witnesses echoed the hubris of their prewar forebears: even as they dismissed the value of the ABC's visual evidence, they could not quite bring themselves to deny that *they*, in their professional wisdom, could identify at least some homosexuals on sight. The psychiatrist testifying for Adele Kaczka, for instance, insisted that the task of classifying gay men was "difficult for an untrained person" even as he conceded that he himself, witnessing the effeminate and intimate conduct recounted by the ABC's investigators, would have suspected that the customers in question were homosexual. At the proceedings against Murphy's Tavern, similarly, Dr. Farb admitted that the flamboyant mannerisms observed by the investigators would "raise some question in [his] mind" about the patrons' sexuality, though he qualified that he would need to "investigate further" to draw any conclusive determinations. Some witnesses were less equivocal. Having admitted that a small minority of gay men in fact conform to the stereotype of the pansy, Dr. Wardell Pomeroy conceded that, if he saw a group of men displaying as many "identifiable manifestations" as the ABC's agents described, he would likely conclude they were queer.[36]

Simultaneously dismissing the trope of the fairy and affirming their own ability to spot gay men on the basis of that trope's rough contours, the experts' testimony partly reflected the limits of their roles as partisan witnesses. Enlisted by bar owners to help discredit the ABC's charges, men like Farb and Pomeroy were compelled to emphasize the shortcomings of the investigators' conclusions even in the face of what they may have seen as genuinely incriminating evidence. Yet that ambivalence also revealed the continuing difficulties, faced by doctors like George Henry and still plaguing medical professionals in the 1950s and 1960s, of claiming unique authority on the social problem of homosexuality: the tension of wresting that subject away from the purview of lay opinion in the face of the undeniable fact that many gay men seemed to bear out the wisdom of public stereotypes. Witnesses like Farb and Pomeroy might have acknowledged that even laypersons could reliably identify a minority of homosexual men and women: those who continued to embrace the conspicuous affectations that much of the queer community had, by the mid-1950s, come to shun. By insisting, instead, that laypersons should not even try their hand at homosexual detection, psychologists attempted to claim exclusive jurisdiction over even those aspects of sexual difference most closely aligned with lay knowledge at the time.

For most liquor officials, this distinction was too fine to parse. Refusing to recognize any meaningful difference between an expert's and an ordinary man's fluency in recognizing homosexuals, judges and liquor officials consistently took the witnesses' testimony, aimed at contrasting their professional insight with the liquor agents' more facile conclusions, to vindicate the agents' own testimony. In the case against Adele Kaczka's N.Y. Bar, the psychiatrist's concession that he himself might have suspected Kaczka's customers of homosexuality doomed the defense. How could Kaczka maintain that the ABC's agents were unqualified to recognize her patrons as homosexuals, Davis questioned, when her own expert had apparently reached the same conclusion? Dr. Farb's concession that the effeminate patrons at Murphy's Tavern "would arouse suspicion in his mind" was equally damning. Farb had intended to distinguish his own inference, built on decades of professional training and intended as a starting point for further inquiry, from the agent's simplistic assumption that the men were clearly homosexual. But as far as Director Joseph Lordi was concerned, his testimony confirmed the wisdom of the investigators' own inferences. "Coincid[ing] with and support[ing] the testimony of the Division agents," Lordi concluded, Farb's expert opinion undermined the bar's own defense.[37]

Davis's and Lordi's point in comparing the various witnesses' testimony may have been that the layman's purported fallibility in identifying gay individuals was irrelevant in those cases where, as it happened, his conclusions turned out to be correct. If Adele Kaczka's own expert confirmed that she welcomed a regular crowd of queer patrons, after all, Kaczka could hardly quibble with the sufficiency of the ABC's evidence. Yet the reasoning at the heart of the directors' opinions also evinced a far greater skepticism of the defendants' strategy, effectively denying the very possibility of expertise at the task of identifying homosexuals. If a professional psychiatrist could recognize gay men on the basis of a certain set of visual and behavioral clues, Davis and Lordi suggested, a liquor agent or a bartender could necessarily do just as well.

That dismissive attitude, indeed, made its way well past the ABC's own staff and into New Jersey's higher courts, in the state's most infamous disposition against a gay-friendly tavern. Arising from the ABC's proceedings against Marion Brown's ill-fated bar in Asbury Park, the appellate division's 1957 opinion in *Paddock Bar, Inc. v. Division of Alcoholic Beverage Control* was notable primarily for its full-throated defense of the agency's use of demeanor evidence to identify suspected homosexuals. As Judge Wilfred H. Jayne reasoned: "It is often in the plumage that we identify the bird." But Jayne also noted that laymen were hardly alone in relying on such observations to detect sexual deviance. "The psychiatrist," he observed, "constructs his deductive conclusions largely upon the ostensible personality behavior and unnatural mannerisms of the patient." On this reading, the psychiatrist's professional inferences, drawn from his observations of a patient in close quarters, were of a kind with a bartender's ability to guess his patrons' sexuality from their casual encounters at a bar. The court apparently declined to consider the possibility that a trained professional could improve on the judgments of a layman.[38]

This lingering resistance to the psychiatrist's claim of any special expertise over the hallmarks of homosexuality went against the rising status of medical professionals in the postwar years, including when it came to the regulation of homosexuality. In this same period, after all, not only popular media outlets but also lawmakers and police agencies commonly embraced the wisdom of expert psychiatrists in dealing with the problem of sexual difference, not least through the sexual psychopath laws whose terms often embraced nonviolent homosexual men. Trial judges, too, welcomed the input of both state-employed psychiatrists and private therapists in reasoning through the homosexuality-related cases that came through their courtroom, happy to defer to their greater authority on the subject (see chapter 3).[39]

The chillier reception of expert witnesses at the state's liquor proceedings was partially doubtless strategic, reflecting the unique institutional demands of those legal settings. Long before an industry of experts arose to challenge the stereotype of the flamboyant homosexual, the presumption that average Americans could easily recognize queer customers had wormed its way into the heart of the liquor boards' operations, providing especially powerful evidence against gay-friendly bars. In that context, what officials like Davis and Lordi were willing to recognize as expert knowledge about homosexuality did not simply follow the shifting contours of public debates about sexual difference, or even their own view of the leading medical consensus. It reflected their investment in what they saw as a functional regulatory regime.[40]

At the same time, however, that skepticism was also likely at least partly genuine, a product of legal actors' own personal and professional experiences with queer men and women in the public sphere. Appellate judges and hearing officers were, for one thing, as susceptible to popular assumptions about homosexuality as anyone else, well-versed in the cultural tropes that shaped public views of queer communities. And their unique professional experience adjudicating charges against gay-friendly bars gave them little reason to question those tropes. From the wealth of lay witnesses—on all sides—who defended their ability to tell homosexuals on sight, to the frequent overlap between the presence of effeminate patrons and more overtly homoerotic conduct, not least to their own intuitions that such flamboyant men *had* to be at least a little deviant, liquor officials' experiences seemed to bear out the adequacy of the public's commonsense presumptions about queer bodies. Even acknowledging the medical profession's deep wisdom on the subject of sexual deviance, and happy to defer to those experts in their own field, these legal actors simply did not see a role for expertise in so straightforward a task as identifying homosexuals in public.

In this regard, the liquor boards' proceedings against gay-friendly bars at midcentury did not just provide an arena for debating the public's conflicting intuitions about sexual difference. They intervened in an ongoing dispute over the boundaries of social and professional wisdom on that topic: the relative authority of experts and laymen in charting the public and legal meaning of homosexuality. Even as the boards' proceedings revealed the fissures underlying the public's supposedly common presumptions about deviance—the difficulty of locating where precisely the boundaries of "normal" masculine or feminine behavior could be drawn—they nevertheless defended the underlying value of that debate, confirming the significance of conventional gender norms as meaningful proxies for same-sex desire. In doing so, too, they defended the authority of the public itself in producing knowledge in a field increasingly dominated by more rarefied voices. As a rising class of self-identified professionals denigrated the layperson's long-standing assumptions about a topic of deep social and political interest, the liquor boards' regulatory proceedings emerged as a space where at least some insights about queer men and women remained squarely within the province of the common man. Before the law, if not in the doctor's office or even in the press, the liquor boards preserved the standing of the layman as the ultimate arbiter of deviance.

Police Expertise and the Politics of Deference

As a battle over comparative authority, indeed, the struggle over expert witnesses at the liquor boards' proceedings spilled well beyond professional psychiatrists. Eager to rebut the charges brought against them, bar owners hardly limited their expert witnesses to medical professionals and researchers. With judges and liquor boards refusing to recognize such conventional scientific authorities, rather, they turned to more creative sources of expertise.

Some looked to the world of leisure, which offered its own ranks of authorities on the proper boundaries of modern manhood and womanhood. Bar owners charged with serving gay men sometimes engaged sportsmen and athletic coaches, those professional observers of rugged masculinity. Prior to retaining Harry Farb, for instance, the owners of Murphy's Tavern called the director of the Newark Athletic Club, Al Thoma, who testified on the basis of his lifelong experience working with quintessentially manly figures like wrestlers and football players that he found nothing unusual about men with high-pitched voices and loose wrists. Nor did Thoma think twice about the sight of men embracing or even touching each other's backsides or privates in public—a common sight, he recounted, in steam rooms, heat rooms, pools, and football fields. Sometimes, he admitted, "I do it myself."[41]

Owners accused of catering to lesbians looked to a different authority, enlisting employees at clothing boutiques to educate the liquor boards about the latest trends in women's couture. At a hearing against Helene's Bar in Roselle in 1961, the manager of a local retail store produced samples of the "mannish type clothing" popular with his female customers, insisting that traditionally masculine items like button-down shirts and pants with flies on the front had become a staple of modern women's apparel. Far from bucking gender conventions, echoed a sales associate at the proceeding against the Keyhole Cocktail Lounge in Montville, trousers, loafers, and pullover sweaters were the leading "casual" fashions of the day.[42]

Bar owners who called athletic coaches or retail consultants to testify on their behalf were essentially bending the meaning of *expertise* on sexual difference as it applied to the liquor boards' antihomosexual campaigns. To the extent that disciplinary charges depended less on patrons' inner desires than on their departure from idealized norms of masculinity or femininity, after all, who better to rebut them than the day's leading arbiters of culture and fashion? The ABC's attorneys demurred from this novel claim—seized, suddenly and quite temporarily, with a newfound respect for the professional training required to render a reliable opinion on homosexuality. As Edward Ambrose protested when Al Thoma took the stand, only a "medical expert or mental expert" such as "a psychiatrist or neurologist" was qualified to testify about the vagaries of distinguishing homosexuals from ordinary men. (When Murphy's Tavern accommodated Ambrose's request and retained a psychiatrist in its subsequent appearance before the liquor board, of course, he promptly objected to that testimony as well.)[43]

More commonly, however, bar owners looked to another category of expert witness. Eager to rebut the liquor boards' testimony on its own terms, litigants in the 1950s and 1960s enlisted a somewhat counterintuitive professional ally: local police officers, who offered to counter the states' evidence with their own observations of a bar's business practices.

Here, again, Clarence Goldberg's defense of Manhattan's Gloria Bar and Grill in 1940 was ahead of its time. In addition to questioning Investigators Wickes and van Wagner on their expert insights into sexual deviance, Goldberg called three New York City policemen, who assured the SLA that they had made no homosexuality-related arrests or received any complaints about untoward activities at the Gloria in all their time on the job. These local officers, Goldberg insisted, were more reliable observers than a pair of liquor agents supplied by the state, since "it is the Police Department" that "is in intimate touch with neighborhood affairs."[44]

In the coming decades, that strategy emerged as a popular defense, especially in New Jersey, where police departments and liquor investigators retained significant independence in their daily operations. Throughout the 1950s and 1960s, current and former police officers commonly took the stand on behalf of suspected gay bars. When the ABC brought charges against the Rutgers Cocktail Bar in 1956, for instance, Rutgers's defense team called not only a professional psychiatrist but also a local policeman, who denied having "observed any objectionable persons or conduct" at the bar. When the ABC charged the Paddock Inn in 1964, the owner engaged Hugh E. Langcaskey, a detective with the Trenton Police Department. In his own experience "drop[ping] in to see who was in the place" on the weekends, Langcaskey informed the board, he had noticed some personal acquaintances and even crowds of local businessmen, but no one who struck him as an "apparent homosexual."[45]

Officers who testified for the defense bucked the general sentiment among police departments in these years, which was hardly sympathetic to gay-friendly bars. Nor did they likely ingratiate themselves with their fellow officers. Policemen who shared the burden of enforcing the liquor laws, and sometimes worked alongside liquor agents on the job, rarely appreciated colleagues who turned against them at trial. In Washington, DC, one officer who ventured to testify against the liquor board in a 1948 case—involving not homosexuals but a number of vice violations including prostitution—recalled being warned by a colleague that his testimony might "get [him] hurt."[46]

Policemen who testified anyway likely had varied motives. Some may have had long-standing relationships with the owners or employees of their local taverns, either through their years on the beat or through more informal interactions in their leisure hours. When three liquor agents visited Hy and Sol's Bar in Newark in January 1960, for instance, the patrons included an off-duty officer who stayed until at least 1 A.M. and insisted that he saw no "effeminate" conduct in his time there. After the ABC initiated proceedings against Herbie's Bar and Grill in Paterson, claiming that a bartender named Raymond propositioned an agent, a retired police captain testified that he had known Raymond for nearly three years and had never seen anything that "would indicate that Raymond was a homosexual or sex deviate." Sometimes, such testimony was easy enough to reconcile with the ABC's charges, but many witnesses were willing to contradict the liquor board's evidence directly, denying what multiple investigators described as overt homosexual behavior. Spending their late-night hours in gay-friendly bars, some of these officers might have been gay themselves— particularly those who had since left the force and felt less need to protect their private lives. Others might simply have been more tolerant of their cities' diverse nightlife in their off-duty hours, happy to patronize neighborhood bars that also served handfuls of queer men and women.[47]

Other officers, of course, likely had more self-serving reasons for testifying. Especially where a local department had opened its own investigation into a gay-friendly bar, the liquor boards' charges did not merely call bar owners' diligence in guarding against gay customers into question. They also put the police's own competence on trial. After the ABC brought charges against the Hotel Penn in Trenton, for example, Sergeant John Prihoda and Officer John Kennedy of the Trenton Police Department acknowledged that they had received a complaint about the bar's patrons, but reported that the owner promised to crack down on any inappropriate behavior. When they dropped in again some days later, they "observed no unusual actions on the part of any patron." In such cases, officers testified partly as a matter of professional pride, vouching for the value of their own enforcement strategies. And sometimes, they testified to cover up their willful *non*enforcement—fueled less by personal sympathy for the gay community than by pecuniary interests. At a time when many gay bars operated on the basis of a reliable system of bribes to local policemen, some officers had both a financial and a reputational investment in helping bar owners dispute the liquor boards' evidence.[48]

If police officers' own motives for testifying varied, bar owner's incentives to call them to the stand were more straightforward. Precisely owing to the counterintuitive nature of such alliances, police officers made for powerful witnesses for the defense: government employees who were held in comparatively high esteem by the courts and harbored no obvious bias toward gay-friendly bars. The very fact that a police officer was willing to testify on a bar owners' behalf spoke to the good order with which his or her establishment was run.

But the reliance on policemen to rebut the liquor boards' evidence also reflected the suspicion, going back to the earliest years following Repeal, that police officers were particularly reliable arbiters of sexual difference. Even as attorneys such as Clarence Goldberg questioned investigators' expert qualifications, in fact, many bar owners who denied knowingly serving queer patrons took the opposite tack: granting the liquor agents' intimacy with the visual hallmarks of homosexuality as all more the evidence of their own innocence. As James and Anne Tumulty insisted at their hearing in 1962, the state's witnesses were "experts" in identifying apparent homosexuals, having spent years patrolling the local nightlife. They themselves were "not so equipped."[49]

That faith in the investigator's professional insight was hardly the invention of creative bar owners. It was the deliberate work of law enforcement officials themselves. Eager to shore up their public reputation after the disastrous experience of Prohibition, which had exacerbated long-running critiques of local departments as bastions of incompetence, brutality, and corruption, reformist police chiefs in the mid-twentieth century embarked on a concerted effort to professionalize their departments. Like earlier efforts at police reform, that project included a range of institutional changes, from streamlining channels of command to imposing heightened personnel requirements. Yet it was also a shrewd public relations effort, aimed at cultivating an air of professionalism and expertise that would entitle officers to greater public respect. That latter project was particularly successful among the courts. Most commonly in cases involving drug dealing but also a range of offenses including burglary and prostitution, judges in the mid-twentieth century came to recognize the policeman's professional training and investigative experience as endowing him with unique insights into the hallmarks of urban crime. At trials, officers increasingly took the stand as expert witnesses, explaining the significance of seemingly innocuous clothing or furtive gestures. At suppression hearings, judges evaluating the constitutionality of police stops deferred to veteran officers' professional judgment, crediting their suspicion that a suspect was engaging in or about to engage in an offense.[50]

Enforcement agents appearing before the liquor boards often echoed this trend. Testifying against the Gloria Bar and Grill in 1940, Investigators Wickes and van Wagner knew enough to disclaim any pretensions to expertise, describing their observations as a matter of common sense, but a number of cooperating policemen lacked their professional modesty. As Patrolman Frederick Schmitt boasted, his "official investigation[s] . . . in connection with homosexuals and degenerates" made him especially confident in his ability to identify groups of fairies. As the years went on, such professional pride became progressively more common, and it spilled out past the police department, into the ranks of liquor investigators themselves. Before Detective Langcaskey took the stand on behalf of the Paddock Inn in 1964, the ABC's own agent touted his special credentials in identifying queer patrons, emphasizing his four years of experience "observing apparent homosexuals." A colleague testifying against Val's Bar in Atlantic City conceded that he was not "a scholar" of homosexual practices, but nevertheless credited his ability to classify Val's flamboyant customers to his years on the job, participating in numerous investigations of gay-friendly bars. In the hearing against One Eleven Wine and Liquors, Inspector Salvatore, a high-ranking investigator with the ABC, went even further: having "specialized in homosexual work for the Division" in his approximately eight years there, he boasted, he could readily detect homosexuals of all ages and in all settings, however hard they might try "to prevent any display of perversion."[51]

Hearing officers and commissioners were not unreceptive to such claims. Just as trial judges embraced narcotics officers as experts in drug-related transactions, so liquor officials in the 1960s acknowledged—even lauded—the "substantial" experience of investigators charged with ferreting out gay bars. Yet at a certain point, investigators' assertions of expertise also ran into some resistance. Even as they acknowledged the agents' unique experience observing gay bars, both the attorneys prosecuting anti-homosexual charges and the officials presiding over the proceedings consistently downplayed such professional experience as a factor bearing on the resolution of the case. In the proceeding against One Eleven, for instance, Director Joseph Lordi simultaneously praised Inspector Salvatore's "considerable on-job training" and, nevertheless, concluded that identifying gay men was a commonsense task, easily accomplished by any "witness with ordinary intelligence." In the case against Murphy's Tavern, too, Lordi hedged his bets, emphasizing the liquor agents' "many years of investigative experience" while disclaiming that identifying gay patrons "may be based on common observation," requiring "no special knowledge or skill." When Murphy's Tavern appealed to the Superior Court of New Jersey, New Jersey's attorney general adopted that same strategy, insisting that an investigator's "special experience . . . enables him to draw more accurate inferences than the casual observer" even as he argued that any ordinary witness could testify about the presence of gay customers.[52]

In proceeding after proceeding, in short, liquor officials and prosecutors toed a fine line, simultaneously acknowledging the professional insights that helped liquor agents identify gay customers and denying that any such insights were actually necessary. Careful not to cast the investigators' inferences too far into the realm of expertise, liquor officials preserved the recognition of homosexuals in some liminal space between common sense and specialized knowledge: an inference that both reflected an investigator's unique professional experiences and was entirely obvious to the layman.

The liquor boards' insistence that their agents benefited from no special talents beyond "common observation" went against the courts' growing embrace of police experience as a source of professional wisdom. And it ignored the fact that, as a practical matter, liquor agents and police officers often *did* have greater experience with the signs of gay life than most Americans. But the boards' skittishness about such expert claims was also unsurprising. Starting with their earliest charges and continuing well into the 1960s, proceedings against gay-friendly bars depended on the presumption that anyone, liquor agent and bartender alike, could recognize homosexual men or women on sight. Equivocating about the value of agents' professional experience allowed liquor officials to maintain this critical presumption, acknowledging the agents' qualifications without going so far to designate their observations expert opinions beyond the defendants' own competence. As Director William Howe Davis emphasized in 1960, rejecting Marion Brown's attempt to deny her ability to spot "queer" customers at her bar, "ABC agents, who have no special faculties in that respect, were readily able to ascertain and recognize" the offending patrons. Surely Brown could have done the same.[53]

The liquor boards' resistance to the specter of the expert investigator, no less than the expert psychiatrist, confirms the depth of their reliance on public authority over the markers of sexual deviance. More than rejecting an unwanted interloper in their proceedings, liquor officials' skepticism of expert testimony on the matter of homosexual identification was, first and foremost, a rejection of expertise itself: a defense of the role of common sense and lay knowledge in defining the boundaries of normal and deviant social conduct, during a period that made increasingly little room for either.

Yet that trend also illuminates the unusual incentives created by the liquor boards' regulatory campaigns, not only for creative bar owners seeking professional allies, but also for law enforcement agents and prosecutors. Buoyed by the gains of the professionalization movement, police officers at midcentury frequently legitimated their enforcement decisions in the field by emphasizing their expert insights about the groups they policed. In the case of liquor regulations, however, far from deferring to investigators' trained judgment in identifying gay bars, both the boards' prosecutors and their hearing officers denied the need for, and indeed the possibility of, any expertise in the task of detecting homosexuals. Working within a legal framework that concerned itself less with the truth of a customer's sexual propensities than with bar owners' presumptive awareness of them, agencies like New Jersey's ABC and New York's SLA did not claim that their officers had any unique fluency in the hallmarks of homosexuality. They chalked up those officers' testimony to the public's shared, inalienable wisdom about sexual difference.

A closer look at the role of specialized testimony in the liquor boards' proceedings reveals the complex, often-curious epistemic politics overhanging the regulation of queer life in the mid-twentieth century: the extent to which the policing of queer social spaces stood at the center of a live debate over who had the standing to proclaim binding truths about homosexuality in America, if not at the doctor's office then at least before the law. At a time when medical and scientific professionals commanded evergreater authority in public discussions of sexual difference, liquor proceedings emerged as a useful arena for testing some of their claims about the nature and social meaning of same-sex desire—a site in which the power of the law consistently held the line of popular intuition and common sense against the aspersions of trained expertise. In that context, the unique logic of the boards' proceedings transformed the political purchase of seemingly familiar forms of expert knowledge about deviance, turning the medical profession's pathological view of homosexuality, for instance, into a useful tool for resisting the suppression of queer social spaces. And it complicated the presumptive value of police expertise itself, harnessing the success of the liquor boards' campaigns to the disavowal rather than the recognition of liquor agents' often-substantial professional exposure to the gay world. In a legal regime grounded on the diffusion of regulatory responsibilities— one perfected not by refining the skills of state officials but by distributing enforcement duties among the broader public—conventional authorities both inside and outside the legal system sometimes found themselves playing a surprising role.[54]

Investigators enforcing the liquor codes, of course, were not the only state agents amassing unique insights into gay life in the postwar years. They were joined on that score by the vice squads proliferating among urban police departments. Responsible for enforcing a range of criminal laws, those units were not beholden to the idiosyncrasies of the liquor boards' regulatory schemes. But they faced their own set of distinctive institutional and legal pressures—not least, criminal courts far more willing to question the value of their charges.

THREE

Plainclothes Decoys and the Limits of Criminal Justice

In the waning hours of March 4, 1939, Investigator Robbins of New Jersey's Division of Alcoholic Beverage Control (ABC) stood in Peter Orsi's bar in Newark when a customer came up and asked him for a drink. As the man made the nature of his interest known, reaching down to stroke the investigator's legs and chest, Robbins remembered his official duties and acted accordingly: having heard enough for his report, he pushed back the man's arms and walked away.[1]

Ten years later, a patron flirting with an undercover agent at a gay bar was likely to face more drastic consequences. As police departments after the end of World War II delegated the investigation of sex-related offenses to a spate of specialized vice squads, a new line of plainclothes officers charged with patrolling their cities' queer nightlife converged on bars, parks, and public bathrooms across the country. Sometimes, these officers helped agents like Robbins gather evidence against gay-friendly venues, but primarily they enforced a range of criminal laws targeting supposedly degenerate sexual practices—not least, men seeking sex with other men. Some officers chafed at what they saw as undignified assignments, hardly the type of intrepid crime fighting they had joined the force to do. Others threw themselves into the task, pursuing suspects through an array of brazen, time-consuming tactics that stretched the boundaries between the solicitor and the solicited.

If some vice officers had their reservations about plainclothes enforcement, however, their operations inspired even greater qualms among the other agents of the criminal justice system, including some prosecutors but most critically the courts. Unlike liquor laws, which were enforced largely within the auspices of a single top-down agency, criminal laws fell to the discretion of multiple arms of government, which often took very different views of the vice squads' work. To be sure, even the most lenient judges rarely accepted homosexuality as a functional lifestyle or questioned the state's right to discourage it. Yet they sometimes balked at the reality of anti-homosexual enforcement, whether owing to a libertarian impulse against prosecuting consensual activities, an incrementalist concern with excessive punishment, a pragmatic objection to wasting government resources, a self-serving interest in clearing their own dockets, or even personal sympathy for the men involved—especially the middle-class defendants who otherwise rarely appeared before the criminal courts. Not least, some struggled with an abiding squeamishness over the unsavory enticement tactics often used by decoys in the field—tactics that struck some courts as more immoral than the practices they aimed to suppress.

Formally, the judge's task left little room for these objections; whatever the court's own views, the penal codes criminalized homosexual solicitation, and even the most aggressive decoy tactics fell short of the legal standard for entrapment. In practice, however, judges exercised substantial discretion in the courtroom, and they used that discretion to dispose of what they saw as morally if not legally problematic arrests. From New York to Detroit to Los Angeles, judges who questioned the wisdom of the vice squads' campaigns imposed relatively lenient sentences, reduced charges, and dismissed cases against sympathetic defendants. Those offended by police enticement tactics narrowly interpreted criminal statutes, generously applied common law defenses, and drew on their discretion over the sufficiency of the evidence to dismiss objectionable charges. The story of gay men's legal struggles against the vice squads is an integral part of the gay community's battle for civil rights, a battle waged primarily by a group of courageous defendants, supportive activists, and the attorneys who championed them in court. But that story also featured another underappreciated set of players: the diverse members of the judiciary, who sometimes saw their work as regulating odious police practices as much as unorthodox sexual conduct, and who proved quite willing to engage creatively with the law to curtail what they criticized, privately if not publicly, as unjust laws and repulsive police methods.

Recognizing trial judges' frequent resistance to the vice squads does not erase the harm that many gay men suffered in the criminal justice system, both at the hands of vice officers and in court. The majority of defendants charged with solicitation were convicted. Many experienced devastating consequences, including fees, jail time, public humiliation, the loss of employment opportunities, and estrangement from friends and family. Nor did the courts' flights of mercy always have their intended effect. Aiming

to soften the law's treatment of gay men, judicial leniency led some officers to feel vindicated, perversely, in serving their own less humane brand
of justice, using loitering or disorderly conduct charges to hassle gay men
in public parks, or turning to violence as a punishment no court could
reduce. The police harassment and abuse of gay men and women is remembered as among the most galling features of gay life in the 1950s and
1960s, an emblem of the law's deep-seated contempt for a marginalized
social group. But that practice did not always reflect a policy of zealous
antihomosexual enforcement. It sometimes reflected a practice of princi-
pled *non*enforcement by the courts, and the resentment that clemency inspired on the ground.[2]

For all those reasons, it is all the more important to disaggregate the
project of antigay policing in the mid-twentieth century. From its greatest
excesses to its buried flights of mercy, the enforcement of misdemeanor
laws against gay men was not a monolithic enterprise. It was the site of a
complex, deep-seated struggle among multiple branches of the legal system, a contest about the proper boundaries of law enforcement as much
as about the law's treatment of sexual difference. Driven by their personal,
political, and institutional interests, judges did not always act as foot soldiers for the legislature's antihomosexual policies, or as rubber stamps for
the vice squads' arrests. They often did their best to mitigate the deepest
harms of those campaigns, constraining and sometimes confounding their
more zealous partners in the criminal justice system. Their efforts simply
did not always unfold as they had hoped.[3]

Turning from the civil to the criminal regulation of queer life, this chapter examines the institutional fissures that accompanied the enforcement of
antisolicitation statutes at midcentury, classically victimless crimes inspiring trenchant moral and practical disagreements among the various arms
of the legal system. That story uncovers the many pressures that shaped
the courts' divergent views of the vice squads' campaigns, from personal
principle to professional self-interest. It reveals the surprising sources of
mercy in the criminal justice system's treatment of gay men, not least the
mitigating influence of outwardly punitive developments like the sexual
psychopath laws. And it exposes the project of antihomosexual policing in
the United States as a fractious battleground over not only the boundaries
of permissible sexual practice, but also the character of the criminal justice
system itself: the wisdom of criminal statutes, the limits of ethical policing, and the power of the courts to determine either. At a time of ongoing
and often vocal debate about the law's proper treatment of homosexuality, these lesser-recognized institutional struggles, no less than shifting po-

litical commitments to the regulation of sexual difference, shaped the legal rights and freedoms of gay individuals.

The Politics and Geography of Plainclothes Policing

A favorite tool of the vice squad, the police decoy, a plainclothes officer set out as bait for criminal activity, was part of a broad system of undercover investigation in the modern police department. In Europe, that system became a formal feature of police work in the early nineteenth century, when a French criminal named Eugene Vidocq turned detective and organized a squad of ex-convicts to infiltrate the Parisian underworld. In the United States, it did not become widespread until the early twentieth century, when the diversifying profile of the American city strained the competence of the uniformed police. Under pressure from private reform agencies, which often hired their own detectives to investigate enclaves of urban vice, police departments established specialized units targeting narcotics, prostitution, liquor sales, and disputes in immigrant neighborhoods. Plainclothes detectives, they realized, were especially useful for enforcing morals regulations: crimes typically carried out in private and among consenting participants, evading detection by more conventional means.[4]

Queer men first encountered the undercover officer soon after Repeal, as liquor boards began dispatching plainclothes agents to patrol disorderly conduct and other licensing violations in bars. At gay-friendly venues, as anywhere else, the agents did their best to fade into the scenery, purchasing drinks and fraternizing with the customers around them. On some evenings, those investigators found themselves welcomed warmly into their city's queer nightlife, fondled or propositioned near the bar. As a rule, however, they were more concerned with enforcing the states' liquor regulations than their sodomy or solicitation laws. Stories of flagrant sexual overtures bolstered the agents' cases against disorderly establishments, and sometimes those agents helped local policemen apprehend the offending customers. But most investigators did not go to bars looking to make an arrest, and they certainly did not go out of their way to pass for the fairies they described in their reports.[5]

Following World War II, the profile of plainclothes enforcement began to change. By the early 1950s, essentially every large police force in the nation had adopted a specialized vice or morals squad aimed at enforcing sex-related offenses. These novel units owed their origins partly to the sex-crime panics of the late 1930s and early 1950s, which not simply pushed legislatures to enact a new breed of sexual psychopath statutes but also fueled demand for more systematic enforcement of existing offenses. They also reflected a broader shift in police organization in these years: a widespread campaign, led by police executives aiming to professionalize police work, to divide investigative tasks into more specialized units. Some modicum of specialization, the logic went, both improved the quality of policing and boosted accountability in each division, ensuring that the laws were actually enforced.[6]

Frequently responsible for a range of offenses, including sex crimes, prostitution, and gambling, vice squads varied in size by city. In San Francisco, the police department's Bureau of Special Services operated a Sex Detail, which was focused solely on violent and nonviolent sex offenders, including suspected rapists, child molesters, and "degenerates." In Washington, DC, the police made do with an all-purpose morals squad staffed by four to six undercover agents—which, despite its small size, proved notoriously effective. Larger cities, including Los Angeles and Detroit, sometimes made room for both a central vice squad and smaller details in each neighborhood division. By the mid-1950s, the Detroit Police Department assigned sixty people to central vice—nearly twice as many as were staffed to the homicide squad—in addition to its "cleanup squads" in local precincts. Departments with fewer resources, by contrast, sometimes divided duties among specialized vice officers and the general detective unit, as in Philadelphia, or relied entirely on the central division.[7]

Vice squads were often inspired by concerns over violent sex crimes, but their daily operations were far likelier to target nonviolent offenders like gay men. To some extent, that pattern was a matter of convenience. As the end of World War II sent waves of gay and lesbian soldiers, emboldened by the friendships they had formed during the war, into the nation's major cities, police departments tasked with patrolling urban nightlife grew familiar with the sites of gay life, including not just bars but also public cruising grounds like street corners, parks, and public bathrooms. For officers pressured by their superiors to maintain their arrest rates, visiting these familiar areas—like, for that matter, frequenting corners popular with prostitutes—was an easy way to boost their productivity.[8]

Yet the focus on gay men also reflected a growing sense that the proliferating enclaves of queer life in American cities genuinely merited the attention of the police. Partly responsible was the sex-crime panic itself, which often led journalists and public officials to conflate homosexual men with a darker category of urban predator. A 1949 article in *Collier's* magazine on sex crimes in Detroit depicted a homosexual cruising for a partner alongside its survey of violent sex offenders. "Suppose he finally snapped up a

child?" the reporter wondered. Local police officials were no less susceptible to these concerns. As a veteran New York Police Department officer
warned in 1959, men who failed to find willing adult partners in parks or
theaters "tend[ed] to go after young children" as a last resort.[9]

Another catalyst was strictly a Cold War innovation. In February 1950,
Deputy Undersecretary John Peurifoy revealed that the State Department
had fired ninety-one employees for alleged sexual perversion. The statistic
sparked an outcry among Senate Republicans eager for a political cudgel
against the Truman administration, who promptly deprioritized the Communist threat and challenged the nation to "think of a person who could
be more dangerous to the United States of America than a pervert." A congressional subcommittee, named the Hoey Committee for its chairman,
Clyde Hoey, soon concluded that gay men and women were "unsuitable"
for federal employment, not least—in a classic example of a self-created
problem—because their illicit sexual practices opened them to blackmail
by foreign agents. Disseminated by publications from the *New York Times*
to *Reader's Digest*, the specter of homosexuals clearing a path for Communist infiltration soon led to a concerted campaign in Washington, DC, to
purge homosexuals from federal employment. It also fueled policing in the
capital and beyond, elevating the problem of the homosexual to a national
concern.[10]

For most police departments, however, the primary impetus for antihomosexual drives was neither the risk to national security nor the alleged
threat to the nation's children. It was the same concern that drove the liquor boards' campaigns against gay-friendly bars in these years: the fear
that unrestrained sites of "depravity," violent or otherwise, were an affront
to the public order. Especially as middle-class Americans eager to return
to domestic normality following the war decamped to the suburbs, police
officials and politicians often saw the growing traces of queer life in their
cities as yet another symptom of what they decried as urban blight, offending the sensibilities of local residents, diminishing the quality of life, and
ushering in economic decline. From DC to Detroit, vice squads commonly
insisted that they cared little about private homosexual activity, focusing
on overt displays that might cause a public nuisance. In Los Angeles, the
vice squad formally structured its campaigns around the "three Cs": citizen
complaints, commercial activity, and conspicuous conduct. In San Francisco, politicians concerned about attracting the right caliber of tourist—
namely, the heterosexual one—directed the police toward the city's more
visible pockets of queer life, tolerating bars while cracking down on bus
stations and bathrooms. Given the lengths to which many bars went to

conceal themselves from public view, indeed, some police departments were happy to turn a blind eye to well-run businesses. Some likely did so for financial considerations, selling their leniency to amenable bar owners, but others did so as a genuine enforcement strategy, preferring to let gay men gather indoors rather than push them out onto the streets.[11]

Animated by these concerns, vice squads in the 1950s turned their attention to the more public pockets of queer life. And, conveniently, they found themselves armed with a number of laws to enforce against them. The harshest penalties attached to sodomy, still considered a felony in nearly every state. But sodomy laws were notoriously hard to enforce, plagued by all the evidentiary burdens of a private morals offense. More useful was a range of misdemeanor charges that could be invoked against men seeking sexual partners in public. The precise statutes varied by state, from California's "lewd vagrancy" law to New York's disorderly conduct statute to a rash of antisolicitation laws in jurisdictions like Michigan, Wisconsin, and DC—some specifically updated to target homosexuality following the war. Regardless, the reach of these laws was similar, allowing police officers to arrest men who tendered a sexual proposition in a public space.[12]

For the same reasons they were so helpful in regulating prostitution and gambling, plainclothesmen were all but essential in enforcing these statutes. Although police departments reported frequent calls from private citizens or business owners perturbed by homosexual activity in the area—in Los Angeles, claims of "numerous complaints" became boilerplate on arrest reports—such calls typically reported unattached men idling in public rather than unwanted sexual advances. Stories of unwilling bystanders actually propositioned by gay men were uncommon, and they rarely led to an arrest. A decoy in the right place at the right time, by contrast, could elicit a solicitation "in a matter of minutes." And he could make multiple arrests in one night. In DC's Franklin Park in the fall of 1948, one decoy officer arrested six men in a single evening. In the quieter Pontiac, Michigan, a campaign in a downtown department store during the 1956 Christmas season yielded fourteen arrests in as many days.[13]

Emboldened by these considerations, plainclothes vice officers soon descended on cruising sites across the country. Decoys waited in bus terminals, public bathrooms, bathhouses, and gyms. They visited bars, hotel lobbies, department stores, and movie theaters. Certain parks became especially well-known as hubs of homosexual activity. As one seasoned Los Angeles Police Department (LAPD) vice officer warned recruits: "Any small plot of grass with a bush may have a homosexual behind it." In Los Angeles, the vice squad focused its attention on the nature area by the Griffith

3.1. Officer Max K. Hurlbut outside Ferndell No. 9 in Griffith Park, Los Angeles.
© Max K. Hurlbut. Courtesy of Max K. Hurlbut.

Park Observatory, and on one particular restroom known as Ferndell No. 9, a "notorious homosexual contact spot." On the East Coast, Washington's Lafayette Park acquired a similar reputation among not only vice officers but also journalists and politicians. In 1947, a reporter discovered a wiretap hidden behind a park bench; although no agency claimed credit for the operation, the press widely attributed it to an investigation targeting sexual deviance. By 1950, the frequent arrests in the park fueled the Republicans' campaign against homosexual federal employees. As the former congressman and then-Senate candidate Everett Dirksen warned that June: "I know about LaFayette Park across from the White House and the men who loitered there. Many found their way into the state department to be blackmailed into selling the secrets of our country."[14]

Operating in the shadow of the federal government's crusade, indeed, the morals squad in Washington became notorious for its antihomosexual campaigns. Partially to credit was the congressional commission organized in response to fears of homosexuals in government. Outraged to discover that policemen in the 1940s booked most offenders for disorderly conduct and released them without further process, the Hoey Committee promptly demanded a stricter program of enforcement. Also significant, however, was the man heading the morals squad, Lieutenant Roy Blick. Commemorated by the press as a "one-man watchdog of the city's morals," Blick led the vice division for roughly twenty years until, after two requests for an extension of tenure, the city finally forced him into retirement in 1964. In his office, Blick kept a gray safe filled with index cards for every suspect arrested by his bureau. When he left the department, he threatened to keep the key. Blick had a genuine, perhaps unusual zeal for the morals squad's antihomosexual campaigns, and in the Lavender Scare he saw an opportunity to enhance his division's prestige. Under his guidance, tales of the morals squad's prolific arrests, many involving government employees, saturated the local papers in the 1950s.[15]

Public parks and theaters were frequented by men of all races and classes, and the vice squads' operations ensnared a range of suspects. As one defense attorney in Los Angeles recalled, his clients over the years included lawyers, doctors, engineers, professors, artists, athletes, and servicemen. The nation's capital, in particular, attracted a steady stream of single government employees, and the morals squad's campaigns there often struck at the heart of the political elite. In the winter of 1954, a police officer arrested Joseph Buscher, an assistant attorney general in Maryland, outside a downtown Greyhound station. Five years later, Walter Jenkins, a senior aide to future President Lyndon B. Johnson, fell prey to a vice sting in the men's room of a YMCA. Such arrests could be trusted to end political careers, but sometimes the consequences were more tragic. On June 9, 1953, Officer John Costanzo arrested twenty-six-year-old Lester Hunt Jr., the son of Democratic senator Lester Hunt of Wyoming, in Lafayette Park. The arrest became a dagger in the hands of the senator's political enemies, who ensured that the younger Hunt went to trial and threatened to drag the charges through the press if his father ran for reelection. The elder Hunt fatally shot himself in his Senate office.[16]

While DC's morals squad courted local headlines for its arrests of white-collar federal employees, departments in other cities concentrated on a different suspect profile: men who were poor, nonwhite, gender nonconforming, or some combination of the three. To an extent, that discrepancy reflected the entrenched habits and presumptions of urban police departments. Mirroring the geography of existing enforcement practices, which had long singled out racial and ethnic minorities for heightened police surveillance, the vice squads' campaigns against so-called urban degeneracy frequently dispatched officers to poor and predominantly black and brown neighborhoods. (At the same time, of course, as they often selectively tolerated criminal economies in those settings, effectively relocating pockets of urban vice from richer to poorer areas.)[17]

Yet the particular logistics of decoy enforcement, too, sometimes served to focus the attention of the vice squads on less ostensibly "respectable" targets. For one thing, the social practices of wealthier gay men, who were more likely to limit their socializing to private gatherings or high-class bars, shielded them from the vice squads' patrols in more public cruising areas. Indeed, since cruising sites like public bathrooms and parks were often chosen for their distance from commercial foot traffic, situated in remote or economically abandoned pockets of the city, patrols there inevitably threw plainclothes decoys in contact with poorer suspects. Meanwhile, officers searching for potential arrests frequently found it easiest to focus on gender-nonconforming individuals. As one LAPD vice officer recalled, "normal" homosexuals, indistinguishable from other men, rarely caught the vice squad's eye; it was "the ones who dress or act aggressively or outrageously that attract[ed] our attention." Relying largely on their visual impressions to identify potential suspects, officers often gravitated toward men who comported most closely with public stereotypes of homosexuality—those flamboyant mannerisms or fashions that, over the course of the 1950s, became increasingly associated with lower-class communities and communities of color.[18]

And sometimes, of course, the harsh treatment of less "respectable" targets was more deliberate. Making their arrests in the anonymity of a bathroom or a darkened park, decoys rarely had the benefit of much identifying information about their targets, but officers who discovered that they had arrested wealthy or socially prominent suspects sometimes did their best, in the words of one contemporary, to "undo" the encounter. An observer at the Detroit Police Department in 1956 remarked on how differently officers treated different classes of men suspected of a sex offense. Booking middle-class defendants, officers frequently spoke kindly, assuring them that no publicity would result. "It happens to a lot of people . . . in all walks of life," one sergeant assured a nervous suspect arrested for solicitation. After a young policeman staking out a Greyhound station arrested a forty-four-year-old physician—an otherwise law-abiding man, he noted, who supported his elderly parents—the officer himself tried to explain away the arrest, speculating that the man's obstetric practice might be to blame. "He does not like to deal with women," he conjectured, "and I think it is because he usually sees women when they are at their messiest."[19]

Policemen rarely showed such forbearance to the cross-dressers or sex workers—effeminate, poor, and often black—who sometimes caught the department's attention. Routine procedure, one Detroit officer confided, was to arrest such "fags" or "queers" on sight and then book them pretextually for suspected larceny, a practice officially rationalized by sex workers' alleged habit of "rolling" their customers. Following the arrest, too, the difference was stark. At the station, officers gathered in groups to "razz" gender-nonconforming suspects as they were booked. In jail, the guards mocked their attire, sometimes forcing them to discard any items of feminine clothing. As these cases suggested, some officers took less umbrage at the homosexual's unorthodox sexual practices than at the cross-dresser's voluntary rejection of conventional masculine norms—fueled in many cases by the low social status of sex workers, and especially black sex workers, in the city's deeply racialized sexual market.[20]

Preceding the task of selecting suspects, naturally, was the task of selecting the decoys themselves. As a general matter, vice officers tasked with enticing homosexual solicitations were chosen on the basis of two factors: age and physical attractiveness. In Pontiac, Michigan, in 1957, one patrolman with a notable resemblance to the screen idol Rudolph Valentino "specialized in the investigation of cases involving male homosexuals." In Philadelphia, the morals squad made do with two "specially selected" officers—both under thirty, "good-looking," and neatly dressed—for all its decoy assignments.[21]

Like most police officers at the time, vice officers were typically white, though large cities with more diverse populations employed the occasional black or Latino officer. At a time when most gay bars were still strictly segregated, in practice if not by legal mandate, these decoys likely helped entice defendants with a shared racial background. But, reflecting the racial suspicions of the day, they also helped build cases against white defendants. Throughout the 1950s, white men who offered white officers a drink or even invited them up to their apartments managed to mount a credible defense that their offers were purely platonic—that they were simply feeling convivial, as one put it, toward a "decent citizen." Some judges hesitated to ascribe such benign motives to a budding interracial friendship. In DC in 1960, sixty-six-year-old Warren Wildeblood struck up a conversation with a young black officer at a bus stop and invited him back to his apartment. Judge Milton Kronheim of the municipal court derided the claim that the two might have had an innocent interest in each other's company. "I can't imagine any credible reason why a white man meeting a colored man as a stranger in front of a bus station at that time of night, should walk . . . towards his home," he concluded, "other than such as has been suggested here."[22]

Rarer still than black or Latino decoys was another category of officer: women. Certainly, female officers were not entirely absent from the vice squads' campaigns. When California's liquor board brought charges against Mary's First and Last Chance Bar in Oakland in 1956, key witnesses included a policewoman who testified that, during one of her many visits to the bar that spring, a female patron complimented her as a "cute little butch" and kissed her. But few departments assigned female decoys to entice suspected lesbians. For the same reasons that lesbian bars sometimes escaped the liquor boards' attention, failing to strike some investigators as meaningful public hazards, vice squads rarely saw plainclothes enforcement against women as a good use of their resources. Lesbians, as Sergeant Glenn Souza of the LAPD explained, were far less likely to solicit strangers than gay men were, preferring to "stick . . . with their own kind." Even if they were worried about the social problem of the lesbian, police departments had their reservations about sending out officers to make arrests. Most departments employed few women to begin with, and plainclothes enforcement, forcing officers into intimate contact with an illicit sexual underworld, struck some police officials as "too degrading" for the gentler sex. When the Tallahassee Police Department found itself in need of a female decoy in the early 1960s, it cast its sights beyond its typical personnel, paying a convicted prostitute $400 a month to entice both lesbians and the occasional political enemy.[23]

If senior officials' concerns about the degrading nature of decoy work were limited to women, vice officers themselves were often less discriminating. As most policemen recognized, vice assignments were a useful step up the ladder of police work, a gateway from uniformed patrols to detective assignments. But many still resented the indignities such work entailed. Decoy patrols forced vice officers into intimate contact with a sexual underworld that many viewed with both derision and distaste, and some officers saw their duties as equal parts petty and demeaning. As Chief Thomas Cahill of the San Francisco Police Department (SFPD) later recalled, most officers assigned to the sex bureau in San Francisco "wanted no part of it." "They'd rather get out and do regular police work," he insisted, "than to be working undercover to entrap people like those."[24]

Some concerns arose from the lowly nature of the underlying offense, far from the serious investigations many officers imagined at the heart of big-city policing. But they also reflected the sense that decoy work was, as some policemen put it, intrinsically "dirty," attaching a shadow of deviance to anyone who performed it. In earlier decades, when many Americans still saw sexual deviance as a matter of gender variation as much as erotic conduct, liquor investigators thought little of inviting physical intimacies in bars. In 1919, indeed, one naval outpost in Rhode Island went so far as to send sailors to initiate sexual acts with suspected homosexuals, all without worrying that the task tarnished the sailors' own sexual identities. By the late 1940s, the public's narrowing conceptions of normative sexual practice made legal officials more nervous about immersing their officers in an illicit sexual underworld. Even beyond the realm of antihomosexual policing, vice assignments in these years often carried a whiff of inevitable corruption. For that very reason, departments like the LAPD set strict limits on all vice rotations: no more than eighteen months per assignment. For sex-related work like prostitution and antihomosexual patrols, some also imposed an additional safeguard, preferring to hire only married officers, who had some buffer against the appearance—or perhaps even the reality—of temptation in the field. Even that buffer did not save officers from ridicule inside the station: the jokes bandied around the coffee room that "it takes one to catch one" or that vice officers "prefer" their line of work in any case. Sometimes, such jokes may have hit close to home. From the sordid tales of policemen demanding sexual favors to more benign rumors of decoys living with male lovers, gay men arrested by officers insisted that the vice squads featured their share of secret homosexuals. But even among the least self-conscious decoys, the teasing made such assignments, as one LAPD officer recalled, among the "less glamorous" aspects of the job.[25]

Some officers, by contrast, took well to the task. Inclined by both a process of self-selection and the professional culture of midcentury police departments toward conservative social values, some policemen likely arrived with a sinister view of homosexuals, happy to do their part to contain what they saw as a degenerate practice. The violence that some suspects suffered at the hands of arresting officers—the black eyes and bloodied lips sighted at police stations—suggested the deep hostility that many policemen felt toward the men they patrolled. Even in the absence of such personal antipathy, officers who simply accepted the law's prohibitions on same-sex practices—a policy vindicated, by many accounts, by the prevailing view of homosexuality as a disease—regarded plainclothes work as a legitimate part of the job, a reasonable if unpalatable strategy to contain a harmful social activity. Some enjoyed the inherent suspense of enticement assignments, preferring work in the field—any work in the field—to the dreary exchange of phone calls required by investigations into gambling dens. Some even found the essentially victimless nature of vice offenses, which more critical colleagues saw as the source of their petty character, part of what made those assignments enjoyable. If decoy work sometimes placed unsavory demands on vice officers, after all, it was still far less unsavory than many other assignments—preferable, as one LAPD officer put it, to "collect[ing] body parts in a tub at an accident scene."[26]

And some decoys, whatever their views before joining the vice squad, learned their enthusiasm on the job. Spending their nights patrolling cruising grounds, pressured if not explicitly directed by their superiors to rack up arrests, those officers inevitably came to take their work seriously. As one Detroit defense attorney remarked in 1957, the officers who pursued gay men in the city's parks and bathrooms reminded him of "an athletic team imbued with a violent determination to win." And anyone "so intent on winning," he reflected, was bound at some point to "commit a foul."[27]

Decoy Tactics on the Ground

As a general matter, vice officers in the 1950s received little guidance in the field. Left to rely on their own instincts, they developed a range of techniques for attracting men seeking partners, varying on the basis of both their aptitude and their appetite for the job.

Most tactics in these early years were straightforward. In bars, officers took their cues from liquor agents, purchasing their alcohol of choice, striking up conversations, or offering to buy their new acquaintances a drink. Sometimes, they insisted, their mere presence was enough to elicit a solicitation. In New York in April 1953, the police officer Howard Koch was sitting alone at Diamond Jim's Bar and Grill when, as he reported, two patrons came up and invited him back home for "a few beers" and "some fun." In more public areas, too, decoys waited to be approached in parks or on sidewalks, or introduced themselves to idling passersby. Simply idling on a park bench was often enough to catch a stranger's eye, but many officers were more proactive, following suspected gay men or inviting them to sit beside them. After a plainclothes decoy arrested Donald Brenke for solicitation in DC in 1951, Brenke recounted that the officer had approached him, proposing that the two men go out for "a good time." The subsequent summer in Lafayette Park, Ed Wallace recalled being hailed by a blond stranger who "began to ask a lot of questions." "Where were you before you came here?" the young man pressed. "Why'd you come out?" When Wallace tried to walk away, the officer followed, continuing to ask where he might be headed next.[28]

In bathrooms, vice officers settled on a more established pattern. From hotels to theaters to public parks, decoys singled out men who appeared to be searching for sexual partners, either through some overt signal, such as a patron exposing himself or masturbating by the urinals, or simply by some telltale trace of effeminacy. Rather than making an arrest on the spot, they would then start up a conversation. When the man turned to leave the restroom, the decoy followed him out. If he made no signs of going, the officer stepped outside first, waiting for the man to follow. Almost invariably, decoys found some way of exposing themselves to suspected cruisers, either pretending to use the urinals or at least drawing back their coats to attract the suspect's eye. Ben Bradlee, a *Washington Post* reporter who later became the paper's executive editor, recalled the morals squad's arrests as a fairly sordid routine: Blick's "apple-cheeked" recruits would drop by public bathrooms, "wave their tallywackers around[,] and see if anybody was interested."[29]

Confident that a friendly word or some exposed flesh would elicit a solicitation, many officers did not bother with much else. But some tried their hand at a more complicated masquerade. As the gay writer Donald Webster Cory observed in 1951, homosexual men encountering each other in public commonly relied on telltale touches of effeminacy to communicate their common purpose: "a softness of tone, an overenunciation of word sounds, an affectation in the movement of the hands." Vice officers were often familiar with these cues; in their work for the liquor boards, after all, some used these same mannerisms to identify gay patrons. But if investigators like Williams Wickes had insisted on maintaining some distance from the fairies they patrolled, the demands of plainclothes enticement work forced decoys to grow more comfortable with imitating those affectations. In the spring of 1954, for instance, Officer Dante A. Longo arrested twenty-five-year-old Paul Ross after Longo's feminine mannerisms and "flirtatious" gestures "inflamed [Ross] beyond his capacity to resist." Ross was so taken aback by the officer's utter change of demeanor following the arrest, he later confided, that he promptly confessed to the offense.[30]

One signal was especially effective. Among gay men's most reliable internal codes, Cory noted, were certain morsels of slang, shared among friends or exchanged by strangers to signal their membership in a marginal sexual community. That distinctive jargon had long provided researchers and state officials with a useful tool for ferreting out suspected homosexuals. During the recent war, one man recalled, military psychiatrists used such argot to identify homosexual recruits, rattling off "the gay language from A to Z" and looking for a sign of recognition. Vice officers hardly boasted the psychiatrist's encyclopedic knowledge, but they also learned that a drop or two of queer slang could go a long way in the field. Decoys found ways to work terms like *gay* into their banter or waited for suspects to do so as evidence of their salacious intent. After Officer John Costanzo arrested a patron in a DC theater in 1952, both Costanzo and a fellow officer testified that the man "had used terms" with a "special significance among sexual deviates." The decoy who approached Ed Wallace in Lafayette Park both dropped and listened for Wallace's use of queer argot: having repeatedly asked Wallace why he had "come out" that evening, the officer arrested him only after he mentioned the "bitches" at a popular gay bar.[31]

As in any police unit, some vice officers were more zealous than others. In DC, Louis Fochett earned a particular reputation for his effective strategies in public bathrooms. A career man with the morals squad, Fochett joined the force in 1946 and served until his early death in 1968. In his private life, he was a father, a Catholic, and a coach in the local elementary school's physical fitness program, but in his professional capacity—as a young man, at least—he was "out every night" catching homosexuals for the vice squad. Fochett developed a consistent, almost trademark tactic. Having spotted a likely cruiser in a public bathroom, he would exchange glances with the other man and then head outside, leaning on the wall by the men's room long enough for the suspect to find him. Sometimes, he would unbutton his coat. If he were still inside the men's room, he would expose himself by unzipping his pants. When the suspect reached toward him, Fochett would ask if he "wanted to take it"—and, receiving an affirmative response, promptly make his arrest. That combination of suggestive body language and aggressive sexual banter was responsible for countless arrests around DC in the 1950s. Fochett became so notorious, indeed, that, when he tried to infiltrate the inaugural meeting of an early gay rights group, the Mattachine Society of Washington, in 1961, the attendees promptly identified him and expelled him from the room.[32]

In smaller towns with less established cruising areas, officers were less prolific, but what they lacked in arrest numbers they sometimes made up for in patience and creativity. In the winter of 1951, a group of police officers driving through the Village of Endicott in upstate New York observed two men in a series of incriminating positions during a traffic stop: the driver's pants seemed to be unbuttoned, and soon afterward his passenger appeared to have a hand on the driver's crotch. One of the officers recognized the passenger as Frank Humphrey, an old acquaintance from his previous job as a taxi driver. Bearing out Oscar Wilde's truism about all the added bitterness of an old friend, Officer Shepard did not arrest either of the men. Instead, he had his colleagues drop him off on the street outside Humphrey's home. When Humphrey finally returned, the officer greeted him by name. "Frank, how are you?" he asked. "I want to see you tonight," he implored. After a few minutes of casual conversation, Humphrey invited Shepard to his apartment for "some beer, candy, and for some fun." Only once they were inside, with the other two officers eavesdropping from the porch, did Humphrey tender a more explicit proposal and Shepard finally make his arrest.[33]

Even Shepard's manipulations, however, paled in comparison to Dale Jennings's infamous encounter in the men's room of Los Angeles's Westlake Park. A founding member of the original branch of the Mattachine Society in Los Angeles, Jennings had always thought it took a certain sloppiness to fall prey to the LAPD's roving decoys. But the story he told was enough to change more minds than just his own. According to Jennings, he was looking for a movie to "fill in an empty evening" in the spring of 1952 when he stopped in to use the men's room in a public park. Inside, he may or may not have exchanged some words with a policeman. The officer may or may not have put his hand on Jennings's crotch. Regardless, although Jennings insisted that he was not interested, the officer followed him out, dragged out a "one sided conversation," and accompanied him over a mile to his home. The officer insisted on coming inside and, once there, strolled to the bedroom, unbuttoned his shirt, and sprawled on the mattress. He urged Jennings to "let down [his] hair" and reminisced about his days in the navy, where "all us guys played around." When Jennings refused to take the bait, frightened now that the man had come to rob him, the officer tried to push Jennings's hand on his own crotch. Only then, Jennings recalled, did the officer identify himself and make the arrest.[34]

For all its outrageous detail, it did not really matter whether Jennings's account was entirely true. As to some of his denials, even his closest friends in the Mattachine Society had their doubts. What mattered was that the tale, in all its disgraceful particulars, resonated with the countless stories of police persecution and harassment of gay men circulating in Los Angeles in the early 1950s. Still a fledging organization shy about negative publicity, the Mattachine Society mobilized around Jennings's arrest, spinning off the Citizens' Committee to Outlaw Entrapment (CCOE) as an ancillary group aimed at combating abusive police tactics. The CCOE turned Jennings's trial into a cause célèbre in Los Angeles's gay circles, spreading flyers and raising significant funding for his defense. Urged on by his friends at the Mattachine Society, Jennings took the unusual step of admitting his homosexuality, but he denied participating in the officer's extended flirtation. The case came down to Jennings's word against the officer's—and, to the surprise of many, Jennings won. The jury came back hung after eleven members voted for acquittal but the twelfth refused to budge, and the city agreed to dismiss the case.[35]

Jennings's victory was celebrated as a landmark by homophile activists: proof that a man could admit to being gay in open court and still win over a jury. Yet it was also a narrow victory. Because Jennings denied any sexual advances, portraying himself as the perfect martyr to the vice squad's operations, his trial did little to address the problem of defendants who succumbed, however gradually, to a policeman's enticements.

Crucially, however, the Jennings trial was hardly the end or even really the beginning of the courts' confrontations with police enticement in the mid-twentieth century. Many cases in these years grappled far more directly with the politics and ethics of the police's antihomosexual campaigns. It simply happened that most of them never reached a jury.

Prosecutors, Judges, and the Politics of Vice Enforcement

Intimately familiar with the vice squads' machinations on the streets, many gay men understandably saw police officers as the face of the criminal justice system as a whole. But the officers who arrested gay men were just one among several groups involved in the administration of the states' antihomosexual laws. And those other groups had their own opinions both about gay men and about the laws enforced against them.

First in line were the prosecutors who chose whether and how to charge men arrested for solicitation. Typically drawn to their line of work by their law-and-order values, many prosecutors zealously pursued homosexual convictions. That petty matters like solicitation often went to younger attorneys, eager to rack up a record of triumphs in court, exacerbated the trend. In Los Angeles, district attorneys maintained "bounce lists" of jurors who had served in unsuccessful prosecutions, striking them from future cases. Some chatted with potential jurors in the hallways, stressing the importance of "clean[ing] up" the city's sexual underworld. Such zeal matched the rigor of the LAPD's vice officers themselves, and indeed the same political pressures that drove a local vice squad's campaigns also guided the prosecution. In DC in the early 1950s, where the panic over homosexuals in federal employment lent the morals squad's pettiest arrests an air of political significance, District Attorney Leo Rover championed a strict program of homosexuality-related prosecutions. As an assistant prosecutor explained in court in 1952, that "the security agencies of the United States immediately fire these people as weak security risks" proved there was "good reason for the Government to prosecute these cases."[36]

But not all Rover's colleagues were as enthusiastic. As Gerald Levie, a Los Angeles–area defense attorney, reported, some prosecutors had genuine compassion for gay defendants. In their private conversations, if not in their public dealings, they did not see consensual sexual acts as a matter for the criminal law. Typically, such compassion did not prevent them from prosecuting gay men, but some did try to temper the legal consequences of a decoy arrest. In Michigan and Wisconsin in the 1950s, district attorneys commonly reduced homosexuality-related charges to lesser offenses like trespassing or disturbing the peace, even at the cost of irritating the arresting officers. As one police sergeant with the Wauwatosa Police Department complained in 1956, a local prosecutor had charged down a defendant—a third-time offender, no less—from sodomy to disorderly conduct without so much as consulting him.[37]

Prosecutors' willingness to reduce solicitation charges reflected the same calculation underlying their growing reliance on plea bargains more broadly: preserving the office's resources by offering attractive plea deals. But it also traced back to a more specific concern: as one contemporary identified it, avoiding "the unnecessary collateral harm" of a homosexuality-related conviction, a whiff of deviance some prosecutors believed would make even career criminals shudder. Such leniency did not necessarily spring from a spirit of liberality toward gay men. To the contrary, prosecutors sometimes invoked that same principle in reducing not only homosexuality-related charges but also a broad range of sex offenses, including adultery, molestation, and even forcible rape. And they did so, in some instances, with the full support of local policemen. Hardly a rejection of patriarchal sexual norms, law enforcement officials' clemency toward homosexual offenders in such cases served a broader principle against prying into the personal and sexual lives of local men—and they were invariably men—whose files passed over the prosecutors' desks.[38]

The right men could often count on particular sympathy. District attorneys deciding to reduce or even dismiss a charge took into account many factors, including the suspect's wealth, educational level, employment, home life, and prior criminal record, all coalescing into some inchoate measure of "respectability." In Detroit, one prosecutor let a businessman who solicited an undercover officer plead guilty to disorderly conduct, concerned that a sex-related conviction would "ruin" his life. The physician arrested at the bus station received no charge at all. (Sensitive to lingering concerns about homosexual men as sexual predators, the prosecutor conceded that the doctor's thriving medical practice arguably cut both ways, since it gave him daily access to unsuspecting men. But nonhomosexual physicians, he reasoned, "have access to women's bodies during the course of their work, and this does not mean that they are more likely to be rapists.")[39]

Prosecutors offered numerous justifications for such leniency, from the greater reputational harms suffered by high-class offenders to their lesser statistical likelihood of recidivism. Some even relied on fiscal conservatism. Since wealthier suspects could afford private psychiatric care, one Detroit prosecutor reasoned, dropping the charges would save taxpayers the cost of any state-financed treatment. Such calculations reflected the same class biases that infused much of the criminal justice system: the sense that only some types of offenders truly deserved punishment. Yet they also suggested a genuine sensitivity to the relative social costs of pursuing nonviolent offenders like gay men, especially when dependents like wives, children, and elderly parents were involved. As some prosecutors saw it, punishing a man's intermittent sexual deviations, relatively petty offenses as they came, hardly justified depriving innocent women and children of a steady source of support—or, perhaps more crudely, casting them on the care of the state.[40]

On the basis of these considerations alone, some prosecutors were happy to reduce or even dismiss solicitation charges, persuaded that the arrest was punishment enough. But even those who personally preferred a more punitive approach sometimes found their hands tied by an external source of pressure: the courts.

Most men who had the misfortune of running afoul of the vice squads' campaigns at midcentury held out little hope for mercy from the court. Living their lives under the shadow of police harassment and enticement—a system that operated, by all indications, under the benign indifference if not approval of local judges—they typically saw the courts as handmaidens of the vice squads' antihomosexual campaigns. And, indeed, many judges had little sympathy for homosexual offenders. Historically, that aversion had emerged in their reticence, echoing the legislatures' euphemistic references to "unnatural" and "infamous" perversions, to describe the precise facts that gave rise to a criminal complaint. By the mid-twentieth century, some courts had grown more willing to discuss the record, and they did not hesitate to decry the defendants' "degenerate" and frankly "bizarre"

sexual practices. That judges frequently served as prosecutors in their earlier careers may have influenced their views. Just a few years after zealously
pressing charges against gay men, Leo Rover was sitting as the chief judge
of the DC Municipal Court of Appeals.[41]

Many judges, however, were more ambivalent about the antihomosexual
laws they enforced. The precise nature of their objections varied, reflecting a range of political views, moral commitments, and institutional interests. Some bristled at petty charges like solicitation as a waste of police
resources. "It is ridiculous that the vice squad will assign 28 men to investigate a misdemeanor while we only have 22 men on the homicide squad,"
one trial judge in Detroit decried. Others, more protective of their personal
time than that of the police, resented the burden those charges placed on
their own dockets. Some judges supported criminalizing homosexual conduct in theory but balked at the steep penalties carried by state laws, from
high minimum sentences to collateral consequences like sex-offender registration. There was, after all, a world of difference between suspending a
liquor license and imposing a jail term or a registration requirement on an
individual defendant—a sentence that might upend an entire life. In New
York, as the journalist Jess Stearn reported in 1961, magistrate judges sensitive to the toll of a prosecution for a sex-related crime, a process some saw
as sufficient punishment itself, "lean backward to give the homosexual the
benefit of the doubt."[42]

Others harbored a deeper concern about the vice squads' campaigns:
Private morality notwithstanding, they simply could not bring themselves
to see consensual sexual intimacies as the proper subject of criminal sanction. For some judges, laws targeting consensual homosexual behavior fell
within a broader principle against what they saw as victimless crimes, from
fornication to petty gambling. But many also had more specific quibbles
with antihomosexual laws. Even as police officials invoked the specter of
the sexual psychopath to justify their efforts, certain segments of the American public, especially among the highly educated, experienced a slow liberalization of attitudes toward sexual difference in the 1950s. Crucial here
was the work of Alfred Kinsey, whose account of the sheer prevalence of
technically illegal sexual conduct among ordinary Americans forced legal
elites to reconsider the wisdom of contemporary criminal laws. In 1954, a
survey of legislators in New England reported that a third supported making their sex laws less punitive. Among the commissions assigned to ap-
praise sexual psychopath laws, too, Kinsey's findings, alongside progressive
psychiatrists' abiding view of homosexuality as a comparatively benign
condition, reduced the appetite for punishing homosexual offenders. In

large part for those reasons, in 1955 the American Law Institute, a window into reformist legal thinking in these years, recommended that consensual sodomy be decriminalized altogether.[43]

Although not all fell within the elite, many trial judges stood directly within this shifting legal culture. And they had the additional benefit of seeing the individual cases brought by the vice squad campaigns—seeing the men, many not unlike their own friends or neighbors, whose lives were shaken by homosexuality-related charges. By the early 1950s, those pressures led some to question the value of punishing private, if unorthodox, sexual activity. In DC, Judge Milton Kronheim, who gladly accepted the factual inference that a white man striking up a late-night conversation with a black man must be serving some illicit sexual impulse, nevertheless emerged as a fervent critic of the morals squad's operations. As Kronheim admitted at one public hearing in 1954, the squad's arrests may have "st[ood] up legally and factually," but "whether any overriding purpose is served by [them] I certainly doubt." A decade later, Stanley Mosk, a California supreme court justice and former attorney general, regretfully recalled his own experience overseeing a sodomy prosecution in the early 1950s. "[The defendants] were subjected to a felony charge for no evident societal purpose," he mused. "I have often wondered how they survived the humiliating exposure of a felony trial and conviction for their private behavior."[44]

Even the most sympathetic judges rarely accepted homosexuality as a functional lifestyle. Suggesting the persisting influence of professional psychiatry, many came at their ambivalence instead from a more practical angle: their belief that homosexuality was not only benign or even common but, more importantly, a medical matter, better entrusted to doctors than policemen or wardens. In Milwaukee in February 1956, a judge presiding over a solicitation charge marveled at the problem of the homosexual in a mix of sexological and psychiatric rhetoric. "Third sex, is it a crime or a sickness?" he pondered aloud. When the *Metropolitan Citizen-News*, a conservative paper in Los Angeles, published an exposé on antihomosexual policing in 1963, two out of four judges interviewed agreed that homosexuals were best seen as medical charges, and the other two claimed joint jurisdiction. Far from quibbling with the social rejection of homosexuality, many judicial shows of leniency reflected a type of pity, encouraged by the medical profession, for gay defendants as a psychiatric rather than a penological concern.[45]

In that regard, judges in the 1950s had one important institutional ally: the state-operated psychiatric clinics funded as part of the sexual psychopath laws proliferating at the time. Those laws, too, after all, had presumed that sex offenders—whether rapists, child molesters, or even arsonists serving some dark sexual pleasure—were neither scofflaws nor hardened criminals but diseased souls, requiring treatment. And they provided a specific infrastructure for such treatment: an array of court-affiliated hospitals whose staff could detain, observe, and (crucially) indefinitely commit any suspect who posed a risk of repeating his crime. As these laws demonstrated, the language of mental illness in the 1950s was a seemingly progressive rhetoric that commonly justified a deeply brutal criminological regime, dramatically expanding the carceral arm of the state. And gay men were among its core victims. Especially in the 1930s and the early 1940s, in the first states to pass sexual psychopath laws, stories emerged of men charged with consensual homosexual acts and committed, sometimes at length, to psychiatric hospitals.[46]

But in practice, the legacy of the sexual psychopath laws was more complicated. Psychiatrists themselves had long questioned the value of such legislation, particularly when it came to consensual homosexual conduct. Many judges and even many prosecutors, it turned out, shared their concerns. Aimed principally at incapacitating violent sex offenders, the statutes' reach was often limited to a narrow set of predatory crimes, if not by their express language then by the prosecutorial discretion they invited. By the mid-1950s, for instance, cases processed under the sexual psychopath laws in Kansas, Wisconsin, and even Michigan—a state distinguished in the early 1950s by its insistence on retaining consensual sodomy within its psychopathy statute—consisted almost entirely of child molestation and rape, with no mention of adult homosexual conduct despite a constant flow of solicitation and sodomy cases through local courts. As a psychologist at Detroit's Psychopathic Clinic explained, district attorneys recognized the draconian consequences of such prosecutions, and they were "very cautious" in invoking them. The prevailing sense, echoed a probation officer, was that the sexual psychopath law was "too rough." Entrusted with a dramatic weapon against sexual deviance, prosecutors and courts did not level it against all possible defendants, but drew what they saw as sensible distinctions among more or less dangerous offenses.[47]

In context, the sexual psychopath laws of the 1950s did not necessarily make homosexual offenders more vulnerable before the law. What they did, rather, was cement the primacy of often-progressive psychiatrists in the criminal justice system, funding a spate of clinics whose employees had a direct line to the court. Most judges took advantage of such professional advice, and they put great weight on the clinics' suggestions. In Kansas, courts frequently followed psychiatrists' recommendations to release sex offenders who they recognized "[are] and will remain deviated" in their sexual practice. In Ventura County, California, the district attorney recounted, courts commonly released homosexual offenders in deference to the state hospitals' "express opinion" that they were "not a menace to the health and safety of others," even though "everyone concerned [was] fully aware" that they would continue their homosexual activities. Far from drawing homosexual offenders into the anathematized category of the psychopath, the infrastructure erected by the sexual psychopath laws often created an institutional advocate for leniency, ushering in both a pattern of reliance on medical expertise and a process for invoking such expertise that urged judges to treat gay men less punitively. An undeniably sinister influence on public debates about same-sex practices, the rise of the psychopath laws, like the medicalization of homosexuality more broadly, often had a surprisingly liberal effect in the particular economy of the courts.[48]

In theory, of course, judges' personal views of homosexuality-related offenses, medicalized or otherwise, were unrelated to their work at trial. Regardless of their personal sympathies, most judges saw their jobs as enforcing the legislature's pronouncements, which still covered a broad swath of gay men's sexual and social practices. But in practice, judges exercised significant discretion in the courtroom. And those who questioned the value of criminalizing homosexuality or balked at the punitive nature of the operative statutes found a number of ways to vindicate their concerns.

Most basically, judges exercised enormous discretion in sentencing defendants, and they often used that discretion to minimize the consequences of a conviction. In New York, where the disorderly conduct statutes exposed defendants to six months' imprisonment and a $50.00 fine, suspects commonly received a $10.00–$25.00 fine. In DC, courts authorized to impose ninety days' jail time and a $100 fine typically allowed defendants to pick among the two, and sometimes tendered significantly lower sentences. One man convicted of indecently assaulting an officer received no sentence at all in exchange for a verbal promise not to repeat the offense. In Los Angeles, where the lewd vagrancy statute authorized up to six months in jail and a $500 fine, defendants were typically fined less than $100 and almost never served jail time, even for repeat offenses. One man, charged seven times for soliciting a police officer—including three instances in a single year and almost always at the same bus terminal—did not serve time on a single arrest.[49]

In many cases, judges' aversion to harsh sentences, and especially jail time, directly reflected their faith in psychiatric care as a superior response to homosexuality-related offenses. In Los Angeles in 1952, a judge waived

jail time for a young man arrested under circumstances strikingly reminis-
cent of Jennings's ordeal after the man promised to retain a psychiatrist.
In Atlanta in 1957, a municipal court judge handed a pastor arrested by
the vice squad a sixty-day suspended sentence, conditioned on his seeking
private treatment. In Detroit, judges who sentenced homosexual offenders
to probation almost invariably imposed a requirement of psychiatric care.
After one suspect, the vice president of a major bank and an avowed family
man, informed the court that he was already receiving private counseling,
the judge dismissed his charges altogether.[50]

As the backgrounds of these men suggest, the courts' deference to psychiatric authority may sometimes have been pretextual, an excuse to show
mercy to otherwise "respectable" defendants—not least considering the
classes of men who could typically afford private care to begin with. Well
beyond the courts, indeed, the rhetoric of mental illness in the postwar
years could be a highly hierarchical instrument, rationalizing wealthy
white men's and women's forays into unorthodox sexuality while continuing to attribute such conduct among black and poor white communities
to more deeply rooted cultural pathologies. But many judges also seemed
genuinely committed to the value of psychiatric treatment, willing to reduce a harsher criminal sentence even for conventionally sympathetic suspects only once the possibility of care was brought to their attention. In
1956, for instance, a Milwaukee judge ready to sentence a nineteen-year-
old defendant to a $100 fine or thirty days' probation changed his mind
after he learned the teenager was receiving private psychiatric treatment,
imposing no additional punishment. And some judges were sensitive to
the plight of poorer and less privileged defendants, waiving fines when the
money could, they believed, be better used to pay medical bills. More than
just facile rhetoric, judges' faith in psychiatry as the proper redress for illicit
sexual conduct genuinely tempered their sentencing practices with a range
of criminal defendants.[51]

Some misdemeanor charges carried unavoidably steep penalties, leaving
the courts minimal discretion in sentencing. Judges who balked at those
punishments nevertheless found ways to avoid imposing them, reducing a
defendant's charges with or without the prosecution's blessing, or acquitting him altogether. Prosecutors grew attuned to these judicial moods. As
early as the 1930s, the Wayne County, Michigan, prosecutor's office instituted an intraoffice review system to screen out excessive criminal charges
brought by young prosecutors. Reserved primarily for felony prosecutions,
the system also covered a number of misdemeanors, including interracial

disputes and solicitation arrests. These latter charges entered the system, as one of its architects explained, after some judges "rebelled" at the number of solicitation cases flooding their dockets, exasperated by the parades of prostitutes and tales of vice officers "pranc[ing] around the restroom." By the mid-1950s, senior prosecutors screened out nearly half the solicitation charges that came through the office—not because of any weakness in the evidence, but because judges did "not want to be bothered with" these types of cases.[52]

In California, a similar dynamic took hold. Judges sympathetic to nonviolent homosexual offenders commonly insisted on having lewd vagrancy charges, which carried a registration requirement, reduced to disturbing the peace or trespassing. In Los Angeles, in particular, courts revolted against the use of the lewd vagrancy law when charging first-time offenders. By the early 1960s, enough courts had taken to dismissing such charges that the city attorney, Roger Arnebergh, threw up his hands, adopting a uniform policy against prosecuting first-time defendants under the provision. Arnebergh was hardly enthusiastic about the change, but, he explained, the courts left him no choice. "We found the judges just would not convict," he told reporters, "so we had to establish this policy to get a conviction at all."[53]

Undoing considerable labor by the vice officers and district attorneys who brought these cases to court, judicial leniency sometimes outraged prosecutors, policemen, and even the public. In Detroit, a trial judge who commonly dismissed solicitation charges against gay men and prostitutes so infuriated the vice squad that its members took to the press, denouncing him in a series of articles in a local paper. In Los Angeles, well after the city attorney resigned himself to reducing lewd vagrancy charges for first-time offenders, law enforcement agencies balked at the constraint. Arnebergh and the head of the LAPD's Hollywood patrol continued to speak out against the reduction policy, insisting that higher penalties for homosexuality-related offenses would help deter more criminal conduct. Adamant that all sex offenders be placed on a sex-offender registry, some local police agencies adopted a formal policy requiring vice officers to arrest gay men on registrable charges whenever possible. And on discovering the pattern of judicial leniency, the *Metropolitan Citizen-News* had a field day, lambasting judges for "coddl[ing]" "sexual deviates" and launching a rash of emergency public responses by police officials, prosecutors, and judicial officers. Facing the critical coverage, at least two judges suggested they would reconsider their sentencing practices; the problem, one professed, was "much more serious than I realized." But aside from that ritual of public self-flagellation, it is unclear whether they ever followed through.[54]

It is important not to overstate the impact of these practices. Beyond Los Angeles and Michigan, where the habit was systematically documented, it remains unclear how widely charge reduction pervaded the courts. Judges like Stanley Mosk in California and Milton Kronheim in DC were, though not unique in their moral qualms, certainly on the liberal end, and even they convicted most defendants brought before them. Even when judges handed out modest sentences or found ways to avoid the registration requirement, the mere fact of a morals-related arrest and conviction blighted a man's record, and the process of fighting the charges cost precious time, money, and mental security. For professionals like doctors, lawyers, and teachers, as well as government employees and service providers requiring state licenses, an arrest sometimes triggered an automatic review that could lead to the revocation of professional credentials. And where, as in Los Angeles and Detroit, judges waived jail time, they often still subjected gay men to burdensome probation conditions—more burdensome, in many cases, than those imposed on heterosexual defendants convicted of similar crimes. The courts' practices did not—indeed, could not—alleviate all these human harms.[55]

But judges' frequent pushback against prosecuting homosexual offenders to the utmost was nevertheless notable—if only to the extent that it pitted them against the other actors in the criminal justice system. From modest sentences to outright acquittals, judges' attempts to mitigate the costs of the vice squads' arrests were systematic enough for prosecutors to take notice and sometimes preemptively change their charging practices. Some of those efforts, such as dismissals and compelled reductions to nonregisterable offenses, genuinely spared defendants the serious collateral harms of a sex-related conviction. Far from dutiful soldiers in the states' antihomosexual campaigns, trial judges in the postwar years entertained often-pervasive doubts about the value of such regulation, and they imposed what some officers and prosecutors experienced, not inaccurately, as meaningful constraints on their efforts to police gay life.

The Problem of Police Entrapment

Ultimately, however, judicial qualms about the wisdom of solicitation laws may have been the least of the vice squads' concerns. Beyond the statutes being enforced against gay men or the mandatory sentences those laws carried, many judges found themselves questioning how precisely the police

enforced them. The extended flirtations at local bars, the suggestive pos-
turing at public urinals—all these techniques rubbed some judges the
wrong way.

Some were open about their reservations. In New York, Magistrate Judge
John M. Murtagh publicly denounced the New York Police Department's
enticement arrests, echoing the same concerns that so commonly hung
over undercover work. Decoy enforcement, he insisted to the reporter Albert Deutsch, pushed officers into "the use of low trickery and deceit," "inevitably corrupt[ing] the men engaged in it." In DC and Detroit, too, a
number of municipal judges aired their views on the vice squads' tactics in
open court. "Ordinarily, this court does not concern itself with matters outside its jurisdiction," Milton Kronheim proclaimed at a 1954 proceeding
involving one of Louis Fochett's flirtations in Lafayette Park. "But I think
the public is in considerable doubt, and I know the court is, as to whether
this is good police work." On Detroit's Recorder's Court in 1957, Judge
Miller chided an officer who had spent half an hour flirting with a suspect.
Such conduct, he announced, did "not seem entirely proper, at least, from
a moral standpoint." Others refrained from such public proclamations but
privately excoriated the vice squad's undercover practices. Asked his views
of the decoys' tactics, one of Miller's colleagues grew red in the face. The
vice squad's campaigns, Judge Stewart denounced, were "atrocious," "horrible," "miserable," and "appalling."[56]

The courts' sensitivity to the morality of the vice squads' conduct, alongside that of the defendant's own, was part of a broader shift in the relationship between the judiciary and the police in these years. Up through
the early twentieth century, judges engaged in little oversight of police
procedures, confronting official misconduct only in civil or criminal actions against individual officers. But beginning in the 1930s, a combination of factors focused their scrutiny on the daily work of law enforcement.
One was the recent experience of Prohibition, a legal experiment that confronted both the public and the courts with seemingly limitless accounts
of corruption, incompetence, and brutality among police officers. Mostly
responsible, however, was an onslaught of developments that challenged
the criminal justice system's treatment of vulnerable suspects, most notably black men but also political dissidents, labor activists, and vagrants.
Emboldened by cases like its high-profile challenge to the racist prosecution of the "Scottsboro Boys," organizations like the National Association
for the Advancement of Colored People protested the discriminatory and
pretextual arrests of black suspects. Scholars and progressive attorneys increasingly challenged broadly phrased loitering laws as the hallmarks of a

police state. Especially as domestic political discourse during the Cold War era charted increasingly existential boundaries between the American state and more totalitarian regimes, a range of policing tactics, from wiretaps to discretionary stops, struck some critics as innately undemocratic. In that context, many judges began to think that the role of courts at trial was not simply judging the evidence. It was also judging the police.[57]

For some, the vice squads' tactics fell directly in the shadow of these concerns. Alongside Judge Kronheim, the DC Municipal Court's most notable critic of the morals squad in the 1950s was Judge Andrew J. Howard Jr., a Howard Law School graduate and one of the few black judges on the court, who earned a reputation for his sympathy for criminal defendants. In 1953, Howard made headlines for "rebuk[ing]" two decoys in his courtroom. "These [m]orals division officers are interested in doing their jobs," he protested, "but I think they're too zealous." In Detroit, judges' impatience with the enticement of homosexuality-related offenses often paralleled their scrutiny of police overreach in other areas of enforcement, most notably against suspected prostitutes—just one component of a broader discomfort with proactive police tactics against relatively petty crimes. Indeed, criticizing antihomosexual enticement as part of a bigger pattern of police misconduct was an attractively modest position, focusing on the evil of state abuses more than on controversial questions of social policy. That modesty made it popular with legal groups that hesitated to defend homosexual practices outright, including the American Civil Liberties Union (ACLU) in the 1950s. Although some members urged a stronger stance, the organization's 1957 policy statement on homosexuality disavowed any interest in challenging state laws against same-sex practices, including sodomy and solicitation offenses. But the ACLU still insisted that police abuses of suspects, including entrapment, were of course "matters of proper concern for the Union."[58]

In some cases, however, judges' objections to enticement bespoke a concern more specific to the vice squads' antihomosexual campaigns: the suspicion, once more, that homosexuality was a medical condition, to be suppressed if not cured through treatment. Set against that presumption, after all, decoys' flirtations in the field were not just manipulative and cruel. They also bred deviance, corrupting men who might otherwise have gone a lifetime resisting their latent sexual urges. These "poor souls that should be pitied and medically treated," as Judge Stewart lamented in 1957, were instead "deliberately, surreptitiously and unethically enticed into committing acts that they may have not committed for years and years and which they may never commit again." That concern was hardly the judge's own conjecture. It reflected the direct input of state psychiatrists—not least the executive director of Detroit's Psychopathic Clinic, who deplored the vice squads' enticement methods and made his criticism known to the courts. Concerned that weak-willed men "succumbed" to vice officers' temptations in public bathrooms, the director made a point of personally visiting each judge on the Recorder's Court and asking him to dismiss homosexual cases "where there was even the slightest doubt as to . . . entrapment." Interviewed in April 1957 about the court's common skepticism of police decoys, he proudly "attributed the present attitude . . . to his influence."[59]

The fear of the decoy as an agent of sexual contagion revealed the genuine distinction drawn by both medical and lay authorities in these years between homosexual *acts* and homosexual *status*: the idea that same-sex conduct was not the province of a discrete personality type, but rather presented a constant risk for even seemingly ordinary men, tempted in a moment of weakness to experiment with deviance. Drawing on that presumption, skillful defense attorneys commonly emphasized their clients' loving wives and well-adjusted family lives, attributing their arrests to an acute bout of personal or professional anxiety—a defense invoked most famously by the White House aide Walter Jenkins, who, on his second arrest in 1964, explained it away as the result of "nervous exhaustion." This was the reason that some judges and jurors dealt so much more leniently with first- or second-time offenders, who plausibly presented themselves as "normal" but for one disastrous decision, than with men who, on the basis of their own admission or their criminal record, seemed committed to a lifetime of same-sex encounters. As Gerald Levie recalled of his work defending gay clients, the worst thing that could happen at trial was for the court to conclude that his client had not only committed a lewd act but was also "in fact a homosexual." Here, indeed, was another way that certain categories of defendant were invariably privileged in the legal system. At a time when government programs like the GI Bill encouraged white men to marry and settle into suburban life at greater rates than their nonwhite counterparts, white suspects coming into court were simply far likelier to have the outward trappings of heterosexual respectability, whatever the truth of the underlying charges.[60]

Gay men themselves, of course, rarely shared the courts' concern about decoys pulling blameless men onto the path of deviance. But they shared the judges' objections to vice officers' manipulations in the field. And they had a common word for those manipulations: *entrapment*. Following Dale Jennings's arrest and trial in 1952, the problem of plainclothes policing became a key concern among homophile activists. The magazine *ONE*, started by a group of Mattachine Society members in the wake of Jennings's trial, began its run with a multipart exposé on police enticement tactics—what one contributor openly denounced as the state's "unscrupulous methods of deliberate entrapment."[61]

In court, that challenge was more difficult to raise. Dismissed by early American courts as a sophistry denounced by God himself in the parable of Eve, the doctrine of entrapment gradually gained ground with state judges over the last quarter of the nineteenth century. By the mid-twentieth century, it had won acceptance throughout the federal system and in forty-eight states, rejected only in Tennessee and possibly New York. But even in jurisdictions that honored the doctrine, the bar for proving entrapment was high. Under the test developed by the Supreme Court in 1932, entrapment required not only evidence of egregious police misconduct but also proof that the defendant had no preexisting predisposition to commit the crime. "The controlling question," the Court explained, is whether the government had charged an "otherwise innocent" person for a crime produced by "the creative activity of its own officials."[62]

Homosexual solicitations presented a particularly difficult case. Even assuming that decoys sometimes goaded vulnerable men to yield to their repressed impulses, arguing that a suspect who solicited an officer in a known cruising site had no prior homosexual tendencies was an uphill battle. As ONE explained to its readers in April 1954, a case of entrapment could be made "if the officer 'picks up' the defendant, gains his acquaintance, proposes the act, and proceeds to overcome the defendant's genuine reluctance and unwillingness," but "IF AND ONLY IF the defendant was in fact unwilling, and the officer's appeals were such as to leave no doubt that he was the procuring party." Measured against that bar, evidence that an officer struck up a conversation in a bathroom or even swished around a park was certainly inadequate. After Dante Longo arrested Paul Ross in 1954, for instance, the court rejected Ross's claims that Longo's "flirtatious" charade had entrapped him into a solicitation. Longo's affectations were "so patently in accord with the procedures of detection authorized" by the Supreme Court, Judge Edward Beard of the municipal court concluded, "that one could almost assume that he held the legal opinion in one hand while he made effeminate gestures with the other."[63]

Even if they could not technically claim that officers "entrapped" gay suspects, however, judges whose dockets swelled with solicitation arrests sometimes grew exasperated with manipulative vice squad tactics. And they found other ways to vindicate their concerns. Most basically, judges who balked at the police's arrests dismissed cases on the insufficiency of the evidence. Particularly in bench trials, the courts were vested with broad discretionary power over judgments of innocence and guilt, and they used that leeway to quash what they saw as questionable charges. In New York, judges who recoiled against a vice officer's manipulations simply rejected the prosecution's evidence. "[While] entrapment at present does not constitute a legal defense," the veteran defense attorney Irwin D. Strauss would assure a new colleague in 1965, "most of our judges upon a recital of facts showing entrapment dismiss the case . . . on the ground of having a reasonable doubt of the defendant's guilt."[64]

In Detroit, too, judges frustrated with the vice squad's enticement tactics, against both prostitutes and gay men, commonly dismissed the ensuing charges or acquitted defendants at trial. Speaking confidentially to researchers in 1956 and 1957, a number openly defended their practices. As Judge Miller confided, he was "constantly on the lookout for defendants being railroaded" by vice officers "over-anxious to secure a conviction." His colleague Judge Doyle shared those concerns. He certainly realized that some men frequented public restrooms or bars to serve their illicit desires, Doyle admitted, but he also knew that vice officers go "in there and hang around and more or less encourage these fellows in order to make a case." Given that fact, he was "reluctant to find the defendant guilty," especially if the offender was a visitor who would soon be on his way back home.[65]

Judge Stewart earned a particular reputation as an enemy of the vice squad, equally recognized by policemen, prosecutors, and defense attorneys who strategized to get their cases on his docket. Presented with a decoy arrest, Stewart would pose three questions to the officer: Did he enter the restroom "due to nature's call" or to make an arrest? Did he make the arrest in the restroom or after he and the defendant left? How much time had elapsed between the initial contact and the arrest? If the officer claimed to have wanted to use the restroom, the judge "knew [the] witness was not telling the truth," and he tended toward dismissal. "If an officer spends over three or four minutes," he reported, "then there is definitely enticement and I will dismiss the case." He did not claim that these tactics rose to the level of *entrapment*—a legal term that, said aloud in court, risked inviting a prosecutorial appeal. But, like his colleagues, he felt that the vice squad's arrests stretched the boundaries of moral police work, and he tried to use his authority to limit their consequences, inside and outside the courtroom. Some years back, Stewart recounted in a 1957 interview, he not only acquitted a schoolteacher "entice[d]" by an officer but even called the defendant's principal, "a good friend," to ensure that the man kept his job.

Now ten years later, he delighted, the teacher counted the judge's own son and numerous children of vice squad officers among his former students.[66]

While some judges weighed the sufficiency of the evidence, others took a more legalistic approach, asking whether the conduct recounted by police decoys fell within the purview of the relevant statutes. In Michigan, the operative law prohibited defendants from *accosting, soliciting,* or *inviting* anyone to commit an immoral act. Several trial judges read that language to bar only "aggressive" solicitations: those in which a defendant boldly tendered a proposal without any apparent encouragement from the officer. In April 1957, Judge Doyle dismissed charges against a man arrested by a decoy who spent over two hours drinking with him at a bar, eventually feigning a stomachache and accompanying the man to his apartment. Privately, Doyle admitted that he had "no stomach" for such cases, in which the officers "practically maneuver" the defendants into a solicitation. But, more publicly, he explained that the defendant's gradual proposal was simply "not the type of accosting and soliciting that the law intended" to cover.[67]

In Wisconsin and Washington, DC, both of which enacted broader prohibitions against *advising* or *inviting* a homosexual act, judges found themselves hard-pressed to read the statutes as requiring a particular level of aggression. Even here, however, judges sometimes rejected the charges when, as one researcher in Wisconsin summarized, an officer was "so active that he, rather than the suspect, d[id] the soliciting." In May 1954, Judge Kronheim acquitted Walter Cox of all charges arising from an encounter with Officer Dante Longo in the men's room of a YMCA. Longo testified that Cox had engaged him in some pleasantries, walked with him to G Street, and then asked if he could "come up" to Longo's room. Cox testified that Longo's behavior was so brazen that he had begun the conversation by asking Longo if the officer was soliciting *him*. "That is a different thing from a solicitation," Kronheim concluded, "and I have no choice but to dismiss."[68]

Judges in New York found themselves grappling with a thornier provision: the confounding Section 722(8), which grafted lewd solicitations onto the preexisting disorderly conduct statute. Read at face value, the law required prosecutors to prove not merely that a defendant loitered for the purpose of soliciting a sexual act but also that he did so with the intent to breach the peace. Some courts saw the latter requirement as a formality, reasoning that anyone bold enough to propose a criminal sex act to a stranger had accepted the risk of disturbing the public. But others questioned that inference. In the spring of 1958, Benito Feliciano approached a vice officer outside a Turkish bath on St. Marks, spent one or two minutes speaking with him, and then tendered a proposal so graphic that the court declined to reprint it. Magistrate Judge Charles Solomon dismissed the complaint. "Ordinary common sense," he reasoned, suggested that disturbing the peace was "just about the farthest thought from [the defendant's] mind."[69]

Some judges focused instead on Section 722(8)'s requirement of a "public" solicitation. Numerous arrests in the 1950s involved an extended flirtation, starting on the street and moving to a defendant's home or hotel room before culminating in a proposition. In 1955, for instance, forty-seven-year-old Clark Kuebler met twenty-eight-year-old Officer Eugene Kelly on a corner in Midtown Manhattan. Kelly claimed that Kuebler introduced himself, proposed a drink at his hotel, and asked Kelly to stay the night. Kuebler insisted that Kelly asked for directions, invited himself in for a nightcap, and finally forced his way into Kuebler's hotel room, threatening to blackmail him as "a God-damn homosexual." But the court declined to resolve their conflicting testimony, disposing of the case on a much simpler point. Even granting Kelly's version of events, Magistrate Judge Hyman Bushel concluded, the only alleged solicitation was tendered inside Kuebler's hotel room, and "under the law the solicitation must occur in a public place."[70]

The precise motives of these judges varied. Many genuinely felt their hands to be tied by the statute, forced to dismiss homosexuality-related charges even as they proclaimed their own "abhorrence" of the defendant's "repulsive" conduct. A particularly strident critic of the law, Magistrate Judge Solomon went so far as to send the legislature a draft amendment, streamlining the language to outlaw all lewd solicitations and, he insisted, making his own job immeasurably more satisfying.[71]

But some judges used such statutory quibbles to vindicate deeper concerns about the circumstances of a defendant's arrest. In Kuebler's case, the magistrate's treatment of an additional charge suggested that he credited Kuebler's testimony over Kelly's; emphasizing the publicity requirement saved him from having to impugn the officer's word directly. Meanwhile, the court reviewing Frank Humphrey's arrest in the Village of Endicott in 1951, where Officer Shepard waited for Humphrey outside his home and all but invited himself upstairs, made little effort to disguise the fact that section 722(8)'s convolutions allowed it to redress criticisms aimed more fundamentally at Shepard's offensive tactics. Formally, the appellate panel reversed Humphrey's conviction on the basis of the same statutory argument used by Magistrate Bushel: the only "public" proposition in the case, consisting of Humphrey's offer of "beer, candy, and some fun," did not amount to a solicitation. But its opinion ventured well beyond the statutory language. Far from importuning a stranger, as Judge Brink saw it, Humphrey himself was "accosted" by a policeman as he returned to his own apartment. If Shepard had not flagged him down, "Humphrey would have gone home, minding his own business." Perhaps, the judge speculated, "the Police felt the end justified the means[, so] they resorted to entrapment." Lacking a formal entrapment defense in New York, Brink could not resolve the case directly on that ground. But he emphasized that Shepard's outrageous conduct was "an additional reason" for construing section 722(8) as strictly as he did.[72]

DC and the Battle for Judicial Review

Perhaps the most tenacious battles between the vice squads and the courts, however, occurred in Washington, DC. Here, too, judges like Milton Kronheim sometimes resisted solicitation charges obliquely, quietly dismissing cases brought by overly aggressive officers. But beginning in the winter of 1952, a watershed decision handed down by the US Court of Appeals jump-started a far more public dispute about the propriety of the morals squad's antihomosexual campaigns.[73]

That decision traced back to September 18, 1948 in Franklin Park, where a twenty-three-year-old vice officer named Frank Manthos sat on a bench, within eyesight but not earshot of his partner. At around 1:00 A.M., forty-one-year-old Edward Kelly, an analyst with the Public Health Service, entered the park. Searching for some overt signs of deviance, Manthos immediately noticed Kelly's "peculiar walk." Subsequently, the officer testified, Kelly sat beside him, and a casual conversation ensued. Manthos introduced himself as "Gaynor," said he was a salesman from Atlanta, and asked what men do "around here for excitement." Kelly told him that the bars were closed this time of night, spoke wistfully of the "gay parties" in Hollywood, and (according to Manthos) lauded California's tolerance of men who want "to get together and have a good time." Eventually, the two agreed to return to Kelly's apartment for a drink and (according to Manthos) "a lot of fun." When they got to Kelly's car, Manthos placed Kelly under arrest.[74]

At trial, the defendant's account was somewhat different. Kelly recounted that he was passing through the park after a late meal, having spent most of the evening with a female friend. He insisted that he sat on a park bench first and that Manthos approached him, taking a seat conspicuously nearby and eventually inviting him to join. He recalled sharing no opinions about California's nightlife and swore that Manthos invited himself over for a drink. The only reason he accepted the young man's request, Kelly explained, was because he was "feeling congenial" after a pleasant, and mildly alcoholic, evening.[75]

The innocence of Kelly's account invites some skepticism. As the historian David Johnson has observed, forty-one-year-old heterosexual men rarely invited attractive twenty-three-year-olds from the city's best-known cruising grounds to their apartments at one thirty in the morning. Unsurprisingly, then, even as Kelly denied any sexual overtones to their conversation, his attorney pursued an additional strategy, effectively accusing Manthos of entrapment. Why would Manthos have pressed Kelly about Hollywood's "gay parties" and where he could find a drink, the attorney implied, if he did not have some ulterior motive in setting up Kelly for arrest? On the stand, Manthos denied knowing that the word *gay* had any suspicious connotations. A gay party, he explained, was simply a "wild party" or an "anything goes" party, filled with "drinking, smoking . . . or gambling." In fact, it came out over the course of the litigation that Manthos had substantial experience with gay parties and defendants alike. Known among the press as the "one-man vice squad," he had been responsible for 150 convictions in just eight months on the force. The same evening that he arrested Kelly, he had arrested six other men for solicitation. Manthos, the attorney suggested, was the DC police force's equivalent of a bounty hunter.[76]

Led by the prominent federal judge E. Barrett Prettyman, the majority in *Kelly v. United States* did not quite accuse Manthos of entrapment. But, considering all the evidence, including Manthos's prolific history of charges, the fact that he was in the park only "for the purpose of making arrests," and the multiple character witnesses who testified on Kelly's behalf, the court chose to credit Kelly's version of events. Nor was it content simply to reverse the conviction in this one case. Stressing the "destructive" nature of a homosexual-related charge, which opened a defendant to blackmail and abuse, Prettyman proposed a set of evidentiary safeguards to be used in all lewd solicitation cases, including a requirement of some corroboration for a decoy's testimony and special deference to any character witnesses called by the defense.[77]

As soon as the *Kelly* decision came out, the morals squad's Roy Blick took to the press, complaining that the new evidentiary rules would "make it more difficult for us to make our cases." Indeed, the *Kelly* rules ushered in an immediate drop in conviction rates for homosexuality-related offenses. Even after the numbers crept back up, judges continued to hold *Kelly* as a shadow over the morals squad, regularly dismissing cases that depended on a single officer's testimony or featured character witnesses for the defense. Frustrated, Leo Rover intervened personally on his office's behalf. At a closed-door meeting with local judges on March 23, 1954, he denounced the shoddy conviction rates, castigating trial judges for applying an unreasonably high standard to prosecutions for morals charges. Never one to shy away from controversy, Judge Kronheim denounced Rover's attempts to influence the judiciary. "How would you like to be charged with such an offense," he demanded of reporters, "and come before a judge who'd been told the conviction rate was too low?"[78]

Failing to obtain the results he wanted under the solicitation statute, Rover turned his attention elsewhere. If a suspect simply touched a vice officer in the course of making an advance, prosecutors realized, they could avoid the judicial pitfalls of *Kelly* by charging him with simple assault. The district attorney's new strategy reinvigorated the city's antihomosexual campaigns. Yet as prosecutors soon discovered, the assault statute did not free them from judicial oversight. To begin with, many trial judges continued to apply the *Kelly* rules when presiding over assault prosecutions. Judge Howard, for one, dismissed so many assault cases on evidentiary grounds that, when the district attorney's office found itself prosecuting an especially high-profile case in his courtroom, it took the unusual step of demanding a jury trial over the defendant's protests. After Howard refused to grant one, Rover managed to get the case transferred—to, of all people, Judge Kronheim, who excoriated the prosecution's lack of corroborating testimony and directed the jury to acquit.[79]

Ultimately, however, *Kelly* may have been the least of Rover's problems. For, while liberal judges strained to dismiss solicitation charges on the grounds of enticement, the law of assault had always come with a roughly equivalent defense: consent. At the appellate level, the first case to raise a consent-based defense originated after Officer Klopfer, on a routine patrol of a movie theater, tried to entice a man into a sexual advance over the course of over forty minutes and in no fewer than two separate bathrooms. As the court summarized, Klopfer had all but arranged the defendant's fateful caress in that case, striking up a friendly conversation in the men's room of the theater, waiting for the suspect outside, strolling with him for seven city blocks, and finally entering a nearby hotel, where, in the court's own words, he "led the way . . . to the men's room and exposed himself in front of a urinal." Uninvited and unanticipated, a homosexual advance might constitute an offensive touching. But where an officer "by his own insidious conduct, by patient and clever encouragement," led a defendant to believe that he welcomed a sexual advance—this, the panel insisted, hardly qualified. "Courts are not so uninformed as not to be aware that there are such things as flirtations between man and man," Judge Cayton wrote for the municipal court of appeals. "And when flirtation is encouraged and mutual, and leads to a not unexpected intimacy . . . such cannot be classified as an assault."[80]

The consent defense reined in the morals squad's more aggressive tactics, though it took some time for judges to agree on what qualified as sufficiently aggressive. When Louis Fochett tried his typical technique with twenty-two-year-old Ernesto Guarro in Keith's Theater in 1955, the same panel that had just thrown out Klopfer's arrest affirmed the conviction. Certainly, Fochett's actions were not as egregious as Klopfer's. Fochett waited for Guarro to make the first approach; he unbuttoned his coat jacket rather than unzipping his pants; the entire encounter lasted only a period of minutes. Yet on review, the US Court of Appeals reversed. "Considering the totality of the policeman's conduct, including his inviting inquiry to the defendant," it concluded, Guarro's mutual flirtation did not count as an assault. Whether he spoke to a suspect for forty minutes or for four, the court suggested, a vice officer's job was to reduce the pandemic of sexual perversion in the district. It was not, through enticing gestures and vulgarities, to extend his own invitation.[81]

Rulings like *Kelly* and *Guarro* set some very real limits on the morals squad's campaigns in DC. But they were also just the most formal traces of a more extended negotiation between the courts, the district attorney's office, and the morals squad about the limits of vice enforcement in the nation's capital—both the proper boundaries of police officers' enticement tactics and the courts' role in monitoring those tactics at trial. As judges skeptical of the morals squad's methods applied new pressure on the district's homosexuality-related prosecutions, the district attorney and Roy Blick first tried to shame the courts into loosening their grip and, failing that, adjusted their arrest strategies to sidestep them. And the courts adjusted in turn, drawing on a range of jurisprudential tools to maintain their oversight over the police's campaigns. Caught within these battles, the morals squad's decoy arrests emerged as the crucible of a far deeper debate about private morality and government power in the 1950s—a contest over not simply the proper uses of public space by gay men but also the value of antihomosexual penal laws, the limits of ethical police work, and the proper place of the courts in determining both.

This is not to say, of course, that judges were always willing to police the vice squads' conduct, in Washington or elsewhere. In DC, *Kelly*'s exhortations notwithstanding, many judges continued to defer to police witnesses at trial. In New York, numerous men were arrested and convicted for disorderly conduct well into the 1960s. In Detroit, one researcher in the 1950s came away disappointed with the courts' reluctance to regulate the police abuses they decried in private. Most, he noted, did not even bother explaining their dispositions in court. As a statistical matter, it would be impossible to estimate the rate of dismissals or acquittals on these grounds.[82]

What is clear, however, is that disputes about the ethics of police practices, no less than about the wisdom of criminal policy, shaped judges' views of the project of antihomosexual enforcement—often irrespective of the technical directives of the law. From coastal California to midwestern Michigan and Wisconsin, from cosmopolitan hubs like New York City to small towns like Endicott, from the elected judges on the Recorder's Court in Detroit to the appointed municipal judges of Washington, DC, from trial judges to appellate panels, courts in the 1950s raised a strikingly consistent set of concerns about the vice squads' plainclothes campaigns—operations some saw as more dangerous than the acts they aimed to stamp out. And they relied on a similar set of professional tools to mitigate those campaigns' bite, from acquitting or dismissing charges on the evidence, to narrowly interpreting criminal statutes, to adopting systematic evidentiary presumptions to hamper the success of future cases. These judges did not typically doubt that the defendants made some sexual overtures to the arresting officers, nor did they pretend that the decoys had committed entrapment under the law. Yet when, in their view, the vice squads' enticement methods exceeded the boundaries of proper police work, they used their discretion over both fact and law to avoid giving those tactics the sanction of their courtroom.

Judicial Leniency on the Streets

By the end of the 1950s, many vice squads had come to feel the scrutiny of the courts. Coming before judges who consistently dismissed seemingly straightforward cases, let off repeat offenders with probation or a fine, or publicly interrogated officers on their flirtations in public bathrooms, officers recognized that their decoy campaigns were raising eyebrows outside the police station.

Like the Michigan officers who took to the local press to denounce uncooperative judges or the LAPD officials who decried judicial leniency to the *Metropolitan Citizen-News*, some vice officers made their outrage well-known. As W. Cleon Skousen, a prominent conservative and former chief of the Salt Lake City Police Department, decried in the police journal *Law and Order* in 1961, vice officers' best efforts to clean up their cities were hampered by "local judges [with] a soft policy toward deviates"—not least, their tendency to "unload" homosexual cases "by turning the deviate loose on [the] condition that he take 'psychiatric treatments.'" Others did not go quite so far, but they privately castigated the courts for what they saw as an abdication of judicial duty. No matter how diligently his unit enforced the state's solicitation laws, one Detroit officer protested, its work was wasted on judges who did not "properly handle their end of the job."[83]

That vice officers recognized the courts' resistance to homosexuality-related charges, of course, does not prove that they saw such interference as a commentary on their tactics. Absent further elaboration, an acquittal or a dismissal might have accommodated any number of judicial humors, from sympathy for a particular defendant to distaste for the solicitation laws to a genuine doubt about a police officer's account.[84]

As local courts continued to scrutinize the vice squads' cases, however, many departments came to recognize the criticism inherent in their holdings. In San Francisco, as early as 1954, an inspector with the SFPD Sex Detail informed the press that vice officers were wary of making any solicitation arrests through the use of plainclothes decoys, concerned that "entrapment cases do not hold up in court." In Philadelphia in 1961, an observer with the morals squad reported that decoys tried to "avoid [any] overt encouragement" of suspected gay men, careful to "rule out any basis for a claim of entrapment" at trial. In Michigan in the mid-1950s, researchers found policemen well-attuned to the breadth of judicial impatience with their solicitation arrests, wary that proactive decoy tactics would get them accused of misconduct. Frustrated by his squad's "difficulties" with the municipal courts, indeed, the head of Pontiac's vice squad proposed a "sort of in-service training program," focused in large part on "how to avoid the appearance of entrapment" at legal proceedings.[85]

Vice officers' sensitivity to these accusations did not mean that they accepted the courts' charges of misconduct, either as a policy or as a legal matter. Familiar with the laws governing arrest, some officers understood that their tactics fell short of the technical standard of entrapment. "Entrapment requires inducing one to commit a crime he is not otherwise disposed to commit," the LAPD officer Max Hurlbut recalled. "We simply make ourselves available to be plucked." Some police officials put the point more strongly. The problem, the deputy superintendent in Detroit explained, was that the courts "have a complete lack of understanding of entrapment." As police executives and some officers realized, the courts' resistance to their arrests reflected less the limits of the law than the judges' personal views of their campaigns.[86]

Recognizing this sometimes-confounding leniency, whatever the reasons behind it, many vice officers altered their approach to antihomosexual patrols to accommodate the judges' preferences. In Detroit, where judges took turns screening petty criminal charges, officers varied their enforcement priorities depending on the judge on call for a particular week or month, devoting less time to decoy arrests when the presiding judge was especially critical of enticement. Once a more amenable judge rotated in, the arrest numbers crept back up. Officers sometimes showed remarkable sensitivity to the moods of different judges, down to the category of solicitation or the type of setup used. In January 1957, officers in Detroit reported that the presiding judge of the early sessions court took particular umbrage at the use of phone calls and hotel bellhops to arrest female prostitutes but was less bothered by their typical decoy tactics. So they focused their efforts that month on streetwalkers and gay men.

Others did not alter their priorities in the field, but they changed the laws they invoked to make their arrests. Sensitive to many judges' distaste for the stigma of a homosexuality-related charge, vice officers learned to avoid the more contentious solicitation statutes in favor of lesser charges like vagrancy or disorderly conduct. By arresting suspects preemptively on these milder charges, officers guaranteed that more defendants simply pled guilty and fewer cases proceeded to court. But they did not actually make any fewer arrests. Exasperated by the courts' persisting scrutiny, some departments cut out the hassle of judicial review altogether. In Detroit's Thirteenth Precinct, officers commonly distinguished between "regular" and "investigation" arrests of gay men and prostitutes, the former aimed at preparing a case for court, while the latter merely cleaned up the streets by detaining suspects overnight and letting them go the following morning. By the mid-1950s, investigation arrests accounted for the vast majority of vice-related arrests—a pattern, Judge Miller confided, that courts recognized but could do little about.[87]

And some officers, frustrated by what they saw as the courts' dereliction in cleaning up the homosexual underworld, took a darker turn. In many cities in the mid-twentieth century, gay men arrested by the vice squad complained of their brutal treatment. The defense attorney Gerald Levie recalled arriving to find his clients with black eyes or concussions, broken lips or eardrums, fractured noses or arms. Although such violent treatment was not "true as a rule," he noted, it occurred with some frequency and went far above the force necessary to detain a suspect. Some officers developed a particular habit of beating or demeaning homosexual suspects. First and foremost, of course, such patterns of brutality revealed the personal antipathy that many police officers in these years felt for what they saw as sexual deviance, a reaction especially pronounced in a profession distinguished by its social conservatism and conventional ideals of masculinity. Many policemen, simply enough, needed no further invitation to violence. But contemporary researchers also reported that some officers who took a heavy hand with gay suspects expressly justified their conduct as compelled, in some sense, by the courts: it was the judiciary's inevitable leniency, supposedly, that made their own brand of justice necessary to vindicate the laws they enforced. At a time when police officers' rising frustration with what they perceived as judicial disrespect for their discretion fueled an increasingly hostile police culture, ongoing conflicts between vice squads and trial judges over the value of antihomosexual enforcement helped legitimate and normalize these violent practices.[88]

More than just inviting us to recognize the intermittent moments of grace in the courtroom, tracing the legal system's internal disagreements over the wisdom of antihomosexual enforcement illuminates the history of gay men's often-turbulent interactions with the police on the streets. An infamous feature of the police's antihomosexual campaigns, the use of petty misdemeanors like loitering or trespassing to intimidate gay men in public spaces—typically remembered simply as the *police harassment* of homosexuals—has been recalled as among the most bitter signs of the state's contempt for gay communities: evidence of vice officers' leeway to use the many tools at their disposal to abuse gay men assembling peacefully in public. And the brutality that some gay men encountered at the hands of officers has seemed to confirm the justice system's indifference to their suffering, suggesting the unchecked violence that hostile policemen could inflict on a community with few friends among the supposed servants of the law.

Yet the police harassment of gay men sometimes arose out of less public, more complex fissures among the officials responsible for overseeing the state's antihomosexual campaigns: the extent to which some judges and even some prosecutors resisted the police's use of more serious criminal statutes. And the brutalities that some gay men suffered, more than simply reflecting the inevitable tension between a criminalized minority and the officers charged with repressing it, sometimes reflected a less visible tension between the police and the *courts*—police officers' response to judges pushing back on what they saw as unreasonable laws or unpalatable police tactics. Aiming to mitigate the harm inflicted on gay men by the criminal justice system, judges' leniency was used by some officers, perversely, to legitimate their reliance on less humane tactics on the ground.

In that, the history of decoy enforcement is as notable for the courts' resistance to the vice squads' tactics as it is for the police's own adaptability to judicial pressures: the mutual give-and-take between the officers who made morals arrests and the judges who sometimes discarded them. Today, as when the American courts began attending to police abuses in the midtwentieth century, scholars and reformers have questioned whether judicial oversight meaningfully trickles down to police work in the field. Officers, they observe, do not always follow their arrests through the prosecutor's office or to the courts. Some never learn whether a case was thrown out or on what grounds. Some, recognizing judges' fickle dispositions, simply wash their hands of the courts, continuing to make what they see as good arrests regardless of what happens at trial.[89]

Yet in the case of the vice squads' campaigns against gay men, many police officers kept carefully abreast of the courts' preferences and opinions. Especially in cities where vice enforcement fell to specialized divisions and most arrests came before the same group of municipal judges, officers recognized that their enticement practices were playing poorly before the courts. And they adapted accordingly, alternating the offenses they investigated, the tactics they used, and the laws they invoked in order to evade judicial criticism. They simply did not always do so in the way the courts expected or hoped.

A deeper look at the internal politics of decoy enforcement, in short, complicates our understanding of the law's relationship with queer life in the mid-twentieth century. The work of antihomosexual enforcement in these years is often remembered as an unrelenting regulatory campaign against a stigmatized community that could expect little sympathy within the legal system. In fact, the history of antihomosexual policing is in key part a story of contestation: a profound moral and institutional struggle over not only the morality of same-sex practices but also the proper character of law enforcement itself. It is a story of creative intervention: an account of how individual judges drew on their various levers of discretion to push back against harsh criminal laws, punitive policies by police departments, and unforgiving legal doctrines. Not least, it is a story about the idiosyncrasies of the law: a tale of how the unique economy of the criminal justice system, embedding a variety of personal and professional pressures, transformed both the incentives of individual actors and the impact of seemingly familiar developments in the history of gay life. These hidden internal struggles, no less than more public debates about the law's proper treatment of sexual difference, shaped the daily realities of gay men's encounters with the police.

If recalcitrant judges sometimes inspired vice squads to adapt their enforcement practices, of course, they were hardly alone. As cautionary tales of undercover decoys circulated in gay bars and cruising sites in the 1950s, vice officers soon found themselves confronting more immediate reasons to reconsider their most overt enticement tactics—reasons that originated not within the courts, but among gay men themselves.

FOUR

The Rise of Ethnographic Policing

In 1956, the psychologist Evelyn Hooker published the first in what would become a series of influential articles on gay life around Los Angeles. At a time when even the most sympathetic discussions of homosexuality often relied on the rhetoric of disease, Hooker ventured to examine gay men not as medical anomalies but as members of a cultural minority: a "world [with] its own language, . . . literature, group ways, and code of conduct." Her studies helped open the door to a newly tolerant discourse on sexual difference. Far from seeking to condemn homosexuality or even to diagnose it, this new line of social research sought to unearth the gay world as its participants experienced it: the fashions common to gay men, the social protocols in gay bars, the verbal codes and physical gestures exchanged by men trying to make new "contacts."[1]

Gathering this information was not an easy task. The very codes that fascinated researchers also insulated the gay world from prying eyes, allowing its members to "recognize . . . and reveal" themselves to kindred spirits while "concealing [their] identity" from outsiders. The key, as the sociologists Donald Black and Maureen Mileski proposed in 1967, was to use the insights gathered by the competent ethnographer to infiltrate the community he hoped to study: to adopt gay men's fashions, slang, and "body idiom" to, in their words, "pass as deviant."

By 1967, of course, "passing as deviant" inside the gay world was hardly a novel phenomenon. Researchers who emulated the homosexual's cultural codes to infiltrate bars and cruising sites were, to the contrary, trying on a camouflage worn long and well by far less academic trespassers: the police.[2]

From Frank Manthos's insinuations about gay parties to Dante Longo's affectations in Lafayette Park, intrepid vice officers had long used gay men's cultural language to ingratiate themselves with suspects. By the end of the 1950s, as gay nightlife in major cities grew simultaneously more robust and more insular, they were often forced to expand their repertoire. Encountering the same resistance that would later frustrate more academic interlopers, decoys adapted to the gay world's defensive codes, from the tacit cues in bathrooms to the spatial organization of pickup bars, by mastering them as a tool of enforcement itself. Some learned these signals from their experiences in the field, which provided an intimate window on the shifting contours of gay life. Others drew on the training programs that proliferated among vice squads in the late 1950s and the 1960s, teaching new recruits what to do—and what not to do—to operative effectively on the streets. Regardless, by the early 1960s, the demands of effective enforcement had transformed vice officers into leading students of the gay world that had sprung up in American cities following World War II, professional speakers of a complex cultural language few others even knew existed.

The ethnographic study of homosexual communities has long held a privileged place in the history of gay life, embraced by homophile activists and lauded by historians as a powerful weapon in the fight for liberation. That project is typically seen to have begun in the 1920s with Ernest W. Burgess's courses on deviance in Chicago and flourished in the late 1950s with the work of progressive allies like Hooker, whose vision of homosexuality as a culture helped undermine the pathological model that fueled the repression of gay men and women following the war. Yet the practice of queer ethnography at midcentury did not unfold solely among sociologists and academic researchers. It developed, perhaps first and foremost, among law enforcement agents carrying out the states' antihomosexual campaigns. And the recognition of gay life as its own "world," governed by its own language and social protocols, was not simply a point of fascination for social scientists or a rallying cry for progressives seeking to recast public discussions of sexual difference. It was a strategic weapon in the hands of the police: both an example of the professional knowledge to which modern police forces frequently aspired and a powerful tool for constricting the social and sexual freedoms of gay men.[3]

Identifying plainclothes enforcement tactics as a form of ethnographic policing is not meant to equate the vice squads' forays into gay culture with those of trained sociologists and academics studying gay life in these years. In effect, police ethnography was to academic ethnography what Cesare Lombroso's criminal anthropology was to anthropology: a politicized project that borrowed some insights and methodologies from a more serious pursuit without its underlying rigor or depth of understanding. Not least, that project typically focused on just one part of queer life—cruising culture—without touching on the complex social and class dynamics surveyed by more academic scholars.

Nevertheless, conceptualizing the vice squads' decoy operations as a form of "queer ethnography" focuses an instructive lens on the work of antihomosexual policing in these years. That framework acknowledges the extent to which vice officers, through their sustained exposure to queer cruising sites, gathered genuinely rarefied insights into little-known aspects of gay life in the mid-twentieth century. It illuminates the extent to which urban policing, aimed at eliminating the public manifestations of same-sex desire and practice, did not merely constrain queer communities but also produced novel and even accurate knowledge about them. And it lays bare how the recognition of the gay world as an organized culture, far from being an inherently progressive paradigm, lent itself directly to the work of restricting gay men's legal and social rights in the United States, as a reliable technology of the police.

It is notable, in context, that at a time when police officers frequently emphasized their intimacy with criminal cultures as a mark of professional sophistication, vice officers who amassed similar insights into the shifting contours of gay life rarely claimed credit for that investigative knowledge. Far from it. Even as police instructors taught new recruits what to wear, how to speak, and how to act in public bathrooms to elicit solicitations from cautious cruisers, officers and prosecutors continued to insist that decoy enforcement required no special skill or effort—that the homosexual's indiscriminate sexual habits, indeed, made such arrests inevitable.

Partly, the vice squads' skittishness about their professional insights reflected the growing discomfort inspired by the police's antihomosexual campaigns, inside and outside the police station. At a time when progressives increasingly questioned the wisdom of criminalizing same-sex acts, even as decoy enforcement itself grew increasingly demanding in the field, depicting gay men as predators liable to approach innocent men and teenagers justified the police's ongoing operations against them, persuading not only the vice squads' critics but also new recruits why loitering in public parks and drinking at gay bars was a valuable use of police time.

Largely, however, that strategy was specifically aimed at the courts, where the vice squads' campaigns continued to inspire some ambivalence. Conveniently for the vice squads, as their more aggressive enticements continued to abrade the humors of some judges, the decoy's fluency in cruising codes and customs did not only evade the suspicions of gay men. It also evaded the scrutiny of the courts. Drawing on a cultural language that gay men developed precisely for its unintelligibility to outsiders, experienced decoys managed to elicit sexual advances that appeared, as officers and prosecutors presented them, all but spontaneous at trial. Even as defendants insisted that the signals and gestures so masterfully emulated by vice officers were their own form of enticement, no different than an overt invitation to participate in a sexual act, judges drawing on their own perceptions of the facts declined to see such seemingly benign conduct as justifying judicial intervention.

More than complicating the politics of queer ethnography in the mid-twentieth century, in this sense, the history of the vice squads' shifting decoy tactics reveals the unusual ways that police insight into gay life played out in court. That story suggests that the police's continuing operations hung on what can be thought of as an *epistemic gap* between the different arms of the justice system: a disconnect between the police and the judiciary regarding not only the ethics of plainclothes enforcement but also the nature of gay life itself. From arrest to conviction, the success of decoy enforcement against an increasingly insular gay world did not simply depend on vice officers' own intimacy with the codes that structured cruising culture, or even on their ability to operationalize those codes in the field. It also rested on the courts' continuing failure to appreciate those codes—on the lag between what the officers who arrested gay men knew about queer life and what the judges reviewing their arrests assumed about that world in court. Historians have frequently remarked on state agencies' imperative to amass knowledge about policed communities as a tool of governance, facilitating and legitimating their enforcement efforts. In the case of the vice squads' contentious decoy campaigns, the police's ongoing power to regulate queer life rested less on the spread of vice officers' novel insights through the legal system than on their limited distribution among its branches, creating knowledge gaps that undercut potential checks on police tactics on the ground.[4]

In that, too, the continuing legal struggles over decoy policing in the 1960s reveal the unusual incentives that the enforcement of antisolicitation statutes created for police officers concerned with their professional status. Since the mid-twentieth century, police officers' claims of unique insight into criminal communities have been seen as a reliable source of institutional authority: a hallmark of professionalism and grounds for deference in court. Yet in the context of the vice squads' plainclothes operations, an area inspiring ongoing disputes about both the wisdom and the ethics of antihomosexual enforcement, police officers and prosecutors defending their arrests frequently found it more useful to downplay the specialized cultural knowledge that facilitated those encounters. Far from automatically entitling officers to deference, the mantle of police expertise at midcentury carried very different meanings within different legal frameworks, sometimes straining rather than bolstering the legitimacy of controversial police methods.

Delving into the shifting landscape of decoy policing in the late 1950s and the 1960s, this chapter traces the complex, sometimes-surprising ways that changing understandings of gay life shaped the possibilities of vice enforcement. Bearing down on the vice squads' evolving tactics casts new light on seemingly familiar phenomena, situating the ethnographic study of the gay world as an early tool of law enforcement and complicating the institutional value of police knowledge as a wellspring of police authority. It unearths the continuing—indeed, accelerating—ambivalence inspired by the vice squads' enticement methods in the 1960s, not only among the courts but within police departments themselves. And it suggests the extent to which the law's encounters with conflicting views of sexual difference in these years—rival accounts of the visual hallmarks, social contours, and even moral significance of gay life—did not necessarily aim to resolve those conflicts in any particular direction, but sometimes to leave room for continuing disagreements. If, beginning in the 1950s, the project of antihomosexual enforcement inspired disagreements between vice officers and judges about the merits of the police's campaigns, those disagreements were sometimes appeased in the 1960s by those actors' diverging views about the nature of homosexuality itself: what the different agents of criminal justice knew, and when, about the patterns of queer life.

Old Policing and the New Gay World

To the frustration of many vice officers, progressive judges were not the only ones mobilizing against police enticement tactics at midcentury. As stories of attractive officers flirting in parks, bars, and bathrooms spread across the country, gay men themselves became increasingly attuned to the specter of police entrapment. And, outraged by this pattern of harassment, they developed a range of strategies for fighting back.[5]

Some strategies were purely legalistic. One of the Mattachine Society's most popular projects in the 1950s was a wallet-sized card entitled "Know Your Legal Rights," drafted by the Los Angeles attorney and homophile ally Herb Selwyn to advise homosexual men on how to handle a potential arrest. Throughout the decade, the activist magazine *ONE* ran a series of exposés on police entrapment, educating its readers about both the range of vice operations and the applicable legal frameworks. Other tactics of resistance were more literal. Although some officers came to the vice squad with stereotypical views of gay men as timid creatures, their experiences in the field soon taught many to appreciate both the diversity of queer life and the anger and desperation inspired by the threat of arrest. In Washington, DC, in 1957, a man who invited the morals squad officer Louis Fochett home only to learn, to his dismay, that Fochett was an undercover agent responded by hitting him on the head with a kettle. A year later, a gay man who solicited Fochett's colleague Robert D. Arscott in Lafayette Park punched the officer in the stomach as he tried to make his arrest.[6]

Perhaps gay men's most effective defenses against the vice squad, however, were purely social. For it said something about the shifting nature of gay life in these years that magazines like ONE and organizations like the Mattachine Society were there to channel gay men's outrage and paternal guidance, respectively. Not coincidentally, homophiles' growing anger at the vice squads arose as the gay men who settled in American cities following the war coalesced into something resembling organized communities. Simultaneously an outcome and a catalyst of that shift, homophile societies helped forge a national communication network among gay men. In Los Angeles and San Francisco and, eventually, New York, DC, and Chicago, the Mattachine Society engaged in public awareness campaigns and organized meetings to bring together local gay residents. Publications like ONE and the Mattachine Review spread among readers in Midwestern towns and cities, introducing them to the life and culture awaiting them in larger communities.[7]

Many gay men and women shied away from homophile groups, concerned about the optics of an organized homosexual lobby, or simply uninterested in turning their personal lives into political platforms. Even among those who avoided politics, however, a robust sense of community sprouted in a worldlier setting: the bars and clubs where queer individuals came to drink or flirt in their leisure hours. From the early twentieth century, gay men and lesbians seeking kindred spirits had often gathered in bars and restaurants, but after World War II the growing size and caution of urban gay communities led to a proliferation of bars catering specifically to a queer clientele. In these exclusively gay spaces, patrons practiced their own language, observed their own social hierarchies, and enforced their own public protocols, from acceptable greetings for an old friend to the proper manner of flirting with a stranger. Such bars were, to be certain, just one nexus of gay culture in American cities in the 1950s, one that self-styled "respectable" homosexuals sometimes avoided altogether. Yet, as the most visible and popular grounds of urban gay life, they were a crucial space for cultivating the contours of a gay community: what researchers would soon come to characterize as a distinct "homosexual world" with its own "language," "norms of behavior," and "group standards."[8]

A core feature of that world was its suspicion of strangers. As Evelyn Hooker noted in 1961, gay culture both provided a source of solidarity within queer social circles and functioned as a type of compass for men looking to find kindred spirits. "Experienced homosexuals" in a new town, she observed, could meet partners and friends by following a "fairly standard" "community map." Anyone who stumbled into those spaces without the proper passkey, on the other hand, was likely to be summarily evicted. In bars, employees and customers developed a set of defenses to keep unfamiliar faces at bay. Bar owners put secret locks on the doors, hired bouncers to vet unfamiliar faces, and distributed membership cards to their regulars. Bartenders served newcomers warm beer, overcharged them for their liquor, or turned off the heat to freeze the interlopers out. In one bar in San Francisco, waiters who noted the arrival of any unwelcome guests—heterosexual couples or groups of women looking for an evening's companion in the worst possible setting—ushered them to the center of the floor, where old-timers showered them with ribald comments until they simply embarrassed the intruders into leaving.[9]

The real shadow overhanging gay communities in these years, of course, was not the errant single woman but the police. Although gay bars often provided an oasis from the outside world, they never quite erased the specter of the vice squad. Particularly as stories of aggressive decoys proliferated among queer communities, one constant feature of gay nightlife, inside and outside the bar scene, emerged as the danger of accidentally making the wrong acquaintance. Avoiding the attentions of an undercover cop became a kind of shared skill, a right of entry. "Ways of recognizing vice-squad officers," as Hooker observed, were among the first morsels of wisdom passed down to younger homosexuals by their elders when they came out.[10]

Eager to negotiate this treacherous terrain—to surveil, in effect, the agents who surveilled them in turn—gay men in the 1950s developed a social language that would in later years become an object of fascination for researchers studying urban subcultures. As early as the turn of the century, naturally, men who sought sex with other men had used certain systematic codes to identify each other in public. The fairy's rouged cheek, the red ties, the cheeky phrases that filled gay-friendly bars in the 1940s—these were all part of a language used by men to signal their sexual interests to potential friends and partners. Some of these early codes themselves were far from self-evident. Yet many, developed in a time of less prevalent police harassment, involved a certain self-conscious theatricality. The man who blondined his hair or swayed his hips at a bar accepted some level of public attention in exchange for finding kindred spirits, or even wore those markers proudly as a gesture of defiance. The social codes that sprang up by the late 1950s, by contrast, were designed to avoid any such conspicuous shows of difference. They tried to attract notice, and often to extend an invitation for a sexual encounter, precisely by avoiding attention.[11]

Among the simplest was the matter of dress. Far from the deliberately flamboyant stylings of the fairy, the majority of gay men in the late 1950s and the 1960s adopted a more innocuous uniform: tailored slacks, often of a lighter fabric; pullover sweaters or button-down shirts; sport coats or short jackets. And, of course, the footwear: instead of lipstick or swishing hips, markers that over the 1950s grew increasingly limited to a narrower and poorer segment of the gay community, the most reliable sign of the urban homosexual emerged as the tennis shoe. This new dress code was self-consciously respectable and middle-class—the type of style, as one straight observer in the 1960s would remark, modeled by "dashing young men in college sportswear advertisements." Yet such fashions were remarkably pervasive, dotting gay bars and pickup sites, and they carried a good deal of symbolic weight. Among gay men themselves, a pair of tight slacks and a sport shirt were enough to raise "suspicions of homosexuality." By the mid-1960s, the tennis shoe had become such a paradigmatic symbol of queerness that one leather bar in San Francisco, hoping to dissociate itself from the city's more flamboyant circles, dangled a cluster of sneakers derisively from the ceiling.[12]

In bars and clubs, too, the tenor of gay nightlife grew more subdued. To be sure, gay bars catered to a broad range of classes, ages, and sexual interests, and they did not conform to any single code of conduct. In some establishments, a more old-fashioned, working-class clientele continued the tradition of the fairy's tongue-in-cheek flamboyance, waving cigarettes and greeting friends with feminine endearments. Other venues tolerated a different display of conspicuous queerness: especially by the 1960s, as younger gay men grew more confident about their place in the urban landscape, some business owners shed the caution of their forebears and operated dance floors in their back rooms.[13]

Most "respectable" gay bars, however, frowned on the hallmarks of the fairy, and overt shows of affection were often limited to the company of friends. Instead, gay men hoping to meet new partners signaled their availability through a complex interplay of verbal, physical, and spatial codes. As researchers in the 1960s would observe, a man looking for a night's companion at a gay bar knew to stay on the outer edges, standing or sitting with his back against the wall and scanning his fellow patrons. Simply eyeing another customer from the walls was enough to communicate sexual interest. "If one watches carefully, and knows what to watch for in a 'gay' bar," Hooker reported, "one observes that some individuals are apparently communicating with each other without exchanging words. . . . [B]y their exchange of glances [these men have] agreed to a sexual exchange."[14]

In establishments catering to both gay and straight customers, patrons could not always rely on such rarefied signals, continuing to depend on more verbal cues. Yet these also grew increasingly innocuous. While some gay men continued to use camp slang and effeminate endearments, many turned to subtler conversational codes. One traveler swore he could find an evening's company in any new town by visiting an upscale hotel bar, striking up a conversation with a likely homosexual, and simply asking "where the activity [was]."[15]

Beyond the bars, in the more public settings shunned by many members of the gay community, men also developed subtle means of extending sexual invitations. In the early 1950s, decoys routinely enticed solicitations in parks and on street corners simply by striking up a conversation with a passing stranger, but by the 1960s such artless gambits rarely worked. In his first month on the job, one decoy in Illinois reported that three-fourths of his flirtations in a local park led to dead ends. Although he was fairly confident about the men's intentions, the vast majority were "'too round-about' in their proposals" to give him grounds for an arrest. In bathrooms, meanwhile, experienced cruisers stopped speaking altogether. Some retreated to the artful glances that had long allowed homosexual men to initiate sexual encounters, catching a fellow occupant's gaze or glancing from his genitals directly to his eyes. Others turned to more idiosyncratic signals, jingling keys to catch a partner's attention or tapping their feet in a bathroom stall. Where someone had cut a hole in the partition, they inserted a finger through the opening and waited for the other man to show his finger in return. Some men could always be less prudent, sticking their tongues through glory holes or masturbating in front of strangers, but for the most part outsiders at cruising grounds remarked on the near-invisible nature of gay solicitations. "These overtures are often so subtle that a casual observer could not recognize them," the lawyer Harold Jacobs observed in 1963.

"Indeed, in some cases the ability to recognize a veiled overture almost amounts to a 'sixth sense.'"[16]

The newly coded nature of gay cruising, of course, did not simply reflect the growing caution with which gay men looked for sexual partners by the early 1960s. It also reflected a shift in whom precisely they were looking for. Historians have noted that the gay life emerging in American cities in the postwar years departed from earlier same-sex arrangements in two subtle but important ways: first, it featured a notion of cultural identification, recognizing gay desires as not merely a matter of private erotic experience but also a source of cultural self-definition; and, second, it involved a certain sense of reciprocity, envisioning the participants in a sexual encounter not as distinct actors separated by sexual role but as two partners with a shared sexual identity. Those differences have been attributed to a range of factors, from the demographic changes occasioned by World War II, to the influence of psychiatric theories of homosexuality divorced from gender variation, to the political strategies of homophile activists, who deliberately recast homosexuals as a social minority to improve their bids for tolerance. Yet that evolving cultural landscape might also be recognized as part of a broader negotiation between the gay world and the police. Wary of plainclothes officers infiltrating their bars and cruising sites, gay men looking for sexual partners learned to limit their search to men who not only evinced a shared sexual desire but also bore the traces of a common membership in an insular sexual subculture: who wore the subtle marks of an increasingly coded gay world.[17]

Police officers who patrolled the sites of gay life—and especially those who worked alongside liquor agents in surveilling queer-friendly bars—sometimes stayed well-abreast of these evolving social patterns. The collegiate fashions popular among gay men in the 1950s, after all, emerged at liquor proceedings as their own indelible marks of queerness.[18]

Yet many officers had more limited exposure to the gay world, and they sometimes struggled to fit that culture into their preexisting presumptions about both gay men and the landscape of crime traditionally imagined at the heart of police work. Speaking to the historian Christopher Agee, one San Francisco Police Department (SFPD) patrolman recounted his bewilderment at entering a gay bar in 1959. "I'[d] never seen anything like this," he recalled. Even detectives in the department's specialized units harbored more than a little confusion at the prospect of an organized gay community. Beginning in April 1955, after an officer with the SFPD vice squad reported a spike in "homosexual activities" around the Bay Area, Chief

Thomas Cahill authorized a formal inquiry into the city's burgeoning queer scene. Headed by a single detective who signed his name simply as "X.," the investigation produced numerous reports over several years, and it gathered some useful information. X. built a topography of San Francisco's bar scene, including the names of popular venues, their shifting geographic sprawl, and the demographics of their clientele. He kept fairly accurate reports on the Mattachine Society, listing its gathering places and outreach projects, as well as the lesbian rights group the Daughters of Bilitis. Confirming a rumor common among members of the gay community, he compiled a list of some fifteen hundred known and suspected homosexuals in the city, including their names, addresses, telephone numbers, and occupations.[19]

In many ways, however, X.'s survey revealed an almost comic misperception of the city's thriving gay culture. Gathering his information primarily through a young prostitute who came to his attention during an investigation of the infamous madam Mabel Malotte, the detective offered a deeply selective view of the city's sexual underground. His earliest report consisted mostly of voyeuristic anecdotes of alleged orgies staged by Malotte's prominent customers: an oil company vice president who hired prostitutes to "purchase for his escapades certain female wearing apparel," an office manager who liked to decorate his body with lipstick, and, of particular note, one Sir Henry, Count Vasco da Gama, a supposed nobleman who "procure[d] lesbians . . . and cheer[ed] on, 'I say, old girl'" while watching them have sex. Later reports took an even more exaggerated tone. The mission behind his research, X. announced in December 1955, was "to form a more perfect union between pimps, prostitutes, con men, stick-up men, freaks, homosexuals, Vasco Da Gama, Professor William K. Schmelzle, and . . . other appropriate agents and agencies." The investigator portrayed the city's gay culture as part of a teeming criminal syndicate, sharing meeting grounds with Malotte's prostitution racket, responsible for thousands of dollars in burglaries across the city, and populated by a host of Mafia-like characters such as "The Lipstick Man" and the realtor Burton Stenberg, "known in the trade as 'Dorothy, the Fruit.'" The Mattachine Society and its members fit indiscriminately somewhere among these criminal elements. Even the SFPD's most dedicated student of the city's queer community, in short, came away with an image of gay life few of its participants would have recognized.[20]

The vice squads' decoy campaigns in the early 1950s were not seen as especially demanding assignments. Decoys had to be young, attractive, and unfazed at the prospect of flirting with other men, but that was about it. By the end of the decade, however, policemen sometimes found themselves struggling to keep up with the demands of policing an organized gay world. And they realized that a bit more sophistication was in order.

The Rise of Ethnographic Policing

In 1957, while agent X. was still delving into San Francisco's sexual underground, the University of Nebraska criminology professor and trained sociologist James Melvin Reinhardt published his own foray into a local gay community. Funded by the Nebraska Police Officers' Association for a readership of "officers, investigators, judges, and prosecutors," Reinhardt's *Sex Perversion and Sex Crimes* was among the first in its field: a "sociocultural" examination of sexual deviation. Reinhardt was particularly interested in the problem of homosexuality, devoting three chapters to the life of America's gay men and women. The centerpiece was a "sociological study of a homosexual 'group' in what may be called a 'natural setting'": a gay social circle in a Nebraska college town.[21]

Drawing on questionnaires and carefully arranged interviews with a group of local men and women, Reinhardt amassed a wide-ranging analysis of the small-town homosexual, from his experience coming out to the possibility of long-term attachments ("possible, but not probable") to his "missionary" work introducing converts to the group. But he was especially interested in the codes his subjects used to communicate in public. "Homosexuals have developed an extensive means of identification," he reported. Familiar words like *fag* or *gay* were enough to "strike responsive recognition" in a gay man. Popular songs like "Margie," sung or whistled by a woman, "would immediately arouse suspicions" in a lesbian. The gay world's semiotics, Reinhardt warned, created some room for confusion: "If inadvertently a 'normal' person uses some of the expressions or mannerisms characteristic of the 'gay world,' it is assumed that the individual is a homosexual." Yet such uses did not have to be inadvertent. In addition to sprinkling jargon throughout his chapters, Reinhardt included a "Gay Glossary" for curious readers, ranging from popular slang (*gay, queer, come out*) to obscure sexual phrases (*bagpipe*) to camp interjections like *coo* and *get you!* "Whoops," Reinhardt instructed, should be "pronounced with a rising inflection and as if it were spelled 'Woo!'" Introducing law enforcement agents to America's gay world, Reinhardt did not simply teach his readers to recognize the language of the homosexual underground. He taught them to speak it.[22]

An overtly scientific endeavor, Reinhardt's study was likely of more academic than practical use. But over the following decade, a similar pedagogical impulse cropped up in law enforcement agencies throughout the country. Responding to the increasingly coded nature of gay life, vice squads in the late 1950s and early 1960s began to experiment with a newly ethnographic approach to decoy enforcement. Drawing both on formal training materials and on their own experiences in the field, officers learned to ingratiate themselves with cautious suspects by adopting the codes, fashions, and customs of the gay world—a process that often demanded patience, subtlety, and insight into a social language few outsiders imagined.

Perhaps the leading hallmarks of that pedagogical project were the training programs that proliferated among local police departments and federal agencies, designed to introduce new officers to the patterns of the modern homosexual. In 1960, the Pennsylvania Chiefs of Police Association, in coordination with the Federal Bureau of Investigation, prepared a twenty-eight-hour course on sex offenses. Among the program's "most notable innovations," the executive director reported, were the five hours devoted to the subject of homosexuality, introducing students to "the customs, language, line of reasoning, principles, and activities of this 'third sex.'" The following year, the San Francisco branch of California's Department of Alcoholic Beverage Control began recruiting local officers to help patrol gay bars after the crowds there learned to recognize its investigators. To acclimate the recruits to their task, the San Francisco Examiner recounted, "State Liquor agents train[ed] the young policemen, instructing them on what to look for, and how to act and dress while in 'gay' bars." The LAPD, known for its robust vice campaigns in the 1960s, offered all new officers a multiday introduction to effective investigation, including several hours on the problem of the homosexual. Taught by a series of instructors until being assigned for a period of years to Officer Max Hurlbut, the course familiarized recruits with the terrain of gay life in Los Angeles, from the homosexual's favored fashions to his preferred gathering places to the work of homophile organizations like the Mattachine Society and Daughters of Bilitis.[23]

A key accessory to this project was an influx of published manuals that, although lacking Reinhardt's scientific rigor, offered officers some specialized insight into the dynamics of gay life. Among the first to discuss antihomosexual enforcement was Frederick Egen's 1959 *Plainclothesman*, a book that promised to teach readers "exactly how . . . the degenerate tries to conceal his activities." *Plainclothesman* provided a cursory overview of bar culture and the cruiser's penchant for public bathrooms but offered few additional specifics; in parks, Egen suggested, officers merely had to "be patient." Over the coming years, such references grew more detailed.

In 1964, John B. Williams, an associate professor of police science at the California State College at Los Angeles and a former LAPD instructor, published the first edition of *Vice Control in California*, covering "homosexuals" among other subjects, and ranging in its advice from gay men's typical appearance to their methods of "recruiting." The book soon emerged as the premier reference on vice control in police colleges across California. That same year, the Florida Legislative Investigations Committee in Tallahassee, known as the Johns Committee after its first chairman, Charley Johns, released a more incendiary document. Aimed principally at government administrators charged with ferreting out gay employees, *Homosexuality and Citizenship in Florida* assured readers that the gay world came "replete with its own language [and] customs." A year after the report was published, Johns Committee chairman R. O. Mitchell boasted that it had been adopted by the Florida Law Enforcement Academy and by police training programs in at least eight cities. By 1971, Denny Pace's *Handbook of Vice Control*, published by the textbook giant Prentice-Hall, would offer its "Guidelines for Recognizing Active Homosexuals" to a national audience.[24]

Coinciding with the growth of gay life in American cities, this proliferation of training materials was part of a broader trend in police administration in the 1960s: a drive, spurred by the proponents of police professionalization, to boost the policeman's public status through more rigorous credentialing and education. As reformist police chiefs like the LAPD's William Parker recognized, academy courses and in-service training programs simultaneously allowed police executives to shape their officers' conduct in the field and, as importantly, bolstered the policeman's claim to some unique insight into crime, entitling him to greater respect from judges and ordinary citizens alike.[25]

Serving that reform agenda, instructional programs frequently responded to the pressures of public and judicial criticism, and vice training was no different. As early as 1957, the head of the Pontiac, Michigan, vice division had proposed an in-service education program to protect his officers from accusations of entrapment in court. Echoing that same ambition, the manuals and training programs that proliferated in the 1960s often focused on reining in decoy tactics likely to offend judges' moral, if not legal, sensibilities. From the LAPD to Philadelphia's morals squad, vice instructors cautioned officers away from brazen conduct known to reflect poorly on the department. Decoys were not to bring up the subject of sex. They were not to accompany a suspect home. They were not to urinate in public or unzip their flies while enticing advances in bathrooms. They were not, certainly, to imitate the mannerisms of the fairy. "It is not sufficient to just avoid evil," as the LAPD's Hurlbut reminded his pupils. "An officer shall also avoid the *appearance of evil*." In theory, such warnings aimed to eliminate controversial enticement tactics, steering new officers away from what some judges decried as overzealous methods. But even absent a meaningful impact in the field, the lessons helped officers deflect criticism in court, assuring judges exasperated by police enticement tactics that their units had more palatable policies in place.[26]

The strategic appeal of such initiatives sometimes outstripped their sophistication in practice. Mirroring the whims and interests of the individual instructors, training programs were wildly inconsistent in even the most professionalized departments. When Hurlbut took over the LAPD's internal vice courses, for instance, he had spent only two months in the division. A voracious reader, he threw together a lesson plan based on his conversations with veterans and a handful of visits to the police library. The final outline surveyed a range of queer history and culture, from homoerotic cave paintings to friendships in ancient Greece, and cited publications including Cory's *Homosexual in America* and John Rechy's novels about queer hustlers. Other materials bespoke less immersive research. Published manuals, especially, sometimes fell short of their claim to describe urban gay life, purveying thin distortions of actual pickup practices or delving into aspects of the gay world with little bearing on genuine police work. The *Handbook of Vice Control* included among its top five hallmarks of the "active" homosexual the gay man's alleged penchant for engaging in "frequent, violent arguments . . . which result in slapping and scratching." Williams channeled a more recognizable trope, advising officers that conversations with more flamboyant homosexuals were "likely to cover music, arts, furniture, and the color of the drapes." Drawing on broad stereotypes of gay life, such materials carried the professional trappings of formal police education, but they were not especially helpful in the field.[27]

Perhaps the clearest disconnect between theory and practice emerged in the manuals' treatment of the lesbian. Although most vice squads disavowed the use of decoys to arrest queer women, regarding the practice as both wasteful and demeaning, manuals commonly included some discussion of "female homosexuals," depicted for the most part as domineering butches eager to recruit "normal" women for their sexual gratification. Instructing his readers on how to spot such predators in public, Williams looked to the same clues commonly invoked by liquor boards: cropped hair, mannish clothing, spare makeup. The *Handbook of Vice Control* turned to more outlandish hallmarks. Although "not quite as easy" to recognize as their male counterparts, Pace speculated, lesbians might wear leather jackets, carry razors and shaving equipment in their purses, or wear "athletic supporters" with an "artificial penis attached for convenience." Painting a sinister and sometimes cartoonish view of lesbian life, characterized by jealous outbreaks, scandalous sexual practices, and the seduction of innocent women, such discussions did their best to depict female homosexuality as a police problem. Yet they had little application to the daily work of enforcement.[28]

Despite the ceremonial tenor of some publications, however, many training initiatives that cropped up among vice squads in the 1960s genuinely tried to fill a pedagogical need. As gay men grew increasingly sensitive to state-authorized interlopers on their grounds, after all, vice squads frequently recognized that effective decoy work required some fluency in the organization of gay life. "The most successful operational thing I learned," as Hurlbut later recalled, "is that homosexual predators must be able to pick out contacts from the general public," based on a glance, a smile, the "choice of words or even accent." Training materials often focused on these cultural codes, not only warning new recruits what *not* to do in order to avoid embarrassing their unit, but also providing affirmative tips on how to entice solicitations in the field. Instructors commonly listed gay men's telltale clothing. "To arrest these predatory homosexuals," as Williams advised, "vice investigators may work undercover by dressing similar to homosexuals—tight pants, sneakers or sandals, tight jackets and sweaters with the sleeves pushed up near the elbows." They recounted the behavioral and spatial codes used by men seeking partners in cruising sites. Placing a light coat or sweater across one's lap, Egen informed his readers, "appears to be the universal signal" among "movie men." Many, like Reinhardt, introduced officers to slang common in the gay community. Teaching policemen to recognize and deploy these signals was a core goal of vice instruction in these years. "An effective police decoy must be indistinguishable from a homosexual," as a survey of criminal justice in 1974 reflected. "Intensive training is sometimes required in . . . dress, mannerisms and slang."[29]

"Required" may have been an exaggeration. As Hurlbut conceded, manuals and academy courses were only the beginning, not the end, of a vice officer's education. Beyond formal training, decoys looked to a variety of sources to refine their tactics, including their own experiences and informal talks with senior colleagues—sources that sometimes but not always aligned with the vice instructors' official policies. Given those diverse influences, training materials familiarizing officers with gay men's fashions, slang, and pickup codes may have echoed rather than prompted vice officers' growing intimacy with the social organization of queer life.[30]

Regardless of the role of formal training in the shifting profile of decoy enforcement in the 1960s, however, there was no question that the shift itself was real. As cruising practices grew more opaque and queer communities became more organized, decoys sent out to arrest gay men often found that the only way to do the job effectively was to master the language of the target group—to "dress, walk, talk and act as . . . homosexuals."[31]

Among the most consistent changes was what plainclothes officers looked like. Decoys had long dressed to accentuate their better features, but even dedicated officers like DC's Louis Fochett did not wear uniquely or symbolically queer fashions. By the early 1960s, decoys sent into cruising zones had acquired a professional uniform. From New York to California, vice officers wore slacks, brightly colored sport shirts or fuzzy sweaters, jackets or sport coats, and, of course, the telltale tennis shoe. In the Center Theater in Philadelphia one night in 1961, a gay man looking for a partner picked an officer in the fourth row wearing a sport coat. In a bar in San Francisco, a patron was approached by a decoy dressed in "a bright shirt and slacks and tennis shoes, the whole bit." Even in Los Angeles, where the LAPD's policy formally warned officers against "embarrass[ing] . . . the Department" by wearing tight pants, shorts, or similarly "obvious homosexual dress," decoys adopted the gay world's collegiate fashions, throwing on white sneakers, slim jeans or slacks, and sweaters or short jackets before heading out into the streets. Officers admitted that their clothing choices were deeply strategic, a necessary step toward blending into bars and parks popular with gay men. As one New York patrolman explained, he wore white pants, light colored sneakers, and polo shirts to gay bars in Greenwich Village to try to "be in with" the homosexual crowds there.[32]

If a sport jacket and tennis shoes were not enough, some officers took more active steps to blend in with the scenery. From the earliest years of decoy enforcement, intrepid officers had attracted suspects by mimicking the stereotypical affectations of the homosexual. By the early 1960s, swishing to attract attention had become a common practice. In Los Angeles, some decoys did their best impressions of the fairy, swinging their hips as they entered bars and public bathrooms. In DC, members of the morals squad habitually "'camped it up'—dressed and acted like stereotyped homosexuals to tempt suspects and provoke advances." As in the gay community itself, where such affections had grown increasingly marginalized, swishing was not as widespread a camouflage as the decoy's collegiate fashions. But

4.1. "A policeman in tight-pants disguise," per *Life* magazine in 1964,
dressed in jeans, a short jacket, and white sneakers. Photograph by
Bill Eppridge © Estate of Bill Eppridge. All rights reserved.

it remained a helpful tool inside a city's campier bars or restrooms, a short-
cut for signaling an officer's membership in one, if progressively narrow,
segment of the gay community. The technique was so useful, indeed, that
some officers insisted on using it despite formal directives to the contrary.
Sensitive to the undignified optics of policemen striving too hard to imitate the fairy, some departments forbade their decoys from swishing on the
job, but individual officers sometimes found the tactic too convenient to
resist, relying on the well-placed gesture to attract suspects even if it flouted
their supervisors' policies.[33]

By the early 1960s, gay men themselves remarked on the artfulness of
that charade. It did not "matter how 'queer' he may look," the Mattachine
Society of New York warned in 1965. Anyone who tried to pick up a gay
man in public "could possibly be a disguised police officer." Sometimes,
indeed, decoys who visited cruising grounds sporting the gay man's fashions and affectations may have been too convincing for their own good. In
February 1960, Robert Arscott, a fairly new fixture on DC's morals squad
who would soon rank among its most prolific officers, was attacked "without provocation" by five young men as he walked into Lafayette Park. The
gang was looking "to make trouble for some 'defenseless homosexual'"
and thought Arscott was the perfect target.[34]

First impressions, of course, were often just the first step on the path to an arrest. As many officers realized, eliciting a solicitation often required not only attracting new acquaintances but also continuing to pass once a conversation began, and the decoy's speech patterns, too, came to reflect a greater immersion in the gay world. Part of that shift entailed the use of slang to disarm potential suspects. By the early 1960s, vice officers had mastered a variety of terms, from familiar codes like *gay* to popular camp endearments like *Nellie* to derisive slang for the police themselves (*Millie, Tillie,* and *Mae*). Even officers who avoided more conspicuous affectations admitted that some verbal reassurance could be invaluable in putting "targets at ease." Some officers learned those codes from their own work in the field, not least observing patrons at gay bars, but many also benefited from the extensive glossaries frequently featured in published manuals. The contents of these lists ranged from tongue-in-cheek expressions (*Mary, Well, get you*) to the varied social roles marking the queer world (*auntie, chicken, trade*) to clinical catalogs of unorthodox sex acts. Both *Vice Control in California* and *Homosexuality and Citizenship in Florida*, for instance, defined a range of practices including not only sodomy and fellatio, but also urolagnia, zoophilia, and triolism. Graphic and overinclusive, such references seemed geared less toward facilitating law enforcement than feeding a voyeuristic curiosity about sexual deviance. But the entries on popular slang, at least, served an overt pedagogical function, teaching readers to speak the gay world's language. The Johns Committee, indeed, took care to instruct readers how to deploy gay jargon in the field, including pointers on how to pronounce camp terms like *chi-chi* ("she-she") or use phrases like *do you* in a sentence ("said as, 'I'd like to . . .'").[35]

Where gay men's appetite for camp dwindled, officers traded drops of slang for more equivocal conversational clues. Some borrowed the technique used so effectively by the gay traveler fond of hotel bars. In Los Angeles, a "standard procedure" among decoys was to approach suspected homosexuals, claim to be new in town, and ask, "Where's the action?" Receiving an encouraging response, an officer would proceed to a more suggestive question, asking a suspect "what [he] like[d] to do" and hoping for a sexual response. Hearing an ambiguous answer like "anything you want," he would press for more details, playing naive or continuing to flirt to extract a more explicit advance. A popular combination of provocation and ambiguity, a similar script cropped up among officers in San Francisco and New York.[36]

Such roundabout conversational gambits did not necessarily yield the most efficient arrests. As among gay men themselves, conversations be-

4.2. A Los Angeles Police Department decoy speaks with a suspect in Hollywood, very possibly the same conversation recorded in *Life*. Photograph by Bill Eppridge © Estate of Bill Eppridge. All rights reserved.

tween decoys and their targets frequently devolved into extended verbal games, each man trying to elicit a sexual advance without saying anything overtly sexual himself. In 1964, a reporter with *Life* magazine recorded the delicate give-and-take that characterized these interactions. Striking up a conversation with a driver on Sunset Boulevard, an LAPD officer needed only a few minutes of "idle talk" before the suspect suggested heading to the officer's apartment. But when the decoy tried to suss out a more graphic proposal, the exchange grew more delicate:

> What's on your mind after we get home? That's what I want to know.
>
> Well, what's on your mind?
>
> Well . . . I don't know. . . . I was just wondering . . . what else you had in mind, if anything.
>
> At this point I don't care.
>
> Well, I don't exactly know how to take that.
>
> Well . . . how do you want it to go?
>
> Like I say, it's up to you. . . .
>
> Well, you call it. . . . I'm your guest. . . .
>
> I know but . . . I wouldn't want to be a presumptive host.

Continuing for some time afterward, the conversation finally got too long for comfort. The two men decided to part ways, one wary of a potential arrest, the other insufficiently assured of it. But others were not as cautious, gradually succumbing to an officer's flirtations.[37]

Circular and meandering, such verbal parries exemplified the effort and patience sometimes demanded of decoys trying to elicit solicitations from gay men, many of whom took extensive precautions to avoid propositioning the wrong target. Indeed, some officers struggling to shake a suspect's mistrust did not content themselves with borrowing the verbal tests developed by gay men to winnow out potential decoys; they also created them. By the 1960s, gay men around Hollywood commonly voiced their belief in a particular policy restricting the vice squads' conduct in the field: that a plainclothes police officer had to identify himself as such if asked, on pain of having any subsequent arrest dismissed in court. The genesis of the rumor had grown murky by the 1960s, but vice officers at the LAPD proudly took credit for its inception, and they did their best to continue its use, reminding suspicious men that vice officers could not lie, or even prompting suspects to confirm that they themselves were not policemen. Arrest records in these years were littered with accounts of gay men demanding some assurance that their new acquaintance was not an officer, hoping in vain to buffer themselves against future charges.[38]

In some settings, simply starting up a conversation with a stranger went against the increasingly codified nature of gay cruising. Officers patrolling those exclusive venues turned to subtler methods of enticement. Sensitive to the signals exchanged by "movie men," decoys in theaters pressed their knees against their neighbors or crossed their legs to make their crotch available. Attuned to the unique structure of the pickup bar, they sent lingering looks to fellow patrons across the room or leaned against the walls and watched incoming customers, wordlessly inviting new arrivals to approach them. At the Mug Bar in Garden Grove one evening, Officer Ricketts of the Garden Grove Vice Detail seated himself at the farthest end of the bar, his back against the wall and his knees opening onto the barroom floor. When Gilbert Mesa walked inside, Ricketts watched him scan the room for potential partners until, presumably resting his eyes on the attentive officer, Mesa came up to lean against him and eventually put his hand on Ricketts's thigh.[39]

In public bathrooms—pickup sites so well-established that they went by the special moniker *tearooms* among those in the know—decoys also grew well-versed in queer men's codes for seeking sexual partners. As in the 1950s, some continued to hover by the facilities or use eye contact to invite sexual overtures. In Los Angeles, vice officers eyed potential cruisers, glancing toward their crotch or locking glances for a moment longer than usual. In Philadelphia, they watched suspects by the urinals, keeping a neutral expression but making it "apparent to the homosexual that he has been noticed." Done correctly, one LAPD officer confided, a meaningful look was as effective as an "outright solicitation" in eliciting an overture.[40]

Many also turned to the more discrete language of the tearoom, often singled out for particular attention in training materials. *Homosexuality and Citizenship in Florida* included a narrative overview of the use of glory holes between toilet stalls, stressing not only the coded nature of such practices but also their intrinsic depravity. "A well dressed teacher . . . places a finger through the hole," one anecdote recounted. "The finger of the unknown occupant . . . appears. The teacher then inserts his sex organ through the hole to perform . . . a homosexual act with a partner he never sees." The *Handbook of Vice Control*, too, covered a range of classic cruising codes, including "giv[ing] prospects the 'eye'" and "playing 'footsie' in a 'tearoom.'" The manual even came with helpful illustrations: one black and white photograph of two feet tapping in a toilet stall, another of a man eyeing a prospective partner by the urinal.[41]

These tactics soon grew common among decoys. Throughout the 1960s, officers hoping to entice an advance peered through glory holes between

4.3. "Playing 'footsie' in a 'tearoom,'" in Denny Pace's *Handbook of Vice Control* (Englewood Cliffs, NJ: Prentice-Hall, 1971). © Prentice Hall, Inc.

4.4. "A toilet snipe looking for a date," in Denny Pace's *Handbook of Vice Control* (Englewood Cliffs, NJ: Prentice-Hall, 1971). © Prentice Hall, Inc.

toilet stalls. They jingled keys or change in their pockets—a technique deemed so suggestive that the LAPD's formal policies prohibited it, alongside skintight trousers and effeminate affectations, as "'trolling' for homosexuals." They tapped their feet to signal their sexual availability. At least one agency in the Los Angeles area insisted that its officers never initiated such flirtations, tapping their feet only after receiving the first move from a neighbor, but some decoys admitted to using the signal to lure out suspected cruisers. In Ohio, one department grew to rely so heavily on the gesture that it did not wait for much more before making an arrest. In the summer of 1966, a twenty-two-year-old in a men's room at the Ohio State University tapped his foot in a toilet stall next to a Columbus policeman. After tapping his shoe in return, the officer waited only for the youth to push his foot beneath the partition before arresting him for disorderly conduct.[42]

From the furtive gestures to the time spent loitering near the urinals, decoys patrolling public bathrooms strove hard to match the subtlety and patience of veteran cruisers. Some, perhaps, stepped too deeply into their camouflage. In New York one evening, two plainclothes officers dispatched to investigate an "invert take-over" of a local YMCA men's room concluded their investigations by trying to arrest each other for solicitation. In DC in 1960, just a few months following Robert Arscott's beating in Lafayette Park, Arscott, Fochett, and a colleague were patrolling the park's restrooms when, seeing what he assumed to be an idling homosexual, Private James Thomas of the park police tried to take one of them into custody. When the officers resisted, Thomas drew on his judo training. He flipped Fochett onto his back in the shrubbery, while Arscott and the third plainclothesman ended up in the bushes. Drawing significant mockery in the local press, the run-in exemplified the risk of public embarrassment that departments like the LAPD warned its decoys to avoid. But it also revealed how completely vice officers sent to entice solicitations in parks and bathrooms sometimes immersed themselves in the world of gay cruising, so thoroughly adopting its trappings that they re-created the very nuisances they were supposedly sent to eliminate.[43]

To be sure, not all policemen went to such lengths to suss out potential solicitations. Some suspects, reflecting a human urge hardly unique to gay cruisers, were always willing to take greater risks in pursuit of sexual gratification. Nor did all police officers have the patience for such understated tactics. In the 1960s, as in previous years, some decoys were overzealous in their pursuit of an arrest, exchanging vulgarities with suspects, rubbing themselves in movie theaters, or openly asking strangers about their favorite sex positions. As late as 1966, Dick Leitsch, the president of the Mattachine Society of New York, wrote to the *Fire Island News* denouncing "the practice of some police officers to caress their pubic regions, simper, wink, try to be seductive and, occasionally, fondle or appear to fondle one another's genitals in public places." Considering that such practices were "not at all common in the homosexual community," Leitsch observed, the police "create[d] more danger of breaching the public peace than do homosexuals."[44]

As a general rule, however, many gay men acknowledged that vice officers in the 1960s had learned to fade disarmingly well into the background of gay life. From public bathrooms to darkened street corners, decoy officers recognized that gay men relied on a set of discreet, often obscure codes to initiate sexual encounters. And they set about mastering those codes themselves, marshaling the tools developed to protect a marginalized community from unwanted exposure in order to infiltrate it. By the start of the decade, the undercover investigators responsible for arresting gay men were no longer fresh faces sent to wait in bathrooms or loiter on the benches of local parks. They were careful students, and often artful imitators, of a complex cultural language few outside the vice squad recognized.[45]

And some, indeed, came to take a certain pride in their insights. In 1958, a man arrested by Louis Fochett in a bathroom at George Washington University protested, as he was booked, that he was sure Fochett had welcomed his advance. Fochett laughed. "Well that is what I am paid to do, you know," he replied. Just some years later, officers with the New York Police Department (NYPD) widely acknowledged the skillful camouflage required of an effective decoy. Charged with infiltrating a "wary . . . 'fraternity,'" the officers who frequented gay clubs and bars to elicit solicitations were known around the department as "actors."[46]

The vice squads' evolving decoy campaigns complicate the conventional narrative of the ethnographic discovery of the gay world in the late 1950s: the telltale fashions, the social protocols of the gay bar, the stealthy signals sent by cruisers in public bathrooms. Embraced by the homophile movement as a tool of social enlightenment, the ethnographic study of gay life is typically identified with a generation of liberal researchers who helped push against the stigmatization of queer men and women in the 1960s. Yet the excavation of the group dynamics, codes, and customs of urban gay communities found many of its first practitioners in another setting: the police departments charged with keeping those communities in their place. In the late 1940s, well before trained sociologists descended on gay life, enterprising policemen borrowed the slang and affectations traded among gay men to trap suspected cruisers. In the mid-1950s, while Evelyn Hooker exhorted her colleagues to consider the group behavior of gay men, criminologists like James Reinhardt were conducting their own inquiries into the social organization of gay life as a tool of informed law enforcement. By the early 1960s, when researchers like Mileski and Black confronted the difficulties of doing fieldwork in gay bars and cruising sites, many vice officers had already mastered the art of turning the idioms, clothing, and body language of the gay world against it. Perhaps novel to some academics in the 1960s, the project of "passing as deviant" was hardly news to local vice squads. It was central to the decoy's effectiveness—and sometimes his professional identity—in an increasingly cautious gay world.

The Invisible Expert

Police departments at midcentury were rarely shy about claiming credit for their professional insights. Police chiefs and reformers bearing the mantle of police professionalism, after all, commonly invoked the officer's unique intimacy with criminal subcultures—a "bond of common knowledge" shared by policemen but "not generally known to the public"—as a hallmark of the modern police department. From veteran detectives to beat cops on the street, the policeman was, in this view, "a specialist in his own line," endowed by training and experience with an unparalleled fluency in the internal operations of urban crime.[47]

It was striking, in context, that vice squads did not similarly advertise the cultural insights that facilitated so many decoy arrests by the 1960s— not outside the police department and sometimes not even within it. To the contrary, even as decoys learned the codes and protocols of cruising culture, mastering a variety of verbal, sartorial, and physical clues to help them entice solicitations, vice officers and the prosecutors defending their arrests continued to insist that decoy work required no particular skill or insight.

That counternarrative started at the root, in the training materials that introduced novice vice officers to the contours of gay life. The same manuals and programs that taught recruits the tools of the successful operator, from the homosexual's dress and jargon to his systematic codes in theaters and public bathrooms, also assured those officers, first and foremost, that no such training was actually necessary. Williams's *Vice Control in California* struck perhaps the most alarmist tone, combining its overview of gay slang and advice that decoys dress "similar to homosexuals" with a denunciation of gay men's indiscriminate and even violent habits. "These 'Hollywood' and 'Greenwich' village 'cannibals,'" the manual decried, "are constantly on the lookout for 'new stuff'—persons who are not homosexuals. If this were not so, it would be an utter impossibility for any Vice Investigator to even make an arrest." Others took a more measured tone but offered a substantially similar account. Despite Hurlbut's later reflections that homosexuals had to "be able to pick out contacts from the general public," his presentation at the LAPD warned fledging officers that the "male homosexual appears incapable of conducting his activities in private or limiting his solicitations to his own kind." The *Handbook of Vice Control*, too, emphasized the ease of decoy enforcement against what it termed "predatory" homosexuals. "Merely being 'one of the group' is sufficient in places where homosexuals congregate," it assured its readers, setting aside the planning and patience that being "one of the group" in cruising grounds frequently entailed.[48]

In many cases, such simplifications echoed a familiar tune. They recalled the persisting specter of the sexual psychopath, depicting gay men as, if not outright child molesters, nevertheless sexual predators, corruptors of innocent men and youth. Indeed, most manuals that decried gay men's supposedly intemperate habits also made a point of emphasizing their preference for youthful victims. The homosexual, as Hurlbut warned in a special section on the gay man's "predatory nature," prefers "the young male adolescent or young male adult to the exclusion of others." At a time when progressive psychiatrists and many judges dismissed the facile conflation of homosexuals and sexual predators, vice manuals did their best to resurrect that concern, denouncing the homosexual's alleged missionary zeal and taste for youth as core justifications for the police's campaigns.[49]

In that sense, indeed, the homosexual's supposedly indiscriminate solicitations were just one part of a larger problem. Alongside their enumerations of gay men's fashions, hangouts, and expressions, vice materials typically spent some time reviewing the dangers of the gay world, of which the seduction of innocent youth was the worst but hardly only variant. Manuals and lesson plans warned of gay men's growing visibility in parks and bars, blemishing the landscape of the American city. They decried the alleged health hazards of gay sex, purportedly a leading transmitter of venereal diseases. Echoing, well into the 1960s, the claims used to purge gay men and women from federal employment in the early 1950s, they denounced homosexuals as security risks, liable to "disclose information of a vital nature" to protect their secret habits. The homosexual's seemingly victimless conduct, such materials suggested, actually had numerous victims, from the nation's children to its public health to the national security—indeed, to the very fabric of civilized society. "Homosexuality," as Hurlbut's presentation intoned by way of its parting words to the LAPD recruits, "is the most disruptive of those forces which tend to destroy the home. Thus, complete destruction of society through homosexual marriages would be its logical conclusion." Ostensibly, the paragraph rounded out the longer list of dangers surveyed by the presentation, but in fact it may have supplanted them, uncovering the more inchoate cultural fears lingering beneath the rhetoric of syphilis and treason. Against a backdrop of what many Americans, especially in conservative institutions like police departments, experienced as an unending barrage on traditional family life—a time of birth control and free love, of Betty Friedan and a growing female workforce—some policemen saw the gay world as just the most galling symptom of a broader breakdown in the civic order.[50]

These manuals and lesson plans revealed the range of considerations used to justify the vice squads' continuing campaigns against the gay world in the 1960s. But perhaps as importantly, they demonstrated the police's instinct to justify those campaigns to begin with. Partly, that instinct looked beyond the vice squad itself. By the early 1960s, police officers had grown well aware of the mounting ambivalence within progressive circles about the nation's punitive sex laws. Williams's warnings about the homosexual's "cannibalistic" habits, for instance, came at the start of a special section addressing public opinion on homosexuality, the only such discussion he saw fit to include among the textbook's many chapters. "Many do-gooders and other misinformed people have been asking for more social and official tolerance toward homosexuals," Williams cautioned, before surveying the many ways those critics went awry. At a time when the vice squad campaigns ran up against not only the courts' often-frustrating scrutiny of decoy tactics but also growing public reservations about consensual sexual acts as a criminal concern, decrying the homosexual's predatory habits allowed vice officers to affirm the value of their continuing patrols, explaining why sending decoys to loiter in bathrooms and drink beer in gay bars was a good use of police time.[51]

Partly, however, that defensive instinct looked inside the police department itself. It was vice officers, after all, who were the primary audience for such training materials, and vice officers for whom instructors like Hurlbut and Williams felt the need to recount the many evils of gay life. By the end of the decade, the *Handbook of Vice Control* would address this conflict head-on, acknowledging the ongoing ambivalence "among personnel about the proper role of police action in this area" before launching into its own overview of the predatory homosexual. To some extent, that ambivalence reflected a long-standing discomfort among vice officers, some of whom had always regarded decoy work as sordid and undignified. But it likely also responded to the more specific demands of decoy work in the 1960s. Throughout these years, police departments continued to insist that they cared little about private homosexual conduct, focusing their resources on stamping out the public nuisance resulting from gay bars and cruising grounds. Yet as the flirtation captured by *Life* magazine suggested, vice officers sometimes found themselves devoting all the more time, effort, and patience to arresting gay men the more discreet and unobtrusive their practices became. The subtle codes and affectations that vice officers used to make themselves attractive targets in cruising sites—the meandering conversations, the carefully chosen clothing, the coded body language—made decoy work increasingly demanding even as they illuminated the relative toothlessness of the problem it addressed: a subculture that neither sought to impose itself on uninterested participants nor, typically, succeeded in doing so.[52]

Some officers essentially admitted as much. As a study of vice enforcement around Los Angeles reported in 1966: "Interviews with enforcement agencies indicate that most homosexuals who are 'cruising' for partners do not brazenly solicit the first available male; rather, they will employ glances, gestures, dress and ambiguous conversation to elicit a promising response . . . before an unequivocal solicitation [is tendered]." Recalling his own time patrolling gay bars and cruising sites, Hurlbut conceded that most gay men presented little threat to the public. "Most gays are 'normal' citizens, just leading a different lifestyle," he stated. Even those who drew police attention through their flamboyance or aggressive solicitation were hardly indiscriminate in their flirtations: "Most (but not all) prefer to approach someone they believe shares their sexual preferences." On the basis of his exposure to gay life, indeed, Hurlbut sometimes suspected that certain colleagues in the LAPD were gay, hiding their private lives at a time when the force refused to employ openly homosexual policemen. "Working Vice," he explained, "gives one an insight into sometimes subtle clues that provide strong, if unsubstantiated, insight." He never voiced his suspicions, hesitant to disrupt a man's personal and professional life "over such a personal issue or lifestyle." Nor did he see himself as unusual on that account. In a decade when most Americans still looked on homosexuality with a combination of pity and disgust, the LAPD was no bastion of liberality, but Hurlbut believed that vice officers were often "more understanding and sympathetic than the Department as a whole." Exposed to the complex reality of gay life, some officers who spent their nights enticing solicitations learned to feel some sympathy for the men they arrested.[53]

Against that backdrop, cataloging the purported dangers of the homosexual did not simply allow vice instructors and police officials to rebut what they saw as a misguided strain of liberality among the public. It also allowed them to redress a strain of resistance among police recruits themselves. Insisting that attracting solicitations was effortless—the inevitable destiny of any man who had the misfortune of entering a cruising site—even as they taught their officers precisely how to dress, talk, and act to resemble gay men themselves, vice instructors did their best to persuade new recruits that this genre of enforcement was genuinely important police work. That process of indoctrination helps explain why vice officers continued to decry the public nuisance posed by the gay world even as the logistics of decoy work in the 1960s frequently confirmed the extent to which that world did its best to avoid any such disruptions. By the same token, of course, it suggests the contingency of that zeal, at least among some officers. At a time when judges continued to scrutinize the vice squads' operations and progressive critics questioned the wisdom of criminalizing homosexuality to begin with, enthusiasm for decoy work even within the police department—a conservative institution but not one impervious to the social moods of the day—could not be presumed but required an active process of reminder and reinforcement.

Ethnographic Policing and the Courts

Ultimately, of course, neither recalcitrant vice officers nor liberal do-gooders were the most frustrating critics of the vice squads' campaigns. That distinction went, once again, to the courts.

Like their predecessors, judges in the 1960s continued to bristle at aggressive enticement tactics, dismissing charges when the sheer flagrancy of an officer's trap offended their sense of moral justice. Often, vice officers' increasingly subtle methods hardly helped, forcing officers into extended flirtations and complex charades that bore all the hallmarks of police manipulation. In the fall of 1965, for instance, Officer Stephen Chapwick spent nearly two hours befriending a wary customer at Julius's Restaurant in Greenwich Village until, at around 1:00 A.M., the man finally suggested that they move the conversation to a more intimate setting. Coming into court, the evidence against the defendant was fairly strong. In addition to the alleged proposition, Chapwick testified that the bar was filled with "wiggling" customers, and Julius's own staff found the customer's behavior sufficiently reckless to warn him that he risked a possible arrest. Yet after reviewing all the evidence—not least Chapwick's concession about the time he spent at the bar—the trial judge dismissed the charges on a reasonable doubt as to the defendant's guilt.[54]

In DC, the new decade began with a particularly high-profile denunciation of police enticement. In 1960, after hearing rumors that Calvin Rittenour offered lodging to stray men in exchange for sexual favors, Officer Robert Arscott called him, posing as a potential guest. Claiming that he was "down and out," Arscott invited himself over to Rittenour's apartment, asked to stay the night, and finally elicited an advance in Rittenour's kitchen. On appeal, the DC Municipal Court of Appeals could have reversed the conviction on a statutory point: a private sexual encounter unfolding entirely in the confines of Rittenour's apartment, the solicitation simply fell outside the scope of DC's indecency statute. But the court insisted on addressing the second, "perhaps more important" problem with Rittenour's arrest. "It is very plain from the officer's own admission," the panel decried, that Arscott "trapped the suspect into making a homosexual proposal and then arrested him." Any subsequent charges amounted to prosecuting Rittenour simply because he was homosexual, and "under our law homosexuality is not a crime."[55]

Fortunately for the vice squads, however, most of their arrests of gay men in the 1960s involved nothing so outrageous. For the most part, decoys describing their encounters in the field did not testify that they invited themselves over to a suspect's apartment. They did not recount spending hours flirting in a bar, or exposing themselves in a public bathroom, or even starting up a conversation in a park. Rather, they often claimed that such advances were essentially spontaneous. They insisted, as in the case against Warren Wildeblood in DC, that the defendant struck up a conversation at a bus stop and then invited the officer to have sex back in his apartment. Or, as in the case against Gilbert Mesa of Garden Grove, that the defendant walked up to the officer in a crowded bar, stood between his legs, and began massaging his inner thigh. As an officer with the NYPD's vice division informed the journalist Jess Stearn in 1961, tactics for making solicitation arrests were "often passive, with plain-clothes men patiently waiting around for the suspect to make an advance."[56]

Sometimes, the officers' claims may have been accurate. Some men, always more reckless than others, needed little encouragement to make an advance. Other times, the decoys probably lied or exaggerated, bending the facts to bolster an arrest report. In 1965, for example, the New York patrolman Martin Sweeney arrested the school counselor Harold Bramson at an Upper West Side bar, claiming that Bramson sat down at his table and offered to "go down on" him. Bramson denied both the approach and the offer and convinced a trial judge to acquit him of all charges. Years later, Bramson admitted that he had in fact tendered a sexual proposal that night, but he insisted that Sweeney had approached him first. Initially mistrustful of the stranger, he had opened up only after a half hour of conversation about their favorite music and the neighboring schools the two had attended in their youth.[57]

Yet in many instances, the officers were likely neither exactly lying nor telling the truth. Even the most seemingly spontaneous solicitations that filled police records in the 1960s, after all, did not appear out of thin air. Without the benefit of any vulgar words or overt gestures, they were the

bounty of systematic codes that gay men had developed precisely to identify willing partners in a crowd. When Gilbert Mesa walked up to Officer
Ricketts at the Mug Bar, for instance, he was not approaching an anonymous stranger in public. He was approaching a fellow patron at a gay bar
who had used classic cruising signals to advertise his sexual availability:
sitting with his back against the wall, watching for new arrivals, keeping
his eyes on Mesa as he scanned the room. Mesa's sexual advance may have
been graphic, but there was nothing spontaneous about it. By the same
token, the many men who propositioned vice officers in public bathrooms
after the officers glanced toward their genitals, "giv[ing] no indication . . .
of either encouragement or disgust," may not have seen themselves as making the first move. As the sociologist Laud Humphreys would detail in his
groundbreaking study of tearoom cruising, watching another man's penis
or looking from his crotch directly up into his eyes, precisely with a neutral
expression, was one of the most "encouraging" signals a man searching for
sex in a public bathroom could give.[58]

Used in the right way, those signals could be as powerful as the most
overt enticements decried by some judges. As Humphreys observed, the
seemingly passive methods used by police decoys in public bathrooms—
tapping their feet, swishing by the urinals, making eye contact—were, to
those who spoke the language, invitations to perform a sexual act. "The
decoy approached after such signaling," he explained, "has already indi-
cated his willingness to play the game." Privately, vice officers conceded
as much. The LAPD's routine practice of making "eye-to-eye contact" with
suspects, one decoy confirmed, was "often tantamount to an outright solicitation." Unsurprisingly, in context, gay men themselves in the 1960s
did not see policemen who wore gay fashions, used queer slang, and eyed
other men in bars or bathrooms as "patiently waiting" for an advance.
They saw them as advertising for a sexual partner. As a 1966 study around
Los Angeles found, although policemen drew the line at overt solicitation,
"homosexuals consider any dress, gestures, or language that tends to affect
the character of a homosexual as entrapment." Such accusations were far
from the legal definition of entrapment, but their broad point was one
that many judges had long endorsed: that a decoy who clearly initiated a
sexual encounter should not be allowed to arrest a defendant for responding in kind.[59]

Here, however, some judges drew a line. Like Judge Doyle in Detroit,
who had accused aggressive vice officers of deliberately "maneuver[ing]"
defendants into advances, most judges were not so naive as to believe that
many solicitations were entirely random. They recognized that decoys vis-

ited cruising grounds for the purpose of arresting gay men, and even that decoys went along with friendly conversations once they started. But it did not follow that an officer's apparently passive presence could be deemed to *entice* a sexual advance. In DC, courts refused to accept the suggestion that mere eye contact sufficed to qualify as enticement. In California, as the attorney Herb Selwyn recalled, a defense based on what a policeman wore or where he sat inside a bar could be a long shot even in cases involving the most established cruising signals. When Gilbert Mesa challenged his arrest at the Mug Bar, his defense did not breathe a word about Ricketts's enticing posture or the looks exchanged by the men before Mesa began his approach, relying only on a familiar statutory quibble about whether Mesa's offer of sex at his apartment counted as a "public" proposition.[60]

Some cases did try to raise the defense squarely. The most high-profile of those, *Robillard v. New York*, traced back to the early morning of May 23, 1965, when at approximately 2:00 A.M. Officer Anthony De Greise walked into the crowded Harbor Bar in Greenwich Village. Over the past fifteen weeks, De Greise had arrested nine other men in the city's gay bar scene. Wearing white pants, light sneakers, and a polo shirt, he ordered a beer and sat down by a pool table where Francis Robillard was shooting billiards with John Wrenn and Leroy Snowden. After several minutes, he recounted, Robillard asked the officer for a light and, when De Greise lit his cigarette, introduced him to his friends. The men spent five or six minutes in friendly banter of a nonsexual nature. Finally, Robillard asked if De Greise visited "this type of bar" often, and De Greise said yes. Wrenn asked whether he wanted to come to a "party," and De Greise again agreed. At that point, the conversation turned more graphic. Having speculated on the likely size of De Greise's "joint," the friends allegedly took turns describing how they planned to have sex with him. After the four exited the bar, De Greise identified himself as an officer and arrested them.[61]

Some men arrested for solicitation had trouble finding a good lawyer, or at least one they could afford, but this case caught the eye of an especially high-powered legal representative: the New York Civil Liberties Union (NYCLU), the New York branch of the American Civil Liberties Union (ACLU). The ACLU's official stance on homosexuality had changed little since its 1957 statement disavowing any interest in challenging laws against same-sex practices. Even as more progressive members advocated internally for change, gay men who wrote the national office for assistance in these years were directed, variably, to local homophile groups or psychiatrists. While the national office dragged its feet, however, local affiliates were far more willing to take on the problem of antihomosexual policing, driven not only by their lingering discomfort with plainclothes decoys but also by the strategic influence of homophile activists. Lobbied by organizations like ONE and the Mattachine Society, branches in Washington, Philadelphia, and California grew increasingly involved in the gay community's legal struggles in the early 1960s, speaking at homophile conferences, decrying the termination of gay employees, and protesting the lack of due process in bar raids. When the NYCLU learned of the arrests at the Harbor Bar that May, it too decided to enter the fray.[62]

At trial, the defendants first tried simply denying the charges. As Robillard and Snowden testified, it was De Greise who approached them at the bar, invited them to his apartment, and insisted on accompanying them when they finally left for the night. By this account, there was no sexual advance to justify the arrests. Anticipating that their story might not sway a judge, however, the NYCLU lawyers also insisted that De Greise invited any advances the defendants may have made. As the officer himself testified, he lit Robillard's cigarette, hinted that he came to gay bars often, and made no objections when Robillard first touched his thigh. Even his clothing, the defense pushed De Greise to admit, was chosen to blend into the cruising scene, an attempt to "be in with the patrons of" a Greenwich Village gay bar. The defense initially meant to make a statutory point of the kind that generous New York judges had long embraced: Robillard and his friends could hardly have risked disturbing the peace if they extended their invitation to someone who gave every indication that he welcomed it. But it soon turned the same evidence into an argument for entrapment. Sitting alone in a gay bar, wearing the gay world's telltale fashions, watching and flirting with other customers, De Greise had essentially invited the three defendants to solicit him.[63]

The trial court was not convinced. Without issuing an opinion, it convicted Robillard, Snowden, and Wrenn of disorderly conduct. Recognizing a potential test case, the NYCLU appealed to the appellate division of the New York Supreme Court, where it revisited, again, the power of De Greise's signals during the encounter. Even if the officer did not tender the first verbal invitation, the attorneys Shirley Fingerhood and Henry di Suvero insisted, "sexual behavior is known to consist of more than words." Just as a prostitute who "dresses in the garb of her trade and takes an appropriate stance" could be convicted of "soliciting even though the customer is the one who speaks the words of invitation," so De Greise's coded fashions, warm responses, and coy admissions about "types" of gay bars were all signals "designed to invite sexual overtures" from the defendants.[64]

Once more without opinion, the court affirmed, and, having exhausted its state options, the NYCLU tried a final hand with the US Supreme Court. Newly helmed by Morton P. Cohen, the defense alerted the Court to the latest research on the symbolic significance of gay cruising signals. Sexual advances in the gay world, Cohen reported on the basis of the 1966 study of vice enforcement in Los Angeles, are typically tendered "only if the other individual appears responsive," an inference based on "quiet conversation and the use of gestures and signals having significance only to other homosexuals." Accordingly, any adoption of specialized gay signals by plainclothes decoys—"*any* dress, language or gestures" that "indicate a desire for a homosexual relationship"—should be recognized in their unique cultural context as overt statements of sexual availability. Absent De Greise's deliberate fashions and subtle signs of sexual interest—obscure codes developed and used only by a self-selected group to discern partners in a crowd—men like Robillard, Wrenn, and Snowden would never have even considered making him their offer.[65]

Opposing the petition, District Attorney Frank S. Hogan rejected Cohen's finer points of sociological analysis. As to the statutory requirement of an intent to disturb the peace, Hogan reasoned that a homosexual solicitation was obviously liable to incite a reasonable man toward violence, "implying, as it does, that the addressee is a pervert." As to entrapment, the doctrine was hardly a constitutional matter, and even if it were, it did not apply to De Greise's arrests at the Harbor Bar. As defined by the Supreme Court, Hogan reminded the Court, entrapment required proof of both a "persistent" policeman and an "innocent" defendant. Here, the defense had neither. Happy to invite a stranger home "after an innocuous five minute conversation devoid of any conversation concerning sex," Robillard, Wrenn, and Snowden clearly had a predisposition toward homosexual conduct, and De Greise himself, merely by engaging in friendly banter with them, did nothing that might reasonably have invited an advance.[66]

The case split the justices' law clerks. Lewis Merrifield, a clerk to the famously liberal Justice William Douglas and himself a critic of police misconduct, was compelled by Cohen's argument that the officer's subtle camouflage precluded application of New York's disorderly conduct laws. "Perhaps the average person would be tempted to hit a person who made homosexual advances," Merrifield granted in his memo. "But I doubt that this can be said of a person who has gone to a homosexual bar, dressed as a homosexual." Yet his colleagues, even on the Court's progressive wing, refused to read as much significance into the cultural intricacies outlined in Cohen's brief. Even if De Greise's "special attire" and friendly banter suggested his "willingness to participate in homosexual activity," concluded the law clerk for Chief Justice Earl Warren, that did not change the fact that "all of the advances were initiated" by the defendants, who must have known that "a total stranger might react violently to their proposals." Justice Abe Fortas's clerk denounced the implication that, merely by sitting in a gay bar dressed as a homosexual, De Greise could be seen as having invited a sexual advance. "If that's entrapment," Daniel Levitt quipped, "then banks 'entrap' bank robbers by virtue of their very existence." Characterizing the defendants' proposition as a spontaneous invitation extended to a "total stranger"—de Greise's special attire and banter notwithstanding— the clerks acknowledged neither the extent to which gay men like Robillard, Snowden, and Wrenn used such deliberate fashions, postures, and conversational clues to identify willing partners, nor the extent to which such codes could start a sexual negotiation before any overt words were spoken. But their skepticism prevailed: the Supreme Court refused to hear the case, leaving any continuing debate about the expressive significance of gay cruising culture to the lower courts.[67]

The clerks' memorandums in *Robillard* reveal the cultural blind spots persisting among courts in the 1960s regarding the codes and customs that governed gay communities. Downplaying De Greise's role in initiating the encounter, the clerks simultaneously denied the cultural insights that many vice officers, including the "actors" at the NYPD, saw as the hallmark of an effective decoy: their ability to use the language of the gay world to infiltrate and participate in urban cruising culture. Looking at the record of De Greise's actions in the Harbor Bar, Kranwinkle and Levitt saw, at most, a gay man drinking beer and answering some casual questions by a pool table. They did not consider that Robillard, Snowden, and Wrenn may have seen anything else.

Here, then, was the final virtue of the police's growing intimacy with queer life in the 1960s. At a time when many judges continued to recoil against what they saw as overly aggressive or manipulative decoy methods, the vice squads' ethnographic tactics did not simply slip past the defenses of gay men in the field. They also slipped past the scrutiny of the courts. Decoys who changed into sneakers and sport coats before heading to Greenwich Village, leaned against the walls in gay bars, or slyly watched suspects in public bathrooms emulated a subtle, often obscure language developed in an exclusive sexual community—a language whose utility depended on precisely how few people were expected to know it. And most judges, clerks, and jurors in the 1960s were not among those few. From arrest to conviction, the success of the vice squads' decoy campaigns thus rested not only on vice officers' own insights into the social organization of

gay life, but also on how very unusual those insights were: on the disconnect between the police officers who appreciated the power of the subtlest
codes exchanged in cruising sites and the judges who sometimes failed to
recognize that such codes even existed.

In this sense, the history of the vice squads' decoy campaigns does not
simply complicate the origins of queer ethnography in the late 1950s, un-
earthing the role of the police in developing new knowledge about gay life.
It also complicates the politics of police knowledge itself, exposing the unusual ways that police officers' cultural insights played out in court. That
story suggests that the vice squads' campaigns against gay men sometimes
hung on a gap between how different actors in the legal system understood
the nature of same-sex practice: a disagreement among judges and vice
squads about not only the ethics of decoy enforcement but also the practices and patterns of urban gay life. To the extent that the codes and contours of gay cruising culture presented such a powerful tool in the hands
of the vice squad, it was not because excavating those codes was an inherently regulatory project, or even because the police were institutionally
motivated to put their insights to such use. It was because of the gap that
such insights opened up between the different legal agents who shaped gay
men's rights and freedoms at midcentury—the divergence between what
the policemen responsible for arresting gay men and the judges responsible for overseeing their arrests knew about the nature of gay life.

In that, too, that history highlights the unusual institutional incentives
created by the police's enticement campaigns. The vice squads' newly ethnographic tactics emerged during the heyday of police professionalization,
when police officers commonly defended the legitimacy of their investigative tactics by emphasizing their expert knowledge about criminal cultures. Yet in the case of the vice squads' operations, law enforcement agents
took precisely the opposite approach. At a time when some judges questioned both the wisdom of criminal sanctions against homosexuality and
the morality of proactive vice squad methods, plainclothes decoys and the
prosecutors defending their arrests often found it more useful to downplay
the cultural insights and investigative skills that made decoys so effective
on the streets. As those operations demonstrate, the promise of police expertise at midcentury—the notion that criminal cultures are governed by a
set of reliable codes and that officers boast some unique fluency in those
signals—did not necessarily bolster the legitimacy of police tactics or inspire deference in court. In the context of the vice squads' antihomosexual
arrests, depicting officers as experts at the controversial task of eliciting

solicitations fed a defense strategy of decrying manipulative decoy tactics. And clever prosecutors did their best to avoid it.

The history of the vice squads' shifting decoy tactics in the 1960s, in short, exemplifies both the continuing controversies inspired by the police's campaigns and the persistent, surprising intersections between changing understandings of same-sex practices and the legal regulation of gay life. That story unearths the regulatory underside of the ethnographic discovery of the gay world, a seemingly liberal project refined and operationalized, in the first instance, by police officers tasked with constricting the freedoms of queer communities. It confirms the growing qualms inspired by the use of plainclothes tactics against what some contemporaries saw as an essentially victimless morals offense: the extent to which the decoys tasked with infiltrating gay social spaces in the 1960s labored to persuade themselves, and others, of the continuing value of their work. Not least, it reveals how, bucking a broader trend among police departments in these years, vice squads defended themselves against external criticism by downplaying the professional insights that facilitated their arrests—avoiding judicial scrutiny, in effect, by obscuring their entanglement in a controversial enforcement tactic. More than the legal system's fissures over the merits of antihomosexual policing, courtroom debates over plainclothes policing in these years unearth the critical epistemic divides that attended the regulation of a contested social practice: how vice officers' and judges' moral disputes about the value of certain police operations were matched, and sometimes ironically mediated, by their definitional disagreements about the very thing being policed.

Plainclothes enticement, of course, was not the only controversial tactic employed by the vice squads in these years. As decoys attuned to the increasingly coded nature of gay cruising did their best to infiltrate that culture, some of their colleagues took a different approach, developing novel ways to observe the cruising world from the outside. Those modes of surveillance avoided the same concerns about the manipulation of innocent suspects. But they soon inspired their own questions about the limits of ethical policing.

FIVE

Peepholes and Perverts

On the night of October 1, 1961, Officer Walter Hetzel of the Long Beach Police Department climbed to the top of an outhouse at the Nu-Pike Amusement Park. There, just off the shore of the Pacific Ocean, by the glow of a nearby Ferris wheel, Hetzel looked down at a scene he would describe in court using far less romantic terms. Enlisted by the Nu-Pike's owner to "do something" about the men who frequented the park's toilets for sex, the department had installed a foot-long pipe through the roof of the men's room, allowing a partial view into each of two separate adjoining booths. And it was through this pipe, that autumn evening, that Hetzel watched two men engage in a sexual act through an opening in the wall, each thinking himself fully shielded from view.[1]

From bars to parks to street corners, vice squads at midcentury patrolled a range of settings popular with men looking for sexual partners. But public restrooms inspired particular interest. More than a place to meet kindred spirits, bathrooms provided a convenient setting for the sexual act itself—a fact that made those facilities, as the vice squads saw it, both a special public nuisance and the rare chance to make felony arrests. Apprehending the men suspected of such practices, however, was more easily said than done. Of all the systematic codes developed by queer men seeking partners in the mid-twentieth century, perhaps none were as systematic or effective as those used to consummate sexual acts in men's rooms. As the sociologist Laud Humphreys observed in his landmark study of tearoom cruising in the late 1960s, men who pursued sexual contacts in bathrooms developed a range of "defenses against outsiders," from body language to spatial cues to audio signals, that allowed them both to initiate encounters and, just as quickly, to conceal them on a stranger's approach. Those safeguards let cruisers pursue their activities beneath the noses of passersby, property owners, and policemen alike—to maintain, as Humphreys put it, "privacy in public."[2]

Frustrated by those codes, officers like Hetzel found themselves forced to adopt a stealthier approach. From one-way mirrors to fake air vents to peepholes drilled directly behind toilets, police departments at midcentury devised a range of surreptitious tactics for spying on the interiors of public bathrooms. The diversity of those tactics is notable in its own right, a case study of the struggle between the police and gay men over the permissible use of public space. Trading in the possibility that innocent citizens might be exposed to careless cruisers for the near certainty that they would be exposed to peering policemen, the police's operations laid bare not just criminalized conduct but also hundreds of law-abiding men, unaware that their most private acts were being watched by the state. More than any other tool of vice enforcement, clandestine surveillance exemplifies the extent to which the states' antihomosexual campaigns redounded to the indignity of all citizens, gay and straight. And it exemplifies the viscerally unpleasant work that vice officers often performed in order to crack down on what they saw as a uniquely outrageous manifestation of gay life. The very sordidness of clandestine surveillance made it an unpopular assignment, begrudged by officers for its demands on both their time and dignity. But the tactic was, they conceded, necessary: the only way to apprehend a group of offenders whose subterfuges let them avoid discovery through less intrusive means.

If clandestine surveillance sat poorly with some officers, of course, it fared even worse with the men arrested through those campaigns. Desperate to clear their names of charges far more serious than solicitation or disorderly conduct, many men prosecuted for cruising mounted robust legal defenses, leaving behind especially detailed records of how the vice squads' campaigns played out in court. Some questioned the reliability of the evidence, impugning the motives and morals of officers who spent their hours spying on public toilets. Others appealed to judicial sympathies, parading their friends, colleagues, and wives as witnesses to their fundamentally decent character—a strategy particularly attractive to defendants whose life histories appealed directly to the judges' own spirit of neighborliness. Those efforts did not typically suffice to win an acquittal, but they often succeeded at painting a rich picture of the men caught in the states' campaigns, as husbands, fathers, and pillars of the community, whose misdeeds, it often appeared, harmed their own happiness and reputations more than society at large.

The legal battles inspired by the vice squads' surveillance arrests provide a unique window into the legal system's continuing controversies over the value of antihomosexual enforcement: why so many trial judges at mid-century pushed back against vice squads' charges against gay men, or at the very least tried to mitigate their harshest effects. More than simply their comparatively liberal views of sexual difference, impatience with petty charges, or even discomfort with aggressive police tactics, trial judges' frequent equanimity toward homosexual offenders also reflected the unique theater of the courtroom, which offered an unusually rich view of the lives caught in the vice squads' operations. If trial judges lacked the police's systematic insight into the social organization of the gay world, after all, they often claimed far superior insight into the human facts of each case, including not only a man's criminal offense but also the broader tapestry of his personal, professional, and civic life. Keeping those details in mind, they often saw the men arrested in public bathrooms less as threats to the community than as decent citizens who had made one mortifying mistake. And at sentencing, they took that view into account.

Beyond questioning the strength of the evidence, some men arrested in public bathrooms challenged the practice of clandestine surveillance itself, a gambit that often took them out of trial and into the appellate courts. The vice squads' surveillance tactics raised close constitutional questions, touching on a range of legal controversies from the courts' willingness to recognize a broad right to privacy to their appetite for flatly prohibiting established police practices. But one factor hanging over all these questions was the appellate panels' precise view of the conduct targeted by the vice squads' campaigns, a vision frequently far afield from both the reality of contemporary cruising practices and the attitudes of lower courts. Even as trial judges dismissed defendants as petty offenders, and as police officials admitted that they turned to clandestine surveillance only because cruisers so assiduously avoided exposure through other means, appellate courts frequently justified those tactics as necessary to beat back an exhibitionistic criminal culture. Drawing on lingering stereotypes of gay men as sexual psychopaths and child molesters, the appellate courts sanctioned an investigative technique adopted in response to the insular habits of cruisers by portraying those men as predators worthy of the police's most intensive campaigns.

The sinister rhetoric buttressing the appellate courts' defense of clandestine surveillance encapsulates how judicial understandings of same-sex practices shaped the legal rights of queer men in the mid-twentieth century. Not only in discretionary matters like sentencing but even in the resolution of constitutional questions, the law's treatment of homosexual offenders came down to the courts' conceptions of who the prototypical homosexual was: the tragic family man evoked by defense attorneys or the violent predator of the sexual psychopath debates.

More fundamentally, however, that rhetoric illuminates the lingering impact of the criminal justice system's divergent understandings of same-sex practices: the extent to which police officers' and judges' distinct presumptions about queer men and their habits buttressed the vice squads' most contentious operations. As with the departments' decoy arrests, after all, it was ultimately not the appellate courts' own sinister view of cruising culture that facilitated police surveillance campaigns in public bathrooms, so much as how that view departed from the police's own perceptions. Exposed to the realities of the urban gay world, vice officers recognized the covert and coded practices that characterized tearoom cruising. They turned to clandestine surveillance largely as a concession to those codes. Yet in court, their controversial tactics survived legal challenge in key part through the appellate courts' insistence that cruisers, far from carefully avoiding public exposure, were constantly on the cusp of revelation— through the courts' blindness, in effect, to the cultural conditions that necessitated the very tactics they assessed.

Drawing on the unusually detailed court records left by the states' sodomy-related prosecutions, this chapter examines the vice squads' surveillance campaigns to shed new light on the ethical and epistemic conflicts inspired by the policing of queer practices at midcentury. Police surveillance operations in the postwar years epitomize the excesses of the states' campaigns against gay men, a regulatory project that always, inevitably, also expanded the states' intrusions into the broader spaces of urban life. They illustrate the extent to which the legal system's ongoing disagreements over the value of antihomosexual enforcement reflected the unique professional experiences of its various agents—not only vice officers exposed to cruising practices in the field, but also trial judges exposed to defendants' wide-ranging legal strategies in court. And they demonstrate how, within that deeply contested space, the continuing vitality of the vice squads' controversial tactics rested in key part on a gap between how vice officers, trial judges, and even appellate panels understood the conduct targeted by their campaigns. More than just the social costs of antihomosexual policing or the power of the trial in fostering divisions in the justice system, the beleaguered history of clandestine surveillance confirms the abiding link between queer men's legal status and the law's divergent views of same-sex practices: the legal system's many ways of understanding—and misunderstanding—the nature of queer life.

Peepholes, Pipes, and One-Way Mirrors

By the time the appellate courts turned to the police's clandestine surveillance campaigns in the early 1960s, neither homosexual trysts in city toilets nor the police's furtive observation of those trysts were novel phenomena. Indeed, it would not be facetious to say that men began using public restrooms for sexual encounters as soon as there were public restrooms. In New York City, the first reports of sex in lavatories date back to 1896, right after the first facilities opened in City Hall and Battery Park. Once the city made toilets available in its subway stations, they became an especially popular destination for anonymous encounters. A private inspector making his rounds in 1927 expressed no surprise when "two sets of legs in [the] toilet enclosure" led him to discover two men "committing an act of perversion" in a Harlem subway station.[3]

Arising long before the emergence of more organized queer communities in the nation's cities, the practice of tearoom cruising in many ways remained separate from the center of gay life in the postwar years. Homophile groups like the Mattachine Society shunned the convention of public sex, hardly an aid to their efforts to cast gay men as respectable citizens. Even the more casual communities that sprouted around working-class bars, often themselves disdained by homophiles for their flamboyance and overt sexuality, looked down on the tearoom as the nadir of the queer social hierarchy.[4]

Nor, for their part, did men who sought sex in public bathrooms necessarily seek the affinity of the organized gay world. At a time when social stigma led many men to downplay their sexual practices not simply to others but also to themselves, it was not medical professionals alone who diverged on whether same-sex desire was a passing temptation or a psychosexual identity. Many frequenters of bathroom cruising sites—often referred to in the sociological literature simply as *cruisers*—declined to identify as homosexual in their daily lives. That may have been particularly true of the most committed cruisers: not self-identified gay men like Dale Jennings, who may have picked up an evening's companion in a bathroom just as they would in a park or bar, but those who declined to bring lovers back to their apartments, preferring to consummate the entire encounter in a bathroom stall. For some, that choice was likely a matter of economic necessity, accommodating the limits of privacy in crowded boardinghouses or homes shared with extended families. But for others, it reflected a deliberately compartmentalized approach to such sexual indulgences. As late as the end of the 1960s, Humphreys found that a majority of cruisers lived otherwise conventional married lives, seeing their homosexual encounters as an intermittent, if unsavory, habit.[5]

Nevertheless, these communities were not entirely distinct. Whether or not they admitted it, many gay men, including wealthier men, cruised for sex in public bathrooms, drawn by the adventure of the setting. Homophile publications like *ONE* commonly referenced cruising in their discussions of police repression. And if cruisers did not constitute as cohesive a social community as the gay men who joined homophile societies or frequented gay bars, the cruising world in many ways arose in parallel to the gay world, fueled by the same pressures and fears of discovery. Not least, it shared the gay world's characteristic incentives toward stealth—some systematic, subtle language for identifying partners.[6]

Starting with the early twentieth century and coalescing following World War II, accordingly, cruising itself developed into something of a systematized subculture, with its own protocols for finding fellow cruisers and carrying out sexual encounters. Some of those codes were shared with gay pickup culture more broadly. Like men looking for an evening's partner, veteran cruisers made extended eye contact, jingled keys or loose change in their pockets, and tapped their feet in toilet stalls. Where previous patrons had cut glory holes in the partitions—the better both to identify potential partners and to hide their activities from others—inserting a finger through the opening was a universal advertisement for a sexual act.[7]

Other codes catered to the particular needs of the cruiser, who not only sought sexual partners but also consummated the act in a semipublic place. Beyond adopting a secret language for initiating sexual encounters, cruisers developed a range of techniques for shielding those encounters once they began, avoiding exposure to the strangers ever at risk of passing by. Popular tearooms were typically chosen for their relative inaccessibility: both their geographic isolation from the crowds, often in remote areas or economically dilapidated neighborhoods, and any physical quirks that revealed when others were approaching, such as creaking entryways or sticky front doors. Positioning themselves by lavatory windows or listening for the sounds of clanging doors, washroom regulars cut short their trysts at the first sign of a stranger's entry. Around more highly trafficked areas, they enlisted third parties to act as lookouts. And even having picked a relatively safe location, experienced cruisers stayed vigilant, keeping their clothing as unperturbed as possible in order to cover their activities at a moment's notice. Altogether, these defense strategies proved quite reliable. Researchers who studied cruising in the 1960s reported that the practice was remarkably discreet, initiated through subtle signals and "abruptly discontinued at [a stranger's] approach." Even when he deliberately walked in on pairs he believed to be having a sexual encounter, Humphreys reported, they had typically abandoned any incriminating acts.[8]

The effectiveness of those codes put the police in a difficult position. On the one hand, the fact that some men used public restrooms for sex was hardly a secret. Although urban Americans often remained oblivious to the gay bars that opened and closed in their cities, the unique nature of the public bathroom—a space used throughout the day by all sorts of men to shield their most private bodily activities—inspired greater sensitivities. By the mid-1950s, popular tearooms provided the police departments with a steady stream of complaints from residents, property owners, and street vendors. Newspapers and radio stations reported on the problem of sex crimes in downtown theaters and bus stations, yet another manifestation of the urban blight that simultaneously resulted from and drove the flight of middle-class Americans from cities following the war. "Any man in his right mind," as one man protested after his arrest in a Los Angeles restroom in 1953, would "kn[ow] what kind of place it was."[9]

For all those complaints, however, few witnesses could claim to have seen a sexual act in progress. As with police reports of homosexual activities in parks and bars, complaints about public bathrooms typically recounted not sexual misconduct, but the incidental traces of a popular cruising ground: holes cut between the stalls, suggestive writing on the walls, accounts of "feminine" men idling around the premises. In the rare case, citizens reported patrons masturbating or even propositioning strangers. But stories of men caught in flagrante by private citizens were all but unheard of. Policemen assigned to patrol cruising sites fared no better. Like Humphreys, police chiefs who sent officers to check on suspected tearooms or tasked plainclothesmen with loitering around the premises found such tactics ineffectual at exposing the illicit acts they were certain occurred inside. As one police department reported in 1963, assigning undercover officers to patrol a known cruising sites by periodically stepping inside the bathrooms "produced no results."[10]

Some departments relied on more proactive tactics. Decoys assigned to loiter in public bathrooms, after all, targeted tearoom cruisers no less than gay men looking for a night's companion. Yet for all their effectiveness when it came to making individual arrests in bars and parks, plainclothes decoys were not an especially useful tool for averting cruising activity in men's rooms. For one thing, while gay bars tended to cluster in urban centers, popular cruising sites were often geographically dispersed, and departments in smaller towns lacked the resources and the sophistication to rely exclusively on undercover officers. Even among well-staffed and highly trained departments, like the Los Angeles Police Department (LAPD), solicitation arrests were often too slow going a tactic to make a real dent in the most active locations. And decoys who spent too much time in a given bathroom risked becoming recognized by veteran cruisers, a significant problem given the vice squads' limited manpower.[11]

Frustrated, many departments thus turned to a more resilient mode of enforcement—one that would allow officers to watch cruisers without their ever realizing they were being observed. Like cruising itself, police surveillance was hardly new to public bathrooms following the war. As early as the 1910s, departments in major cities sent officers to keep watch for sexual misconduct from secret cavities in public lavatories. Despite its extended pedigree, however, clandestine surveillance was not an especially popular tactic. To begin with, there were the frustrating logistics of mounting an effective operation. Although some bathrooms came with natural observation spots, such as open windows or large air vents, devising an effective post often required time, planning, and effort. Those resources were entirely wasted once word that a particular site was being watched got out, a significant risk given cruisers' many strategies for identifying and alerting each other to the police's surveillance campaigns.[12]

Beyond its practical inconvenience were the mixed feelings surveillance inspired among vice officers themselves. Certainly, some policemen approached such assignments with relative equanimity, recognizing them as both easy and relatively restful, far from the hazards that accompanied more dangerous work in the field. Some even managed to find hidden perks to the task. Describing his typical routine patrolling a May Company department store in 1956, one LAPD veteran moonlighting as a security guard confided that he often stretched out his time observing the men's room from a utility closet in order to enjoy a cigarette. "It is a nice place to smoke," Officer Charles Glazer explained. "Besides you are not supposed to smoke in public."[13]

For the most part, however, surveillance work elicited a particular distaste within the vice squad. In a realm of enforcement that some officers already saw as lowering the dignity of the department, spying on men's bodily functions—sexual and otherwise—in public bathrooms struck many as an especially tawdry task. As Max Hurlbut of the LAPD recalled: "I never knew a Vice Officer who enjoy[ed] 'toilet duty.'" Some channeled their discomfort into black humor, spreading urban legends of cruisers impaled by icepicks or penises protruding through glory holes only to be sliced off by unappreciative neighbors. Others balked at the assignment altogether. In the Miami Police Department in the early 1960s, the vice division included among its members one Sergeant John Sorenson, a devoutly religious man known to both the gay community and the local press for his unusual fervor for antihomosexual arrests. Eager to stem the ostensible tide of degeneracy in his city, Sorenson distributed, at his own cost, booklets to youths he suspected of homosexuality, warning of their eternal damnation. Asked whether such fatalistic literature might push impressionable readers toward suicide, he conceded: "It's a possibility." Yet Sorenson had his limits, refusing to accept any clandestine surveillance assignments. Even among those officers who most ardently supported the vice squad's work, the work of watching homosexual intimacies in public bathrooms sometimes proved too much to stomach.[14]

For others, of course, that was precisely what made clandestine surveillance worth the effort. Most police officials justified surveillance by invoking the same rhetoric used to explain decoy campaigns, denouncing cruisers as both a public nuisance and a threat to public safety. But there was, to the minds of some officers and politicians, a difference between men who solicited other men in gay bars and those suspected of having sex in public bathrooms. The unique aversion inspired by such public activities was the reason that publications like *Homosexuality and Citizenship in Florida* focused on tearoom cruising in denouncing the "abomination" of homosexuality. Defendants arrested on these types of charges, and especially men of color, commonly reported abusive treatment by arresting officers: unprovoked bursts of physical aggression, mockery on the ride to the station, and a refusal, as though in a sudden fit of modesty, to apprise suspects of the actual charges against them. If vice officers sometimes dismissed decoy arrests as relatively petty cases, few lodged the same complaint about the charges brought through their surveillance operations.[15]

And if the goal was punishing that particular brand of criminal conduct, then, for all its shortcomings, clandestine surveillance boasted some unmatched advantages. Most obviously, the tactic avoided the shortfalls of uniformed and decoy patrol, eluding veteran cruisers' warning systems and immune to concerns about facial recognition. Departments that took the time to devise an effective observation post were often amply rewarded for their efforts. A two-week campaign in a railway station in Palo Alto in 1956 yielded criminal charges against twenty-three suspects. A single sting at the Lincoln Park Zoo in Oklahoma City in 1958 led to ten arrests. One observation post in a Long Beach restroom in the early 1960s ended in charges against seventy men over the course of a year.[16]

Clandestine surveillance also offered police departments something few other tactics promised: it was their best and often effectively their only option for making felony arrests. The harshest weapon in the states' legal arsenal against gay men, laws against actual sex acts were notoriously hard to enforce, plagued by all the evidentiary problems of a crime typically committed privately between willing participants. Encounters in quasi-public spaces like bathrooms provided a key exception. Appreciating that rare opportunity, some officers approached clandestine surveillance less with an eye toward preventing public sex than toward subjecting it to the gravest possible punishments. From Los Angeles to Minnesota, departments frequently left the physical hallmarks of an active tearoom undisturbed, declining to plug glory holes or erase suggestive graffiti that might attract new cruisers to the site. And although some agencies, including the LAPD, instructed their officers to intervene the moment they had grounds for an arrest, many officers continued to observe suspected cruisers until they saw some evidence of penetration, waiting for a flirtation to turn into a felony. Some units openly encouraged the practice. Unsurprisingly, by the mid-1960s, in the Los Angeles area surveillance was responsible for a full 93 percent of all felony indictments.[17]

Buoyed by these considerations, the use of clandestine surveillance proliferated following the war, from coastal hubs like Los Angeles and New York City to smaller cities in Kansas, Georgia, and Ohio. Surveillance typically occurred on public property, such as train stations, bus terminals, parks, libraries, and beaches. Responding to the complaints of local business owners, however, it also reached a range of private establishments, including theaters, department stores, amusement parks, and gas stations. The technique even made its way onto military grounds. In 1958, investigators with the Department of Defense photographed a series of sexual encounters in a men's room on the second floor of the Pentagon. Although no agency ever claimed responsibility for the operation, the Office of Naval Intelligence admitted that it used the photographs in investigating homosexuality among its sailors.[18]

Especially in the early 1950s, the logistics of surveillance were fairly straightforward. Police departments often did little planning, relying on preexisting openings built into the structure of a public restroom to spy on the activities inside. At one bus terminal in Los Angeles in 1950, officers observed men having sex from a pair of windows on the sides of the men's room. In Columbus, Georgia, policemen climbed to a canopy roof abutting a bus station men's room and watched the interior through an open window.[19]

As the decade progressed, some departments also grew more resourceful, deliberately adapting the physical features of the men's room for law enforcement purposes. Failing to find adequate preexisting openings, some officers and business owners drilled peepholes that looked directly into the bathroom stalls. In a park by Playa del Rey in Los Angeles, for instance, policemen carved a series of peepholes facing the toilets on the other side, allowing them to take turns peering into each stall from a neighboring chamber. In San Francisco, the owners of the Paris Theatre drilled "observation holes" through the marble wall right behind the toilet, offering officers a particularly intimate view of their customers. Illicit sexual activities—as well as other "uneventful" acts—occurred "almost directly in front of" their eyes. Most departments trusted that a restroom's patrons would overlook such subtle alterations, but some took greater precautions. In addition to the handful of active peepholes in the Playa del Rey men's room, vice officers made use of a "decoy": a more conspicuous hole carved in the center of one stall, promptly labeled by observant cruisers ("Cop's Peephole. Beware") and plugged up with toilet paper. The false security created by the plug, Officer Richard Barlow explained, made his observations through the remaining peepholes all the more productive.[20]

Other departments turned to more innovative camouflage. Many repurposed common architectural features, like utility closets, metal vents, and air ducts above the ceiling, as makeshift observation stations. In an Emporium department store in Santa Clara in 1962, patrolmen armed with radio transmitters and cameras crouched in a small passage space above the men's room, looking through two overhead air vents into the enclosed toilet stalls below. At the Art Theater in Los Angeles, police officers climbed into a plumbing access hole just above the sink, watching the restroom through a screen covering their entrance.[21]

In some cases, law enforcement agents installed false air vents purely as a cover for their observations. In the summer of 1963, the manager of Camp Curry, a privately operated resort in Yosemite National Park, began receiving unusually graphic complaints: patrons in the men's room had idled and even approached other men for acts of "a homosexual nature." A survey of the grounds confirmed that someone had cut waist-high holes in the toilet stall partitions and that men "whose appearance suggested homosexuals" loitered about the premises. The walls surrounding the bathroom stalls were mounted fairly high, beginning eighteen inches above the ground. Yet the park's law enforcement specialist, Ranger Twight, concluded that that design prevented his agents from catching sight of any criminal activity, making "undercover observation of [the] rest room . . . necessary." On his advice, the manager cut observation holes in the ceiling above each toilet stall and covered them with wire screens. Starting at roughly 11:00 P.M. each night, Twight and a photographer stationed in the attic used those vents to observe the sexual—and scatological—acts taking place below.[22]

As in the operation at Camp Curry, photo and video technologies played an ever-greater role in clandestine surveillance in the postwar years. As far back as the 1910s, some police departments had taken photographs of the offending restrooms, trying to give judges and jurors a better sense of the spaces where their operations took place. By the 1960s, officers commonly brought cameras and even video recorders to their nightly stings, capturing images of the suspects themselves. Some turned to even more advanced technologies. In 1962, Philadelphia's morals squad advised a local YMCA to invest nearly $2,000 in video surveillance equipment. Mounted behind one-way aluminum screens in the men's room, the cameras transmitted live footage of homosexual encounters directly to the building's security detail. By the end of the decade, departments in beach cities like Miami and Laguna Beach—as well as the less exotic Lake Milton, Ohio— had availed themselves of similar techniques. Such documentary evidence bolstered the prosecution's case in court, assuaging judicial concerns about uncorroborated police testimony. It also allowed the police to prolong the usefulness of any given surveillance site, gathering evidence against numerous men before exposing their operation through an arrest.[23]

Perhaps the most notorious surveillance operation of the 1960s, however, traced neither to the locker rooms of Philadelphia nor to the beaches of California but to the industrial town of Mansfield, Ohio. Officers with the Mansfield Police Department had long seen the men's room in the city's Central Park as a dangerous area, "frequently the site of beatings and robberies." In the summer of 1962, they also came to suspect it as a site of homosexual activity, after a young man arrested for assaulting a teenager confessed that he was thrown "along the path of sex deviation" after receiving a blow job inside. Further investigation confirmed that a hole three-fourths of an inch wide had been cut between two stalls—too small to use for sexual encounters, but providing a convenient signaling system for cruisers. Armed with this information, the department embarked on a rigorous campaign to stamp out the lavatory's seedier uses. It first tried sending plainclothes officer to loiter around the grounds in hopes of stumbling on criminal activity, but that strategy, Police Chief Clare Kyler reported, "proved fruitless." Frustrated, it turned to clandestine surveillance as "the only type of investigation which would be of any use."[24]

Prior to the investigation, a paper towel dispenser with a small mirror had hung over a service closet by the door. Over a weekend of advertised renovations, the Mansfield Police Department replaced the mirror with one-way glass and hollowed out the dispenser to fit a camera. The plan was to station one officer inside the closet with instructions to film men "acting suspiciously or committing acts of sexual perversion." The Mansfield police took every precaution to make their campaign as effective as possible. Officers repainted the walls a lighter shade of gray and installed brighter light bulbs to optimize film quality. They mounted an exhaust fan to cover the vibrations of the camera. They even equipped the photographer with a stack of paper towels so that he could periodically refill the dispenser's dramatically reduced capacity. Once the finishing touches were set, Lieutenant Bill Spognardi and two colleagues took turns manning the post.

5.1. The interior of the men's room in Mansfield's Central Park, as printed in the *FBI Enforcement Bulletin*, June 1963. The storage closet with the towel dispenser is visible in the back. Courtesy of United States Department of Justice.

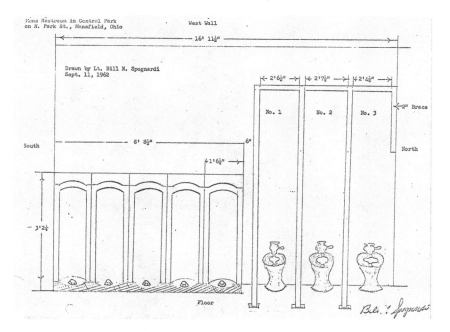

5.2. A diagram of the Central Park men's room, drawn by Lieutenant Bill Spognardi of the Mansfield Police Department. From the Collections of the Kinsey Institute, Indiana University. All rights reserved.

Originally intended to last throughout the summer, Mansfield's operation was cut short after two weeks, when Spognardi broke cover to arrest a man who had exposed himself to a teenager. Yet after just those fourteen days, the police department found itself in possession of some seventeen hundred feet of film, capturing at least sixty-five men engaging in sexual misconduct—as well as dozens who committed no criminal acts of any sort. The sting was a media coup. Over the next four years, the pages of the *Mansfield News-Journal* swelled with accounts of the trials of and the sentences handed down against the men caught on Spognardi's camera. Kyler himself adroitly fed the public interest, playing on the public's lingering concerns about sexual psychopaths to aggrandize his department's efforts: while admitting in a professional journal that the investigation began with a defendant accosting a teenage boy, he informed the *Mansfield News-Journal* that he was inspired by the "brutal murder of two little girls." "Any sex deviate," he explained, "may be a potential killer."[25]

The operation in Mansfield's Central Park, like those at the YMCA and Yosemite's Camp Curry, epitomized the range and innovation of the

5.3. Lieutenant Bill Spognardi manning a hidden camera in the Central Park men's room, as printed in the *FBI Enforcement Bulletin*, June 1963. Courtesy of United States Department of Justice.

police's campaigns against public cruising in the 1960s. Suspecting that certain men's rooms were used for sexual activities, but also well aware that such encounters could rarely be spotted by more straightforward patrols, vice squads marshaled an impressive array of technological and human resources to bring those surreptitious activities to light. The surveillance campaigns they staged were hardly the most convenient tool of law enforcement or one that officers enjoyed having to use. But they were, as policemen saw it, a matter of necessity: often the only effective technique with which to combat a criminal practice that thrived through a set of effective strategies for avoiding exposure, to ordinary citizens and police officers alike.[26]

And if that tactic functioned by exposing *all* users of public bathrooms to the vice squad—not only men engaging in sodomy or even more ambiguous flirtations but also numerous men who used the restrooms for their designated purpose—well, that was simply a collateral cost. Certainly, some departments tried to reduce the humiliation of innocent citizens. In Mansfield, Spognardi ran his camera only when he spotted suspicious activity. In Camp Curry, Ranger Twight began surveillance at 11:00 P.M., after "general family use of the restroom had ceased." But even patrons spared the camera were exposed, in the first instance, to the view of hidden police officers, often in the midst of their most private bodily acts. As Ranger Twight admitted, each night of observation revealed "probably 25 or 30" men who "just went in to use the toilet for a toilet."[27]

Sodomy Laws on the Books and in the Courts

For the men arrested as a result of the police's surreptitious campaigns, of course, the costs of clandestine surveillance went beyond the humiliation of a fleeting exposure. Reflecting the public's shifting, highly localized understandings of sexual morality, the penalties for consensual sodomy varied dramatically, from a one-year maximum in New York, where the legislature reclassified sodomy as a misdemeanor in 1950, to a possible life sentence in Georgia or Nevada. After Illinois became the first state to decriminalize sodomy in 1961, a gay man having sex in Quincy could face no penalty at all, while an acquaintance two miles across the river in Missouri exposed himself to decades in prison.[28]

The enforcement of those statutory punishments varied more widely than the punishments themselves. In some states, including coastal hubs like New York and California but also midwestern and even some southern states like Michigan, Wisconsin, Minnesota, and Florida, judges frequently treated sodomy charges much as they did solicitation cases, releasing defendants with probation, a fine, and a push toward psychiatric treatment. Sensitive to the unique stigma attaching to a sodomy conviction, some used their discretion to reduce the charges. In Kansas, one judge habitually arranged for defendants to plead guilty to lascivious conduct, a misdemeanor. In St. Petersburg in 1966, a trial judge opted to stay one defendant's conviction entirely, placing him on probation without further tarnishing his criminal record.[29]

California may have exemplified the frequent disconnect between sodomy laws on the books and sodomy cases in court. In the early 1950s, at the height of the sexual psychopath panic, the state legislature passed a series of provisions raising the penalties for anal and oral copulation. Yet while those amendments took a symbolic stand against the supposed evils of sexual deviance, the far more influential change was a separate provision adopted in 1950, empowering judges to treat oral copulation as either a felony or a misdemeanor. That shift likely addressed a practical concern facing the state's prosecutors in the late 1940s. As one study in Los Angeles reported, judges in these years convicted almost all defendants charged with homosexuality-related misdemeanors yet less than half of defendants charged with felony offenses, a trend prosecutors attributed to the excess penalties carried by such charges. The legislature's amendment invigorated those conviction rates, even as it largely tempered their bite. By the mid-1960s, even as vice officers surveilling restrooms patiently waited for suspects to commit a felony offense, Los Angeles judges resolved nearly 99 percent of those felony charges as misdemeanors, either through their discretion under the oral copulation statute or simply by demanding a reduction of the charges. And they sentenced almost all defendants, regardless of the final charge, to probation and a fine.[30]

In other jurisdictions, defendants were not so lucky. In Georgia, Texas, Ohio, and North Carolina, men convicted of sodomy served time in jail well through the 1960s. Saddled with mandatory minimums, some judges had no choice but to incarcerate defendants, frequently sentencing them to the lowest possible term. Others, particularly in socially conservative states, felt few qualms about imprisoning men for consensual sexual conduct. Those judges were not necessarily blind to the public's growing tendency to view homosexual desire as a medical condition rather than a penal concern. But they did not appreciate the efforts of progressive psychiatrists to tell them how to apply the nation's criminal laws. "Whether Sodomy and homosexuality be a crime or a disease," one Dallas trial judge insisted as late as 1971, "the confessed practitioners thereof should be isolated from the society upon which they prey." Here, too, of course, particular categories of defendants could expect especially severe sentences. In North Carolina in 1962, one man arrested for sodomy in a private home pled guilty, received a five- to seven-year sentence, and was released well in advance of that time. His codefendant, a sex worker named Maxine who audaciously appeared in court wearing women's clothing, went to trial and was sentenced by the same trial judge to twenty to thirty years.[31]

Beyond jail time, of course, defendants caught in the vice squads' surveillance campaigns suffered a variety of social and civic consequences. In many states, defendants convicted of sodomy were required to register as sex offenders, permanently added to a roster of potential suspects for new sex crimes in their area. Members of the military were almost always assured of a dishonorable discharge. Immigrants, considered guilty of a crime of "moral turpitude," could be deported. And local newspapers frequently printed the names of men arrested in public bathrooms, following their ordeals through conviction and sentencing, and sometimes costing them friendships, relationships, and jobs well in advance of their trials.[32]

Given those painful penalties, the prospect of challenging the vice squads' surveillance arrests in court daunted many defendants. Eager to put the experience behind them with no additional publicity, many pled guilty. Even those who went to trial—an option often limited, in practice, to those who could afford a lawyer—typically tried to minimize the ensuing exposure, opting for bench trials rather than juries despite defense attorneys' common insistence that juries, emotional and unpredictable, promised a greater likelihood of acquittal.[33]

Yet some men, desperate to avoid both the social and the legal consequences of a sodomy-related conviction, were willing to do anything in their power to clear themselves of the charges. And they devised a range of tactics for challenging those accusations at trial.

Clandestine Surveillance in Court

The earliest recorded challenge to a clandestine surveillance arrest in the United States dates back to 1930, when a twenty-six-year-old Bostonian, a design school graduate, appealed his conviction for public lewdness in a railroad station to the Supreme Judicial Court of Massachusetts. Rehearsing a legal claim that would later be echoed by countless men fighting their solicitation charges, he insisted that his behavior, pursued in the privacy of a men's room with no observers present, did not qualify as "public" under the statute.[34]

In the coming decades, such legal challenges would become increasingly pervasive, and they would cover a range of litigation strategies. Mostly, they came from wealthy or middle-class defendants able to afford creative lawyers, although poorer men, relying on flat-fee representation or the goodwill of ideologically sympathetic attorneys, could also mount a defense. Some civil rights–minded lawyers, harboring a long-standing interest in police misconduct, turned sodomy trials into referenda on the vice squads' tactics, challenging the reliability and the morality of police evidence procured through espionage in public bathrooms. Others focused on the good character of their clients, vaunting those men's family ties and professional connections as evidence that they could not have engaged in such sordid sexual acts. In either case, defendants invited the courts to debate the deeper moral questions raised by the vice squads' surveillance operations, from the limits of ethical policing to the social costs of sodomy arrests to the nature of same-sex desire itself.[35]

Like the unfortunate Bostonian, some men tried to avail themselves of purely technical challenges. In New York, defendants arrested for disorderly conduct insisted that their activities, pursued with no witnesses present, failed to disturb the peace. In California, men protested the admission of inflammatory evidence or objected to what they saw as improper jury instructions, denying them the benefit of a fair trial. Exploiting the courts' inclination toward legalistic thinking, such challenges sometimes succeeded at fending off convictions, but they also came with a daunting cost. Focusing on the statutory language or errors of courtroom procedure, they effectively conceded the substance of the underlying charges, a position few defendants wanted to take. Accordingly, most men turned to a more straightforward tactic: they simply denied that the acts alleged by vice officers ever took place.[36]

Many began by tackling the inherent unreliability of the prosecution's evidence, often procured late at night and through makeshift observation stations. Typically charged solely on the basis of eyewitness testimony, defendants pointed to the dim lighting conditions inside public toilets. They noted the cramped angles afforded by slatted doors, air vents, and peepholes cut into bathroom walls. After a Venice Beach officer crouching behind a toilet stall claimed to catch Alfred Mason performing oral sex on Rodney Owens in 1953, Owens turned the officer's very proximity into a weakness: given the officer's own claim that Owens "stood up and [Mason] immediately started copulating his penis," he argued, his back should have blocked the officer's view of the alleged act.[37]

Most men limited themselves to cross-examining the arresting officers, but those with sufficient means called expert witnesses to bolster their defense. When a policeman accused Robert Roberts of cruising in a rest area in Monterey County, California, Roberts's well-funded defense engaged a private detective, a professional photographer, and an optometrist to attest that the lighting conditions would have prevented any clear identification. Arrested at a bus terminal at Pico and Rimpau in Los Angeles, Paul Bentley, a detective by trade, accepted the social costs of publicizing his arrest and prevailed on four colleagues to replicate the vice squad's operation. Based on the angle and the lighting of the window, all four agreed, the officers could not possibly have gotten a clear view inside.[38]

Defendants who challenged the state's evidence frequently offered more innocent accounts, insisting that the officers had confused a benign encounter in a men's room for something more sinister. Arrested in a New

York subway in 1955, Frederick Liebenthal explained that he felt a spell of nausea brought on by a new medication and had braced himself against a neighbor's stall. Accused of entering another man's stall in a Los Angeles department store in 1956, Wilburn Strahan insisted that he noticed another customer feeling unwell and stepped inside to check on him. In Strahan's case, especially, the district attorney insisted on a less upstanding motive: having already noted Strahan's job as schoolteacher working primarily with black and Latino students, he pressed Strahan to admit that he approached his codefendant only "because he appear[ed] to be of Mexican origin." Implying that both Strahan's conduct in the restroom and his daily work catered to some perverse attraction to his pupils, the question simultaneously evoked the lingering shadow of the child molester, casting all homosexual men as latent predators, and exploited the persisting distrust among some courts of spontaneous courtesies between men of different races.[39]

That police officers sometimes mistook the nature of such benign encounters, defendants suggested, was no accident—and not simply due to the poor lighting conditions. If vice officers so commonly assumed the worst, rather, it was because the very nature of surveillance work made such assumptions inevitable. Some defendants made a show of sympathy for the policemen assigned the unpleasant task of patrolling suspected tearooms. As one of Russell Sellers's attorneys speculated, officers tasked to the "disgusting activity . . . of being a 'peeping tom'" were undoubtedly "most eager to detect some act upon which to base an arrest." After enough hours spent watching scatological functions of an "innocent . . . [but] disgusting nature," echoed the lawyer for Guilford Shaw in Santa Monica, "revulsion alone" would compel a vice officer to "end the matter by seeing what was not there."[40]

Other defendants took a less generous view, openly impugning the morals of men willing to spend their time watching bodily functions in public toilets. As Paul Bentley's attorney decried in 1950, echoing the same concerns that drove judicial skepticism of plainclothes decoys in these same years, "the known propensities and prepossessions of vice squad officers" left no man "safe from the charge of homosexuality." Some implied that vice officers derived more than professional satisfaction from their work. Prior to bemoaning the lot of policemen sequestered behind public toilets, Sellers himself tried a more aggressive strategy. "You like your work?" his attorney pressed Officer Gibson on the stand. "Have you ever asked for a transfer?" Turning the focus of the trial from the defendant's conduct in a public bathroom to the policeman's own, that strategy echoed the suspicion, intimately familiar to vice officers, that such degrading work had to say something perverse about the men who performed it. And it seized on the intrinsic absurdities of the vice squads' salacious observations in public bathrooms, perhaps as deviant by prevailing standards as the behavior they observed. As one defendant snapped at his 1963 trial, bristling at the suggestion that he was cruising for sexual partners at a movie screening: "Maybe the police go looking for queers [in theaters] but I was just trying to see the picture."[41]

Sensitive to the value of public embarrassment as a trial strategy, some lawyers went out of their way to drag the indignities of surveillance work into the center of the proceedings. Frank C. Wood Jr., a Los Angeles lawyer and homophile ally who handled a number of high-profile cases in the early 1960s, made a habit of testing vice officers with graphic questions about their observations. Had the witness noticed whether the defendant's penis was circumcised or whether it had "any abnormality about it?" Did he inspect the sex organ for fecal matter prior to arrest? Meanwhile, Russell Sellers's lawyer introduced a parade of defense witnesses who testified, earnestly and with good humor, to Sellers's history of idling on the toilet due to his chronic constipation. Invited to challenge the evidence, the prosecutor demurred: "I don't care to inquire on the subject." Such exchanges were often directly relevant to the case, offering an innocent explanation for a defendant's conduct or testing the sharpness of an officer's recollections. Yet they also reflected a more impressionistic strategy: emphasizing the sordidness of the vice squads' surveillance operations—and, in that, the questionable value of the ensuing arrests.[42]

Judges did not take such challenges lightly. If the courts sometimes dismissed solicitation prosecutions as a waste of judicial resources, judges recognized accusations of sodomy in public bathrooms as "very serious charge[s]," and they did their best to let defendants develop their cases in full. In some cases, judges and even jurors—men and women alike—went so far as to leave the courtroom and visit the site of the defendant's arrest, examining for themselves whether an officer could reliably have seen what was transpiring inside. Presiding over Paul Bentley's trial in Los Angeles, for instance, Judge Edwin Jefferson, a relatively new appointment to the superior court and one of the nation's first black judges to reach that position, staged a spontaneous field trip to the men's room at Pico and Rimpau, where the arresting officer and a clerk took turns hoisting him up to the window and letting him peer onto the stalls. "Perhaps it was not very dignified," he conceded back in his courtroom, "but I was interested to see whether or not that which the officer said he did see could be seen." Prosecutors around Los Angeles soon grew wary of bringing felony charges where the officer failed to get a clear view of the sexual encounter, handling such arrests as misdemeanors even where they had little doubt about the activities involved.[43]

Nor were the defendants' moral aspersions against policemen who spent their time spying on public toilets lost on the courts. Diligent prosecutors recognized that judges and even juries might find the vice squads' surveillance tactics as offensive as the defendant's sexual transgressions, and they did their best to make sure that such qualms did not cost them a conviction. At the jury selection for Oscar Maldonado and Joseph Holman's trial in 1963, for example, the district attorney preemptively tried to screen out potential critics: "Does any of you feel that . . . if you hear evidence that the police have been watching a particular place that you won't listen to such evidence because you feel that the police shouldn't do such things?" Sensitive that juries at criminal trials sat in judgment of the state as much as of the defendant, prosecutors, no less than defense attorneys, acknowledged that the unsavory nature of clandestine surveillance might rob the police of the moral high ground.[44]

If these strategies aimed to rebut the state's charges by turning the court against the state's witnesses, some defendants also tried a more affirmative approach. More than attacking the vice squad's tactics, defendants emphasized their own good character, hoping to convince the jury that they were simply not the type to commit the crimes in question. The most obvious line of attack here was the character witness. Although suspects at all stages of criminal proceedings tried to capitalize on their apparently respectable backgrounds, those who proceeded to trial had the option of introducing formal testimony to that effect, calling relatives, friends, and coworkers to testify about their upstanding moral profiles. Wilburn Strahan, a high school teacher, summoned four colleagues, including his principal, to vouch for his reputation for "sexual morality." Russell Sellers cut more directly to the chase, calling two supervisors, a clergyman, and a policeman neighbor to share their opinions of his "reputation . . . for morality, chastity and as to homosexuality." "Very good," they invariably replied, presumably meaning substantial for the first two and negligible for the last. The strategy worked best for men with deep-rooted professional and residential ties—the middle-class, often suburban defendants whose lives aligned with the courts' own ideals of civic respectability—but it held appeal even for less privileged men. Joseph Holman, a black veteran fired from his nursing job following an arrest in a Los Angeles theater, could not prevail on his colleagues to testify on his behalf. But he still called a longtime friend, a mother, who assured the court of his "good moral character."[45]

As capable defense attorneys realized, such evidence simultaneously played two roles. Formally, it aimed to undercut the state's allegations, but as importantly, it simply made the defendant more sympathetic to a jury, showcasing the personal bonds that enabled him to call so many supporters despite the mortifying charges against him. For that reason, character witnesses remained popular despite the questions they raised about why a man's coworkers or neighbors had any insight into his private sexual practices. As the prosecutor trying Wilburn Strahan demanded of the defendant's colleagues, with more than a whiff of incredulity: "You have discussed the sexual traits or habits of Mr. Strahan, have you, with anyone?"[46]

Wary of that critique, some defendants turned to another type of witness. Many men arrested in public bathrooms led seemingly traditional lives outside the tearoom, and those men called their girlfriends, fiancées, and wives to vouch for their history of heterosexual relations. As Russell Sellers's wife informed the court, she and her husband had a "happy domestic life," including engaging in "normal marital sex relations . . . from time to time." Here, again, such evidence strengthened a defendant's case in multiple ways, both distancing him from popular stereotypes of men perverse enough to have sex in public bathrooms and emphasizing the domestic costs of a conviction—casting the prosecution, simply enough, as breaking up a happy home. Sensitive to that dynamic, indeed, Paul Bentley's lawyer made a point of pressing Mrs. Bentley not just on the couple's satisfying sex life but also on the domestic hearth that the vice squad's charges so rudely interrupted. She only learned about her husband's arrest, Mrs. Bentley testified, when she reached out to inform him that the chicken dinner she had spent the afternoon preparing was awaiting him at home.[47]

Some men turned to that other great authority on a man's sex life: the psychiatrist. In solicitation cases, psychiatrists often played a more informal role in the proceedings, urging judges to exercise leniency toward admittedly guilty suspects behind the scenes. At the trials arising from the vice squads' sodomy arrests, they commonly took the stand to challenge the state's evidence itself, sharing their expert judgments that a defendant simply lacked the psychological predisposition to engage in sodomy in public bathrooms. In addition to his wife, Russell Sellers called Dr. Clemson Marsh, who offered to draw on his training and experience to assure the court that Sellers was not, "in any degree or to any extent, a homosexual." Oscar Maldonado, the son of a well-off Puerto Rican family, engaged an especially well-credentialed witness: a former chief psychiatrist with the air force and an instructor at Columbia University, with an extensive history of treating deviates. On the basis of his professional observations,

Dr. Walter Briehl testified that a trained doctor could spot both overt and latent homosexuals, and that nothing about Maldonado's personality suggested "any homosexual propensity."[48]

From wives to expert psychiatrists, defendants' bids to establish their robust heterosexual sex lives depended on a fundamentally essentialist view of homosexuality: the notion that same-sex acts were committed by a discrete personality type, one devoted to sexual deviance, and thus incompatible with evidence of sexual normality in other spheres. As Dr. Briehl explained, oral sex with another man was a "sexual psychopathy," practiced by men whose psychological profile drew them to such perverse behavior. "The very nature of the crime," echoed Sellers's attorney, "makes the doer a peculiar and different person." Such arguments put the defendants' strategy at odds with the persisting belief, fanned by psychiatrists in these years, that homosexuality afflicted more members of the population than commonly imagined, tempting even seemingly "normal" defendants in a moment of weakness. And they put sodomy charges at odds with the vice squads' solicitation cases, where defense attorneys frequently requested— and judges granted—leniency precisely on the theory that homosexual desire was fleeting and pervasive. Defense lawyers in those cases portrayed their clients as family men lured in by an officer's temptations, emphasizing their domestic life as proof that their alleged sexual acts were aberrational. In sodomy prosecutions, such evidence emerged under a very different guise: evidence that those acts did not happen at all.[49]

In part, that disconnect reflected the divergent strategies pursued by defendants in such cases. Charged with solicitation, many men found it easier to concede the act and point to mitigating circumstances, hoping for leniency from the courts. Men facing the more serious charge of sodomy were often desperate to deny the allegations entirely, and they marshaled every possible argument to distance themselves from the purported crime. Yet the coexistence of these defenses also demonstrated the flexibility of the psychiatric model of homosexuality in the mid-twentieth century. That medicalization of same-sex desire is sometimes remembered as a key entry in the struggle to define homosexuality as an essential part of sexual identity rather than a transient behavior, the unique property of a homosexual "person." But in the courtroom, at least, its uses were more complex. By defining homosexuality as a pathology, doctors cast that condition as simultaneously anomalous and universal, implying both that same-sex desire distinguished those who experienced it from ordinary men and that such desire might, under the right conditions, afflict any number of seemingly normal patients. Defense attorneys recognized this ambiguity, and they exploited it to their advantage, emphasizing either the exceptionality or the pervasiveness of same-sex desire given the charges at hand.[50]

Prosecutors, for their part, recognized the utility of classifying same-sex desire as a mental illness; it was that view that drove the sexual psychopath laws and continued to justify so much vice policing in these years. But in these courtroom battles, at least, they had less to gain from an essentialist theory of deviance. In the trial against Russell Sellers, the assistant district attorney resisted the suggestion that Sellers's psychological predisposition had any bearing on his guilt. Claiming that the defendant did not engage in sodomy because a doctor did not diagnose him as homosexual, Mervyn Aggeler derided, was akin to arguing that a man was innocent of theft because a psychiatrist had not diagnosed him as a kleptomaniac.[51]

As to the defendants' wives, too, prosecutors drew a different lesson from the testimony. Far from being doting partners in fulfilling marriages, they implied, defendants who frequented public bathrooms for sex were faithless and ungrateful husbands who turned to cruising for the excitement their wives failed to provide. Some took direct aim at the veneer of serene domesticity evoked by the defense. At Paul Bentley's trial, while the defense emphasized the dinner lovingly prepared and left cooling at home, the district attorney pushed Bentley to admit that his wife's nagging about the bills led him to Pico and Rimpau in the first place. Most emphasized a different type of marital discord. Vice officers commonly testified that suspects ascribed their conduct to their wives' sexual unavailability, blaming recent bouts of illness or, sometimes, even less sympathetic excuses. "My wife just had a baby a few days ago," Wilburn Strahan purportedly explained to his arresting officer. "This is the only thing I can do." Portraying the defendants as unsatisfied husbands led to their transgressions by an unrequited desire for *marital* sex, such evidence reaffirmed the permeable view of deviance, recasting cruisers as less perverse in their desires than unable to control their sexual urges, however they might be gratified. And it chipped away at the sympathies evoked by the defense, identifying the defendants' wives as the hidden victims of their crimes—the duped spouses sitting at home with the children or the chicken—even as it obliquely blamed those women for their husbands' wandering.[52]

The courts struggled to make sense of these conflicting paradigms. Given the long-standing role of character witnesses on behalf of criminal defendants, few hesitated to allow colleagues or neighbors to vouch for a man's moral character, nor did they quibble with wives testifying for their husbands. But the expert witness inspired more dispute. In the case against Sellers, for instance, both the trial judge and the appellate court agreed with the district attorney. Given that "the law makes no distinction . . . as to the type of person who may commit the act," Judge H. J. Borde noted, Dr. Marsh's testimony that Sellers was not a "homosexual" simply had no bearing on the case. Just four years later, the Supreme Court of California changed course. Considering the "accepted fact that homosexual acts . . . constitute abnormal conduct indulged in by persons with a propensity for it," it reasoned in 1954, evidence of the defendant's "sexual normality" could help prove "the nonperformance of [those] acts." The California courts' shifting positions on the value of expert testimony mirrored the growing prestige of professional psychiatry over the course of the 1950s, both inside and outside the courtroom. Yet it also suggested a lingering ambivalence about the theory of contagious homosexual desire espoused by psychiatrists: the courts' simultaneous embrace of that uncertain model and urge to assert some reassuring boundaries over it. To describe same-sex attraction as a temporary affliction, even a sympathetic one under some circumstances, was not to say that anyone could fall victim to it—and certainly not that anyone would follow through.[53]

Given that appetite for some firmer boundaries, in fact, even judges who excluded expert testimony may have been driven less by the relevance of the evidence than by more tacit considerations. Sellers's own trial was a case in point. Even as Judge Borde dismissed Dr. Marsh's appraisal of Sellers's sexual profile as immaterial, he allowed no fewer than six of Sellers's friends and colleagues to testify for precisely the same purpose, inviting them to vouch for Sellers's reputation "as to homosexuality." Borde's resistance to the learned doctor, it appeared, had less to do with the content of his testimony than the package it came in. That skepticism echoed a common judicial concern about unnecessary expert testimony: the fear that well-credentialed witnesses would overawe the jury, substituting their own conclusions for the jury's appraisal of the facts. But it also evoked a broader dispute over the role of expertise in the state's antihomosexual campaigns: a struggle, mirroring the liquor boards' resistance to expert witnesses in these same years, over who had the right to implicate or clear a man of deviance in court. As medical professionals in the 1950s claimed ever-greater public authority on questions of sexual difference, including as much-valued consultants for courts dealing with homosexuality-related offenses, some judges nevertheless opted for the wisdom of friends, neighbors, and colleagues as the more reliable witnesses to a man's sexual normality.[54]

This, then, was how trial judges often saw the vice squads' clandestine surveillance operations: as windows into complex, often painful family and community dramas. While prosecutors denigrated defendants as perverts and philanderers, deserving the sanction of the criminal law, defendants cast themselves as husbands and fathers, teachers and veterans, friends and colleagues—not hardened criminals or threats to the community, but ordinary men who, with the court's mercy and their family's support, could return to live productive and even happy lives.

In that context, it is notable how many wives stood by their husbands, both during and after their brush with the vice squad. Invariably, women who testified on behalf of their husbands opened themselves up to public humiliation, submitting themselves to prying questions about their sex lives. Some also took a more active role in the defense. Following Wilburn Strahan's arrest in a department store restroom, his wife of six years, a young architect, used her drafting skills to prepare a diagram of the men's room as a visual aid. After two officers arrested Hugh Coyle on a municipal pier in St. Petersburg, his wife, Alice, took it on herself to write the judge requesting an early termination of his probation. The couple hoped to move back to Pennsylvania, Alice explained, where Hugh could get treatment at the veterans' hospital and she could find a job to help support them. Some women who stayed and cared for their husbands even after their public betrayal may have felt trapped in their marriages, dreading the life of a single mother at a time when divorce was still typically seen as a personal and social tragedy. But some likely remained genuinely invested in their marriages, willing to forgive spouses who continued to fulfill their expectations of caring partners and fathers in all other aspects of their lives.[55]

And if their families could forgive them, why not the courts? With multiple police witnesses attesting to the charges, defendants' evidence of their personal virtues rarely managed to raise a reasonable doubt about their guilt. But it often succeeded in humanizing them, giving trial judges a compassionate glimpse into the men's private lives that invited leniency at the sentencing stage. Numerous judges relied on the defendants' impeccable personal records and civic reputations, including family ties, professional potential, and military service, to justify reduced charges or suspended sentences. In the case against Oscar Maldonado and Joseph Holman, for instance, the judge drew on both men's sterling probation reports to explain a relatively lenient disposition. At the trial against Frederick Liebenthal, it was the defendant's deep social bonds, from his support of his elderly mother to the mentorship of his rabbi, that convinced Judge Acquavella to suspend his month-long sentence.[56]

Some judges, moved by the evidence, questioned the value of bringing the defendants into the criminal justice system to begin with. Satisfied that Hugh Coyle, a husband, father, and military veteran, was "not likely again to engage in a criminal course of conduct," the trial judge presiding over his St. Petersburg trial placed him on probation while withholding any formal judgment of guilt. Touched by the drama of Wilburn Strahan's young marriage, so sorely tested by his arrest, Judge Thomas Ambrose excused Strahan from any jail time and then all but apologized for the law that bound him, despite his best attempts at leniency, to place Strahan on the sex-offender registry. "I was just as well aware as possibly could be as to the distress in his life and family," Judge Thomas Ambrose explained. "I would have been personally glad to have taken any other way out, but it was not possible." Recognizing the defendants' arrests as one unfortunate chapter in an otherwise promising social and professional life, trial judges did not see these men as sexual predators or even ongoing threats to the public order. They often saw—and treated—them as ordinary citizens who had made one embarrassing, regrettably public mistake.[57]

Clandestine Surveillance and the Constitution

For all their attempts to expose the indignities of clandestine surveillance, there was one question that defendants in the 1950s rarely raised: whether the practice was legal to begin with. The oversight was not surprising. Setting aside the abiding humiliation of conceding the charges, a near-inevitable implication of challenging the vice squads' tactics, it was unclear that defendants had any legal grounds for such a challenge. Most obviously, surveillance may have implicated the Fourth Amendment's guarantee against unreasonable searches, but in the 1950s state courts granted scant remedies for such violations. Rarely, a state constitution empowered judges to exclude illicitly obtained evidence: in Los Angeles, for instance, one young lawyer experienced both the embarrassment and the good fortune of appearing in court before his former law professor, who held the evidence inadmissible and dismissed the charges. But such cases were few and far between.[58]

That changed in 1961, when the US Supreme Court in *Mapp v. Ohio* held that the Fourth Amendment forbade the states from using evidence obtained through an illegal search at trial. Expanded and emboldened by the new federal rule, the prohibition against unreasonable searches soon emerged at the center of the states' surveillance cases. As it happened, the definition of an "unreasonable search" in this period was undergoing some uneasy shifts. On the one hand, the early 1960s witnessed a growing concern with personal privacy, fueled by the proliferation of innovative, affordable surveillance technologies available to police departments, businesses, and consumers alike. From best-selling books like Vance Packard's *The Naked Society* to court cases involving wiretaps and secret informants, public and legal debates grappled with what seemed to be the badges of an increasingly totalitarian society—"a world," *Life* magazine warned in 1966, "suddenly turned into a peephole and listening post." Those fears would ultimately lead the Supreme Court in 1967 to broaden the reach of the Fourth Amendment, from protecting property to shielding a more inchoate expectation of privacy.[59]

At the same time, some observers in the 1960s were starting to fear that the Fourth Amendment had, to the contrary, grown too broad. More than simply proliferating evidentiary challenges at state trials, the Court's decision in *Mapp* inspired an outcry among police executives and conservative politicians outraged that judges were "handcuffing" the police in their battle against crime. Soon enough, festering tensions between big-city police departments and the black and Latino residents who bore the brunt of their abuses would erupt in a series of violent clashes, ushering in a law-and-order politics that would culminate most famously in Richard Nixon's successful 1968 bid for the White House. Against that backdrop, some courts in the 1960s began to retreat from the defendant-friendly rule announced in *Mapp*. Many did so, in part, by limiting the class of cognizable searches under the Fourth Amendment—carefully weighing how much encroachment on personal privacy, and of what kind, they were willing to tolerate as the price of protecting the public safety.[60]

It was into that debate that the burgeoning battle over the vice squads' surveillance tactics entered. The first major cases to tackle the issue arose in 1962 in California, a state that would emerge as a key battleground in the fight over the legality of clandestine surveillance—not necessarily because the tactic was unusually pervasive there, but because the state's famously progressive supreme court began the debate on an unusually defendant-friendly note. One case traced back to the Long Beach vice squad's stakeout on the roof of the Nu-Pike Amusement Park, during which Officer Hetzel witnessed Robert Bielicki and another man engage in intimacies through an opening between two fully enclosed booths. The other originated at the Emporium department store in Santa Clara, where a policeman perched above an air vent videotaped Paul Britt engaging in oral sex beneath the partition between two stalls. Bielicki came to court with a particularly zealous attorney—Frank Wood, of the graphic inquiries into an officer's anatomical observations—but both men raised essentially identical arguments. Echoing the tenor of the times, they presented the issue as one not of homosexual rights but of personal privacy for all citizens in such delicate settings as public bathrooms. "Never in counsel's experience," as Wood proclaimed, "has he encountered a more brazen invasion of human rights or a more callous effrontery to human dignity."[61]

The lower courts found these claims unavailing, compelled by the prosecutors' argument that the defendants had no right to privacy in what was essentially a public space. But the Supreme Court of California sided with the defense. Between its stand for gay-friendly bars in *Stoumen* in 1951 and its own adoption of a Fourth Amendment exclusionary rule six years prior to *Mapp*, the court had proven itself quite liberal on questions of criminal procedure and civil rights alike, and unsurprisingly, given that reputation, it dismissed the vice squads' tactics as an impermissible assault on privacy. Bielicki's arrest at the Nu-Pike was the easy case: enclosed from all sides by floor-to-ceiling walls, the defendant clearly had some expectation of seclusion from prying eyes. Yet even in *Britt*, where the defendant pursued his encounter on the floor beneath the stalls—"clearly observable," the district attorney emphasized, "to any person of the general public who might have entered"—the court could not condone the arrest. Conceding that a policeman might have spotted Britt's encounter "*had* [he] been observing from a public, common use portion of the restroom," the fact remained that "he was not so stationed" and that "the subject evidence was not so obtained." Hypotheticals about what an officer might have seen on entering the bathroom could hardly support such a flagrant violation.[62]

Bielicki and *Britt* immediately reined in police surveillance operations in California. Even outside the state, the opinions had a wide impact, providing a blueprint for judges evaluating surveillance campaigns and a warning for departments planning them in Minnesota, Ohio, Maryland, Pennsylvania, and Florida. Indeed, the court's suggestion that police observations were limited to publicly accessible angles governed the Mansfield Police Department's sting in the summer of 1962, which was designed in consultation with a local prosecutor and with *Bielicki* squarely in mind. For all the department's precautions in that case, perhaps the most significant detail was the angle of the hidden camera, mounted exactly at eye level and adjacent to the bathroom door. As a judge considering a subsequent Fourth Amendment challenge observed, that post "necessarily place[d] the officers' view at the eye level of one who would be standing in the open part of the lavatory," avoiding any constitutional concerns.[63]

Yet while the Mansfield police plotted to accommodate the demands of *Bielicki*, not all departments proved equally eager to embrace those restraints. Around Los Angeles itself in the early 1960s, police departments commonly complained that the supreme court had taken much of the efficiency out of clandestine surveillance. Some curtailed their campaigns, limiting their observations to public areas of the restroom like sinks and urinals. Others abandoned the tactic altogether, refocusing their energies on decoys and uniformed patrols. At a time when police officials frequently chafed under the courts' procedural reforms, taking their grievances to local politicians and the press, some judges were not insensitive to this concern. As Judge Herbert Walker of the Los Angeles Superior Court protested soon after *Bielicki* was released, if the Fourth Amendment barred vice squads from surveilling crime-infested bathrooms, "we might as well fold up the police department and these courts." And those pragmatically minded jurists soon went on the retreat.[64]

In California itself, that trend began after an officer crouching behind a toilet stall witnessed Lynn Norton and Franklin Strong engage in a sexual encounter in San Francisco's Paris Theatre. The case came to trial while *Bielicki* was still pending, early enough that the trial judge commended Norton's attorney for his "novel" constitutional claim. That very novelty, however, disinclined him to suppress the evidence. "In view of the volume of cases that comes through these courts," Charles Peery reasoned of the vice squad's tactics, "the Court can take judicial notice . . . in the ordinary instance this is just the sort of thing that happens."

By the time Norton's case reached the appellate court, both *Bielicki* and *Britt* had come down, and the panel had to find a stronger rationale if it wanted to uphold the vice squad's tactics. The circumstances of Norton's arrests were similar to those two cases, with one difference: the stall that housed Norton had only three walls, leaving it visible from the urinals across the room. To the appellate court, that fact was dispositive. Unlike Bielicki, Norton had pursued his encounter "in the plain view of any member of the public who might happen to use the restroom." Indeed, "had the police entered the public part of the restroom they could have observed such activities in the same way." Under such circumstances, the defendant had no right against surveillance, clandestine or otherwise.[65]

To vice squads, the implications of *Norton* were clear. In order to avoid the heavy hand of *Britt* and *Bielicki*, police officers had only to prevail on city planners to remove the doors from public toilets, exposing potential cruisers—and everyone else—to view. But the legal distinction between the cases was less obvious. The court in *Britt*, after all, also presumed that anyone walking into the men's room could have seen Britt's encounter; it still insisted that the police had no right to watch that act from overhead. In the Mansfield case, too, the court distinguished Spognardi's operation on the basis of the public angle provided by his hideout, despite the fact that the stalls had no doors and many acts caught on his camera spilled into the common spaces.[66]

In the coming years, this constitutional question would continue to divide the courts. In Pinellas County, Florida, in 1964, Judge Charles Phillips extended the reasoning in *Bielicki* to exclude surveillance evidence of a sexual act inside an open stall. In California, even after *Norton* came down, trial judges in neighboring appellate districts insisted on suppressing evidence of encounters in publicly visible areas of the restroom. In the winter of 1963, for instance, Judge Edmund Cooke dismissed all charges against two men arrested by the LAPD for a sexual act performed by the urinals of the Art Theater. "I think every type of person would like to see this activity curtailed and controlled," Cooke conceded, "but it can't be done by . . . an invasion of the right of privacy by a police officer."[67]

Other judges swung in the opposite direction. In Pinellas County itself, after the trial court presiding over Hugh Coyle's case adopted Judge Phillips's rule, the appellate panel reversed, recognizing no right that "one committing a crime . . . [be] put upon notice by police officers that he is being watched." Meanwhile, after Ranger Twight arrested Joseph Smayda and Wendell Gunther at Yosemite's Camp Curry in 1963, Smayda and Gunther had the unusual experience of fighting their charges in federal court, and those judges rejected *Britt's* suggestion that even a fully enclosed toilet stall shielded its occupants from police observation. Twight had deemed his surveillance operation necessary to uncover any evidence of sexual misconduct, and the prosecution agreed. "Because of the physical set-up in the restrooms," the prosecutor explained, the rangers "couldn't physically observe this activity. So they undertook to cut holes in the ceiling and watch from up there." But the courts found a way to differ. As the district judge observed, the toilet stalls were hardly private, revealing as they did "whether the man had his pants up or down in the customary fashion." "It would have been easy for any member of the public to see the offense," echoed Judge Duniway on the court of appeals, since "any member of the public could have peered over the door, or the side partitions, or under either, or pushed open the door." Duniway shared Judge Cooke's unease at the prospect of peering policemen in public toilets. But Twight's attempts to drive out public sex acts from Camp Curry's bathrooms, he concluded, were well worth the sacrifice.[68]

As these divergent holdings suggested, constitutional challenges to the vice squads' surveillance campaigns did not necessarily come down to clear legal rules or factual distinctions. They entailed close judgment calls about how much protection the law *ought* to accord to individuals in toilet stalls, weighing the value of police surveillance in those quasi-private spaces against its social costs: whether "the nature of the place, the nature of the criminal activities," and the public's right to be free of such depredations, as Judge Duniway tallied them, justified the "uncomfortable . . . thought that our own legitimate activities in such a place may be spied upon by the police." As vice squads and cruisers both pushed the limits of conventional decency in their struggle over the acceptable use of public space, courts had to decide which unsavory practice in public toilets—intermittent sexual encounters or systematic police surveillance—they preferred the public to bear.[69]

And in resolving that particular question, one consideration that frequently shaped the courts' decisions was their view of the precise activities implicated in the vice squads' operations. Rejecting the evidence in *Bielicki*, the Supreme Court of California had characterized the defendants' conduct as an essentially victimless morals offense, posing no obvious danger to the public. "Authority of police officers to spy on occupants of toilet booths," the panel insisted, could hardly "be sustained on the theory that if they watch enough people long enough some *malum prohibitum* acts will eventually be discovered."[70]

The courts defending the vice squads' practices saw matters differently. The operative paradigm was perhaps best expressed in a California case that arose on the heels of *Norton* itself, tracing back to another surveillance arrest in a doorless stall. On appeal, the case came up to a familiar face: Judge Edwin Jefferson, who, continuing a pathbreaking career, had been elevated to the appellate court some three years earlier. Like Judge Peery, Jefferson had seen his share of sodomy cases since Paul Bentley's trial in 1950. And although Bentley had struck Jefferson as harmless enough, deserving no more than a misdemeanor conviction and probation, from the appellate bench he remembered that onslaught of cases rather differently. "Judges can take judicial knowledge from the case files in their own courts," Jefferson wrote in *People v. Young*, that public bathrooms "are often the locale of [such vices] as sexual perversion, sale of narcotics, petty thefts, robbery and assaults," all at significant "peril to immature and innocent youth." Conflating cruisers with violent criminals, Jefferson's view harkened back to the persistent suspicion of queer men as sexual predators, forcing their desires on unwilling victims. But even to the extent that he recognized the relative stealth that characterized contemporary cruising, he suggested that such habits made cruisers all the more dangerous. By "leaving a 'spotter' or 'lookout' at the door to warn other perverts or degenerates of the approach of police," Jefferson speculated, such criminals "could conduct their illicit activities in full view of impressionable youths." Far from an overreaction to a *malum prohibitum*, on this view, the vice squads' campaigns were a core tool in the police's drive against a predatory culture.[71]

Young's bleak vision became a rallying cry for judges and prosecutors defending the vice squads' surveillance campaigns, filling briefs and opinions from California to Minnesota to Pennsylvania. Meanwhile, after admitting the evidence against Hugh Coyle in St. Petersburg in 1966, a Florida District Court of Appeal added its own take on the public interests at stake. "It is a matter of common knowledge," Judge Kanner wrote for the panel, "that public restrooms are often selected by persons of sick or depraved minds as favorite locales for perpetration of indecent or illegal acts." Coyle's own offense, performed in an open stall "where anyone who might have entered" could have seen it—and the arresting officers did—supposedly illustrated the brazenness of such criminals. In fact, the policemen in that case had observed and apprehended Coyle from a private storeroom, to which they retreated only after having identified him, on the basis of "their long experience" as vice officers, as a likely cruiser—confirming, if anything, the necessity of clandestine tactics to capture actual sexual activity. Regardless, Judge Kanner's "common knowledge" of cruisers' perverse practices made short work of any claim that the defendants had a right to privacy in a bathroom stall.[72]

The sinister vision of cruisers revealed in these opinions echoed the pathological view that had fueled the criminalization of same-sex practices for decades, depicting homosexuality as one step on a path leading inexorably toward more predatory passions. The district court presiding over Gunther and Smayda's trial, indeed, articulated those concerns in no uncertain terms. "Insofar as the protection of society is concerned," Judge MacBride demanded, "how am I to know that the next time in their curiosity about some of these homosexual experiences they might want to find out what it's like with a 14-year-old boy or a 13-year-old boy or some juvenile? And then they go from that to . . . one of the heinous sex crimes that are constantly in the papers." That this suspicion cropped up among courts presiding over sodomy arrests was hardly surprising. As some courts saw it, the relative gravity of sodomy charges—and not just sodomy but *public* sodomy—mapped most closely onto the fears of so-called degeneracy that the sex-crime debates of the early 1950s had inspired.[73]

Nevertheless, the view of the prototypical cruiser expressed in such opinions, as an exhibitionist waiting to corrupt the nation's youth, departed fairly dramatically from that of trial courts handling the bulk of the police's sodomy arrests in these years. In California, even as Judge Jefferson decried the epidemic of "perverts [and] degenerates" in public bathrooms, trial judges disposed of nearly all cruising charges as misdemeanors, meriting no jail time. In the case against Hugh Coyle, after Judge Kanner railed against Coyle's "depraved" activities, the trial judge spared him so much as a formal conviction, placing him on probation while staying any adjudication of guilt. Some trial judges, indeed, discussed defendants' offenses in terms that recalled a social gaffe more than a danger to the community. As Magistrate Judge James R. Creel of New York explained, his goal in referring cruisers to probation was not to impose "punishment" but to "enable them to live happier lives and to escape that kind of embarrassment in the future." The appellate courts' denunciations of the perverts and criminals who had sex in public bathrooms, in short, expressed a very different vision of cruising than that populating the trial courts in the same years—and even, sometimes, the same cases.[74]

To some extent, that disconnect likely reflected the personal views of individual judges, whose perspectives on same-sex practices varied even in comparatively liberal states like California. It also reflected the unique institutional pressures of the appellate courts, where the sinister image of the homosexual was most frequently rehearsed. It was one thing, after all, to show leniency in sentencing individual defendants or to dismiss charges out of distaste for a particular arrest. It was another flatly to invalidate a police tactic used by law enforcement professionals to preserve the public safety. Unlike trial judges tailoring their sentences to the specifics of each case, moreover, appellate courts faced a more technical task: evaluating whether the Constitution barred a tactic long used to suppress crime in public bathrooms. Such courts were primed to perceive cruising simply as another police problem among many, conflating defendants, as did Judges Kanner and Jefferson, with the more predatory criminals who occupied the police's time.

Precisely in that regard, of course, the divergent visions of the cruiser emerging among appellate and trial courts in these years also confirmed the humanizing power of the courtroom. From the divergent impressions left by Hugh Coyle on the appellate and the trial judges presiding over his case to Judge Jefferson's shifting solicitude toward Bentley personally and "degenerate" cruisers more abstractly, the comparatively lax treatment received by defendants in the lower courts revealed the expressive impact of the trial process, which not only exposed judges to the vice squads' voluminous arrests but also illustrated their moral ambiguity. Drawing on those experiences, some trial judges prided themselves on developing a more nuanced view of sexual difference than most Americans of the day. After a juror at Wilburn Strahan's trial fretted that Strahan might pose a risk to her young children, for instance, Judge Thomas Ambrose attributed her concerns to the average citizen's "ignorance of the situation." Of course "we do not regard homosexuals as a menace to society in general," he assured Strahan's counsel, but "these people don't distinguish between the grouping of sex deviates that we do." It is notable, in context, that Gunther and Smayda's trial, distinguished both by Judge McBride's unusually sinister rhetoric and by a startlingly high sentence under the California statute, was the rare case to come before a federal trial judge, who would have lacked the routine exposure to cruisers that state judges commonly acquired.[75]

Regardless, in the coming years, the nature of urban cruising practices rose to the center of legal struggles over police surveillance. Recognizing the extent to which the courts' view of same-sex conduct could determine the outcome of a case, prosecutors and defense attorneys turned the defendants' constitutional challenges into the sites of an ongoing debate about the nature of cruising itself. And in that, echoing the failure of most commentators to distinguish between the two, into a debate about the nature of gay life more broadly: who the typical homosexual was, what he wanted, and what danger he posed to the public.

The prosecution, unsurprisingly, took its lead from Judge Jefferson. District attorneys at trial had long made passing references to the evils of cruising, but in the aftermath of cases like *Young* and *Coyle*, that rhetoric emerged as an abiding feature of surveillance cases. At the proceedings against Oscar Maldonado and Joseph Holman in Los Angeles, for instance, the prosecutor initially presented a third man spotted with the defendants—by all accounts, a willing participant—as "the alleged victim," at one point controversially describing him as a "young" white blond. At Alvin Buchanan's trial in Dallas, the prosecutor pressed each witness about the lavatory's proximity to local playgrounds, schools, and children's hospitals, going so far as to invite one officer to speculate whether a child might have been able to "see under [the stall]." In their briefs addressing the defendants' Fourth Amendment challenges, meanwhile, government lawyers parroted Jefferson's and Kanner's sordid assessments of the cruiser's "depraved" practices, importing the paradigm of the predatory homosexual into the heart of their constitutional arguments. Perhaps, as one attorney in Pennsylvania put it, the challengers "prefer[red that] these perverts solicit young, impressionable male persons" out of police view.[76]

The defense pushed back against that narrative. Taking up the same educational project begun in solicitation cases like *Robillard*, which had challenged the New York Police Department's decoy operations largely by emphasizing the systematic nature of gay pickups, defendants sought to reintroduce queer life to the courts not as a dangerous psychopathy but as a self-contained, if unorthodox, subculture. That effort included questioning the lingering conflation of homosexuals with more dangerous criminal offenders. "Contrary to popular opinion," as one defendant caught in the Mansfield Police Department's sting protested to the court, medical research suggested that "sexual deviation between consenting adults affords no basis for an inference that such adults tend to violence or child molesting." It also included attempting to shift the courts' view of tearoom cruising itself—not least by undermining the claim, so popular among prosecutors, that the men arrested in public bathrooms committed their acts in full view of unfortunate passersby.[77]

That strategy emerged most clearly, once again, in California, where homophile activists in Los Angeles and San Francisco had spent the early 1960s making inroads with the local branches of the American Civil Liberties Union (ACLU). By the middle of that decade, the organization's local attorneys stepped forward to submit amicus briefs in cases challenging the vice squads' surveillance tactics—and, like in *Robillard*, their interventions included drawing on contemporary studies to refute prosecutors' claims that cruisers posed a danger to innocent strangers. Considering most cruisers' care to avoid bystanders, as an attorney with the ACLU of Northern California argued on behalf of Robert Roberts in May 1967, the defendant's alleged sexual encounter could hardly have been spotted by more casual patrols. Had the police relied on less surreptitious tactics, the "act discovered would not have taken place." After an officer peering through an air vent arrested Leroy Triggs in Los Angeles in 1970, attorneys with the ACLU of Southern California branch tried a similar tactic. "Studies would indicate that the persons involved in this activity . . . expect privacy from the public," A. L. Wirin, Fred Okrand, and Laurence R. Sperber informed the court—an expectation borne out not only by the negligible number of arrests involving public complaints but also by cruisers' systematic tactics to avoid exposure, including the lookouts cited by Judge Jefferson. Far from throwing themselves into the public eye, those studies suggested, "homosexual solicitations are so discreet as to be beyond notice of non-homosexuals."[78]

The states' representatives derided such pedagogical efforts. The salient question, as the attorney general in Roberts's case pointedly reminded the court, was not whether the defendant's act would be deterred by a policeman in the restroom but whether it would be "deterred by the approach or presence of young boys." The very fact that Leroy Triggs pursued a sexual encounter "when it was likely that people would still be using the park restroom," echoed Deputy Attorney General Douglas Noble, demonstrated "his indifference to public observation." Even if he "intended to conceal his act," he certainly "did not choose an effective way to do it."[79]

In 1972, nearly ten years following its opinions in *Bielicki* and *Britt*, the Supreme Court of California finally reentered the debate. In the intervening decade, the context surrounding the vice squads' tactics had shifted in multiple ways. Concerns about private and state surveillance had wound their way to the highest level of political debate in California, leading to a 1969 law banning the use of one-way mirrors in public bathrooms. Urban police departments, not least the LAPD, had sustained withering attacks from progressive critics over their treatment of urban protestors and antiwar demonstrators. Queer activists emerged as a newly vocal public presence, waging a series of protests against police misconduct culminating most famously in the riots at Manhattan's Stonewall Inn in 1969. Not least, these years featured an increasingly open public debate on the subject of homosexuality, as mainstream media outlets frequently cast gay life in the nation's cities not as a predatory criminal underground but as an insular and relatively benign urban subculture.[80]

In that context, perhaps it was overdetermined that the Supreme Court of California in *People v. Triggs* reaffirmed the principle that patrons using public bathrooms had a right to privacy against police surveillance, a right "not diminished or destroyed because the toilet stall being used lacks a door." In supporting that conclusion, the court cited a number of factors, including the new antisurveillance law and the language of *Bielicki* itself. But it also made a point of engaging the conflicting views of cruising practices presented by the prosecution and the defense. As Chief Justice Wright observed: "The Attorney General claims that criminal acts are often committed inside rest rooms within plain view of any member of the public who should happen to enter." Were that the case, however, "the police need not resort to clandestine observation to apprehend individuals involved in such activities. When law enforcement officers suspect that crimes are being perpetrated, they are as free to enter rest rooms as is any member of the public." Rejecting the prosecution's claims that clandestine surveillance was necessary to contain a brazen criminal culture, Wright acknowledged a fact that police departments, and sometimes prosecutors, had recognized for years: that the police resorted to surveillance methods only because the reality of cruising culture prevented those acts from revealing themselves in any other way.[81]

The California courts' extended battles over the constitutional status of clandestine surveillance, from *Bielicki* in 1962 to *Triggs* in 1972, illustrate the extent to which judicial understandings of same-sex practices shaped the legal rights of queer men in the mid-twentieth century. More than simply discretionary matters like sentencing or even the inherently equitable decision to dismiss charges, the resolution of constitutional questions raised by the vice squads' operations sometimes came down to the courts' underlying conceptions of queer life and practice. The police's controversial surveillance tactics survived for years in California owing in significant part to some appellate judges' insistence that men perverse enough to have sex in public toilets posed a direct danger to the public, indifferent to or even gratified by the prospect of exposing themselves to strangers. And those tactics were rejected, finally, in part through a rejection of that presumption itself, aided by defense attorneys' ongoing efforts to convince the courts that cruisers in fact resolutely sought to avoid public exposure, and had developed a number of highly systematic, highly effective strategies to that end.

Beyond the importance of judicial views of same-sex practices, the courts' ongoing confrontations with surveillance tactics in the 1960s confirm the lingering effects of the legal system's disagreements about gay life. As a practical matter, as police officials in these years recognized, surreptitious surveillance methods were necessary to arrest cruisers precisely because those men were so difficult to apprehend through other means. Frustrated by the failures of more casual patrols, agencies like the Mansfield Police Department turned to surveillance as the only tactic that "would be of any use." But as a legal matter, judges repeatedly concluded, those tactics were justified precisely because cruisers were predatory, exhibitionistic, delighting in showing themselves off to innocents and especially children. Not unlike the vice squads' decoy arrests in these same years, the continuing vitality of the police's surveillance campaigns depended on a persisting gap in the legal system's views of cruising practices, dividing what vice officers, trial judges, and appellate panels assumed about the men brought into court.

The history of the vice squads' clandestine surveillance operations in the postwar years, in sum, encapsulates the complex epistemology of vice enforcement at midcentury. That story reveals how different legal agents involved in the regulation of queer life, from vice officers to trial judges, developed often-distinct perspectives on the men who fell within their purview, drawing on their unique experiences and particular institutional competencies. It suggests how those differences, in turn, fueled continuing fissures over the value of the vice squads' operations, not only between the judiciary and the police but also, on some issues, between trial judges and the appellate courts. And it confirms the extent to which the vice squads' most controversial tactics were sustained, over the course of the 1960s, by the justice system's lingering disagreements about the nature of queer life itself. At a time of ongoing debate regarding both the ethics of the vice squads' campaigns and the contours of same-sex practices, exacerbated by the distinct institutional perspectives of different agents in the legal system, the police's continuing reliance on surveillance tactics depended on police officers' and judges' divergent understandings of the criminalized conduct at hand. And the work of resisting those tactics was, in key part, a matter of catching the courts up to the police's understandings, to help bridge that influential gap.

Creative defense attorneys, of course, were not the only ones discussing the underappreciated contours of gay life in the 1960s. By the middle of that decade, debates about the nature of both gay communities and vice policing in the United States had spilled out beyond the courts, to the pages of the popular press. There, too, the vice squads' unusual intimacy with the codes and contours of the gay world would occupy a central role. But it would soon acquire a novel significance.

SIX

The Popular Press and the Gay World

In the spring of 1963, a journalist on assignment for *Harper's Magazine* prevailed on a friend to take him inside one of New York City's gay bars. There, in the dusty haze of the dance hall, William Helmer was taken aback to discover something that vice officers across the country had long recognized—something that liquor investigators and hearing officers had long tried to deny. Peering around the bar, he saw all the hallmarks of a popular nightspot: "dim lights, loud noise, cigarette smoke, music." But "no one," he marveled, "who 'looked' homosexual."[1]

Helmer's account was just one in a series of journalistic forays into gay life in the 1960s. As gay men and women settled into the nation's cities, and as homophile groups like the Mattachine Society ventured to take their grievances over legal discrimination public, media outlets from the *New York Times* to popular magazines like *Life* reasoned that the homosexual had become "such an obtrusive part" of urban life that he demanded public discussion. Yet journalists were bewildered to discover that this new denizen of the urban landscape was not the familiar fairy of years past. He did not sway his hips. He did not speak in a particularly high-pitched voice. Walking among the public, the modern homosexual often appeared to be "the most masculine-looking person in the world." Having withstood decades of attack by psychiatrists, sexologists, and tenacious bar owners, the stereotype of the pansy was finally meeting its death in the press. And with it, a core presumption underlying many Americans' relationship with homosexuality in these years: that, although explaining or treating so-called sexual deviance might be a task best entrusted to doctors, when it came to spotting the homosexuals among it, the public knew everything it had to know.[2]

Appalled, now, to discover that the public had been quite mistaken on that score, the media took it upon itself to restore some order. With a keen eye for detail and a zeal sometimes befitting a zoological expedition, popular outlets in the 1960s offered a sustained tutorial on the codes and customs of urban homosexuality. From gay men's slang to their preferred neighborhoods to their favorite fashions, journalists made up for the public's ebbing mastery over the gay body by honing its mastery over the hallmarks of gay life, reducing the gay world to an object of shared knowledge. And in doing so, it re-created the ostensibly visible gay body itself. Redefining the social significance of previously innocuous items like tennis shoes, sweaters, and polo shirts, the press updated the stereotype of the overt homosexual for a new era, teaching Americans blind to the gay world around them where to look and what to look for in order to recognize the new—the modern—homosexual.

The media's "discovery" of gay life in the 1960s has sometimes been remembered as a watershed moment in public debates about homosexuality, a shift away from the pathologizing rhetoric of deviance and crime and toward a more nuanced view of gay life as just one gradient in a diverse urban landscape. Yet among the press, as among the police in these same years, recognizing the gay world as an urban subculture was not necessarily a liberal impulse. Introducing mainstream Americans to contemporary gay life, the media's ethnographic accounts did not rebut the disease model of homosexuality, nor did they always paint homosexuality as a benign variation in a pluralistic metropolis. They often served a deliberate project of social regulation: a self-conscious attempt to give Americans who had lost their grasp on a rapidly shifting urban culture a new way to isolate, scrutinize, and regain control over an unwelcome interloper.[3]

To offer this tutorial, of course, the press first needed a source. And it promptly discovered one—not, for the most part, among gay men themselves, or the doctors and ethnographers who made it their professional work to examine gay life in these years, but among those other professional students of the gay world: vice officers. Whether instructing journalists on the dynamics of queer culture, shepherding reporters around gay bars, or showcasing their own often-impressive ability to blend into popular cruising sites, vice officers emerged as the most prominent face of the media's ethnographic tutorials on gay life in the 1960s, masters of a subculture most Americans knew little about.

More than merely revealing the public's shifting presumptions about urban gay life, in this sense, the media's forays reflected the shifting role of the police themselves: the emergence of vice officers, alongside doctors and empirical researchers, as professional authorities on the problem of sexual difference. In court, hemmed in by the evidentiary demands of the liquor codes or by judges' often unpredictable humors, police officers typically disclaimed any unusual intimacy with the social organization of the gay world, denying the genuine cultural insights that facilitated their arrests. But privately, at least, some had grown to pride themselves on their rarefied knowledge of their cities' sexual underworlds. And in the court of public opinion, they could not always resist stepping forward to claim credit for that professional skill.

It was a final irony, then, that before the press as before the bench, the vice officer's unique insights into the customs of gay life did not always redound to his advantage. Reporters often presented vice officers as professional authorities on a taboo subject, models of a cultural sophistication to which their readers should aspire. But as Americans discovered the daily realities of vice enforcement, the vice officer's familiarity with the gay world did not reliably emerge as an impressive vocational skill. It often turned into a source of embarrassment. Dismayed by the vice squads' sordid tactics, critics lodged all the familiar objections rehearsed by progressive judges in the 1950s, from the squandering of police manpower to the inherent immorality of entrapment tactics. Some also raised a more delicate concern: the suspicion that the vice squads' masterful charades bespoke more than a professional interest. Sensitive to the questionable optics of their operations, police departments soon rushed to downplay their involvement with gay bars and cruising sites, especially when it came to plainclothes patrols. By the late 1960s, the police officer's role at the center of media exposés on gay life had led, ironically, to a retrenchment of the vice squads' antihomosexual campaigns—a backlash against a police force whose greatest professional talents consisted, it appeared, of blending into a prurient sexual marketplace.

Turning from the work of vice enforcement to the pages of the popular press, this final chapter examines how the media's growing attention to gay life in the 1960s inspired a vocal reappraisal of both the queer communities thriving in the nation's cities and the vice squads' campaigns against them. Situating the media's discovery of the gay world within the history of vice enforcement highlights the intimate relationship between state regulation and popular understandings of same-sex practices: the abiding tie between even the most seemingly liberal public discussions of homosexuality and the continuing surveillance of gay life. It confirms the dawning recognition of the vice officer as a type of epistemic authority over sexual difference: a professional expert, no less than more traditional medical or scientific authorities in the postwar years, who helped shape public understandings of queer communities. And it provides a final reason for why vice officers in these years so commonly downplayed their professional intimacy with gay cruising culture—one that responded not to the pressures of the legal sphere, but to a deeper tension underlying the public's relationship with sexual difference. At a time when gay life inspired in many Americans competing reactions of profound curiosity and profound aversion, vice officers' expertise in that ostensibly deviant sexual culture did not bolster their standing in public debates about sexual difference. It undermined the legitimacy of their operations, casting the specter of deviance on the experts themselves. The mounting public criticism of the vice squads' antihomosexual campaigns in the 1960s reveals the delicate politics overhanging any claims of professional intimacy with queer social and sexual practices at midcentury: the disconnect between expertise and public authority over a subject as taboo as the urban gay world.

The Visible, Invisible Homosexual

The 1960s were, by all counts, a time of rising visibility for gay life in the United States. After decades of rigorous censorship, the Motion Picture Academy of America repealed the Hays Code, allowing directors newfound latitude in depicting homosexuality on the screen. In bookstores and on newsstands, publications by gay authors and magazines like *ONE*, recently still regulated under the obscenity laws, cropped up alongside monographs by psychiatrists and mainstream periodicals like *Life*. Out in the streets, a new generation of gay men settled into their favorite neighborhoods: Rittenhouse Square in Philadelphia, Civic Center in Denver, Bughouse Square in Chicago, Hollywood Boulevard in Los Angeles, and the Lower East Side, the Upper West Side, and Greenwich Village in New York. And homophile organizations like the Mattachine Society stepped into a newly public role. From Philadelphia to San Francisco, established groups like the Mattachine and newcomers like the Janus Society invited lawyers and psychiatrists to deliver lectures on the plight of gay men and women. In Los Angeles, the ONE Institute of Homophile Studies, the new pedagogical affiliate of *ONE* magazine, offered courses providing "parents, ministers, doctors, lawyers, psychologists, sociologists and the public" a better "understanding of homosexuality." In New York, the Homosexual League's Randy Wicker, among the brashest activists of his day, organized an hour-long program on homosexuality on the local radio in 1962.[4]

It was not long before the press took notice. Perhaps the first extended study of gay life in American cities was *The Sixth Man*, a book-length investigation of New York's gay community published in 1961 by the journalist Jess Stearn, formerly of the *New York Daily News* and *Newsweek*. Taking its title from gay men's startling purported numbers, *The Sixth Man* was deeply contemptuous of the "glittering make-believe world" it uncovered, but found a substantial readership. A year later, *Philadelphia Magazine* published a more sympathetic account of Philadelphia's gay population. Assigned to the reporter Gaeton Fonzi, soon to become more famous for his coverage of the Kennedy assassination, the twenty-page article focused less on gay men's personal failings than on their systemic abuse by the legal system. And in March 1963, William J. Helmer offered the readers of *Harper's* a complex social analysis of New York's "middle-class" homosexuals, from the relationship between wealth, education, and status in gay circles to the socioeconomic dimensions of swish affectation.[5]

Only with two higher-profile offerings, however, did the homosexual truly emerge as front-page news. The first appeared in December 1963 in the *New York Times*, after the paper's executive editor, startled by the sight of gay couples while apartment hunting in Manhattan, assigned Robert C. Doty to conduct a comprehensive investigation. Doty, in turn, looked to Randy Wicker. Hoping for a sympathetic account in line with the *Times's* treatment of the city's racial and religious minorities, Wicker agreed to educate Doty on the city's gay fringes. But the piece that went to press took a more apocalyptic tone. "Sexual inverts have colonized three areas of the city," Doty warned. "The city's homosexual community acts as a lodestar, attracting others from all over the country."[6]

The article was a media sensation, covered by peer publications as an event in its own right. But not even Doty could have anticipated the attention that would descend on the gay world in June 1964, when *Life* magazine dispatched a two-part study of the American homosexual to living rooms across the nation. Written by Paul Welch and Ernest Havemann and illustrated by the photographer Bill Eppridge, "Homosexuality in America" tried to restore some calm to the discussion, gently mocking Doty's dread in the face of a homosexual invasion (as ventriloquized by Havemann: "Do the homosexuals, like the Communists, intend to bury us?"). Drawing on interviews with Don Slater, the editor of *ONE*, and featuring multiple photographs inside local gay bars, the article was lauded by homophile organizations as a "milestone" publication "unlike anything ever done on the subject in modern mass media." Other readers were less appreciative. One Brooklynite and self-proclaimed world traveler, by his own account no "prude" to the ways of the world, protested that the "article on homosexuals nauseated [him]."[7]

By that point, there was no turning back. In the coming years, the popular press filled with high-profile forays into the nation's gay communities: a five-day series in the *Washington Post*, a six-part study in the *Denver Post*, a seven-part exposé in the *Atlanta Constitution*, and a four-part series in the *Chicago Daily News*, as well as features in magazines like *Time* and *Look*. Hugh Hefner's *Playboy*, largely silent on the subject in prior years, cited extensively from Welch's "excellent article" in a segment of Hefner's "Playboy Philosophy," and the magazine's Reader's Forum soon came to feature a running exchange on the proper treatment of gay men. Within a few years, it was rare for journalists to join the debate about homosexuality without some preliminary observations on the prominence of that debate itself. As *Time* observed in 1966: "It used to be 'the abominable crime not to be mentioned.' Today it is not only mentioned; it is freely discussed and widely analyzed."[8]

That the subject was so widely discussed did not mean the discussion was enthusiastic. As some journalists went out of their way to qualify, they had not delved into the gay world out of any special fondness for the topic. To the contrary, the gay world itself had allegedly compelled their hand. "Discarding their furtive ways and openly admitting, even flaunting, their deviation," warned the introduction to Welch's essay in *Life*, gay men had "forced [themselves] into the public eye." Homosexuals, echoed his colleagues, were coming "out of the shadows," "emerging openly in the city," "becoming so shrilly obvious that the average person no longer can close his eyes." Whether or not there were actually more gay men in the nation's capital, concluded Jean White for the *Washington Post*, "they certainly are more visible."[9]

At the same time, the American homosexual was becoming, paradoxically, increasingly *in*visible. Psychologists and sociologists had long disdained the myth of the flamboyant fairy, but well into the 1960s the average American's conception of gay men revolved around what White described as "the 'limp wrist' stereotype." Now, reporters tasked with investigating the urban homosexual were startled by his inconspicuous outward appearance. When Helmer visited his first gay bar, he marveled at the unremarkableness of the scene. By the middle of the decade, the homosexual's lack of identifying features recurred in the press with almost obsessive frequency. "The male homosexual is popularly thought to be effeminate and sissyish," the prominent psychiatrist Irving Bieber warned readers of the *New York Times Magazine*. "The confusing and uncomfortable truth is that only a minority of homosexuals conform to these stereotypes."[10]

That truth was so uncomfortable because it challenged a central tenet of the public's relationship with sexual difference in the twentieth century: the popular presumption, encapsulated by the pansy craze of the 1930s though extending well beyond it, that the homosexual was easily identifiable, conspicuous in his physical difference from the ordinary man. Just like the Chicagoan who boasted of his ability to "spot one a block away," many Americans in the 1960s maintained a certain arrogance toward the gay men living among them. "Most normal persons believe they have [an infallibility] in spotting deviates," Doty mused. As late as 1967, a *Playboy* reader derided the suggestion that there might be anything tricky about identifying homosexuals: "Every one of them is as effeminate as a soprano and can be spotted 20 feet away by any sophisticated student of psychology." It now turned out that such confidence had been misplaced. Far from a commonsense intuition, the identification of gay men was a feat that evaded even trained professionals. "Fully 85% or more of homosexuals," Havemann cautioned in *Life*, "cannot be spotted for certain even by the experts."[11]

This discovery filled journalists with a distinct alarm. For many, the newfound invisibility of the homosexual seemed to exacerbate all the familiar dangers associated with gay men at midcentury: the concern about venereal diseases, the fears about national security, the lingering whispers of sexual predation. The "problem" of homosexuality, as the introduction to *Life*'s exposé cautioned, was an issue with which "parents especially are concerned."[12]

Reporters also emphasized the risk to another vulnerable population: the women fooled by the camouflaged gay men in their lives. Judges in the 1950s often spoke sympathetically of the family men arrested by undercover officers, tempted into yielding to their repressed desires, but reporters unveiled a darker scenario: gay men who deliberately led double lives, marrying as a smokescreen for the urges they had no intention of resisting. In the *New York Times*, Doty quoted a homophile activist seemingly boasting that many men pulled off a "successful lifetime masquerade": "wives, children," the whole bit. In *Life*, Welch recounted that vice officers frequently arrested suburban husbands in the city's gay havens. "These guys tell their wives they're just going to the corner for the evening paper," an officer with the Chicago Police Department (CPD) explained. The homosexual's talent for disguise could apparently exact a heavy emotional toll. As *Time* recounted in 1966: "Psychoanalysts are busy treating wives who have suddenly discovered a husband's homosexuality." Subverting the domestic ideals that provided the linchpin of American political character in the early Cold War, the newly stealthy homosexual did not simply pose a threat to national security. He threatened the security of the home itself.[13]

Perhaps the most striking concern overhanging the media's accounts, however, was something harder to pin down. More than the loss of domestic happiness or international power, some journalists lamented the loss of cultural primacy to which the public's blindness to the gay world subjected it. When, in his 1957 study of gay life, the criminologist James Reinhardt reported that queer individuals relied on "the ignorance of the general public" to infiltrate America's cities, it was hard to miss a certain soupçon of smugness. Throwing down the proverbial gauntlet, one subject allegedly told him: "We're safe in this town." Now, as the popular press descended on queer life in the early 1960s, the gay world's supposed self-satisfaction about evading the attention of the public became a recurring theme in its reports. The *Washington Post* opened one column with an implicit challenge from gay men to straight readers. "If someone came through the door now," Clark Polak, the president of Philadelphia's Janus Society, informed reporters, "I bet you couldn't tell whether he was one of us." Discussing the proliferation of gay slang in American cities, Doty cautioned that gay men "would speak of a 'gay bar' or a 'gay party' and probably derive secret amusement from innocent employment of the word in its original meaning by 'straight'—that is, heterosexual—speakers." When *Life* turned its attentions to the subject just a few months later, it only confirmed Doty's worst fears. The same issue that educated readers on the contours of what it called the "'Gay' World" also ran an advertisement for Betty Crocker cake mixes, blithely enticing shoppers with "their gay yellow 'New! Improved!' tags." Having slumbered while gay men organized into robust urban communities, straight men and women had not just left themselves blind to the curious world around them. They had opened themselves up to its mockery.[14]

It was for all these reasons, the popular press insisted, that it waded into the distasteful subject of gay life. "The myth and misconception with which homosexuality has so long been clothed must be cleared away," *Life* explained in the summer of 1964, "not to condone it but to cope with it."[15]

The Gay World and the Emergence of the Police Expert

To educate the public about the American homosexual, of course, the press first had to gather some wisdom on the subject. The most obvious authorities were professional psychiatrists and psychoanalysts, who entered the 1960s as the nation's foremost experts on sexual difference. And, indeed, medical professionals featured prominently in journalists' accounts. In the *Times*, Doty turned to the psychoanalyst Irving Bieber, the primary author of a recent best-selling book on homosexuality, to explain the homosexual's "neurotic" fears of female sexuality. More progressive writers like William Helmer and the *Washington Post*'s Jean White cited Sigmund Freud's early work, including a letter assuring a concerned mother that her son's sexuality was "nothing to be ashamed of." Nearly every newspaper included at least one installment devoted to the psychology of sexual deviance, while Havemann's entire contribution in *Life* examined the latest scientific insights into "the nature, cause and extent of homosexuality."[16]

Ultimately, however, journalists who turned to the wisdom of medical professionals encountered the same limitations faced by bar owners calling expert witnesses in these years. Alarmed by the growing boldness of the urban homosexual, they did not want to know where he came from or whether he could be cured. They wanted a more holistic view of what he was actually like. As Jess Stearn explained in *The Sixth Man*, the goal was to expose the "everyday aspects of the homosexual's world—his social adjustment to himself, his job, friends, and family."[17]

That pedagogical project was hardly unprecedented. By the time the popular press discovered the American homosexual, the study of gay life had been taken up by a cadre of professional researchers and sociologists, who trained their lens on the internal dynamics of the gay world's social and sexual cultures. Journalists' passing references to the scientific nature of their own reporting suggested some awareness of these academic counterparts. As *Newsweek* noted of Doty's article in the *New York Times*, the piece brought a much-needed "sociological" approach to the debate. But in practice, journalists made little use of social scientists in their investigations. For the first half of the decade, the sole references to academic authorities in the popular press focused on Evelyn Hooker's studies of gay men's psychological health—the finding, novel in itself, that gay men were as high-functioning and well-adjusted as their heterosexual peers. Only in 1967, when the magazine *Look* ran the belated overview "The Sad 'Gay' Life," did Hooker receive credit for her more ethnographic work on gay enclaves: what the reporter Jack Star characterized, borrowing her jargon, as "near-communities" with their own "special institutions." Either too academic or too radical for popular consumption, progressive researchers found themselves largely ignored as reporters began their own forays into gay life.[18]

Instead, reporters looked to less rarefied authorities. First among those

were gay men themselves. Shepherding reporters around bars and neighborhood haunts, activists like Randy Wicker and Don Slater played a key
role in shaping the first wave of coverage. Yet they, too, carried a whiff of
political radicalism that few publications openly supported, and their participation was all but expunged from the published versions. More useful,
and more commonly credited in the final press accounts, was another ever-
present fixture of gay life in the 1960s: the police.[19]

In some ways, the vice squads' central presence in media exposés may
have been overdetermined. Throughout the postwar period, when the press
broke its typical silence on the subject of homosexuality, it was the policing of gay life that usually caught its attention. Beginning in the late 1940s,
sensationalistic reports on the sexual psychopath placed homosexuality
at the center of the police war against degeneracy in American cities. Well
through the 1960s, local newspapers like the *Mansfield News-Journal* ran
stories on successful police stings in popular cruising sites and the prosecutions that followed.[20]

Unsurprisingly, then, when journalists seized on the urban gay world in
the 1960s, the police continued to provide a core point of entry into that
phenomenon. Stearn's overview of queer life in *The Sixth Man*, for instance,
drew extensively on interviews with New York policemen, who often displayed a wide-ranging fluency in the gay world's language and culture.
"Mabel and Flo are common names for the passive type," one inspector informed Stearn, before rattling off a series of anecdotes about "rough trade"
loitering on street corners, a hustler killed "in a tizzy" by a "queen," and the
tendency of some homosexuals to "be very bitchy." When the *Denver Post's*
Bob Whearley tried to infiltrate Denver's gay bar scene, he literally found
himself following in the footsteps of the vice bureau. Lacking an insider
like Don Slater to shepherd him through Denver's gay nightlife, Whearley
turned to a "detective-friend" who escorted him to a popular downtown
bar. Curious about a Valentine's Day pageant at the Tick Tock Inn another
evening, he found two vice inspectors already there. Even Fonzi's article for
Philadelphia Magazine, more critical of the vice squad than most, owed a
debt to the police. One of Fonzi's sources was a study of the morals squad
by the law student Richard Elliott, itself an exemplar of how the police
relayed insider information about the gay community to the public. Introduced to gay culture almost exclusively through his observations with the
morals squad, Elliott identified terms like *cruisers* as "police parlance" for
the gay underworld.[21]

Drawing on these diverse authorities, journalists did their best to provide readers an unfiltered view of urban gay life. They charted the neigh-

borhoods where gay men gathered, from Greenwich Village to Rittenhouse and Bughouse Square. They reported where gay men vacationed: New York's Fire Island, "the more or less exclusive domain of the gay crowd." They recounted the professions in which gay men typically worked: "arty" fields like fashion, hairdressing, interior design, dance, and theater. (In many of these industries, Jean White warned, homosexuals "hire their own kind and set up a 'homosexual closed shop.'" Doty, characteristically, espoused a darker theory, blaming the proliferation of gay designers for the pandemic of "hipless, bosomless" fashions befalling the nation's women.) As though ensuring that no readers of theirs would repeat Doty's embarrassing stumble onto the gay world's unique lexicon, reporters taught the public how the gay man spoke, embedding terms like *gay, straight, camp,* and *flaming* directly into their narrative accounts.[22]

Wading into somewhat more nuanced waters, the press surveyed the gay world's complex bar scene. In almost every city, journalists confided, gay men had their choice of drinking venues: mixed bars, welcoming men and women alike; drag bars, where performers entertained devoted crowds with the familiar stylings of the fairy; cocktail bars catering to a "cuff-linky" clientele, where no drops of effeminacy were tolerated; leather or S&M bars, popular with the gay world's more aggressive fringes; and, of course, cruising bars, where men came to pick up new sexual partners. Bar culture was a mainstay of academic research into gay life in these years, a fact not lost on many reporters. As *Time* explained in 1966: "Sociologists regard the gay bar as the center of a kind of minor subculture with its own social scale and class warfare." Unsurprisingly, then, it was the coverage of bars that most conspicuously recalled the scientific tone of that ethnographic project. Welch's article in *Life* opened with an account of the homosexual's mating patterns more befitting a nature documentary than a popular magazine: "In Hollywood, after the bars close for the night, Selma Avenue . . . becomes a dark promenade for homosexuals. Two men approach one another tentatively, stop for a brief exchange of words, then walk away together. . . . [T]he vignette is repeated again and again until the last homosexual gives up for the night and goes home." He described a similar scene in bars: "Throughout the evening there is a constant turnover of customers as contacts are made and two men slip out together. . . . As closing time—2 A.M.— approaches, the atmosphere grows perceptibly more tense. It is the 'frantic hour,' the now-or-never time for making a contact." Fonzi, too, remarked on "the courting ritual" in pickup bars, canvassing the scene with an eye for the kind of precise visual detail that might best be described as zoological: "At the bar, a bird-like figure is perched sideways, thin legs crossed in

6.1. The "frantic hour" on Los Angeles's Main Street, in *Life*'s "Homosexuality in America."
Photograph by Bill Eppridge © Estate of Bill Eppridge. All rights reserved.

front of him. . . . He stares boldly at every new arrival, puffs daintily on a cigarette, [and] motions to the stool beside him." On these pages, the homosexual emerged less as a human being than as a member of an exotic ecosystem, an organism destined for an inevitable exchange of anonymous partners, driven by the least noble urges of the species.[23]

The gay world's pickup culture was central to the media's vision of gay life. In their initial accounts, reporters like Fonzi and Helmer had made a point of qualifying that most homosexual men "have never been to a gay bar"—that some, in fact, "have little or nothing at all to do with gay society." But more prominent publications like *Life* and the *New York Times* soon advanced a different narrative. Meaningful, long-lasting relationships, they insisted, were a rarity in the gay world. Slinking from pickup bars to darkened city streets, the average homosexual could expect little more than a parade of late-night sexual contacts, always chasing the next encounter, always at risk that his "promiscuous" tendencies would throw him in the path of the police. By 1966, the *Atlanta Constitution* would profile two "quiet" gay men, both respectable professionals who disdained the gay world's more flamboyant elements, who nevertheless spent most of their leisure time in bars around the city. "It is loneliness," Hebert reported, that "drives [them] and other homosexuals to their 'gay' bars."[24]

Both the self-consciously academic tone of such accounts and their inherent reductivism were, of course, critical to the media project. As the press admitted, its intimate investigations were an essentially remedial measure: an attempt to compensate for the gay body's newfound invisibility by training the public in the codes of gay life itself. If the outdated stereotype of the fairy had left Americans blind to the queer communities invading their cities, the media's tutorials rebuilt their cultural mastery by teaching readers all there was to know about those communities—by reducing the gay world itself to an object of scrutiny. Far from exposing the limits of the media's pseudoscientific pretensions, as some scholars have suggested, the oversimplifications that pervaded so many journalistic reports captured the very heart of their investigative project: an attempt to map the many lifestyles, social classes, and sexual subcultures of the gay world onto one easily comprehended set of stereotypes, as the first step toward reasserting some control over that group.[25]

Nothing better illustrated that ambition than the coverage of the gay world's clearest outward feature: its clothing. In 1963, when *Harper's* Helmer first noticed gay men's "slim-cut and youthfully styled" fashions, he marveled at how very unexceptional they were. The sport coats, sweaters, and tailored slacks sighted in gay bars were entirely nondescript, the

6.2. "A homosexual sits on a rail in Los Angeles's Pershing Square,"
in *Life*'s "Homosexuality in America." Photograph by Bill Eppridge

type of clothing worn by "dashing young men in college sportswear adver-tisements." But journalists soon set about ensuring that their readers not fall for the same camouflage. In the *New York Times*, Doty noted gay men's "tight slacks" and "short-cut coats" as among their many unknown eccen-tricities, alongside their secret bar scene and exclusive "jargon." In *Life*, Welch drilled his readers in the gay world's fashions: the "tight pants, baggy sweaters and sneakers" seen in Greenwich Village, the "tight pants, sneak-ers, sweaters or jackets" sported by decoys, the "fluffy-sweatered" young men in local parks. Bill Eppridge's photography even provided a visual guide, inviting readers to detect the subtle patterns in a spontaneous array of gay men on the city streets. Like any complex culture, some journalists conceded, the gay world featured a range of subgroups and fringes—not least the "leather" crowd, with its leather jackets and chains. Yet those de-viations were, it appeared, the exception that proved the rule. As the owner of one San Francisco leather bar confided to Welch, niche establishments like his were a haven against the "fuzzy sweaters and sneakers . . . you see in the other bars."[26]

Soon enough, those lessons would take root. Heavily influenced by Welch's piece, Jean White's series for the *Washington Post* in 1965 did not bother explaining the gay man's unique fashions, but rather trusted its read-ers to recognize those items as the telltale signs of homosexuality. "In the larger cities," she observed, men "walk along the streets in tight-cut pants, with long hair and short jackets, and unabashedly declare their homosexu-ality for the world to see." In the *Atlanta Constitution* in 1966, Dick Hebert echoed that "you can tell the types [of gay men] by their dress and their manners," including not just the butches in their sport coats but also the "nelly" homosexuals in their "accepted 'queen' clothes—blousy sweaters, tight jeans, tennis shoes." By that spring, even the New York Civil Liberties Union (NYCLU) could presume that the public understood the sly signifi-cance of tennis shoes, sweaters, and tapered pants. Denouncing the New York Police Department's practice of impersonating gay men, a spokesman for the group had only to remind journalists that "a large number of police spend their duty hours dressed in tight pants, sneakers and polo sweaters." By the middle of the decade, in short, the same casual fashions that had confounded journalists just a few years earlier could be invoked as the red flags of sexual difference.[27]

In this sense, the media blitz that descended on the gay world in the early 1960s did not simply attempt to compensate for the loss of the physical flamboyance that had long characterized public understandings of queer men. It restored that flamboyance itself. Far from destroying the

6.3. Urban gay street life in New York City, in *Life*'s "Homosexuality in America."
Photograph by Bill Eppridge © Estate of Bill Eppridge. All rights reserved.

myth of the self-revelatory homosexual body, readily identifiable by the average American, the popular press's rediscovery of the gay world updated that stereotype for a new era, redefining the so-called overt gay man from the cabaret pansy—all limp wrist, high voice, and swishing hips—to the Greenwich Village barhopper, in his tight slacks, tennis shoes, and fluffy sweaters.

The media's shifting accounts of the gay world's trademark fashions captured the abiding contradiction at the heart of the press coverage of gay life in the 1960s. As those surveys repeatedly insisted, gay men were growing bolder, "more in evidence" than ever before—but readers still needed to be taught where to go and how to spot them. Overt homosexuals were flooding metropolitan centers, "flaunting" their deviation into the public eye—but the press had to explain the fashions and behaviors that made them overt to begin with. For all their ostensible outrage about the brazen visibility of the modern gay world, publications like the *New York Times* and *Life* played a large role in calling attention to the "flagrant" homosexuals who, journalists insisted, forced themselves on a supposedly unwilling public. Training their readers in the cultural significance of such previously ambiguous items as sport coats and white socks, the mainstream press essentially produced the queer visibility it then denounced as justifying its boundary-pushing investigations.

The media's role in constructing the "overt" homosexuals invading the nation's cities confirms the intractable relationship between alleged public disorders like the gay world and the state of public knowledge about that group—the extent to which, not just before the liquor boards but also in the press, the offensive flamboyance of gay men always depended in large part on the public's deliberate attempts to gain some fluency in their culture. Especially as gay communities in the 1960s grew more established in American cities, no doubt some men proclaimed their sexual identities for all to see, wearing unorthodox clothing or unabashedly strolling the streets hand in hand with their partners. Yet as the press trained its readers in the many fashions adopted by gay men partly for their very inconspicuousness, the badge of difference was also imposed on some men who never tried to advertise themselves to the public. Just as the liquor boards' definition of disorderly conduct rested less on the behavior of gay crowds than on the public's familiarity with their habits, the flagrancy of the "flagrant" homosexual depended as much on how gay men chose to present themselves as on how the public expected them to look. Once you learned to recognize them, after all, even a sweater or a pair of tennis shoes could become the red flag of the "'nelly' queens" and "screaming faggots."[28]

The media's discovery of the gay world in the 1960s has been described as a landmark in cultural representations of gay communities. By the same token, the dawning public recognition of gay men as members of an urban subculture, organized around its own social structures and customs, has often been remembered as a leap forward in the push for liberation, recasting homosexuals not as clinical patients or sexual predators but as members of functional communities. Among the press as in the hands of the police, however, recognizing urban gay life as a subculture was not necessarily a liberal impulse. Introducing mainstream Americans to the contours of queer life, media forays into the gay world were a key tool in the social regulation of sexual difference—an often-explicit attempt to give a citizenry that found itself lost in a rapidly diversifying metropolis a new way to recognize and isolate the so-called sexual deviant.

That regulatory drive emerged in numerous ways, from the overtly scientific tone that some journalists brought to their investigations to the reassuring reductivism with which they ironed out the gay world's cultural complexities, turning the gay bar from just one pocket of queer social practice to the cornerstone of the "lonely gay life." Perhaps most clearly, however, it emerged in the policeman's role as the poster child for the media's project: in journalists' reliance on vice officers as the preeminent authorities on the codes and customs of gay life. As they rose from the pages of the popular press, indeed, vice officers did not simply provide convenient source material for the media's tutorials. They provided a model of those tutorials in action. In New York, Doty observed, even as the average American gauchely misused words like *gay*, the NYPD assigned its anti-homosexual patrols to "specialists known in the department as 'actors,'" who infiltrated gay bars, clubs, and cruising grounds to make arrests. In Chicago, police officers prowled through gay bars "pretend[ing] they're queer," blending easily into the coded gay world.[29]

Welch's article in *Life* went one step further, not only assuring the public of the policeman's mastery of gay signals, but shadowing a plainclothes decoy on a typical evening around Hollywood Boulevard. Presaging the media's pedagogical project, Welch reported, the Los Angeles Police Department (LAPD) had compiled "an 'educational' pamphlet for law enforcement officers" titled "Some Characteristics of the Homosexual," introducing recruits to the contemporary gay world. If the scare quotes implied some skepticism about the manual's reliability, the next paragraphs revealed the effectiveness of the LAPD's training at work. As Welch informed his readers, the vice squad ran "an undercover operation in which officers dressed to look like homosexuals—tight pants, sneakers, sweaters or

6.4. A decoy "in tight-pants disguise" and his partner arrest a suspect in Hollywood, in *Life*'s "Homosexuality in America." Photograph by Bill Eppridge

jackets—prowl the streets and bars." Accompanying photographs depicted one youthful decoy in jeans and white sneakers, captioned by *Life*, "a policeman in tight-pants disguise." The following page provided a transcript of his conversation with a suspected cruiser, a slow, repetitive exchange in which the decoy tried to suss out what the man might have "on [his] mind." Demonstrating the officer's fluency in the fashions and protocols of a subculture most Americans barely imagined, the account situated the public and the police on opposite sides of the discovery of the gay world. At a time when most readers still relied on Welch and Doty for the meaning of white socks and tennis shoes, vice officers—those professional students of queer life—had already mastered that world's unique cultural language as a core tool of the trade.[30]

Beyond popularizing a newly sociological account of homosexuality, media forays into gay life in the 1960s thus reflected the shifting social role of law enforcement itself: a growing recognition of vice officers, alongside more familiar medical and academic professionals, as public authorities on the modern gay world. Facing off against defensive bar owners and suspicious judges, policemen at liquor proceedings and criminal trials had legitimated their arrests by disclaiming any unusual intimacy with queer life—by denying the genuinely rarefied insights that often allowed them to bring their charges in the first place. But in the court of public opinion, some officers ventured to take greater credit for their professional knowledge. As the public sought some greater understanding of an urban subculture long entrusted to the attentions of the police, the police ethnographer received the recognition he often forwent in more legal settings.

Police Misconduct and Police Expertise

It was perhaps inevitable, in context, that the media's accounts did not simply bring newfound scrutiny to the gay communities living in the nation's cities. They also cast new levels of scrutiny on the police themselves. Journalists like Doty and Welch had portrayed the vice officer's intimacy with gay cruising culture as a mark of authority, the hard-earned insight of the skilled investigator. But some readers greeted those insights with a bit more skepticism.

For one thing, despite their reliance on policemen as field guides to the urban gay world, most journalists did not present the vice squads' antihomosexual campaigns as unalloyed goods. Even writers who personally sympathized with those initiatives acknowledged that the police's tactics inspired their share of critics. Writing for the *Chicago Daily News*, Lois Wille, warmer than many toward the local vice squad, made room in her reporting for an interview with Pearl M. Hart, a civil rights attorney and (unbeknownst to readers) a cofounder of the Chicago branch of the Mattachine Society. "No, it isn't entrapment," Hart conceded of the vice squads' decoy operations. "But I would say it's unethical."[31]

To the police, such criticism was far from novel. Indeed, if gay communities had to adjust to the onslaught of press attention in the 1960s, the nation's police forces in these years were far more accustomed to the media spotlight. The growing coverage of urban vice squads emerged alongside two ongoing debates about the limits of police power in the United States, both of which dovetailed, conveniently enough, with the work of antihomosexual policing itself.

The first of these involved the historic, seemingly unyielding problem of police brutality, long concentrated on the nation's black communities and now illuminated by the newly active civil rights movement. Beginning with the birth of the modern police department, newspapers like the *New York Times* had cataloged the myriad abuses inflicted by policemen on civilians, from the street violence of the nineteenth century to the "third degree" used to interrogate suspects in the early twentieth. In the 1960s, a series of spectacular confrontations between police officers and black demonstrators in the South reignited those concerns, as raw footage of Alabama sheriff Jim Clark corralling peaceful marchers with bullwhips, or Birmingham public safety commissioner Bull Connor unleashing dogs and fire hoses on black schoolchildren, horrified people across the nation. Northern departments often protested the negative coverage, resentful of what they saw as an unfair conflation of their professionalized forces and the excesses of southern sheriffs. But in the North, too, simmering tensions between police departments and the poor, primarily black communities they often targeted—as well as, increasingly, the anti–Vietnam War demonstrators with whom they clashed—sometimes erupted in violence. Although polls suggested that the majority of Americans, especially white Americans, continued to support policemen over their detractors, the persisting headlines spotlighting racism and brutality left the departments' media image in a self-described crisis. As one former commissioner lamented in the *New York Times* in 1966: "Never before in the 150-year history of law enforcement has the police 'stock' been at a lower point."[32]

The second debate touched on a quieter form of police violence. At the height of the Cold War, when politicians commonly defined American freedom in contrast with the shadow of the totalitarian state, some of the police's own investigative excesses struck critical observers as uncomfortably blurring the line. These excesses included novel surveillance technologies like wiretapping, a practice that drew immediate comparison to Nazi Germany and Soviet Russia when officially sanctioned by Congress in 1954, and that continued to rile commentators well through the 1960s. Among commentators from law school students to Supreme Court justices, indeed, anxieties about Orwellian encroachments on privacy often made room for the vice squads' clandestine surveillance tactics. But perhaps the most heated rhetoric of totalitarianism settled on another hallmark of the police state: the undercover agent.[33]

Perfected by investigators during the Prohibition era, the "ugly and evil business" of entrapment gained particular notoriety in cases involving alcohol and narcotics. In court, of course, that doctrine was largely a formality, but in popular debates it emerged as a libertarian bête noire, a testament to all that made policing antidemocratic. By the 1950s, the rhetoric of entrapment suffused commentaries on tactics ranging from informants sent to infiltrate black political organizations by the House Un-American Activities Committee (a practice borrowed, the *Cleveland Call and Post* decried, "from the Communist world") to the use of unmarked cars to catch speeders on local highways (a ruse, according to multiple politicians, that "smacks of Gestapo tactics"). In some cases, indeed, the growing antipathy to undercover agents supplanted the historic concerns with disorder that prompted so much vice policing to begin with. After male members of the Hartford Police Department went undercover as women in the winter of 1960 to investigate a spate of public gropings, a trial judge dismissed the ensuing charges on the grounds that the officers acted as agents provocateurs by (of all things) violating an ordinance against public cross-dressing. Asked to explain the provenance of the "musty" law, a baffled policeman lamented, "Search me." Against the backdrop of the vice squads' antigay arrests, the irony was unmistakable: an undercover decoy campaign thwarted by the city's own ancient antidrag laws, fallen so thoroughly into disuse that no one remembered why they were enacted to begin with. But the case also exemplified a broader shift in public priorities. By the early 1960s, many Americans recognized that it was not only gay men who passed so stealthily among them. It was also the police.[34]

The vice squads' antihomosexual campaigns had never truly evaded such criticism. Throughout the 1950s, local newspapers in DC reported on trial judges rebuking overeager decoys like Louis Fochett and Dante Longo. After the *Washington Post* regaled its readers with Frank Manthos's arrests in Franklin Park in 1948, some questioned the ethics of the practice. "Am I the only one of your readers to have had a slightly queasy feeling on reading of the multiple exploits of the Police Department's 'one-man vice squad?'" wondered one Virginian. By the time the DC Municipal Court of Appeals in the *Rittenour* case in 1960 all but accused Robert Arscott of entrapment, the *Post*'s own editorial board welcomed the case as "a service to common sense and common decency"—not, to be sure, because it sanctioned homosexual conduct, which was "offensive to the morals and mores of Western civilization," but because that case pushed back on "another form of immorality." Opposed to entrapment as inimical to the freedoms of a democratic republic, the *Post* was happy to fold the police's antihomosexual excesses into the critique.[35]

The media's extended surveys of gay life in the 1960s brought a fresh level of scrutiny to these tactics. As journalists detailed the vice squads' often painstaking attempts to infiltrate the gay world—the bar raids, the flirtations, the peepholes carved in public lavatories—some readers found themselves less scandalized by the American homosexual than by the police. Their reactions took many forms, echoing the objections of judges who had long bristled at the vice squads' arrests. After *Life* treated its readers to an evening with the LAPD, some readers wrote in to marvel at the waste of public resources. "That police entrapment conversation in L.A. was absurdity at its height," decried one letter. "As a taxpayer, I revolt against the spending of such huge funds for harassment and entrapment of [consenting adults]." Such concerns were only exacerbated by media depictions of gay life as its own world, with its unique institutions and social customs. That sociological account, after all, not only revealed the robustness of urban queer culture but also exposed the patience and effort required by the vice squads' efforts to entice queer suspects. Certainly, not everybody shared the outrage: after running its own exposé on Colorado's "militant" homosexuals, the *Denver Post*'s board implored the city to add more officers to its vice squad, an "expense the citizens of the community would gladly bear." But as media accounts increasingly recast the American homosexual from an unstable predator to a member of an insular, if unorthodox, urban subculture, many began to question his place on the police agenda.[36]

Others were perturbed less by the cost than by the cruelty of the vice squads' tactics, reaching well beyond the boundaries of what they saw as good police work. A year following Welch's exposé, an editorial in *Life* took a more critical tone. Although ultimately declining to endorse the decriminalization of sodomy, it decried the enforcement of sodomy laws in practice, an endeavor made "unjust and repugnant [by] its peephole and entrapment methods." That objection appealed to a range of civil rights groups increasingly venturing to ally with homophile activists in these years, including the American Civil Liberties Union (ACLU) and the Council on Religion and the Homosexual, an organization founded in San Francisco by progressive clergymen outraged by police abuses of gay men and women. In 1965, the council released its widely publicized *Brief of Injustices*, decrying the San Francisco Police Department's reliance on entrapment tactics—what the *Brief* defined as "attractive young police officers in civilian clothes making themselves receptive targets for approach and solicitation." In court, vice officers' ventures into queer fashions, slang, and cruising codes might not have been egregious enough to prove that they initiated a solicitation, justifying judicial intervention. But in the far more flexible arena of public opinion, they were more than sufficient to raise some eyebrows about the nature of the vice squads' tactics.[37]

As among judges who recoiled against police enticement in the 1950s, these critiques sometimes reflected the unique nature of antihomosexual enforcement, and especially the persisting hold of psychiatry over public discussion of sexual difference—the fear that decoys tempted vulnerable suspects to submit to their latent sexual curiosity. As Saul Bellow mused in a 1961 novel, imagining an enticement arrest: "You don't destroy a man's career because he yielded to an impulse in that ponderous stinking cavern . . . where no mind can be sure of stability, where policemen . . . tempt and trap poor souls."[38]

Yet the specter of the overaggressive decoy also tapped into a more universal critique of proactive policing. Not coincidentally, public attacks on the entrapment of gay men often appeared alongside broader denunciations of police abuses. Excoriating "New York's Finest" in the liberal magazine *Commentary*, for instance, Thomas Brooks listed the vice squads' entrapment arrests among a litany of sins including brutality, racism, and entrenched conservatism. "So far as the police are concerned," he concluded, "drug addicts, homosexuals, derelicts, and (occasionally) off-beat citizens are fair game." A frequent critic of antihomosexual abuses, the *New Republic* ran its repudiations of the vice squad alongside its reports on the police harassment of Vietnam War protestors, civil rights activists, and black youth. Especially as media accounts recharacterized gay men as members of an urban subculture—what homophile activists had long presented as a minority group like any other—the vice squads' campaigns in bars and cruising sites struck progressive readers as yet another exhibit in the shameful history of police officers going out of their way to harass vulnerable populations.[39]

And some worried, to the contrary, that the vice squads' excesses were not limited to homosexuals at all. As early as 1961, when the *San Francisco Examiner* reported on the local liquor board's attempts to "train" policemen to imitate gay men, one alarmed citizen wrote to the *New-Call Bulletin* to decry the agency's "Gestapo-like tactics." Clarifying that he himself had "never been a patron of this type of bar," the writer nevertheless insisted that the Department of Alcoholic Beverage Control's crusade was a threat to all citizens, "only one more step to the building of a police state." By the middle of the decade, others echoed the fear that the vice squads' campaigns impinged on the liberties of homosexuals and heterosexuals alike. In 1966, after a judge in Ohio convicted a cruiser of disorderly conduct on the basis of his alleged use of homosexual "signals" in a university bathroom, a university employee wrote to *Playboy* in fear that he might soon fall victim to a false arrest. "I'll probably get a case of inflamed bladder now, because I'll be afraid to go into the restrooms," he bemoaned. "How can an ordinary heterosexual know what the 'signals' are and be sure he won't innocently use one of them?" In its own way, the employee's complaint lamented the same cultural ignorance that journalists like Doty had tried to correct a few years earlier, but the stakes had changed. Where Doty warned that a straight man's inadvertent use of queer codes might attract a gay man's derision—or, at worst, his undesired attention—by 1966 some readers were more worried about attracting the attention of the police.[40]

Behind these pragmatic concerns about the squandering of state resources or even the inherently undemocratic nature of plainclothes policing, however, lurked another criticism of the vice squads' operations—one driven less by wastefulness or potential unfairness than by the strange intimacies those operations required. As details of their nightly immersions in queer life entered the media spotlight—the time spent "peeking through little holes into men's rooms," or loitering suggestively by public urinals—vice officers' unusual acquaintance with the urban gay world began to strike some readers as, to put it mildly, a dubious professional accomplishment.[41]

As it happened, the explosion of media attention in the 1960s came on the heels of a high-profile cautionary tale of the state's excessive entanglements with the gay world. The agency involved in that case was not the police, but a legislative commission: the Florida Legislative Investigation Committee, initially headed by Charley Johns, whose 1964 pamphlet *Homosexuality and Citizenship in Florida* was adopted as a training guide by law enforcement units across the state. Proposing to share some "basic knowledge" about homosexual men with government employees as well as any "individual concerned with the moral climate of the state," the Johns Committee minced no words about its regulatory ambitions, and some citizens applauded the effort. As one Miami resident wrote after hearing the pamphlet described in the press: "I admire you very much for publishing this booklet and I do hope it will shock our State Legislature into making some new and stiff laws to control these sex deviates."[42]

Unfortunately for the Johns Committee, most citizens who actually read *Homosexuality and Citizenship in Florida* were shocked less by the gay world than by the pamphlet's own sensationalistic indulgences. Eager to impress readers with the sordid nature of queer life, the booklet veered into graphic detail, from a step-by-step guide to the use of glory holes to an official glossary that devolved into a voyeuristic catalog of sexual fetishes. But the text paled against the illustrations that accompanied it. Eager to impress readers with the gay world's purportedly depraved sexual appetites, the Johns Committee punctuated its accounts of gay men's cruising practices and alleged taste for young partners with photographs that made *Life*'s peek inside the interior of a gay bar seem staid in comparison. First was the cover, an intimate photograph of two nude men kissing printed in bright purple ink. Readers who ventured further inside were rewarded with more explicit

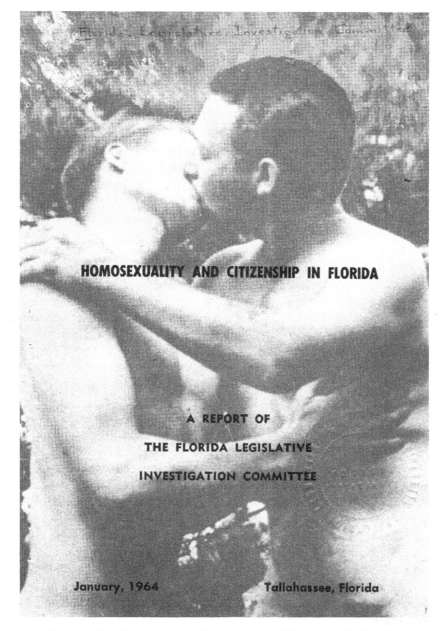

HOMOSEXUALITY AND CITIZENSHIP IN FLORIDA

A REPORT OF

THE FLORIDA LEGISLATIVE

INVESTIGATION COMMITTEE

January, 1964   Tallahassee, Florida

6.5. The cover of the "Purple Pamphlet." *Homosexuality and Citizenship in Florida: A Report of the Florida Legislative Investigation Committee* (Tallahassee: Florida Legislative Investigation Committee, 1964). Courtesy of the P. K. Yonge Library of Florida History, Special and Area Studies Collections, George A. Smathers Libraries, University of Florida.

imagery, including erotic prints of young boys and a snapshot of two cruisers having oral sex through a partition in a public bathroom. Within a year, the Guild Press, a gay publishing house in DC, was distributing bootleg copies of the "Purple Pamphlet," as it came to be known, as novelty pornography.[43]

Homosexuality and Citizenship in Florida turned into an instant scandal for the Florida legislature. The state attorney of Dade County dismissed it as "obscene and pornographic," a "means of engendering homosexuality" among the youth rather than restricting it. The state representative Fred Karl lambasted the Johns Committee for effectively disseminating gay erotica, decrying "anyone, and especially a committee of the legislature, [that] engaged in the publication of such vile material." The attacks soon spread beyond Florida's borders. An editorial in the *Nation* marveled at the Johns Committee's "strange preoccupation with homosexuality." The committee's "war to protect the people of Florida from . . . dangerous homosexuals," echoed the *New Republic*, "has taken a rather odd turn." Engendering homosexuality among Florida's youth, as these insinuations suggested, was not the sole concern raised by the pamphlet's graphic detail. As during the Lavender Scare, when political cartoonists lampooned Senate Republicans' zeal for tracking down suspected homosexuals in the State Department, the sheer prurience of the Purple Pamphlet called the Johns Committee's own motivations into question. Forced to defend its use of state funds on such salacious reading material, the committee disbanded in the summer of 1965, a victim of having succeeded perhaps too well at its goal of exposing the American homosexual.[44]

The Johns Committee was unique in its investigative excesses; other police efforts to infiltrate the gay world inspired no such outpouring of raw derision. Nevertheless, as journalists exposed the complexity of both the gay world and the vice squads' attempts to patrol it, the suspicions generated by *Homosexuality and Citizenship in Florida* did not disappear alongside it. With details of the police's intimate intrusions flooding the popular press, critics refocused the skepticism that had greeted the Johns Committee's "odd" fixation on homosexuality on the vice squads' ongoing campaigns: what the *New York Post*'s James Wechsler denounced in 1966 as a "preoccupation" among police officers with "hounding" homosexuals.[45]

The first to spot this potential opening into the sympathies of the American public were gay men themselves, who commonly and strategically mocked the tenuous lines between vice officers and the alleged degenerates they patrolled. Interviewed by Jess Stearn, one gay man derided the NYPD officers who "postur[ed] for a half hour" in public bathrooms. "They should be the ones charged with loitering," he insisted. Speaking with the

Atlanta Constitution's Dick Hebert, another recounted that decoys routinely "expose[d] themselves" to cruisers, making "themselves more than available" for sexual overtures. (With either impressive artlessness or impressive dryness, he added: "I don't believe it's a policeman's job to do that. . . . Of course I don't know what else they do.") When *Playboy* clarified that the signal for which the Ohio university student had been arrested was tapping one's foot in a toilet stall, one reader wrote to express his astonishment. It must set "some kind of record when a homosexual like me learns 'tricks of the trade' he knew nothing about from *Playboy*, which you learned from the police department," marveled A. J. Seagrams. "And *I'm* considered abnormal!" Encapsulating the curious flow of information created by the media's tutorials on gay life in the 1960s—popular magazines obtaining insider knowledge about queer practices from the police force and then relaying it to the public—Seagrams's complaint captured the intrinsic dubiousness of a law enforcement agency apparently more sophisticated in the ways of gay sex than some gay men.[46]

Others adopted a more aggressive rhetoric. Whether out of derision for the vice squads' crusades or genuine skepticism of the decoys who flirted so convincingly with their targets, many gay men had long suggested that officers who frequented queer cruising sites for a living were gay themselves. One San Franciscan remembered marveling at the police department's staffing choices. "Often the most handsome, hung, desirable-looking cops were used for these plainclothes operations," he remarked. "I often wondered who did the selecting." In Los Angeles, another gay man insisted that the plainclothes officers who walked the streets "teasing" homosexuals were part of the problem they policed: "Most of these guys were living with other cops themselves, you know?" Speaking to Stearn in 1961, multiple New Yorkers implied that decoys who enticed solicitations were more than professionally invested in their work. "It takes one to know one," Stearn summarized. Or as one subject more colorfully put it: "It takes lavender to smell lavender."[47]

In part, such winking insinuations were a defensive polemic, an attempt to embarrass the officers who tormented gay men by launching presumably offensive aspersions against their own sexual practices, even out of earshot. But the persisting rumor that police decoys "must" have been gay to perform their duties well also reflected another shadow overhanging the project of infiltrating the gay world in these years: the persisting claim, both in and beyond the gay community, that gay men boasted a unique ability to identify kindred spirits. Sensitive to the vice squads' mounting arrests, most gay men by the 1960s had discarded the truism that they could invariably recognize fellow homosexuals, but in public, at least, many continued to defend the proposition. In the *New York Times*, Doty contrasted the average man's blindness to homosexuals with gay men's own claimed "infallibility in identifying others of their kind." Most gay men, echoed Stearn in the *Sixth Man*, are "confident they can tell a homosexual anywhere"—gifted, as one interviewee put it, with "a sixth sense nonhomosexuals can never develop."[48]

Should skeptical readers have hesitated to take gay men at their word, those boasts received significant support from the nation's leading experts on sexual difference. Psychiatrists first espoused gay men's ostensible powers of self-recognition as early as the 1930s, when the professional journal *Mental Hygiene* reported that "homosexuals recognize each other intuitively as well as through experience." Over the coming decades, that notion emerged as a key plank of the medical profession's turn against the myth of the fairy. Far from advertising their difference, the psychoanalyst Abram Kardiner insisted in 1954, "homosexuals recognize one another by mysterious signs to which the heterosexual male is blind." Even as most people struggled to spot homosexuals, echoed Irving Bieber in 1964, gay men identified each other through "subtle behavior cues," often adopted "without [their] even being consciously aware of it." His intuition for picking out fellow homosexuals, some doctors deduced, meant that the gay man rarely approached partners who did not share his predilections. As Columbia University's David Abrahamsen speculated: "It is as though there is a mutual sexual attraction between them."[49]

Coming from either authority, the gay world's remarkable talent for self-identification was of course overstated—unsurprisingly so, since, in both cases, that claim intersected with deeper institutional interests. Among gay men themselves, that proposition was part of the same power play underlying the public's confidence that it could identify queer men on sight, a rebuttal to the arrogance and contempt with which popular culture treated the fairy. Among psychiatrists, it served a different political gambit: turning the identification of homosexuality into a matter of trained expertise. Psychiatrists' insistence on the difficulty of classifying gay men inflated their own professional status, narrowing the field of those fluent in the diagnosis of sexual difference. Only coincidentally did that claim also concede that the expertise involved in spotting homosexuals was not always a scientific talent; it was, in most cases, a skill honed and practiced by gay men themselves.[50]

Regardless, by the 1960s, faith in the homosexual's alleged instincts for detecting kindred spirits led some members of the public to suspect that there was not just something abnormal about one man soliciting another man. There was also something abnormal about being solicited. As the advice doyenne Ann Landers recounted in a 1964 column: "I've had many letters from boys who are filled with fear because a number of homosexuals have made passes at them. They are afraid something must be wrong with them or they would not attract 'queers.'" Police officers were not immune to this concern. In *The Sixth Man*, Jess Stearn described an interview with one NYPD detective, apparently not a member of the vice squad, who went out of his way to humiliate a gay man who had propositioned him on the streets of Herald Square. The officer, Stearn explained, "half-resent[ed] the fact that he had been singled out by a 'fairy.'"[51]

Whether out of political sympathy or an appreciation of the absurd, critics outside the gay community soon caught on to the critique. Decrying the vice squads' enticement arrests, some civil libertarians deliberately blurred the line between predator and prey, depicting the decoy in terms that made him indistinguishable from any other member of the queer marketplace. In Chicago, the attorney Pearl Hart recounted that attractive decoys "go out almost on the make, you might say," flirting with gay men and plying them with drinks. "Cruising gay bars," the progressive journalist Webster Schott echoed in the *New York Times* in 1967, policemen affecting gay mannerisms tried to "ensnare homosexuals." Some critics made their implications clearer. Decrying the criminal justice system's abuses of gay men, *Philadelphia Magazine*'s Gaeton Fonzi consulted an expert to illuminate some officers' unusual zeal for vice enforcement. "Those who seem to crack down the hardest on homosexuals," one psychiatrist explained, "are probably fighting their own tendencies in some way." (This psychiatric theory, too, was not lost on gay men protesting the police's tactics. Writing to *Playboy*, one described the visible erotic excitement of two decoys he encountered in the field. "Need I remind your sophisticated readers," he concluded archly, "of Freud's discovery that those who enjoy persecuting homosexuals are persons fighting their own subconscious impulses in that direction?") Grappling with the vice squads' intrusions into the gay world, journalists and doctors, no less than gay men themselves, found themselves questioning the motives behind those regulatory campaigns.[52]

Among vice officers, these insinuations were nothing new. The ribald teasing around the station room—the jokes that "it takes one to catch one," or that decoys, as the LAPD's Max Hurlbut recalled it, "enjoy the job a little too much"—were part of what many officers resented about the work. Some decoys shrugged off such insults in good spirits. The Los Angeles civil rights attorney Herb Selwyn remembered accidentally approaching an arresting officer while trying to identify a new client in court. "I know I look like a fag," the officer reassured him, without a hint of embarrassment. "That's why they chose me for this assignment." But others approached the inevitable cases of mistaken identity with less magnanimity. Stearn had detailed the annoyance of the plainclothes detective propositioned in Herald Square, but the city's gay community preferred a different anecdote. While waiting to testify in court in Manhattan, one decoy officer found himself accidentally called to the stand in the defendant's place. After an aide alerted the presiding judge to his mistake, a wave of suppressed laughter in the courtroom left the young officer "blush[ing]." Aware that their jobs forced them to cross social boundaries no ordinary man was expected to transgress, some vice officers grew self-conscious about what their consummate camouflage implied about their own sexual lives.[53]

Against this backdrop, critics' insinuations about the motives behind vice officers' unusual immersions in gay culture hit a nerve. When journalists like Welch first turned to police departments to mine their unique exposure to the gay world, some officers openly emphasized their insights as the hard-earned wisdom of professional investigators charged with patrolling a secretive sexual underground. But officials better attuned to the demands of public relations soon grew sensitive to the optics of their antihomosexual campaigns. Interviewed by Jean White for the *Washington Post*, a police official eager to appease critics like *Life*'s outraged taxpayer denounced rumors that the morals squad spent its days peeking through the windows of men's lavatories. "Our officers may go in for five or ten minutes and then leave to come back again," he insisted. "They don't sit by hours at peepholes. They don't have the time." Speaking to the *Chicago Daily News*'s Lois Wille, Lieutenant O'Grady qualified that the CPD's vice squad focused its energies primarily on prostitution and "the crime syndicate." His officers were "not interested in going after queers."[54]

Police spokespeople made a particular point of downplaying the queer camouflage that outlets like *Life* presented as the vice officer's most immersive, most impressive professional skill. On Long Island, the Suffolk County Police Department dismissed accusations that officers "pos[ed] as homosexuals" to entice solicitations. The policemen who arrested gay men across Fire Island, explained one detective, were simply "patrolling public areas and observing the obvious." Although the NYPD never denied that its operations sometimes required officers to dress like gay men, it insisted that these assignments entailed no special effort. "Plainclothes men in general," Chief Inspector Sanford D. Garelik informed the *New York Times* in 1966, dress "to fit their surroundings." By 1967, one decoy with the San

Jose Police Department felt compelled to write personally to correct the record. In the course of his six months on the homosexual detail, James Wittenberg insisted in a letter to *Playboy*, he and his partner "dressed conservatively, in Levis, sport shirt and loafers," and "never employed verbal advances or other enticements to aid in making our arrests." Recalling the liquor boards' creative attempts to separate telltale homosexual fashions from the generic men's clothing of the day, Wittenberg's "conservative" fashions drew some fine distinctions around what contemporaries identified as paradigmatically gay dress. But his instinct to defend himself confirmed the pervasive suspicions attaching to police officers who stepped too tightly into the shoes of the men they monitored.[55]

Perhaps no department was more attuned to the sensitive optics of decoy policing than the LAPD, an agency distinguished in the 1960s both by its aggressive enforcement policies and by its robust training programs. By the spring of 1964, the department had already instituted a set of internal policies governing plainclothes tactics in the field, prohibiting controversial practices like officers wearing tight trousers, exposing themselves by the urinals, or generally "lending themselves to the character of the homosexual." Policemen sent out to infiltrate gay cruising sites, the department warned, should "avoid any conversation or action which could be construed as willing participation and result in public criticism or embarrassment of the officer." To some extent, such precautions aimed to appease judges skeptical of the vice squads' aggressive enticement tactics, but the emphasis on "public . . . embarrassment" also reflected a broader concern: the recognition that, in the words of one contemporary study, "society does not approve of officers who dress and act like homosexuals."[56]

Nor, the department suspected, of officers specially trained do so. After *Life* magazine invited the reading public on an evening with an LAPD decoy in 1964, the department took multiple issues with its reporting. At the station, officers grumbled that Welch's article was a boon for cruisers, alerting them to decoys' most effective tactics. Some objected to the inclusion of certain quotations by an inspector interviewed for the piece, which they felt did not cast him in a favorable light. But the department seemed especially sensitive to Welch's claims about its educational materials: the revelation, soon echoed in Hugh Hefner's "Playboy Philosophy," that the LAPD had compiled an instructional pamphlet called "Some Characteristics of Homosexuals." A curious *Playboy* reader reported that, after he wrote in to request a copy, the LAPD denied the materials had ever existed, dismissing Welch's earlier report as based on "a misunderstanding." Technically, the LAPD may have been right; the "pamphlet" in question, whose description closely matched the training outline used by vice instructors like Max Hurlbut, was likely not a circulating manual but an excerpt from the presentation. But the LAPD's skittishness about any additional inquiries into its training materials, no less than its prohibitions on overly convincing decoys, revealed its hesitation to appear too invested in learning the ways of the gay world.[57]

In the coming years, as critics continued to question the ethics of and the motivations behind the vice squads' enticement tactics, some departments began to take more concrete steps to attenuate their entanglements with gay life. In DC, where the *Washington Post* had long derided decoy efforts to entice gay men in parks and bars, the seeds of change were sown in 1964, when the police department finally compelled Lieutenant Roy Blick to retire as head of the morals squad. His successor, Inspector Scott Moyer, soon set about repairing the unit's sordid reputation. By January 1965, when Jean White joined the growing chorus of journalists reporting on the gay world, the squad was already distancing itself from the decoy's most embarrassing camouflage: allegations that officers "camped it up," "dress[ing] and act[ing] like stereotyped homosexuals to tempt suspects." When White visited the headquarters, she reported that the officers who greeted her were all "clean-cut men with normal clothes and haircuts." In the months following her report, the city went even further, drastically reducing the squad's decoy assignments and relegating the policing of cruising spots like Lafayette and Franklin Parks entirely to the park police. By January 1966, the policy change had ushered in a 50 percent decrease in all homosexuality-related arrests. Long a critic of Blick's "disgusting practice" of enticement, the *Post* welcomed the new policy as "an enlightened and eminently healthy reform."[58]

Meanwhile, in New York City, homophile activists' complaints that policemen impersonated gay men to entice solicitations soon reached the ears of Mayor John Lindsay's administration. Critical to this endeavor was a pair of carefully cultivated institutional allies. First was the NYCLU, which by the middle of the decade emerged as a vocal enemy of the NYPD's enticement tactics, fighting Francis Robillard's arrest at the Harbor Bar in court while decrying vice officers in "tight pants, sneakers and polo sweaters" to the press. Second, and perhaps more surprising, was the local tabloid the *New York Post*. That partnership began in late December 1965, when the Homophile League's Randy Wicker and Dick Leitsch, the president of the Mattachine Society of New York, invited one of the *Post*'s reporters to spend an evening taking phone calls from gay men arrested by the police. Outraged by what he heard, Joseph Kahn promptly ran his own multipart exposé—

not, this time, on the city's hidden gay enslaves, but on the vice squad itself. A few months later, following a meeting orchestrated by another ally of the Mattachine Society, the *Post*'s editorial page editor, James Wechsler, joined the fray, running a scathing column denouncing the vice squad's "medieval harassment" of gay men. Like many critics of the day, Wechsler decried the wastefulness of such enforcement efforts, protesting the "squandering of police manpower" on flirting with gay men in bars. But he also cast more delicate aspersions on what he described as the police's fixation on anti-homosexual patrols—a practice, he implied, that not only wasted officers' time but also subjected them to all the well-recognized temptations of vice work. "One wonders how the members of the special squad tell their wives and children of their achievements," he mused. "Are policemen who engage in the entrapment of prostitutes happier spirits?"[59]

The NYCLU's efforts to convince the courts to intervene in *Robillard* were set to fail, but these more public criticisms, measured against the more elastic standard of popular opinion, had more luck. On April 1, 1966, feeling the heat of mounting criticism, Chief Inspector Garelik publicly addressed the concern that the NYPD's officers entrapped gay men into committing sexual advances. Garelik emphasized the relatively minor role played by antihomosexual work in his officers' agenda, a peripheral concern compared with the time spent on drugs, crowd control, and other police business. Even when police officers turned their sights to the gay community, he insisted, entrapment went strictly against department policy. Declining to estimate the pervasiveness of enticement tactics among his officers, Garelik invited the public to report cases in which they felt a decoy's tactics contravened his directives.[60]

The offer was not well received. The NYCLU derided Garelik's "naiveté" about his own department's undercover practices, while the *Post* soon ran a second editorial against the department's "entrapment" methods, protesting that it was Garelik's "responsibility, not the public's," to bring officers in line with official policy. A month later, on May 11, Police Commissioner Howard R. Leary capitulated to public pressure, issuing a formal policy forbidding police officers from enticing gay suspects. The move was widely celebrated, heralded by legal groups from the NYCLU to local bar associations as an important step toward police reform. Dick Leitsch himself lauded the new policy as "the best thing that ever happened."[61]

This wave of policy shifts and clarifications, limited to a handful of cities with especially vocal critics of the vice squads, did not signal the end of enticement tactics. Undeterred by public criticism, some police officials proudly defended their undercover practices. As the head of one morals squad insisted: "I don't care how my men catch them, so long as they catch the right ones. . . . Rats must be trapped." Even in cities like New York and Los Angeles, neither the police departments' prohibitions on embarrassing decoy methods nor their formal bans on entrapment extinguished the practice of officers impersonating gay men in parks and bars. In Manhattan, prosecutors continued to charge suspects approached by undercover officers. Around Hollywood, gay men reported officers flirting and exposing themselves in public bathrooms well through the end of the decade. Police departments' pains to distance themselves publicly from controversial plainclothes tactics, in short, hardly bespoke a genuine commitment against the "evil business" of entrapment.[62]

It did, however, reveal the public stigma attaching to vice officers who appeared too intimate with the contours of the gay world. Reporters like Welch and Doty had portrayed the policeman's unique insights into gay life as a valuable skill, both a useful resource for their tutorials and a professional accomplishment in its own right. Speaking to the *Washington Post*'s Jean White, indeed, one officer invoked the vice squad's superior knowledge about gay men as a shield against external criticism. "People can't understand a problem they don't see," he insisted. "We see them." Yet as the media exposés revealed the blurred lines between vice officers and cruisers in the field, the decoy's fluency in cruising culture did not simply cast him as a professional authority on an allegedly deviant underworld. It painted him with the brush of deviance itself. Initially happy to tout their knowledge to curious reporters, vice officers soon discovered that, before the press as before the bench, displaying too much intimacy with gay cruising practices undermined support for their arrests—not merely by raising doubts about the wisdom or fairness of their tactics, but also by impugning the motives driving their "preoccupation" with gay life.[63]

To some extent, that backlash may have charted the fault line between more and less palatable modes of expertise on sexual difference in these years: the inherent intellectualism of studying the origins of same-sex desire versus the nightly realities of same-sex practice. After all, no one seriously impugned the strange fixations of psychiatrists like Irving Bieber or psychoanalysts like Edmund Bergler, no matter how much insight they claimed into sexual deviance—even as Kinsey's investigators in the late 1940s faced immediate criticism for their attention to abnormal sexual behavior. The public's skepticism of professional decoys, sufficiently fluent in the gay world's cultural codes to trigger gay men's own "sixth sense" in recognizing others of their kind, reflected a key distinction between the type of expertise required to recognize a gay body and the type required to pass as one.[64]

Yet that backlash also reflected a deeper tension underlying the vice squads' claims of expertise on the contours of gay life: the inherent paradox of staking out public authority on the basis of the police's unusual intimacy with a subculture defined by its very insularity and prurient desire. At a time when much of the American public greeted the homosexual with competing reactions of profound curiosity and profound distaste, taking the time to learn too much about the gay world—enough, indeed, to fade seamlessly into its exclusive sexual marketplace—did not necessarily bolster the vice officer's professional authority when it came to the problem of the urban deviance. It undermined his legitimacy, casting the specter of prurience on the expert himself.

From *Life*'s evening trailing a decoy around Sunset Boulevard to the rush to disavow plainclothes enticement tactics some years later, the mixed reactions that greeted the vice squads' campaigns in the 1960s suggest both the genuine substance and the treachery of the police's unusual insights into gay life in the postwar decades. A closer look at the media's growing debates about homosexuality reveals the gradual emergence of police officers as professional authorities on sexual difference: epistemic agents who produced novel insight into and shaped the public's own understandings of gay men's social and sexual practices. It illuminates the regulatory underside of public curiosity about homosexuality—a project aimed, from the pansy craze of the 1930s through the media forays of the 1960s, at reasserting some sense of mastery over a discomfiting social group. And it unmasks the profound social anxieties, alongside more familiar concerns about wasteful or unethical policing, that counseled vice officers against claiming too much credit for their expertise in infiltrating the gay world. The police's intimate, immersive forays into queer cruising culture did not simply, ironically, expose the harmless nature of most gay life. They ran headlong into the inherent gap between professional expertise and public authority on a stigmatized subject like queer cruising: the inevitable point at which the policeman's unusual insight into a criminalized sexual subculture transformed into its own stamp of deviance.

That treacherous cultural boundary may help explain the ironic denunciations of the "overt" homosexual that emerged in the media's forays into gay life in the 1960s: the transformation of the rarefied codes in which the press systematically trained its readers into the flamboyant hallmarks of the shameless homosexual. Especially pronounced in light of the press's still-recent consternation over gay men's startling invisibility, that transformation echoed a familiar pattern, tracing back at least to the provocative entertainment culture of the early twentieth century, of emphasizing the effortlessness with which urban Americans recognized the queer body. As early as the 1930s, liquor proceedings against gay-friendly bars had relied on the assumption that any self-respecting urbanite could identify a homosexual on sight—even as bar owners denied any such powers of perception. In Blair Niles's 1931 novel *Strange Brother*, cousin Phil, spotting a group of queer men entering a crowded nightclub, had shrugged off the simplicity of recognizing such "degenerates"—even as the protagonist, June, marveled at the spectacle, suggesting that there was not necessarily anything so simple about it.[65]

From the pansy craze of the Prohibition era to the media's discovery of the gay world three decades later, the persisting impulse to characterize the homosexual body as something obvious, something *self-revelatory*, did not simply allow the public to declare its superiority to the so-called sexual deviant, nor did it simply allow some of its members to advertise their greater sophistication. It also shielded the public's appetite for greater insight into the elusive sexual subcultures emerging in American cities from the aspersions that inevitably attended any show of excessive curiosity about sexual difference. Simultaneously flattering the average American's ability to identify gay men and denying that this ability was an accomplishment of any sort, the persisting, persistent myth of the overt homosexual assured the American public of its control over the growing pockets of gay life in the nation's city while allowing it to preserve a comfortable distance from that phenomenon—to know everything it had to know, without knowing too much, about a still-taboo social group.

Epilogue

In the fall of 1967, the Supreme Court of New Jersey finally heard argument on an issue that had, for some decades, lingered over one of the state's most powerful weapons against gay life: whether the "presence of apparent homosexuals in so-called 'gay' bars," as New Jersey's Division of Alcoholic Beverage Control (ABC) insisted, justified the suspension of a liquor license. That issue came to the court on the backs of three familiar institutions: Val's Bar in Atlantic City, which had retained the Kinsey Institute's Wardell B. Pomeroy to testify on its behalf; Murphy's Tavern in Newark, whose owners called both an esteemed psychiatrist and an athletic coach to challenge the ABC's demeanor evidence; and One Eleven Wine and Liquors in New Brunswick, where Inspector Salvatore had made the impolitic decision to crown himself a "specialist" in identifying homosexuals. The appeal was watched closely by bar owners, civil libertarians, and homophile activists, fresh off a recent victory against the New York Police Department's enticement tactics across the river. The Mattachine Society of New York submitted an amicus brief in the case.[1]

In an opinion issued on November 6, the court sided with the defendants, holding that the ABC's ban on the "mere congregation" of queer patrons was "legally unsupportable." Its opinion reflected a liberalizing view of public accommodations law in general, endorsing a growing tolerance for marginalized groups like gay men and women in the public sphere. It also reflected a shifting view of homosexuality itself. Drawing on the wisdom of researchers like Wardell Pomeroy and the noted sociologist Edwin M. Schur, the court emphasized both the public's growing liberality toward sexual difference and the discreet, self-contained nature of gay life. It took particular issue with the theory that gay bars might lead to a proliferation of deviance in American cities, inviting ordinary patrons, as the ABC's assistant director had warned just a year earlier, to give in to their own buried sexual impulses and "do things [they] otherwise would not." That familiar account of same-sex desire, as a pathology ever at risk of ensnaring hapless victims, was a mainstay of the medical model of homosexuality in the mid-twentieth century, invoked by both legal officials justifying their antihomosexual campaigns and defense attorneys resisting the ensuing charges. But it was, in the court's view, undercut by the work of sociologists like Schur, as well as homophile writers Donald Webster Cory and John LeRoy, who reported that most patrons in gay bars "already are involved in the homosexual life," and that such gatherings "can scarcely be said to produce homosexuals." Against that backdrop, the panel concluded that gay men and women who did not engage in any overtly sexual conduct—conduct, it qualified, still "manifestly offensive" to prevailing moral standards—had an equal right to frequent places of public accommodation. A month later, the New York Court of Appeals went one step further. Evidence of disorderly behavior under the liquor law, it held, could not "distinguish between the activities of homosexuals and th[ose] of heterosexuals," prohibiting sexual displays by both or neither. The liquor boards' effective bans on bars serving queer patrons were, it seemed, on their way out.[2]

The mid-1960s were in many ways the high-water mark of antihomosexual policing in the United States. In fits and starts over the latter half of that decade, following slightly different time lines in different cities, the pervasive surveillance that hung over gay life following World War II began to wind down. In New York and Washington, DC, mounting criticism of plainclothes decoys among journalists and civil libertarians compelled the vice squads to retreat from their controversial enticement tactics. In San Francisco, a confrontation between the police and attendees at a New Year's Eve ball in the last hours of 1964 sparked widespread condemnation among the city's legal elite, ushering in a détente in bar raids, a gradual decline in decoy patrols, and, by the fall of 1966, a community liaison between the police and the gay community. In Los Angeles, a series of violent bar raids, including high-profile encounters at the Black Cat and the Patch Bar, spurred a wave of newly vocal activism, leading to the city's first pickets against antigay abuses in the early months of 1967, the launch of *The Advocate* magazine later that fall, and the organization of the Metropolitan Community Church, dedicated to outreach among queer communities, in 1968. Across the country, rising concerns about proliferating surveillance technologies, culminating in the Supreme Court's 1967 opinion in *Katz v. United States*, led many courts to prohibit the clandestine observation of at least enclosed toilets by the early 1970s.[3]

It was not, of course, that the project of antihomosexual policing ceased in the United States. Well into the 1970s, gay men reported that vice squads sent officers to entice suspected cruisers in bathhouses, bus stations, and bathrooms—a practice that has persisted, on a lesser scale, to this day. Constitutional challenges to clandestine surveillance, although growing increasingly rare, continued to make their way through the appellate courts into the 1980s. And setting aside those favorite tools of the vice squad, police officers continued to use loitering statutes, disorderly conduct laws, and simply the power of the badge to badger, if not outright brutalize, queer men and women in bars, parks, and other public spaces.[4]

But that regulatory project redirected itself, for the most part, into a different manner of policing—one embodied in perhaps the single best-remembered confrontation between the police and the queer community in the United States, arising in the early morning of June 28, 1969, at New York City's Stonewall Inn. It was no coincidence, after all, that when the policing of homosexuality reclaimed the national spotlight during the Stonewall riots, the catalyst was not a plainclothes operation or a clandestine surveillance post but a raid carried out primarily by uniformed policemen, against a bar popular not only with middle-class men but also with hippies, homeless teenagers, and drag queens and trans women of all races. The images of that night were, increasingly, the face of antigay policing in America: a project pursued largely by uniformed officers, focusing on the spectacular use of force and intimidation to keep a marginalized community in its place. And a project that increasingly focused, like so many police abuses in the coming decades, on the poor, the gender nonconforming, and the black and brown members of the queer community, who would continue to bear the weight of police scrutiny even as more "respectable" segments fought their way into the fold of state protection.[5]

The vice squads' most infamous antihomosexual campaigns in the mid-twentieth century were thus, in a meaningful sense, a regulatory bubble: a relatively contained period when the suppression of gay life drew uniquely sustained and pervasive police attention. Beginning shortly before World War II and continuing for roughly two decades afterward, the most infamous emblems of those campaigns—the enticement tactics, the surveillance posts, the infiltration of gay bars by liquor agents—were fueled by a combination of political, institutional, and cultural trends, from a growing concern with predatory sex crimes to the shifting organization of police departments to the changing demographics of the city. And they were eventually sidelined, once again, by a range of factors, some more and some less specific to the work of antigay policing itself. Those factors included gay activists' and civil libertarians' progressively vocal assaults on the vice squad, just one iteration of a long-simmering dispute about the proper limits of law enforcement in the United States. They included a growing commitment to personal privacy—and sexual privacy specifically—as a fundamental right in a democratic society, constitutionalized by the Supreme Court in *Griswold v. Connecticut* in 1965, which emboldened both organizations like the American Civil Liberties Union and individual Americans to mount newly substantive assaults on sodomy statutes. They included an ascendant countercultural movement, originating outside the gay community but intersecting with many of its political platforms in the late 1960s, that rejected traditional sexual and social mores, anti-homosexual and otherwise.[6]

Not least, the gradual demise of the vice squads' campaigns reflected a shift in the nation's understanding of homosexuality itself, which invited a reappraisal of the nature and the merits of the vice squads' tactics. As mainstream Americans discovered a vision of urban gay life long familiar to the nation's vice squads—one that recognized same-sex practices not as a medical illness or a criminal concern, but as part of a complex, mostly self-contained cosmopolitan subculture—many found themselves questioning both the ethics of the police's immersive operations in gay bars and bathrooms and the motives of the officers who carried such assignments out. In that context, many police departments began to reassess their commitment to the work of antihomosexual enforcement—a project that, critics and officers alike increasingly suspected, was simply more trouble than it was worth.

Precisely because of their relative concentration in the years following World War II, however, the police's antihomosexual campaigns offer a rich case study of the operations of vice enforcement in the United States: an illuminating look into the law's contested, ultimately doomed attempts to regulate the ever-shifting boundaries of allegedly deviant sexual practices. And they suggest that this project was more diverse, and far more complicated, than typically thought.

For one thing, the history of antihomosexual policing uncovers the remarkable contestation that accompanied the surveillance of queer communities in the mid-twentieth century, a project that stoked trenchant disagreements about both the value of the vice squads' operations and the proper contours of the criminal justice system. The work of antihomosexual enforcement is often remembered as a single dark shadow overhanging gay life in the United States, an unforgiving regulatory campaign targeting an unpopular social group. But especially when it came to the criminal law, the policing of consensual same-sex conduct inspired diverse and sometimes deeply felt reactions among the different agents of the law, accommodating a range of political, personal, and institutional concerns. Those frictions, in turn, fueled an array of enforcement innovations among courts and police departments, empowering judges to resist what they saw as unjust charges and leading vice officers to adapt their tactics to evade judicial scrutiny.

The project of policing queer life in the United States, in short, did not simply reflect the state's shifting policies on nonnormative sexual practices, or even the political pressures that often fueled drives against urban vice. It also reflected a set of less visible institutional struggles that shaped, sometimes more and sometimes less intentionally, the gay community's encounters with the law. The history of antihomosexual enforcement uncovers the critical role of lower-level state actors in shaping legal policy, departing from and frequently subverting the legislative enactments and political pronouncements that dominate more public debates. It illustrates the profound discretion and elasticity that characterize the American justice system—a form of discretion that allows for the abuse of power, certainly, but that also created pockets of institutional resistance against what some agents saw as immoral, if not illegal, police practices. And it shows that the roots of resistance against the vice squads' repressive campaigns— including the critiques lodged so powerfully by gay activists, civil libertarians, and progressive journalists in the 1960s—were built into the operation of the criminal justice system itself, rehearsed and refined a decade earlier by the judges who administered the law on the ground.

At the same time, the history of antihomosexual policing unearths the intimate relationship between the regulation of queer life and public understandings of sexual difference: the extent to which, in an age of conflicting cultural and professional claims about the very nature of same-sex desire, the law's operations against gay men and women provided a key site for determining the authority and ultimate legacy of those competing views. A recurrent, high-stakes arena for disputing the outward hallmarks and social meanings of sexual difference, legal debates over vice enforcement provide a striking window into the complex politics underlying popular understandings of "deviance" at midcentury, from the class tensions undergirding supposedly shared norms of masculinity to the relative value of commonsense or expert insights about gay life. More than just showcasing those debates, the states' legal proceedings directly intervened in them, applying the weight of the law to recognize certain claims as authoritative over others—to establish binding truths about queer social and sexual practices, if not in the doctor's office then at least before the law.

The persistent intersections between public understandings of queerness and the policing of sexual difference invite us to revisit the legacy of certain familiar moments in the history of gay life in the United States. From the popular trope of the fairy to the medicalization of same-sex desire to the dawning recognition of gay men and women as part of a cultural minority, the twentieth century's rotating paradigms of homosexuality are known to any historian of sexuality, part of a well-recognized narrative about the public's ever-shifting relationship with gay life. In the legal sphere, however, those paradigms were typically invoked by individuals with their own ideological commitments and institutional interests, and the roles they ultimately played there were often at odds with their more familiar public politics. A deeper look at the operations of antihomosexual policing reveals the slippery legacy of historical flash points whose cultural impact has been extensively debated: how seemingly progressive moments of public recognition fed directly into the regulation of queer life, or how outwardly conservative, often painful developments mediated the punitive impact of the law.

Recognizing these surprising effects does not mean that we must disavow the value of otherwise progressive cultural moments, or forgive the harm caused by more sinister ones. This book does not come to bury the pansy craze, much less to exalt the medicalization of homosexuality in the mid-twentieth century. But it does suggest that any account of evolving public debates about homosexuality in these years must grapple with the diverse consequences of those debates—the ways they played out not only in the press or in popular opinion, but also in the courts. Today, as progressive psychiatrists and social scientists have continued to offer up their expertise in legal battles over gay rights—defending the psychological adjustment of gay families, for instance, in defense of marriage equality—it is common to think of the public politics of expert knowledge about controversial social issues as coextensive with its impact in the courtroom. But that has hardly always been the case. Far from a microcosm of broader cultural disputes about deviant practices, legal proceedings aimed at regulating gay life at midcentury embedded their own institutional norms and pressures, which transformed the significance of seemingly familiar ideas as they entered the legal arena. The history of antihomosexual policing demonstrates that any attempts to understand the link between public culture and the law, and especially the regulation of marginalized groups, must not only recognize how popular presumptions about those groups drive public or political demand for regulation. They must also recognize how such presumptions animate the legal frameworks and institutional dynamics through which those groups are policed.[7]

Finally, the history of antihomosexual policing illuminates the state's own complex, often-conflicting understandings of gay life in the mid-twentieth century: both the extent to which the vice squads' campaigns produced new knowledge about the communities they targeted and the profound ambivalence that such knowledge inspired in the legal system. Exposed by their nightly patrols to the shifting organization of gay life, vice officers in these years amassed a body of rarefied insights into the urban gay world, insights they used to bolster the efficiency of their campaigns. And they ultimately helped introduce those insights to the broader public, emerging at the forefront of the media's discovery of the "gay world" in the 1960s. Yet their familiarity with cruising culture often remained, in effect, a hidden expertise. Even as vice officers grew fluent in the cruising world's special language, and even as they used that language to expand their campaigns, policemen and the prosecutors who defended their arrests did not emphasize their intimacy with gay life. From liquor proceedings to decoy arrests to clandestine surveillance operations, they routinely legitimated the vice squads' operations by denying those professional insights, downplaying the social codes and cultural presumptions that often drove the police's most effective campaigns.

Sometimes, that dynamic served the strict requirements of the law: liquor regulations, for instance, that hung on a bar owner's rather than a liquor agent's familiarity with gay life. Often, it accommodated the humors of individual judges, many of whom disdained the police's tactics even when they technically stayed within the limits of the law. And in some cases, the vice squads' professional modesty reflected the delicate cultural status of homosexuality itself. In an age when popular discussions of homosexuality commonly strove to reassure the public of both its insight into and its distance from that uncomfortable phenomenon, vice officers' ambivalence over their own insight into queer life suggested the paradox of the very concept of expertise on a subject like the gay world: the persisting skepticism attaching to anyone who claimed too much intimacy with a taboo sexual culture.

The history of antihomosexual policing exemplifies the complex politics of expertise surrounding a fraught topic like sexual deviance in the mid-twentieth century. The field of science and technology studies has yielded numerous fruitful meditations on the interplay between expertise and deference in the political and private spheres, examining both the use of expert claims to bolster political legitimacy and the ever-present contingencies of marshaling support for expert authority among the public. The project of antihomosexual enforcement is a model of that very process, a study of how legal actors conferred and withdrew expert status on the basis of not only the quality or content of the underlying knowledge, but also the broader institutional, ethical, and political considerations at play, from a court's preferred outcomes to its confidence in its own commonsense presumptions. But that history also demonstrates an additional wrinkle: the extent to which some subjects intrinsically resist claims of authority based on expertise, owing not simply to their politicized or supposedly self-evident nature, but to the suspicions they arouse about the motives necessary to amass such expertise, or the uses to which such expertise will be put. In the case of the vice squads' antihomosexual campaigns, vice officers' unique insights into a criminalized sexual subculture did not support their claims to public authority. They cast the specter of sexual deviance on those officers themselves. The curious legacy of the vice squads' professional intimacy with queer life reveals the tension between expertise on and authority over a social practice defined, in the popular imagination, as both alien and alienating to the ordinary man.[8]

Since its proliferation through the American courts in the mid-twentieth century, the promise of police expertise—the presumption that trained, experienced officers develop some unique insights into the cultures they patrol—has stayed on the forefront of debates about police power. Whether ascribed to judges' sensitivity to the relative competence of the police or their institutional biases toward the prosecution, the trope of the expert investigator is commonly derided by defense attorneys, civil rights groups, and academics as an unearned transfer of power to the police. Yet in the case of the states' antihomosexual campaigns, both in the courtroom and before the press, the specter of police expertise played a more ambiguous role. Far from an automatic claim to deference, the persuasive value of the vice squads' intimacy with queer practices depended on a range of considerations, including the perceived wisdom of criminalizing those practices and the propriety of the police tactics in question. That story supports the view that judicial deference to police expertise is more instrumental than institutional, a way to let judges reach their preferred outcomes in any case.

But it also identifies a new wrinkle for those concerned with insufficient judicial scrutiny of problematic police tactics: the extent to which such failures of oversight might, in some cases, arise not from the courts' inflation of the possibilities of police knowledge, but from their inability to recognize them.[9]

Perhaps most importantly, the history of antihomosexual policing unearths the crucial role of epistemic gaps in the administration of contested criminal laws: the extent to which the states' continuing campaigns against queer men at midcentury rested on the legal system's capacity to sustain, at any one moment in time, multiple competing understandings of queer life. That story provides a valuable counterpoint to histories and political studies examining how legal institutions expand their power through the accumulation, dissemination, and consolidation of knowledge about policed populations. Against the backdrop of ongoing disputes about both the ethics of the vice squads' tactics and the nature of queer practices themselves, the reach of the state's immersive, intrusive antihomosexual campaigns did not necessarily depend on the spread of social insights about gay life through the justice system. It sometimes depended, to the contrary, on ignorance: the selective distribution of those insights among different legal actors, opening up gaps in how the police and those who might exert political or legal pressure against them understood the very thing being policed. Ultimately, this book suggests, it was precisely the legal system's lingering disagreements over the nature of queer life that bolstered the vice squads' sometimes controversial operations. And it was, in key part, the bridging of those disagreements—the growing recognition among judges and the public of a cultural reality long known to many vice officers—that ushered out the vice squads' most aggressive tactics, raising questions about the value and the propriety of those campaigns.

The immersive policing of gay communities depicted in this book has, for the most part, remained a twentieth-century story, with mercifully little place among police departments today. Parts of it, such as the unique social anxieties hovering around gay life in the 1960s, might be specific to that tale. Yet the broader project of enforcing contested laws against marginalized populations, with all the intrusive tactics it entails—the surreptitious surveillance posts, the reliance on plainclothes officers, the pervasive infiltration of communities—is far from a remnant of history. It remains a mainstay of policing against a range of criminalized conduct, including but not limited to narcotics, prostitution, criminal solicitation, terrorism, and gang activity. Here, too, tactics like enticement have inspired qualms among judges and commentators. And here, too, critics have questioned the courts' limited cultural understandings of the communities involved, which sometimes lead them to rely unquestioningly on representations offered by the police.

It is worth asking, then, how far the trends examined in this book may extend beyond the vice squads' antihomosexual campaigns, into the work of policing today—even if those trends might not immediately be obvious. It is in large part the historic nature of antihomosexual policing, after all, that makes some of these dynamics visible, partly through the chronological shifts revealed, but primarily through the demystification of cultural insights that were once more closely held by the police. Only through the collective work of scholars reconstructing the customs and contours of queer life over the past decades can we now recognize, through the lens of history, the gaps that divided the vice squads from the courts. The painful, contested tale of the state's attempts to regulate gay life in the United States may be a classic case of history not simply showing us a shameful past but also casting light into the hidden corners of the present: a study of how, in a system administered by multiple agents of the law, the repression of marginalized social practices reflects the legal system's many ways of understanding—and misunderstanding—the thing being policed.

ACKNOWLEDGMENTS

The writing of a book sometimes feels like a solitary endeavor, but it always reflects the insight, kindness, and support of countless colleagues, mentors, friends, and strangers. I am grateful for an opportunity to recognize them here.

First and foremost, I want to thank the scholar who has most deeply shaped my academic career, my extraordinary adviser Nancy Cott. From the moment I met her, Nancy has been both my most trusted critic and my most valuable supporter. Whether reading and rereading multiple drafts of the manuscript, checking in with articles and literary references of interest, or advising me over coffee in my first years of teaching, Nancy has been an incredible mentor, a formidable example of a historian and a teacher, and a dear friend. The work of nurturing a young career is an act of extraordinary generosity, and I could not have asked for someone more generous than Nancy; I only hope to live up to her example.

Over the past three years, this book has been enriched by thoughtful feedback and warm support from my wonderful colleagues at Harvard Law School, many of whom read each chapter (sometimes more than once) and helped refine ideas over coffees, lunches, workshops, and unceremonious office calls. I am immensely grateful to Nikolas Bowie, Molly Brady, Tomiko Brown-Nagin, Glenn Cohen, Andrew Crespo, Benjamin Eidelson, Einer Elhauge, Richard Fallon, Noah Feldman, Martha Field, Charles Fried, Jeannie Suk Gersen, John Goldberg, Janet Halley, Vicki Jackson, Elizabeth Papp Kamali, Lewis Kaplow, Michael Klarman, Adriaan Lanni, Kenneth Mack, Bruce Mann, John Manning, Martha Minow, Robert Mnookin, Intisar Rabb, Daphna Renan, William Rubenstein, Carol Steiker, Nicholas Stephanopoulos, Matthew Stephenson, Cass Sunstein, Laura Weinrib, and

Crystal Yang. Janet, in particular, has been a disciplinary kindred spirit and moral champion for the project throughout my time here.

Beyond my home institution, I have been lucky to benefit from the keen insights of numerous friends and colleagues, among historians and scholars of the criminal law alike. My deepest thanks go to Christopher Agee, Monica Bell, Rabia Belt, Mary Sarah Bilder, Susanna Blumenthal, Dan Coquillette, Daniel Farbman, Sarah Barringer Gordon, Jill Hasday, Bert Huang, Aziz Huq, Sarah Igo, Jeremy Kessler, Genevieve Lakier, Serena Mayeri, Bernadette Meyler, Maria Ponomarenko, John Rappaport, Daniel Richman, Sarah Seo, Amanda Shanor, Jocelyn Simonson, David Sklansky, and Timothy Stewart-Winter, and to the many participants at the Boston College Law School Legal History Roundtable, the Law of Policing Conference, the Minnesota Law School Faculty Workshop, the Stanford Law School Faculty Workshop, and the University of Pennsylvania Law School Legal History Workshop. I am especially indebted to Margot Canaday, Marie-Amélie George, and Karen Tani, who astounded me with their generosity and volunteered to read the entire finished manuscript, each dramatically improving it. Finally, although I regret that I cannot thank them by name, the anonymous readers chosen by the University of Chicago Press provided astute and gracious guidance at two stages of the project, inspiring and encouraging me to make this a stronger book.

This project began at what is now Harvard's American Studies Program, where, in addition to Nancy, I was lucky to be surrounded by a set of remarkable professors and colleagues. Robin Bernstein, Lizabeth Cohen, Jill Lepore, and Afsaneh Najmabadi helped me see myself as a historian and pushed me to make the most of all my sources. Mario Biagioli, Peter Galison, Sheila Jasanoff, and Andrew Jewett introduced me to the sociology of knowledge, a theoretical framework that continues to underpin my research to this day. My fellow graduate students, and especially fellow historian of sexuality Stephen Vider, read my earliest forays in this field and provided valuable feedback and friendship. Arthur Patton-Hock performed minor miracles to ensure that my research stayed on track alongside my legal studies and obligations.

Beyond those mentors and colleagues, I am indebted to a number of generous scholars who, having no obligation to do so, volunteered their time and expertise to help guide this project into a book. George Chauncey inspired me to become a historian when I was an undergraduate and provided essential commentary as an outsider reader on my committee; his example as a scholar and public intellectual remains an inspiration. Russell Robinson, William Rubenstein, and Kenji Yoshino read the full manuscript in my year on the teaching market and took the time, far beyond what their roles demanded, to provide kind encouragement and constructive comments for revision.

One of the many privileges of my profession is teaching remarkable students who are willing to give their time and insight to help refine one's work. For exceptional assistance in polishing the manuscript, improving it in style and substance, I am grateful to Jordan Ascher, Rachel Casper, D Dangaran, Alexander Guerin, Ben Gunning, Jason Harary, Xinchen Li, Nora McDonnell, Grace McLaughlin, Heather Pickerell, Jacob Steinberg-Otter, and Leah Weiser.

I owe special thanks to Susan Smith, who has kept the preparation of this book, along with the remainder of my professional life, running smoothly over the past three years. From painstakingly tracking down elusive permissions and missing sources to coordinating with research assistants, Susan has been essential to the project.

A history with a national scope necessarily draws on numerous archives, libraries, and collections—which is to say that it depends on the kindnesses of many strangers. I want to thank the staff at the California State Archives, the Dauphin County Law Library, the GLBT Historical Society, the Kinsey Institute, the Library of Congress, the New Jersey State Law Library, the New York City Bar Association, the New York Public Library, the New York Supreme Court Archives, the ONE National Gay and Lesbian Archives, the San Francisco Historical Society, the University of Chicago Special Collections, the Yale Beinecke Rare Book Library, and the National Archives in Washington, Chicago, Kansas City, Atlanta, Philadelphia, and San Francisco for their diligence, enthusiasm, and professionalism. I am particularly grateful to Lee Grady at the Wisconsin Historical Society, Dan Jordan and Andrea Kishner at the New York County Lawyers' Association, Carmen Santiago at the New York Civil Liberties Union, Ray Shine at the San Francisco Police Officers Association, and Kris Turner at the University of Wisconsin Law School Library, who went out of their way to facilitate my research.

In addition to professional librarians and archivists, I am grateful to several scholars and private individuals who helped enrich my sources, graciously sharing their own time and research with me. Marc Stein and Joyce Murdoch generously offered scans and leads from their archival work to help supplement my records. Officer John Mindermann and the legendary civil rights attorney Herb Selwyn spoke with me, multiple times, about their recollections of midcentury policing. Officer Kevin Mullen welcomed me into his home and shared his collection of police reports. The

Philadelphia attorney Richard Elliott mailed me a copy of his manuscript on the city's morals squad in the 1960s. The late, great policing scholar Herman Goldstein arranged my access to the field reports of the American Bar Foundation, warmly welcomed me to Madison, and shared his own memories of vice enforcement in Detroit. For particular gratitude, I have to single out Lieutenant Max K. Hurlbut, formerly of the Los Angeles Police Department. With remarkable generosity and trust, Max responded to countless questions, shared photographs from his days on the force, and even read the manuscript upon completion. Despite anticipating differences of opinion, he never hesitated to advance the project of learning; this book would be a different, and weaker, project without him.

Finally, I want to express my gratitude to the friends and family who encouraged, inspired, entertained, and distracted me throughout the years it took to turn this book into a finished product. Thank you to my academic friends for motivating me with your own terrific projects. Thank you to my nonacademic friends for making me believe my book might interest someone outside the discipline. My husband, Greg Schmidt, has lived alongside this project for years, celebrating new leads and breakthroughs, commiserating about setbacks, enduring lost evenings and weekends, and reading each word of the manuscript at least twice over, offering valuable substantive and stylistic edits. His support of this book is among the least of the things I am indebted to him for, but it is among them.

Most of all, I want to thank my parents, Gregory and Kseniya, and sister, Katrine, who raised me on books, entertained my many historical obsessions, encouraged me to enter academia, and paid for those good deeds with countless holidays and family vacations spent sharing me with this project. They always encouraged me to do what I love—this book included. For that, and for much more, I am deeply grateful.

ABBREVIATIONS

ABF American Bar Foundation, The Administration of Criminal Justice in the United States Study Records, 1956–62, Wisconsin Historical Society, Madison

BAA *Baltimore Afro-American*

Bulletin Bulletin of the New Jersey Department of Alcoholic Beverage Control (1933–47), and Bulletin of the New Jersey Department of Law and Public Safety, Division of Alcoholic Beverage Control (1947–), New Jersey State Law Library, Trenton, NJ

CDN *Chicago Daily News*

CDT *Chicago Daily Tribune*

CSA California State Archives, Sacramento

EWBP Ernest W. Burgess Papers, University of Chicago Library

Field Report Field Report, American Bar Foundation, The Administration of Criminal Justice in the United States Study Records, 1956–62, Wisconsin Historical Society, Madison

GLBTHS GLBT Historical Society, San Francisco

HC *Hartford Courant*

LAT *Los Angeles Times*

MNJ *Mansfield News-Journal*

MSC Mattachine Society Collection, International Gay Information Center, New York Public Library, New York

MSP Mattachine Society Project, ONE Archives

NYAN *New York Amsterdam News*

NYPL New York Public Library, New York

NYSC New York Supreme Court Records Room, New York

NYT *New York Times*

ONE Archives ONE National Gay and Lesbian Archives, University of Southern California Library, Los Angeles

RG276 Record Group 276, National Archives and Records Administration, Washington, DC

***UCLA Law Review* Study** "The Consenting Adult Homosexual and the Law: An Empirical Study of Enforcement and Administration in Los Angeles County," *UCLA Law Review* 13 (1966): 643–832

WP *Washington Post*

NOTES

INTRODUCTION

1. Field Report 31075, March 22, 1957, 3.
2. *Murphy's Tavern, Inc. v. Div. of Alcoholic Beverage Control*, Supreme Court of New Jersey, A-8, No. 5433 (1967), Appendix, 562–563a.
3. Max K. Hurlbut, "Presentation," January 1965, 12, ONE Subject Files Collection: "Los Angeles Police Department—Entrapment & Vice," Coll1012.001, item 88, ONE Archives; *UCLA Law Review* Study, 694 and nn. 47 and 53; Paul Welch, "The 'Gay' World Takes to the Streets," *Life*, June 26, 1964, 72; "Playboy Forum," *Playboy*, February 1965, 37–38.
4. For general histories, see John D'Emilio, *Sexual Politics, Sexual Communities: The Making of a Homosexual Minority in the United States, 1940–1970* (Chicago: University of Chicago Press, 1983); George Chauncey, *Gay New York: Gender, Urban Culture, and the Making of the Gay Male World, 1890–1940* (New York: Basic, 1994); Nan Alamilla Boyd, *Wide Open Town: A History of Queer San Francisco to 1965* (Berkeley and Los Angeles: University of California Press, 2003); Lillian Faderman and Stuart Timmons, *Gay L.A.: A History of Sexual Outlaws, Power Politics, and Lipstick Lesbians* (New York: Basic, 2006); Timothy Stewart-Winter, *Queer Clout: Chicago and the Rise of Gay Politics* (Philadelphia: University of Pennsylvania Press, 2016), chaps. 1–2; Marc Stein, *City of Sisterly and Brotherly Loves: Lesbian and Gay Philadelphia, 1945–1972* (Chicago: University of Chicago Press, 2000); Genny Beemyn, *A Queer Capital: A History of Gay Life in Washington, D.C.* (New York: Routledge, 2015); Charles Kaiser, *The Gay Metropolis, 1940–1996* (New York: Houghton Mifflin, 1997); Gary Atkins, *Gay Seattle: Stories of Exile and Belonging* (Seattle: University of Washington Press, 2003); Elizabeth Lapovsky Kennedy and Madeline D. Davis, *Boots of Leather, Slippers of Gold: The History of a Lesbian Community* (New York: Penguin, 1993). For histories of regulation, see Margot Canaday, *The Straight State: Sexuality and Citizenship in Twentieth-Century America* (Princeton, NJ: Princeton University Press, 2009); David K. Johnson, *The Lavender Scare: The Cold War Persecution of Gays and Lesbians in the Federal Government* (Chicago: University of Chicago Press, 2004); Stacy Lorraine Braukman, *Communists and Perverts under the Palms: The Johns Committee in Florida, 1956–1965* (Gainesville: University Press of Florida, 2012); Allan Bérubé, *Coming Out under Fire: The History of Gay Men and Women in World War II* (New York: Free Press, 1990); Douglas M. Charles, *Hoover's War on Gays: Exposing the FBI's*

"Sex Deviates" Program (Lawrence: University Press of Kansas, 2015). Two notable, if brief, exceptions are Christopher Lowen Agee, *The Streets of San Francisco: Policing and the Creation of a Cosmopolitan Liberal Politics, 1950–1972* (Chicago: University of Chicago Press, 2014), chap. 6; and Emily Hobson, "Policing Gay L.A.: Mapping Racial Divides in the Homophile Era, 1950–1967," in *The Rising Tide of Color: Race, State Violence, and Radical Movements across the Pacific*, ed. Moon-Ho Jung (Seattle: University of Washington Press, 2013), 188–212.

5. On censorship, see Andrea Friedman, *Prurient Interests: Gender, Democracy, and Obscenity in New York City, 1909–1945* (New York: Columbia University Press, 2000); Martin Meeker, "Behind the Mask of Respectability: Reconsidering the Mattachine Society and Male Homophile Practice, 1950s and 1960s," *Journal of the History of Sexuality* 10 (January 2001): 78–116; Craig M. Loftin, ed., *Letters to ONE: Gay and Lesbian Voices from the 1950s and 1960s* (Albany: State University of New York Press, 2012), 121; Whitney Strub, "The Clearly Obscene and the Queerly Obscene: Heteronormativity and Obscenity in Cold War Los Angeles," *American Quarterly* 60 (June 2008): 373–98. On the military, see Bérubé, *Coming Out under Fire*; Canaday, *Straight State*.

6. William N. Eskridge Jr., *Dishonorable Passions: Sodomy Laws in America, 1861–2003* (New York: Viking, 2008), 1–6, 13–23.

7. Eskridge, *Dishonorable Passions*, 14–23; Stephen Robertson, "Shifting the Scene of the Crime: Sodomy and the American History of Sexual Violence," *Journal of the History of Sexuality* 19 (May 2010): 223–42; Chauncey, *Gay New York*, 2–3.

8. On the sex crime panic, see Estelle Freedman, "'Uncontrolled Desires': The Response to the Sexual Psychopath, 1920–1960," *Journal of American History* 74 (June 1987): 83–84, 92–93; Andrea Friedman, "Sadists and Sissies: Anti-Pornography Campaigns in Cold War America," *Gender and History* 15 (August 2003): 213–39; Stephen Robertson, *Crimes against Children: Sexual Violence and Legal Culture in New York City, 1880–1960* (Chapel Hill: University of North Carolina Press, 2005), chap. 10; Chrysanthi S. Leon, *Sex Fiends, Perverts, and Pedophiles: Understanding Sex Crime Policy in America* (New York: New York University Press, 2001). For rising urban communities, see Bérubé, *Coming Out under Fire*, 244; D'Emilio, *Sexual Politics*, 31–33. On the Lavender Scare, see Johnson, *Lavender Scare*; Robert D. Dean, *Imperial Brotherhood: Gender and the Making of Cold War Foreign Policy* (Amherst: University of Massachusetts Press, 2001).

9. Marketing Laws Survey, *State Liquor Legislation* (Washington, DC: US Government Printing Office, 1941). On professionalization, see Robert M. Fogelson, *Big-City Police* (Cambridge, MA: Harvard University Press, 1977), 177–79. For statutory expansions, see Eskridge, *Dishonorable Passions*, 57–59, 94–99; Steven A. Rosen, "Police Harassment of Homosexual Women and Men in New York City, 1960–1980," *Columbia Human Rights Law Review* 12 (1980): 159–90; Freedman, "'Uncontrolled Desires,'" 97–98; Marie-Amelie George, "The Harmless Psychopath: Legal Debates Promoting Decriminalization of Sodomy in the United States," *Journal of the History of Sexuality* 25 (2015): 225–61. On the use of loitering laws, see Risa Goluboff, *Vagrant Nation: Police Power, Constitutional Change, and the Making of the 1960s* (New York: Oxford University Press, 2016), chap. 5.

10. Gerald J. Levie, "Vice and Victim (Police Entrapment)" (1975, typescript), 46, ONE Archives Manuscripts Collection, Coll2012.175, ONE Archives.

11. The emphasis on the legal system's antipathy toward gay men and women characterizes most of the social and legal histories noted above, including especially

Eskridge, *Dishonorable Passions*; D'Emilio, *Sexual Politics*; Faderman and Timmons, *Gay L.A.*; Stewart-Winter, *Queer Clout*; Stein, *City of Sisterly and Brotherly Loves*; Johnson, *Lavender Scare*; Atkins, *Gay Seattle*. Legal scholars have also argued that the law's treatment of gay men reflects judges' overwhelmingly sinister view of queer practices. See Larry Cata Backer, "Constructing a 'Homosexual' for Constitutional Theory: Sodomy Narrative, Jurisprudence, and Antipathy in United States and British Courts," *Tulane Law Review* 71 (1996): 529–96. A notable exception is David Sklansky, "'One Train May Hide Another': *Katz*, Stonewall, and the Secret Subtext of Criminal Procedure," *UC Davis Law Review* 41 (February 2008): 875–934.

12. The story told here thus echoes the work of legal scholars like Malcolm Feeley and Lawrence Friedman, who have examined courts as complex institutions guided by their own incentives, norms, and culture. Malcolm Feeley, *The Process Is the Punishment: Handling Cases in a Lower Criminal Court* (New York: Russell Sage, 1979), chap. 1; Lawrence Friedman, *The Legal System: A Social Science Perspective* (New York: Russell Sage, 1975), 1–24.

13. This story, too, echoes seminal sociological work on courts as creative problem solvers. Feeley, *The Process Is the Punishment*, 283–84; Issa Kohler-Hausmann, *Misdemeanorland: Criminal Courts and Social Control in an Age of Broken Windows Policing* (Princeton, NJ: Princeton University Press, 2018), 13. It also joins a line of valuable histories examining how lower-level public actors use their discretion to shape legal policy. Michael Willrich, *City of Courts: Socializing Justice in Progressive Era Chicago* (New York: Cambridge University Press, 2003); Mae Ngai, *Impossible Subjects: Illegal Aliens and the Making of Modern America* (Princeton, NJ: Princeton University Press, 2004); Canaday, *Straight State*, 4–7; Marie-Amelie George, "Bureaucratic Agency: Administering the Transformation of LGBT Rights," *Yale Law and Policy Review* 36 (2017): 83–154; Charles R. Epp, *Making Rights Real: Activists, Bureaucrats, and the Creation of the Legalistic State* (Chicago: University of Chicago Press, 2009); Karen Tani, *States of Dependency: Welfare Rights and American Governance, 1935–1972* (New York: Cambridge University Press, 2016).

14. This book thus joins recent histories situating queer legal struggles within broader debates about governance and rights making at midcentury. Robert Self, *All in the Family: The Realignment of American Democracy since the 1960s* (New York: Hill & Wang, 2013); Clay Howard, *The Closet and the Cul-de-Sac: The Politics of Sexual Privacy in Northern California* (Philadelphia: University of Pennsylvania Press, 2019); Agee, *Streets of San Francisco*, chap. 6.

15. Robert Beachy, "The German Invention of Homosexuality," *Journal of Modern History* 82 (December 2010): 810–11, 814; Arnold I. Davidson, *The Emergence of Sexuality: Historical Epistemology and the Formation of Concepts* (Cambridge, MA: Harvard University Press, 2001), 4–7; Gert Hekma, "A History of Sexology: Social and Historical Aspects of Sexuality," in *From Sappho to De Sade: Moments in the History of Sexuality*, ed. Jan Bremmer (London: Routledge, 1989), 176–77; Paul Robinson, *The Modernization of Sex: Havelock Ellis, Alfred Kinsey, William Masters and Virginia Johnson* (1976; reprint, Ithaca, NY: Cornell University Press, 1989); Henry L. Minton, *Departing from Deviance: A History of Homosexual Rights and Emancipatory Science in America* (Chicago: University of Chicago Press, 2002); Jennifer Terry, "Anxious Slippages between 'Us' and 'Them': A Brief History of the Scientific Search for Homosexual Bodies," in *Deviant Bodies: Critical Perspectives on Difference in Science and Popular Culture*, ed. Jennifer Terry and Jacqueline Urla (Bloomington: Indiana University Press, 1995), 129–69.

16. For the dominance of psychiatrists, see D'Emilio, *Sexual Politics*, 16, 144; Jennifer Terry, *An American Obsession: Science, Medicine, and Homosexuality in Modern Society* (Chicago: University of Chicago Press, 1999), 309–21; Ellen Herman, *The Romance of American Psychology: Political Culture in the Age of Experts* (Berkeley and Los Angeles: University of California Press, 1995); Kenneth Lewes, *Psychoanalysis and Male Homosexuality* (Northvale, NJ: Jason Aronson, 1995); Minton, *Departing from Deviance*, 232–33. Medical and scientific authorities were, of course, not alone in shaping popular views of homosexuality. On the arts, see Michael S. Sherry, *Gay Artists in Modern American Culture: An Imagined Conspiracy* (Chapel Hill: University of North Carolina Press, 2007). On film, see Harry M. Benshoff, *Monsters in the Closet: Homosexuality and the Horror Film* (Manchester: Manchester University Press, 1997). On political debates, see K. A. Cuordileone, *Manhood and American Political Culture* (New York: Routledge, 2005).

17. For the activist turn, see Minton, *Departing from Deviance*, 239–45; D'Emilio, *Sexual Politics*, 153. On sociological studies, see Chad Heap, *Slumming: Sexual and Racial Encounters in American Nightlife, 1885–1940* (Chicago: University of Chicago Press, 2009), 84, and *Homosexuality in the City: A Century of Research at the University of Chicago* (Chicago: University of Chicago Press, 2000); Minton, *Departing from Deviance*; D'Emilio, *Sexual Politics*, 109–17. Homophile activists also strategically defined homosexuals as a political minority. Daniel Hurewitz, *Bohemian Los Angeles and the Making of Modern Politics* (Berkeley and Los Angeles: University of California Press, 2008).

18. For the corrosive effects of medicalization, see D'Emilio, *Sexual Politics*, 162; Minton, *Departing from Deviance*, 2–3; Regina Kunzel, "Sex Panic, Psychiatry, and the Expansion of the Carceral State," in *The War on Sex*, ed. David Halperin and Trevor Hoppe (Durham, NC: Duke University Press, 2017), 239–40; Eskridge, *Dishonorable Passions*, 94–95; Atkins, *Gay Seattle*, chap. 2; Robertson, *Crimes against Children*, chap. 10. Some scholars have noted the impact of progressive psychiatrists on high-level policy debates. George, "Harmless Psychopath," 227–29; Freedman, "'Uncontrolled Desires,'" 95. My focus, however, is on how medicalization tempered the law's daily applications. Allan Bérubé has noted how progressive psychiatrists pushed the military toward leniency, though he reads the sexual psychopath laws purely as a conservative retrenchment. See Bérubé, *Coming Out under Fire*, 149–74, 258–59.

19. For an instructive discussion of how idiosyncratic legal institutions can illuminate broader public understandings of sexuality, see Regina Kunzel, *Criminal Intimacy: Prison and the Uneven History of Modern American Sexuality* (Chicago: University of Chicago Press, 2008), 5.

20. My reasoning about the social construction of expertise is deeply indebted to the history of science and science/technology studies, which have long examined how expert claims are established through a complex of self-interested and often deeply politicized institutional alliances. Brian Wynne, "Misunderstood Misunderstandings: Social Identities and Public Uptake of Science," in *Misunderstanding Science? The Public Reconstruction of Science and Technology*, ed. Alan Irwin and Brian Wynne (Cambridge: Cambridge University Press, 1996), 19–46; Stephen Hilgartner, *Science on Stage: Expert Advice as Public Drama* (Stanford, CA: Stanford University Press, 2000); Michael Lynch, "The Discursive Production of Uncertainty," *Social Studies of Science* 28 (1998): 829–67; Bruno Latour, *The Pasteurization of France*, trans. Alan Sheridan and John Law (Cambridge, MA: Harvard University Press, 1988); Arnold I.

Davidson, "Styles of Reasoning, Conceptual History, and the Emergence of Psychiatry," in *The Science Studies Reader*, ed. M. Biagioli (New York: Routledge, 1999), 124–36; Sheila Jasanoff, "The Eye of Everyman: Witnessing DNA in the Simpson Trial," *Social Studies of Science* 28 (October–December 1998): 713–40.

21. On medicalization, see n. 18 above. On the pansy craze as a moment of relative tolerance, see chapter 1, n. 3, below.

22. For scholarship examining public culture as a window into legal battles, see Michael Klarman, *From Jim Crow to Civil Rights: The Supreme Court and the Struggle for Racial Equality* (New York: Oxford University Press, 2004); Leslie Friedman Goldstein, *The Constitutional Rights of Women: Cases in Law and Social Change* (Madison: University of Wisconsin Press, 1979); Robert F. Nagel, *Judicial Power and American Character: Censoring Ourselves in an Anxious Age* (New York: Oxford University Press, 1994), introduction; Corinna Barrett Lain, "Countermajoritarian Hero or Zero? Rethinking the Warren Court's Role in the Criminal Procedure Revolution," *University of Pennsylvania Law Review* 152 (2004): 1414–15.

23. Agee, *Streets of San Francisco*, 76–78.

24. For liberationist accounts, see Heap, *Homosexuality in the City*, 34; Minton, *Departing from Deviance*, 239; D'Emilio, *Sexual Politics*, 109–17.

25. See esp. Canaday, *Straight State*, introduction; Freedman, "'Uncontrolled Desires.'" Steven Maynard has also examined how antihomosexual policing contributes to public knowledge by bringing homosexuality to the public's attention. Steven Maynard, "Through a Hole in the Lavatory Wall: Homosexual Subcultures, Police Surveillance, and the Dialectics of Discovery, Toronto, 1890–1930," *Journal of the History of Sexuality* 5 (October 1994): 239–41.

26. On midcentury professionalization, see Samuel Walker, *A Critical History of Police Reform: The Emergence of Professionalism* (Lexington, MA: Lexington Books, 1977), 139–66; Fogelson, *Big-City Police*, 146–49, 155–64, 177–82. On Prohibition, see Humber S. Nelli, "American Syndicate Crime: A Legacy of Prohibition," in *Law, Alcohol, and Order*, ed. David E. Kyvig (Westport, CT: Greenwood, 1985), 128. On judicial deference, see Anna Lvovsky, "The Judicial Presumption of Police Expertise," *Harvard Law Review* 130 (June 2017): 1997–2081.

27. For conventional accounts of deference, see Kit Kinports, "Veteran Police Officers and Three-Dollar Steaks: The Subjective Objective Dimensions of Probable Cause and Reasonable Suspicion," *University of Pennsylvania Journal of Constitutional Law* 12 (2010): 754–57; Jennifer E. Laurin, "Quasi-Inquisitorialism: Accounting for Deference in Pretrial Criminal Procedure," *Notre Dame Law Review* 90 (2014): 816; Eric J. Miller, "Challenging Police Discretion," *Howard Law Journal* 58 (2015): 533; Anthony O'Rourke, "Structural Overdelegation in Criminal Procedure," *Journal of Criminal Law and Criminology* 103 (2013): 410; L. Song Richardson, "Police Efficiency and the Fourth Amendment," *Indiana Law Journal* 87 (2012): 1161.

28. Nikolas Rose and Peter Miller, "Political Power beyond the State: Problematics of Government," *British Journal of Sociology* 43 (June 1992): 175, 179. See also Ian Hacking, *The Taming of Chance* (Cambridge: Cambridge University Press, 1990); Theodore M. Porter, *Trust in Numbers: The Pursuit of Objectivity in Science and Public Life* (Princeton, NJ: Princeton University Press, 1995); Lorraine Daston, *Classical Probability in the Enlightenment* (Princeton, NJ: Princeton University Press, 1988); James C. Scott, *Seeing Like a State: How Certain Schemes to Improve the Human Condition Have Failed* (New Haven, CT: Yale University Press, 1998). On Foucault, see esp. Michel Foucault, *Discipline and Punish: The Birth of the Prison*, trans. Alan Sheri-

dan (New York: Pantheon, 1977), and *The History of Sexuality*, vol. 1, *An Introduction*, trans. Robert Hurley (New York: Random House, 1978). For scholars examining how the regulation of homosexuality embeds distinctive views of homosexual men and women, see Canaday, *Straight State*; Freedman, "'Uncontrolled Desires'"; Backer, "Constructing a 'Homosexual' for Constitutional Theory," 546–47; Joey L. Mogul, Andrea J. Ritchie, and Kay Whitlock, *Queer In(Justice): The Criminalization of LGBT People in the United States* (Boston: Beacon, 2011), 22–26, 69–72.

Consistent with the foregoing discussion, my invocations of state power are intended to evoke not a unified or intentional entity, but rather the work of discrete, often-conflicting agents in imposing what are nevertheless coercive legal duties and prohibitions on private citizens. See Kimberly J. Morgan and Ann Shola Orloff, *The Many Hands of the State: Theorizing Political Authority and Social Control* (New York: Cambridge University Press, 2017), introduction; James T. Sparrow, William J. Novak, and Stephen W. Sawyer, eds., *Boundaries of the State in US History* (Chicago: University of Chicago Press, 2015), introduction.

29. On racial and class disparities in policing, see Khalil Gibran Muhammad, *The Condemnation of Blackness: Race, Crime, and the Making of Modern Urban America* (Cambridge, MA: Harvard University Press, 2010); Samuel Walker, *Popular Justice: A History of American Criminal Justice* (New York: Oxford University Press, 1998); Elizabeth Hinton and DeAnza Cook, "The Mass Criminalization of Black Americans: A Historical Overview," *Annual Review of Criminology* 4 (2021): 261–86. On similar disparities in the enforcement of early sodomy laws, see Mogul, Ritchie, and Whitlock, *Queer (In)Justice*, xviii, 15–16; Eskridge, *Dishonorable Passions*, 17. For a comprehensive review of recent histories, see Hinton and Cook, "The Mass Criminalization of Black Americans." For further discussion, see esp. chapter 3 below.

30. On the lesser attention paid to lesbians, see Johnson, *Lavender Scare*, 12, 155; Margot Canaday, "Heterosexuality as a Legal Regime," in *The Cambridge History of Law in America*, ed. Michael Grossberg and Christopher Tomlins (Cambridge: Cambridge University Press, 2008), 460. For further discussion, see chapters 1 and 3 below.

31. For the sociohistorical analysis of expertise, see n. 20 above, esp. Wynne, "Misunderstood Misunderstandings," 19–46; Jasanoff, "The Eye of Everyman," 713–40.

32. On the historically shifting cultural and sexual identities of men and women engaging in same-sex practices, see Ian Hacking, "Making Up People," in *Reconstructing Individualism: Autonomy, Individuality, and the Self in Western Thought*, ed. Thomas C. Heller et al. (Stanford, CA: Stanford University Press, 1986); Joan W. Scott, "The Evidence of Experience," *Critical Inquiry* 17 (1991): 773–79; Foucault, *History of Sexuality*, vol. 1; Davidson, *Emergence of Sexuality*.

CHAPTER ONE

1. "Editorial Paragraphs," *The Nation*, December 13, 1933, 663. On the repeal of the Eighteenth Amendment, see Michael A. Lerner, *Dry Manhattan: Prohibition in New York City* (Cambridge, MA: Harvard University Press, 2007), chap. 12.

2. Chauncey, *Gay New York*, 196–98, 306; Heap, *Slumming*, 91–93.

3. On pansy entertainments as flights of relative tolerance, see Chauncey, *Gay New York*, 3–4, 331–35; Heap, *Slumming*, 280–81; Boyd, *Wide Open Town*, 26–29; John Loughery, *The Other Side of Silence: Men's Lives and Gay Identities* (New York: Henry Holt, 1998), 40–42, 49–59. While this book is the first to connect the pansy craze to the legal regulation of gay life, the broader insight that knowledge about marginalized communities might have regulatory dimensions is familiar to historians and

literary critics. Foucault, *Discipline and Punish*; Lee Edelman, *Homographesis: Essays in Gay Literary and Cultural Theory* (New York: Routledge, 1994); Terry, *An American Obsession*; Jacqueline Urla and Jennifer Terry, "Introduction: Mapping Embodied Deviance," in Terry and Urla, eds., *Deviant Bodies*, 1–18; Scott Herring, *Queering the Underworld: Slumming, Literature, and the Undoing of Lesbian and Gay History* (Chicago: University of Chicago Press, 2007). Critics have also examined the negative cultural externalities of gay visibility, such as perpetuating stereotypes and fostering a false sense of liberalism. Leo Bersani, *Homos* (Cambridge, MA: Harvard University Press, 1996), 11–15; Suzanna Danuta Walters, *All the Rage: The Story of Gay Visibility in America* (Chicago: University of Chicago Press, 2001), 10, 13, 20.

4. On the liquor laws, see Leonard V. Harrison and Elizabeth Laine, *After Repeal: A Study of Liquor Control Administration* (New York: Harper & Bros., 1936), esp. 7–8; National Conference of State Liquor Administrators, *Methods Employed to Correct and Prevent Violations of Alcoholic Beverage Control Laws: A Survey* (Sacramento, CA, 1946). For state agencies, see Marketing Laws Survey, *State Liquor Legislation*, 371 (California), 637–38 (New Jersey), 661–62 (New York). For the range of agencies generally, see National Conference of State Liquor Administrators, *Survey of State Liquor Control Laws and Regulations Relating to Enforcement* (Sacramento, CA, 1944). New Jersey's ABC was initially called the Department of Alcoholic Beverage Control but was soon renamed the Division of Alcoholic Beverage Control. For clarity, I use the latter throughout.

5. On the early policing of drinking and public culture, see Fogelson, *Big-City Police*, 20–21; Walker, *Popular Justice*, 60–62. On the emergent gay nightlife in the early twentieth century, see Chauncey, *Gay New York*, chap. 9; Heap, *Slumming*, 236. See also further discussion below. For growing police crackdowns, see Chauncey, *Gay New York*, chap. 11, esp. 331–35.

6. On the BOE, see Agee, *Streets of San Francisco*, 84–85. For dispositions of the New Jersey and New York commissioners, see "Home Rule on Liquor," *New York Daily News*, October 29, 1936, 35; Joseph Lawrence, "New State Liquor Czar a Bird Fancier and Nature Lover, but Record Shows Him Bad Medicine for Lawbreakers," *Brooklyn Daily Eagle*, March 12, 1936, 3; "New Jersey Loses a Valuable Public Servant," *Red Bank Daily Register*, April 25, 1940, 6; "Liquor War: Second Phase," *Hackensack Record*, December 16, 1935, 5. For political pressures, see "Editorial Views of Other Papers: D. Frederick Burnett," *Red Bank Daily Register*, April 25, 1940, 6 (Burnett quoted); "State Liquor Authority Warns Legislature against Change," *Binghamton Press and Sun-Bulletin*, March 9, 1937, 1, 8. On the request regarding female impersonators, see "Burnett Prepares to 'Clamp Down': Night Clubs Must Eliminate 'Female Impersonators' or Lose Licenses," *Asbury Park Press*, July 27, 1934, 1; "Bars—Where Men Are Men and Women Must Be Women," *Camden Morning Post*, July 28, 1934, 1, 11.

7. For New York, see *Gloria Bar & Grill v. Bruckman*, 259 A.D. 706 (N.Y. App. Div. 1940), Record on Review, 7. For California, see *Stoumen v. Reilly*, 37 Cal. 2d 713, 715 n. 1 (1951). In the 1950s, some jurisdictions did enact laws explicitly targeting establishments serving homosexuals. William N. Eskridge Jr., "Law and the Construction of the Closet: American Regulation of Same-Sex Intimacy, 1880–1946," *Iowa Law Review* 82 (1997): 1083–86, 1086 n. 301.

8. For the drafting of Rule 4 by Burnett, see James S. Brown, "Investigators Must Hold Their Liquor with Ease," *Asbury Park Press*, May 25, 1967, 1, 6; *In re Peter Orsi*, Bulletin 326, no. 1, 1939, 2. For Burnett's broad ambitions, see "Bars—Where Men Are

Men," 11. For invocations of Rule 4 against drag performances, see *In re Club Harmony*, Bulletin 794, no. 10, 1948, 10–11; *In re P.A. Colored Democratic Club*, Bulletin 852, no. 7, 1949, 12; *In re Polka Club, Inc.*, Bulletin 1045, no. 6, 1955, 8–9; *In re Andy's New Log Cabin, Inc.*, Bulletin 1496, no. 3, 1963, 9. Sometimes patrons joined the festivities, organizing drag parties. *Polka Club*, Bulletin 1045, no. 6, 1955, 8; *In re Tollins' Bar*, Bulletin 1441, no. 5, 1962, 9–10. For *fag*, *fairy*, and *female impersonator* used interchangeably, see *In re Log Cabin Inn*, Bulletin 279, no. 8, 1938, 11; *In re Jessie Lloyd*, Bulletin 1045, no. 7, 1955, 10, 11; *McCracken v. Caldwell*, Bulletin 456, no. 3, 1941, 3–4; *In re M. Potter, Inc.*, Bulletin 474, no. 1, 1941, 1.

9. For New York, see *Gloria*, Record on Review, 6–7, 90; *Loubor Rest., Inc. v. Rohan*, 197 N.Y.S.2d 429 (App. Div. 1960), Record on Review, 7–8. For New Jersey, see *Murphy's Tavern, Inc. v. Davis*, 70 N.J. Super. 87 (App. Div. 1961), Appendix to Brief for Appellant, 6a–22a; *Paddock Bar, Inc. v. Div. of Alcoholic Beverage Control*, 46 N.J. Super. 405 (App. Div. 1957), Brief and Appendix for Appellant, 5a–19a. For Pennsylvania, see *In re Revocation of License of Clock Bar, Inc.*, 85 Dauph. 125, 126–27, 131 (Pa. C.P. 1966); *In re Anthony Wayne's Bar & Rest., Inc.*, 209 Pa. Super. Ct. 756 (1967). For California, see *Stoumen v. Reilly*, 222 P.2d 678 (Cal. Dist. Ct. App. 1950), Opening Brief for Appellant, 4–5; *Benedetti v. Dep't of Alcoholic Beverage Control*, 9 Cal. Rptr. 525 (Ct. App. 1960), Appellant's Opening Brief, 2–6.

10. Brown, "Investigators Must Hold Their Liquor with Ease," 6. For previous careers, see *Paddock Bar*, Brief and Appendix for Appellant, 29a; *Gloria*, Record on Review, 314, 333; *Murphy's Tavern*, Supreme Court, Appendix, 393a. For law enforcement backgrounds, see "Fire Department Aide Charges Dry Raid Entrapment," *Brooklyn Daily Eagle*, March 16, 1931, 2 (Prohibition agent); *Gloria*, Record on Review, 141–43; *Paddock Bar*, Brief and Appendix for Appellant, 44a; Warren Hall, "Guard N.Y. Vice King's Enemies as Jail Looms," *New York Daily News*, December 22, 1935, 34.

11. For police enforcement duties, see *Annual Report of Commissioner*, Bulletin 62, 1935, 1–3. For examples, see *M. Potter*, Bulletin 474, no. 1, 1941, 1; *Williams v. Newark*, Bulletin 571, no. 5, 1943, 6, 8; *In re One-Thirty-Five Mulberry St. Corp.*, Bulletin 892, no. 2, 1951, 2–4; *In re Bader's Bar*, Bulletin 1073, no. 4, 1955, 5–7; *In re Hotel Penn*, Bulletin 1453, no. 2, 1962, 5, 9.

12. For cooperation in New York, see Edward P. Mulrooney et al., State of New York, *Report of the State Liquor Authority, January 1, 1935 to December 31, 1935* (Albany, NY: J. B. Lyon, 1936), 8. For officers and agents working alongside each other, see *Fasone v. Arenella*, 139 N.Y.S.2d 186, 187 (N.Y.C. Magis. Ct. 1954); *Gloria*, Record on Review, 279–94; *Times Square Garden & Grill, Inc., v. Bruckman*, 256 A.D. 1062 (N.Y. App. Div. 1939), Record on Review, 44–45; *Kershaw v. Dep't of Alcoholic Beverage Control of Cal.*, 155 Cal. App. 2d 544 (1957), Brief of Respondents, 3–4; *Lynch's Builders Rest., Inc. v. O'Connell*, 303 N.Y. 408 (1952), Record on Appeal, 27–29, 34, 60–62, 75. For more limited police involvement in New Jersey, see *Log Cabin Inn*, Bulletin 279, no. 8, 1938, 11–12; *In re Joseph & Sarah Silidker*, Bulletin 405, no. 5, 1940, 10–11; *One-Thirty-Five Mulberry*, Bulletin 892, no. 2, 1951, 3–4; *In re Casino*, Bulletin 1050, no. 1, 1955, 4. For growing cooperation in later years, see *Bader's Bar*, Bulletin 1073, no. 4, 1955, 7; *Skip's Bar, Inc. v. Mun. Bd. of Alcoholic Beverage Control of Newark*, Bulletin 1392, no. 1, 1961, 2; *In re Casino*, Bulletin 1456, no. 3, 1962, 7. For continuing conflicts, see *In re Murphy's Tavern, Inc.*, Bulletin 1374, no. 2, 1961, 7; *In re Club Delite, Inc.*, Bulletin 1495, no. 6, 1963, 11; *Hotel Penn*, Bulletin 1453, no. 2, 1962, 8.

13. Thomas Cahill, interview by Paul Gabriel, July 28, 1997, 111, OHC No. 97-026, GLBTHS. For incentives not to close bars, see Agee, *Streets of San Francisco*, 76–79;

Field Report 11180, January 26, 1957, 5; Jess Stearn, *The Sixth Man* (New York: Doubleday, 1961), 157; Max K. Hurlbut to author, October 16, 2017, item 12. On graft, see Agee, *Streets of San Francisco*, 80–82; Stein, *City of Sisterly and Brotherly Loves*, 158; Donald Webster Cory and John P. LeRoy, *The Homosexual and His Society: A View from Within* (New York: Citadel, 1963), 107.

14. For examples of group visits, see *Gloria*, Record on Review, 68–69; *Polka Club*, Bulletin 1045, no. 6, 1955, 8; *In re N.Y. Bar*, Bulletin 1063, no. 1, 1955, 1, 2; *One-Thirty-Five Mulberry*, Bulletin 892, no. 2, 1951, 3. For drinking habits, see *Gloria Bar & Grill v. Bruckman*, 259 A.D. 706 (N.Y. App. Div. 1940), Brief for Petitioner, 13–15; *Polka Club*, Bulletin 1045, no. 6, 1955, 8; *N.Y. Bar*, Bulletin 1063, no. 1, 1955, 3; *Kershaw v. Dep't of Alcoholic Beverage Control of Cal.*, 155 Cal. App. 2d 544 (1957), Appellant's Brief, 11–19. For intimate encounters, see *Gloria*, Record on Review, 69 ("fondle"); *Peter Orsi*, Bulletin 326, no. 1, 1939, 1 ("effeminate"). See also *Stanwood United, Inc. v. O'Connell*, 283 A.D. 79, 80–81 (N.Y. App. Div. 1953); *Giovatto v. O'Connell*, 278 A.D. 371 (N.Y. App. Div. 1951), Papers on Appeal, 27–41. For active encouragement, see *One-Thirty-Five Mulberry*, Bulletin 892, no. 2, 1951, 4 ("take care"); *Lynch's Builders Rest. v. O'Connell*, 102 N.Y.S.2d 606, 607–8 (App. Div. 1951); *Snug Harbor Inn*, Bulletin 1161, no. 3, 1957, 7; *Hotel Penn*, Bulletin 1453, no. 2, 1962, 7; *Times Square Garden*, Record on Review, 27; *In re Hoover's Tavern*, Bulletin 1474, no. 2, 1962, 8. For just a few examples of charges alleging sexual conduct toward officers or among customers, see *Lynch's Builders*, 102 N.Y.S.2d at 607; *Peter Orsi*, Bulletin 326, no. 1, 1939, 1; *Jessie Lloyd*, Bulletin 1045, no. 7, 1955, 10; *N.Y. Bar*, Bulletin 1063, no. 1, 1955, 2–3; *Maxwell Cafe, Inc. v. Dep't of Alcoholic Beverage Control*, 142 Cal. App. 2d 73 (1956), Respondent's Brief, 5.

15. For owners stopping dancing, see *In re Doc's Tavern*, Bulletin 1168, no. 3, 1957, 6; *Club Delite*, Bulletin 1495, no. 6, 1963, 11. For bathrooms, see *In re N.Y. Bar*, Bulletin 1126, no. 3, 1956, 4. For owners restraining overt affection, see, e.g., *Murphy's Tavern*, 70 N.J. Super. at 92; *In re Topsy's Hideaway*, Bulletin 1259, no. 4, 1959, 8; *Hotel Penn*, Bulletin 1453, no. 2, 1962, 8; *Hoover's Tavern*, Bulletin 1474, no. 2, 1962, 8; *In re Murphy's Tavern, Inc.*, Bulletin 1677, no. 1, 1966, 2. For scolding, see *In re Hy and Sols Bar*, Bulletin 1356, no. 2, 1960, no. 2, 1960, 5 (quoted); Helen P. Branson, *Gay Bar* (San Francisco: Pan-Graphic, 1957), 43 (quoted).

16. For liability based on frequent or overt solicitation, see *One-Thirty-Five Mulberry*, Bulletin 892, no. 2, 1951, 4; *Maxwell Cafe, Inc. v. Dep't of Alcoholic Beverage Control*, 142 Cal. App. 2d 73, 76–77 (1956). For employees, see *In re Zaro's Bar & Grill*, Bulletin 1150, no. 2, 1957, 3. For officials dismissing charges for insufficient evidence of knowledge, see *Lynch's Builders*, 102 N.Y.S.2d at 607–8 (quoted); *Stanwood*, 283 A.D. at 81; *Giovatto*, Papers on Appeal, 98–100; *In re Herbie's Bar & Grill*, Bulletin 1087, no. 7, 1955, 9; *In re Fireside Tavern, Inc.*, Bulletin 991, no. 5, 1953, 12. For examples of defense witnesses claiming they missed any solicitations, see also *Peter Orsi*, Bulletin 326, no. 1, 1939, 1–2; *In re Entertainer's Club*, Bulletin 1088, no. 2, 1955, 2, 3–4; *In re Storky's, Inc.*, Bulletin 1263, no. 2, 1959, 6; *In re Tumulty*, Bulletin 1466, no. 1, 1962, 2; *Stanwood*, 283 A.D. at 81.

17. *Peter Orsi*, Bulletin 326, no. 1, 1939, 1; *Times Square Garden*, Record on Review, 27–29, 49, 90. For other examples, see *Bader's Bar*, Bulletin 1073, no. 4, 1955, 7; *In re Pappy's Bar*, Bulletin 1418, no. 1, 1961, 2; *In re Fun House*, Bulletin 929, no. 3, 1952, 4; *In re Midtown Bar & Cafe*, Bulletin 1366, no. 6, 1960, 11; *Casino*, Bulletin 1456, no. 3, 1962, 8; *In re Your Girls, Inc.*, Bulletin 1713, no. 2, 1967, 12.

18. For denunciations, see *In re Val's Bar, Inc.*, Bulletin 1685, no. 1, 1966, 1, 2–3

(quoted); *One-Thirty-Five Mulberry*, Bulletin 892, no. 2, 1951, 3; *McCracken*, Bulletin 456, no. 3, 1941, 4; *In re Blue Room*, Bulletin 1403, no. 3, 1961, 6. Others expressed perplexity but also relative tolerance. *In re Redman's Cafe, Inc.*, Bulletin 1354, no. 2, 1960, 4; *Hotel Penn*, Bulletin 1453, no. 2, 1962, 7; *In re Wardell Hotel*, Bulletin 1529, no. 2, 1963, 7; *In re Rutgers Cocktail Bar*, Bulletin 1133, no. 2, 1956, 3. For internal conflicts, see *Club Delite*, Bulletin 1495, no. 6, 1963, 10 (quoted); *Pappy's Bar*, Bulletin 1418, no. 1, 1961, 2 (quoted).

19. Transcript of Renewal Hearing, September 27, 1939, at 5, in *Gloria Bar & Grill v. Bruckman*, 259 A.D. 706 (N.Y. App. Div. 1940) Case File, NYSC; *Gloria*, Record on Review, 64–65, 182–84 ("well-known"); *In re Paddock Bar*, Bulletin 1202, no. 5, 1958, 11 ("want any"). For other bars employing apparently gay staff, see *Zaro's Bar*, Bulletin 1150, no. 2, 1957, 3–4; *Topsy's Hideaway*, Bulletin 1259, no. 4, 1959, 7–8; *In re Jockey Club*, Bulletin 1259, no. 5, 1959, 9. For the involvement of organized crime, see Jack Star, "The Sad 'Gay' Life," *Look*, January 10, 1967, 30–33; Robert C. Doty, "Growth of Overt Homosexuality in City Provokes Wide Concern," *NYT*, December 17, 1963, 1, 33; Stewart-Winter, *Queer Clout*, 24–25. For maternal relationships, see Branson, *Gay Bar*; *Paddock Bar*, Bulletin 1202, no. 5, 1958, 11 ("boys"); *N.Y. Bar*, Bulletin 1063, no. 1, 1955, 3–4; *In re Connie Gannitti*, Bulletin 1218, no. 2, 1958, 4.

20. For precautions, see *In re Ally-Ally*, Bulletin 1757, no. 1, 1967, 1, 3 ("well-behaved"); *Snug Harbor Inn*, Bulletin 1161, no. 3, 1957, 6–8; *In re Garden State Club*, Bulletin 1153, no. 1, 1957, 2–3; *Kerma Rest. Corp. v. State Liquor Auth.*, 21 N.Y.2d 111 (1967), Brief of Respondent, 15. Many, like their more grudging peers, prohibited any flamboyant or overt sexual conduct. Branson, *Gay Bar*, 75; *Hoover's Tavern*, Bulletin 1474, no. 2, 1962, 8; *Doc's Tavern*, Bulletin 1168, no. 3, 1957, 6; *Topsy's Hideaway*, Bulletin 1259, no. 4, 1959, 8. For owners standing up to liquor agents, see *In re Latin Quarter*, Bulletin 1471, no. 2, 1962, 4 ("Tell"); *In re Anthony's Bar*, Bulletin 1289, no. 7, 1959, 14 ("Show"). See also *In re Paddock Bar*, Bulletin 1368, no. 5, 1960, 15; *Hoover's Tavern*, Bulletin 1474, no. 2, 1962, 8.

21. For attempts to disperse customers as evidence, see *Times Square Garden*, Record on Review, 26–27; *Peter Orsi*, Bulletin 326, no. 1, 1939, 1; *Bader's Bar*, Bulletin 1073, no. 4, 1955, 7; *Fun House*, Bulletin 929, no. 3, 1952, 4; *Casino*, Bulletin 1456, no. 3, 1962, 8; *Pappy's Bar*, Bulletin 1418, no. 1, 1961, 2; *Your Girls*, Bulletin 1713, no. 2, 1967, 9. For complaints, see *Blue Room*, Bulletin 1403, no. 3, 1961, 6; *McCracken*, Bulletin 456, no. 3, 1941, 4; *One-Thirty-Five Mulberry*, Bulletin 892, no. 2, 1951, 3.

22. *Pappy's Bar*, Bulletin 1418, no. 1, 1961, 2; *Connie Gannitti*, Bulletin 1218, no. 2, 1958, 4; *Jessie Lloyd*, Bulletin 1045, no. 7, 1955, 11 (quoted).

23. For reputation evidence, see *In re Clover Leaf Inn*, Bulletin 1256, no. 3, 1959, 11; *Kershaw*, Brief of Respondents, 8 ("haven"); *Vallerga v. Dep't of Alcoholic Beverage Control*, 343 P.2d 54 (Cal. Dist. Ct. App. 1959), Respondents' Brief, 4. For paraphernalia, see *In re Paddock Bar*, Bulletin 1159, no. 2, 1959, 5; *Clock Bar*, 85 Dauph. at 127. For precautions as proof of knowledge, see *Kerma*, Brief of Respondent, 15; *Snug Harbor Inn*, Bulletin 1161, no. 3, 1957, 6–8; *Ally-Ally*, Bulletin 1757, no. 1, 1967, 2–3.

24. Chauncey, *Gay New York*, chap. 1; Boyd, *Wide Open Town*, chap. 1; Heap, *Slumming*, 43–44; James F. Wilson, *Bulldaggers, Pansies, and Chocolate Babies: Performance, Race, and Sexuality in the Harlem Renaissance* (Ann Arbor: University of Michigan Press, 2010), 34–36; Ernest Hemingway, *The Sun Also Rises* (New York: Charles Scribner's Sons, 1926), 28 (chap. 3).

25. For arrests, see "Citizens Claim That Lulu Belle Club on Lenox Avenue Is Notori-

ous Dive," *NYAN*, February 15, 1928, 1; "Police Arrest Impersonator," *Atlanta Daily World*, March 3, 1937, 6; "Two Eagle-Eyed Detectives Spot 'Pansies on Parade,'" *Inter-State Tattler*, March 10, 1932, 2; La Forest Potter, *Strange Loves: A Study in Sexual Abnormalities* (New York: Robert Dodsley, 1933), 184; Samuel Kahn, *Mentality and Homosexuality* (Boston: Meador, 1937), 217. For the ambivalent treatment of plays, see Kaier Curtin, *"We Can Always Call Them Bulgarians": The Emergence of Lesbians and Gay Men on the American Stage* (Boston: Alyson, 1987), 56 (quoted), 69–71, 109–11; Jon Tuska, *The Complete Films of Mae West* (New York: Citadel, 1992), 47.

26. Gerry, "Men Tenors, Women Wear Tuxedos at Costume Ball," *BAA*, February 22, 1930, A5 (quoted). For New York, see Chauncey, *Gay New York*, 291–98. For Chicago, see Myles Volmer, "The New Year's Eve Drag," 1, folder 2, box 140, EWBP. For Philadelphia, see "Police Keep Crowd of 200 from 3rd Sex," *BAA*, April 8, 1933, 1; "'Pansies' Ball Shocks Staid Philadelphians," *Norfolk Journal and Guide*, April 15, 1933, 8. On the popularity of the Hamilton Lodge Ball, see "Society Sees 3rd Sex Cavort at Harlem Ball," *BAA*, March 5, 1932, 3; "3,000 Attend Ball of Hamilton Lodge," *NYAN*, March 1, 1933, 2; Chauncey, *Gay New York*, 310. For newspaper coverage, see also "Annual 'Pansy' Ball Colorful," *BAA*, March 26, 1932, 12; "'Pansies' Ball Shocks Staid Philadelphians," *Norfolk Journal and Guide*, A8; Ralph Matthews, "Is the Reign of Harlem's Twilight Men at an End?," *BAA*, October 5, 1935, 16; "When 'Odd Fellows' Cavorted," *NYAN*, March 5, 1938, 2; "The Third Sex Called 'Pansies,'" *BAA*, July 4, 1931, 20. On relative tolerance, see Thaddeus Russell, "The Color of Discipline: Civil Rights and Black Sexuality," *American Quarterly* 60 (March 2008): 101–28.

27. On New York and Malin, see Chauncey, *Gay New York*, chap. 11, esp. 315–18; Julian Jerome, "Floor-Show," *Vanity Fair*, February 1931, 68–69, 86. For other cities, see Heap, *Slumming*, chap. 6 (Chicago and Bartlett); "Hollywood Adds 21 New Nightery Spots," *Variety*, September 27, 1932, 58 (Los Angeles); "Night Club Reviews— CLUB GREYHOUND," *Variety*, August 21, 1935, 58 (Cleveland). See also *Call Her Savage*, dir. John Francis Dillon (Fox Film Corp., 1932).

28. For examples, see "Bizarre Doings Friday at Hamilton 'Ball,'" *NYAN*, February 27, 1937, 1; Chauncey, *Gay New York*, 321–28. For Malin, see Jerome, "Floor-Show," 86 (quoted).

29. On the popularity of female impersonators, see Marybeth Hamilton, "'I'm the Queen of the Bitches': Female Impersonation and Mae West's *Pleasure Man*," in *Crossing the Stage: Controversies on Cross-Dressing*, ed. Lesley Ferris (London: Routledge, 1993), 107–11; Hurewitz, *Bohemian Los Angeles*, 26–35. On female impersonators as illusionists, see Hamilton, "'I'm the Queen of the Bitches,'" 111; John F. Kasson, *Houdini, Tarzan, and the Perfect Man: The White Male Body and the Challenge of Modernity in America* (New York: Hill & Wang, 2001), 92–98. For coded references to the pansy craze, see Ralph Matthews, "Boys Will Be Boys, but More Profitable Being Girls!," *BAA*, October 9, 1937, 11 (quoted); "Harlem and Park Avenues Step Out Together at Twilight Folks' Ball," *BAA*, March 5, 1938, 17 (quoted); Geraldyn Dismond, "New York Society," *BAA*, March 5, 1932, 3; Romeo L. Dougherty, "My Observations: People of the Half-World and Other Things," *NYAN*, April 14, 1934, 6; Roi Ottley, "This Hectic Harlem," *NYAN*, December 27, 1933, 7. For Nesbit, see Potter, *Strange Loves*, 5–6 n. 1. See also Jimmy Durante and Jack Kofoed, *Night Clubs* (New York: Knopf, 1931), 34–35. For the patron, see "Told to Me by a Mr. X.," folder 11, box 98, EWBP.

30. *Gloria*, Record on Review, 101, 183 (quoted); Conrad Bingham, "Notes on the Ho-

mosexual in Chicago," 5–9, folder 10, box 146, EWBP. For additional discussions of the exploitative nature of the craze, see Chauncey, *Gay New York*, 327–29; Heap, *Slumming*, 231–33, 265.

31. C. J. Bulliet, *Venus Castina* (New York: Covici, Friede, 1928), 7 ("chorus"); "Under Hypnosis," September 24, 1932, folder 3, box 98, EWBP ("not true"). For cabaret performers in full drag, see Jack Lord and Jenn Shaw, *Where to Sin in San Francisco* (San Francisco: Richard F. Guggenheim, 1939), 93; "Night Club, Coffee Cliff," December 2, 1930, box 35, Committee of Fourteen Records, NYPL.

32. "(Homosexual) Ferry's, Punks, Etc.," January 8, 1937, folder 18, box 209, EWBP ("block away"); Blair Niles, *Strange Brother* (New York: Horace Liveright, 1931), 96, 55. For bar patrons, see *Times Square Garden*, Record on Review, 160–61, 182, 187 ("observation"), 196; *Paddock Bar*, Bulletin 1159, no. 2, 1959, 6; *Paddock Bar*, Brief and Appendix for Appellant, 73a, 75a, 79a; "Ballyhoo Café, 11:30," September 24, 1933, folder 2, box 98, EWBP.

33. For Linker, see *Times Square Garden*, Record on Review, 109. For Wickes, see *Gloria*, Record on Review, 296, 333, 335–36. For other examples, see *Times Square Garden*, Record on Review, 34, 36, 40, 42; Certified Transcript of Minutes of Hearing Held January 8th, 1940, at 75, in *Gloria Bar & Grill v. Bruckman*, 259 A.D. 706 (N.Y. App. Div. 1940) Case File, NYSC; *Gloria*, Record on Review, 174; *Gloria*, Transcript of Renewal Hearing, 3; *Salle De Champagne, Inc. v. O'Connell*, 278 A.D. 912 (N.Y. App. Div. 1951), Record of Proceedings, 20–22; *Stanwood United, Inc. v. O'Connell*, 283 A.D. 79 (N.Y. App. Div. 1953), Record on Review, 35; *Stoumen v. Reilly*, 222 P.2d 678 (Cal. Dist. Ct. App. 1950), Brief for Respondents, 19; *Peter Orsi*, Bulletin 326, no. 1, 1939, 1; *Rutgers Cocktail Bar*, Bulletin 1133, no. 2, 1956, 2; *Log Cabin Inn*, Bulletin 279, no. 8, 1938, 11–12; *M. Potter*, Bulletin 474, no. 1, 1941, 1. For reliance even in cases with overt sexual conduct, see *One-Thirty-Five Mulberry*, Bulletin 892, no. 2, 1951, 3; *McCracken*, Bulletin 456, no. 3, 1941, 3–4.

34. *Gloria*, Transcript of Renewal Hearing, 3 (quoted). See also *Gloria*, Record on Review, 174; *Gloria*, Certified Transcript of Minutes of Hearing Held January 8th, at 75; *Times Square Garden*, Record on Review, 32, 35, 40, 42, 54, 73–74. For a West Coast example, see *Stoumen*, Brief for Respondents, 19. For Wickes's entertainment experience, see *Gloria*, Record on Review, 333.

35. For the quotations, in order, see *Gloria*, Record on Review, 141–42, 311, 195–96, 311, 339.

36. *Times Square Garden*, Record on Review, 37. See also *In re Peter Orsi*, Bulletin 390, no. 1, 1940, 1.

37. *Times Square Garden*, Record on Review, 168; *Gloria*, Certified Transcript of Minutes of Hearing Held January 9th, 1940, at 61, in *Gloria Bar & Grill v. Bruckman*, 259 A.D. 706 (N.Y. App. Div. 1940) Case File, NYSC. For similar denials, see *Peter Orsi*, Bulletin 326, no. 1, 1939, 2; *Lynch's Builders Rest. v. O'Connell*, 303 N.Y. 408 (1952), Respondent's Brief, 23; *Fasone*, 139 N.Y.S.2d at 188. For Palma, see *Clover Leaf Inn*, Bulletin 1256, no. 3, 1959, 11. For similar objections, see *In re Paddock Inn*, Bulletin 1543, no. 3, 1964, 8, 11; *Murphy's Tavern*, Supreme Court, Appendix, 484a.

38. For owners questioning the significance of unorthodox demeanor, see *In re Clover Leaf Inn, Inc.*, Bulletin 1159, no. 1, 1957, 2 ("oddly"); *McCracken*, Bulletin 456, no. 3, 1941, 4 ("effeminate side"); *Gloria*, Certified Transcript of Minutes of Hearing Held January 9th, at 61; *Murphy's Tavern*, Bulletin 1374, no. 2, 1961, 7; *Wardell Hotel*, Bulletin 1529, no. 2, 1963, 6–8. For more discreet codes, see *Lynch's Builders*, Record on Appeal, 80; *Times Square Garden*, Record on Review, 93.

39. *Stanwood United, Inc. v. O'Connell*, 306 N.Y. 749 (1954), Brief of Petition-Respondent, 19; *Peter Orsi*, Bulletin 326, no. 1, 1939, 2; *N.Y. Bar*, Bulletin 1063, no. 1, 1955, 4 (Kaczka); *Garden State Club*, Bulletin 1153, no. 1, 1957, 3 (Bolcato); *Wardell Hotel*, Bulletin 1529, no. 2, 1963, 4–5.

40. *Times Square Garden*, Record on Review, 158; *Gloria*, Record on Review, 314, 321. For officers distancing themselves from gay men, see also *One-Thirty-Five Mulberry*, Bulletin 892, no. 2, 1951, 5.

41. *In re McClyment et al.*, Bulletin 491, no. 3, 1942, 6, 7; *Rutgers Cocktail Bar*, Bulletin 1133, no. 2, 1956, 2, 4–5 (reversed by Director). For other examples, see *In re Torch*, Bulletin 945, no. 5, 1952, 5; *Fireside Tavern*, Bulletin 991, no. 5, 1953, 12.

42. *Peter Orsi*, Bulletin 326, no. 1, 1939, 2. For similar cases, see *Paddock Inn*, Bulletin 1543, no. 3, 1964, 11–12; *Jessie Lloyd*, Bulletin 1045, no. 7, 1955, 10–11.

43. *Gloria*, Record on Review, 142 (van Wagner), 311–12, 321 (Wickes).

44. On duties to act, see Chauncey, *Gay New York*, 339, 341–42; Charles A. Reich, "The New Property," *Yale Law Journal* 73 (April 1964): 767–68. Late in the editing process, I became aware of work making a similar claim about duties of knowledge with regard to patrons' intoxication levels. Mariana Valverde, *Law's Dream of a Common Knowledge* (Princeton, NJ: Princeton University Press, 2003), chap. 7.

45. On the BOE's practices, see Boyd, *Wide Open Town*, 110–11. On the Black Cat, see ibid., 145–46; *Stoumen v. Reilly*, 222 P.2d 678, 682 (Cal. Dist. Ct. App. 1950) ("persons"); *Stoumen*, 37 Cal. 2d at 716 ("mere proof"). On the court's liberalism, see Kathleen A. Cairns, *The Case of Rose Bird: Gender, Politics, and the California Courts* (Lincoln: University of Nebraska Press, 2016), 57–61.

46. *Fasone*, 139 N.Y.S.2d at 187–89. For higher New York courts, see, e.g., *Kerma Rest. Corp. v. State Liquor Auth.*, 278 N.Y.S.2d 951, 952 (N.Y. App. Div. 1967).

47. For federal policy, see Canaday, *Straight State*, introduction. For *Stoumen*'s restrictive effects, see Boyd, *Wide Open Town*, 122–28. For legislative interventions, see also Agee, *Streets of San Francisco*, 86–87; *Nickola v. Munro*, 328 P.2d 271, 274 (Cal. Dist. Ct. App. 1958); *Benedetti v. Dep't of Alcoholic Beverage Control*, 9 Cal. Rptr. 525, 526–28 (Ct. App. 1960). For judicial resistance, see *Kershaw v. Dep't of Alcoholic Beverage Control of Cal.*, 155 Cal. App. 2d 544, 550–51 (Cal. Dist. Ct. App. 1957); *Nickola*, 328 P.2d at 274–75; *Vallerga v. Dep't of Alcoholic Beverage Control*, 343 P.2d 54, 58–59 (Cal. Dist. Ct. App. 1959); *Vallerga v. Dep't of Alcoholic Beverage Control*, 53 Cal. 2d 313, 318 (1959).

48. *Fulton Bar & Grill, Inc. v. State Liquor Authority*, 205 N.Y.S.2d 37 (App. Div. 1960), Papers on Appeal, 40–41; *Fulton Bar & Grill, Inc. v. State Liquor Auth.*, 205 N.Y.S.2d 37, 38 (1960). For Handy's, see *Kerma*, 278 N.Y.S.2d at 952; *Kerma Rest. Corp. v. State Liquor Auth.*, 21 N.Y.2d 111 (1967), Record on Review, 40.

49. For the ABC's switch to Rule 5, see *Murphy's Tavern*, 70 N.J. Super. 87, Appendix to Brief for Appellant, 51a; *One Eleven Wines & Liquors, Inc. v. Div. of Alcoholic Beverage Control*, 50 N.J. 329, 331–32 (1967); *Polka Club*, Bulletin 1045, no. 6, 1955, 8 (emphasis added); *Paddock Bar, Inc. v. Div. of Alcoholic Beverage Control*, 46 N.J. Super. 405, 407 (App. Div. 1957). For examples of continuing reliance on demeanor evidence, see *Entertainer's Club*, Bulletin 1088, no. 2, 1955, 3–4; *Paddock Bar*, Bulletin 1159, no. 2, 1959, 6; *One Eleven Wines*, 50 N.J. at 333–34.

50. *Paddock Bar*, 46 N.J. Super. at 408 (emphasis added).

51. *M. Potter*, Bulletin 474, no. 1, 1941, 1.

52. For cases focusing on sexual conduct, see *Loubor Rest., Inc. v. Rohan*, 197 N.Y.S.2d 429 (1960), Respondents' Brief, 5–9; *Kerma*, Brief of Respondent, 8, 12; *Ekim Broad-*

way Rest. Corp. v. State Liquor Auth., 18 A.D.2d 619 (N.Y. App. Div. 1962), Papers on Appeal, 31; *Maxwell Cafe*, Respondent's Brief, 4–13; *Kershaw*, Brief of Respondents, 4–7. For New Jersey's continuing emphasis on demeanor, see *Casino*, Bulletin 1050, no. 1, 1955, 4; *Bader's Bar*, Bulletin 1073, no. 4, 1955, 5–6; *Doc's Tavern*, Bulletin 1168, no. 3, 1957, 6; *Storky's*, Bulletin 1263, no. 2, 1959, 5; *Anthony's*, Bulletin 1289, no. 7, 1959, 14; *Hy and Sols Bar*, Bulletin 1356, no. 2, 1960, 4–5; *Midtown Bar & Cafe*, Bulletin 1366, no. 6, 1960, 11; *In re First Circle Inn, Inc.*, Bulletin 1413, no. 2, 1961, 6; *Wardell Hotel*, Bulletin 1529, no. 2, 1963, 3, 9–10; *In re Club Coronet, Inc.*, Bulletin 1123, no. 2, 1956, 3; *Paddock Bar*, Bulletin 1368, no. 5, 1960, 15.

53. On the lower profile of lesbian life before World War II, see Faderman and Timmons, *Gay L.A.*, 87–88; Lillian Faderman, *Odd Girls and Twilight Lovers: A History of Lesbian Life in Twentieth-Century America* (New York: Columbia University Press, 1991), chaps. 3–4. For broader restraints on women generally, see Elizabeth Sepper and Deborah Dinner, "Sex in Public," *Yale Law Journal* 129 (2019): 86–96. For women's growing role in the public sphere, see Susan M. Hartmann, "Women's Employment and the Domestic Ideal in the Early Cold War Years," in *Not June Cleaver: Women and Gender in Postwar America, 1945–1960*, ed. Joanne Meyerowitz (Philadelphia: Temple University Press, 1994), 86–87, 90–91, 94–95; Faderman, *Odd Girls*, 161–63. There is a documented history of lesbian bar life in some cities by the 1940s. Kennedy and Davis, *Boots of Leather*, 34–38; Roey Thorpe, "The Changing Face of Lesbian Bars in Detroit, 1938–65," in *Creating a Place for Ourselves: Lesbian, Gay, and Bisexual Community Histories*, ed. Brett Beemyn (New York: Routledge, 1997). For mixed bars, see *Rutgers Cocktail Bar*, Bulletin 1133, no. 2, 1956, 2–3; *In re Torch's Lodge Bar*, Bulletin 1150, no. 1, 1957, 1; *Garden State Club*, Bulletin 1153, no. 1, 1957, 2–3; *Connie Gannitti*, Bulletin 1218, no. 2, 1958, 4; *Clover Leaf Inn*, 1256, no. 3, 1959, 11; *Jockey Club*, Bulletin 1259, no. 5, 1959, 10; *In re Pine Brook Diner & Marge's Keyhole Cocktail Lounge*, Bulletin 1406, no. 2, 1961, 2–3; *In re King Bar & Liquor Store*, Bulletin 1437, no. 3, 1962, 5–6; *In re Jack's Star Bar*, Bulletin 1667, no. 3, 1966, 7; *In re Chez'l Cocktail Lounge*, Bulletin 1721, no. 1, 1967, 1–2; *Kershaw*, Appellant's Brief, 30–31. For primarily lesbian bars, see *Blue Room*, Bulletin 1403, no. 3, 1961, 6; *In re Speedway Inn, Inc.*, Bulletin 1241, no. 3, 1958, 6–7; *In re Edna's Rendezvous*, Bulletin 1378, no. 3, 1961, 7–8; *In re Helene's*, Bulletin 1405, no. 3, 1961, 9–10; *Clover Leaf Inn*, Bulletin 1159, no. 1, 1957, 1–2; *In re Famous Bar*, Bulletin 1345, no. 6, 1960, 10; *In re Pelican Bar*, Bulletin 1242, no. 3, 1958, 7; *In re Latin Quarter*, Bulletin 1444, no. 3, 1962, 5–6; *Club Delite*, Bulletin 1495, no. 6, 1963, 9–10. In referring to primarily lesbian bars, I intend to say not that men never patronized these bars but that queer women predominated and drove the ensuing charges.

54. For the general, if comparatively milder, harassment of lesbian communities, see Faderman and Timmons, *Gay L.A.*, 89–93; Beemyn, *A Queer Capital*, 141; Boyd, *Wide Open Town*, 90–96; Kennedy and Davis, *Boots of Leather*, 41–42. For raids especially, see Kennedy and Davis, *Boots of Leather*, 35, 63–64; Faderman, *Odd Girls*, 162–66, 185. For the sergeant, see "Vice Hunting in Los Angeles," *Los Angeles Free Press*, March 17, 1967, 1, 20. For overlap with other vice-related charges, see Boyd, *Wide Open Town*, 87–88, 91–95.

55. For the prevalence and significance of butch/femme, see Kennedy and Davis, *Boots of Leather*, 5–6; Faderman, *Odd Girls*, chap. 7. For makeup and grooming, see *Pine Brook Diner*, Bulletin 1406, no. 2, 1961, 3 ("slight traces"); *Edna's Rendezvous*, Bulletin 1378, no. 3, 1961, 8; *In re Hollywood Cafe*, Bulletin 1393, no. 2, 1961, 5; *In re*

Francis Lachnicht, Bulletin 1436, no. 3, 1962, 3; *Casino*, Bulletin 1456, no. 3, 1962, 5–6, 8; *King Bar*, Bulletin 1437, no. 3, 1962, 5. For clothing, see *Jack's Star Bar*, Bulletin 1667, no. 3, 1966, 7; *Helene's*, Bulletin 1405, no. 3, 1961, 12; *King Bar*, Bulletin 1437, no. 3, 1962, 5–6; *Chez'l Cocktail Lounge*, Bulletin 1721, no. 1, 1967, 2–3; *Hollywood Cafe*, Bulletin 1393, no. 2, 1961, 4; *Blue Room*, Bulletin 1403, no. 3, 1961, 5; *Helene's*, Bulletin 1405, no. 3, 1961, 10–12 ("red sweater"); *Lachnicht*, Bulletin 1436, no. 3, 1962, 3; *Kershaw*, Appellant's Brief, 28–29.

56. *Jack's Star Bar*, Bulletin 1667, no. 3, 1966, 7–8 ("filthy," "vile," "roughly"); *Chez'l Cocktail Lounge*, Bulletin 1721, no. 1, 1967, 2–3 ("back-handed," "daintier"); *Hollywood Café*, Bulletin 1393, no. 2, 1961, 5 ("whiskey," "filthy"); *King Bar*, Bulletin 1437, no. 3, 1962, 6 ("indecent"); *In re Club Tequila*, Bulletin 1557, no. 1, 1964, 2 (billiards).

57. For "straight" girlfriends, see *Latin Quarter*, Bulletin 1471, no. 2, 1962, 3–4; *Casino*, Bulletin 1456, no. 3, 1962, 7; *Latin Quarter*, Bulletin 1444, no. 3, 1962, 6; *Famous Bar*, Bulletin 1345, no. 6, 1960, 10. For growing distinctions between gay men and female impersonators, see *In re Walter Sherry*, Bulletin 1236, no. 3, 1958, 6; *In re Val's Bar*, Bulletin 1747, no. 2, 1967, 5, 7–8. For the anxieties inspired by women's increasing public presence more broadly, see Hartmann, "Women's Employment and the Domestic Ideal," 96; Elaine Tyler May, *Homeward Bound: American Families in the Cold War Era* (New York: Basic, 1988), chap. 4.

58. On Bentley, see Wilson, *Bulldaggers*, 155–56, 181.

59. For heterosexual observers, see Martin Hoffman, *The Gay World: Male Homosexuality and the Social Creation of Evil* (New York: Basic, 1968), 55 (quoted); William J. Helmer, "New York's 'Middle-Class' Homosexuals," *Harper's Magazine*, March 1963, 86. On collegiate fashions, see also Maurice Leznoff, "The Homosexual in Urban Society" (MA thesis, McGill University, 1954), 164; Welch, "The 'Gay' World," 68. Some men who adopted collegiate fashions continued to display stereotypically swish mannerisms. *Redman's Club Café*, Bulletin 1354, no. 2, 1960, 4; *Pappy's Bar*, Bulletin 1418, no. 1, 1961, 1; *Val's Bar*, Bulletin 1685, no. 1, 1966, 2; *Murphy's Tavern*, Bulletin 1677, no. 1, 1966, 2; *Fulton Bar & Grill*, Papers on Appeal, 40.

60. For telltale fashions, see *Garden State Club*, Bulletin 1153, no. 1, 1957, 2; *Anthony's*, Bulletin 1289, no. 7, 1959, 14; *Kershaw*, Appellant's Brief, 28–29; *Redman's Club Cafe*, Bulletin 1354, no. 2, 1960, 4; *Pappy's Bar*, Bulletin 1418, no. 1, 1961, 1; *Tumulty*, Bulletin 1466, no. 1, 1962, 2; *Murphy's Tavern*, Bulletin 1677, no. 1, 1966, 2, 5; *Val's Bar*, Bulletin 1685, no. 1, 1966, 2; *Ally-Ally*, Bulletin 1757, no. 1, 1967, 2. For incriminating conduct, see *Paddock Inn*, Bulletin 1543, no. 3, 1964, 9–10 ("bowl[ed]"); *In re Charmac, Inc.*, Bulletin 1637, no. 1, 1965, 1; *In re One Eleven Wines & Liquors*, Bulletin 1656, no. 5, 1966, 5; *Jack's Star Bar*, Bulletin 1667, no. 3, 1966, 7; *Murphy's Tavern*, Supreme Court, Appendix, 383a–385a, 408a, 427a; *One Eleven Wines & Liquors, Inc. v. Div. of Alcoholic Beverage Control*, 50 N.J. 329 (1967), Petition for Certification, 3 ("straws and cherries").

61. For parsing of fashions, see *Fulton Bar & Grill*, Papers on Appeal, 40–41; *Kifisia Foods, Inc. v. New York State Liquor Auth.*, 281 N.Y.S.2d 611 (1967), Record on Appeal, 55, 67, 78. For singing, see *Paddock Inn*, Bulletin 1543, no. 3, 1964, 9–10.

62. *Kifisia*, Record on Appeal, 55; *Club Tequila*, Bulletin 1557, no. 1, 1964, 2. For similar fashions in gay and lesbian bars, see *Pappy's Bar*, Bulletin 1418, no. 1, 1961, 2–3; *King Bar*, Bulletin 1437, no. 3, 1962, 5; *Ally-Ally*, Bulletin 1757, no. 1, 1967, 2; *Helene's*, Bulletin 1405, no. 3, 1961, 12. For the California case, see Kershaw, Appellant's Brief, 31.

63. *Murphy's Tavern*, 70 N.J. Super. 87, Appendix to Appellant's Brief, 58a ("shows"); *In re Hoover's Tavern*, Bulletin 1521, no. 1, 1963, 1, 5 ("perfume"); *In re Paddock Inn*, Bulletin 1342, no. 1, 1960, 3–4 ("swish[ed]"). See also Gaeton J. Fonzi, "The Furtive Fraternity," *Greater Philadelphia Magazine*, December 1962, 53. For the universality of fashions and behaviors, see *Kifisia*, Record on Appeal, 69–71, 62–63; *One Eleven Wines*, Petition for Certification, 4; *One Eleven Wines*, Bulletin 1656, no. 5, 1966, 6; *Murphy's Tavern*, Supreme Court, Appendix, 493a, 405a–406a ("haircut").

64. *Paddock Inn*, Bulletin 1543, no. 3, 1964, 11; *Murphy's Tavern*, Supreme Court, Appendix, 494a–495a, 516a. For additional examples, see *In re Ron-Day-Voo*, Bulletin 1625, no. 2, 1965, 8; *Murphy's Tavern*, Bulletin 1374, no. 2, 1961, 7–8; *Club Delite*, Bulletin 1495, no. 6, 1963, 11–12.

65. For defenses of patrons' fashions as modern, see *Val's Bar*, Bulletin 1747, no. 2, 1967, 8; *Latin Quarter*, Bulletin 1444, no. 3, 1962, 7; *Kershaw*, Appellant's Brief, 30; *Pine Brook Diner*, Bulletin 1406, no. 2, 1961, 4–5; *Jack's Star Bar*, Bulletin 1667, no. 3, 1966, 10. For Pearl's, see *Kershaw*, Appellant's Brief, 17, 25.

66. *Kershaw*, Appellant's Brief, 30 (rings); *Rutgers Cocktail Bar*, Bulletin 1133, no. 2, 1956, 4 ("riffraff"); *Murphy's Tavern*, Supreme Court, Appendix, 396a, 403a, 643a. For other examples, see *Ally-Ally*, Bulletin 1757, no. 1, 1967, 2; *Paddock Inn*, Bulletin 1342, no. 1, 1960, 1–4.

67. For bars emphasizing the respectability of patrons, see *Lynch's Builders*, Respondent's Brief, 23.

68. For friction with locals, see *Your Girls*, Bulletin 1713, no. 2, 1967, 9; *Hotel Penn*, Bulletin 1453, no. 2, 1962, 7. On the significance of Ivy League fashions, see Daniel Horowitz, *On the Cusp: The Yale College Class of 1960 and a World on the Verge of Change* (Amherst: University of Massachusetts Press, 2015), 46–51, 152–54; *Kifisia*, Record on Appeal, 82, 55 (Brakatselos).

69. On the precarity of elite masculinity during the Cold War, see Dean, *Imperial Brotherhood*, 65, 89–96; Johnson, *Lavender Scare*, chap. 3.

70. *Club Tequila*, Bulletin 1557, no. 1, 1964, 2, 4; *Pine Brook Diner*, Bulletin 1406, no. 2, 1961, 5–6.

71. *Pine Brook Diner*, Bulletin 1406, no. 2, 1961, 5–7.

CHAPTER TWO

1. *Gloria*, Brief for Petitioner, 10–11; *Gloria*, Record on Review, 311.

2. For the early emphasis on the body, see Beachy, "German Invention of Homosexuality," 810–11, 814; Davidson, *Emergence of Sexuality*, 4–7; Hekma, "A History of Sexology," 176–77.

3. For the continuing interest in physiology among sexologists, see Havelock Ellis, *Studies in the Psychology of Sex*, vol. 1, *Sexual Inversion* (Watford: University Press, 1900), 121 (quoted); Hekma, "A History of Sexology," 180; Minton, *Departing from Deviance*, 11–13; Terry, "Anxious Slippages between 'Us' and 'Them,'" 130–35; Siobhan Somerville, "Scientific Racism and the Emergence of the Homosexual Body," *Journal of the History of Sexuality* 5 (October 1994): 247–56. For the growing influence of a psychological approach, including the influence of Freud, see Beachy, "German Invention of Homosexuality," 801–38; Davidson, *Emergence of Sexuality*, 12–21; Robinson, *Modernization of Sex*, 5–6.

4. Arthur Weil, "Sprechen anatomische Grundlagen für das Angeborensein der Homosexualität?," *Archiv für Frauenkunde und Konstitutions Forschung* 10 (1924): 23–50; George W. Henry and Hugh M. Galbraith, "Constitutional Factors in Homosexual-

ity," *American Journal of Psychiatry* 13 (May 1934): 1250–55 (see also 1250 ["physiological"]). On the Committee for the Study of Sex Variants, see Minton, *Departing from Deviance*, 33–57; Terry, *An American Obsession*, chap. 6; George W. Henry, *Sex Variants: A Study of Homosexual Patterns*, 1 vol. ed. (New York: Paul B. Hoeber, 1948), xiii.

5. For the history of criminal anthropology, see Stephen Jay Gould, *The Mismeasure of Man* (New York: Norton, 1981), 123–30. For its intersection with sexology, see Somerville, "Scientific Racism," 248–53; Britta McEwen, *Sexual Knowledge: Feeling, Fact, and Social Reform in Vienna, 1900–1934* (New York: Berghahn, 2012), 9. For the quotation, see Austin Flint, "A Case of Sexual Inversion, Probably with Complete Sexual Anesthesia," *New York Medical Journal* 94 (December 1911): 1111. For studies emphasizing the homosexual's physical inferiority, see Potter, *Strange Loves*, 99–101; A. L. Wolbarst, *Sexual Perversions as a Scientific Problem* (Girard: Haldeman-Julius, 1947), 4; Weil, "Sprechen anatomische"; Henry and Galbraith, "Constitutional Factors in Homosexuality," 1255–57.

6. Weil, "Sprechen anatomische," 33, 36; Henry, *Sex Variants*, 1046; Henry and Galbraith, "Constitutional Factors in Homosexuality," 1260. On the disconnect between Henry's statement and his research, see Minton, *Departing from Deviance*, 48–49, 107, 115–16. For additional examples, see Potter, *Strange Loves*, 99–100; Wolbarst, *Sexual Perversions as a Scientific Problem*, 4.

7. Joseph Wortis, "A Note on the Body Build of the Male Homosexual," *American Journal of Psychiatry* 93 (March 1937): 1123–25; Thomas V. Moore, "The Pathogenesis and Treatment of Homosexual Disorders: A Digest of Some Pertinent Evidence," *Journal of Personality* 14 (September 1945): 61.

8. Henry, *Sex Variants*, 283, 242, 303; Wortis, "A Note on the Body Build of the Male Homosexual," 1123–25; Moore, "The Pathogenesis and Treatment of Homosexual Disorders," 61. See also Kahn, *Mentality and Homosexuality*, 71; Lewis M. Terman and Catharine Cox Miles, *Sex and Personality: Studies in Masculinity and Femininity* (New York: McGraw-Hill, 1936), 248. For psychoanalytic theories of homosexuality as the product of improper gender modeling, see Irving Bieber et al., *Homosexuality: A Psychoanalytic Study* (New York: Basic, 1962), 44–117; David Abrahamsen, *Crime and the Human Mind* (New York: Columbia University Press, 1944), 118–19.

9. Kahn, *Mentality and Homosexuality*, 138; Henry, *Sex Variants*, 303. For Henry's accounts of patients with apparently masculine physiques, see ibid., 105–6, 115, 125, 156–57. Most doctors acknowledged that some homosexuals were entirely masculine, though they emphasized the preponderance of the effeminate type. Potter, *Strange Loves*, 97–99; Kahn, *Mentality and Homosexuality*, 70; Wolbarst, *Sexual Perversions as a Scientific Problem*, 4.

10. Kahn, *Mentality and Homosexuality*, 138; Henry, *Sex Variants*, 117–18, 219, 229, 477. On the exclusionary aspirations of scientific discussions of sexual deviance in these years, see also Urla and Terry, "Introduction: Mapping Embodied Deviance," 11.

11. For the army's early practices, see Army Regulation 40-105, "Standards of Physical Examination for Entrance into the Regular Army, National Guard, and Organized Reserves" (Washington, DC: US Government Printing Office, 1922), 25–26, folder 19, box 20, World War II History Project Papers, GLBTHS ("stigmata"); Frank T. Woodbury and James A. Moss, *Manual for Medical Officers: Being a Guide to the Duties of Army Medical Officers* (Menasha, WI: George Banta, 1918), 124; Bérubé, *Coming Out under Fire*, 13–14. For screening standards during World War II, see Mobilization Regulations, "Standards of Physical Examination during Mobilization,"

March 15, 1942, folder 16, box 20, World War II History Project Papers, GLBTHS. For rates of rejection, see Carleton Simon, "Homosexualists and Sex Crimes," September 21–25, 1947, 4, Kinsey Institute for Research in Sex, Gender, and Reproduction Library and Special Collections, Indiana University. For another example of state officials' buy-in to homosexual anthropometry, see Eugene W. Green and L. G. Johnson, "Homosexuality," *Journal of Criminal Psychopathology* 5 (January 1944): 467–73.

12. Bérubé, *Coming Out under Fire*, 18–19, 22. For the New Yorker, see ibid., 8.

13. J. Paul de River to Fiorella LaGuardia, April 5, 1941, folder 10, box 20, World War II Project Papers, GLBTHS; Samuel J. Kopetzky to Dr. J. Paul de River, April 23, 1941, folder 10, box 20, World War II Project Papers, GLBTHS. For the military's failures and frustrations weeding out homosexual conduct, see Bérubé, *Coming Out under Fire*, chap. 6. For indoctrination lectures, see Chief of Naval Personnel, "Lecture to Be Utilized in the Indoctrination of Recruits," January 12, 1948, folder 3, box 22, World War II Project Papers, GLBTHS.

14. William C. Menninger, *Psychiatry in a Troubled World* (New York: Macmillan, 1948), vii ("as a result"). For the military's growing dependence on psychiatric analysis, including to identify homosexuals, see Herman, *Romance of American Psychology*, chap. 4; Naoko Wake, *Private Practices: Harry Stack Sullivan, the Science of Homosexuality, and American Liberalism* (New Brunswick, NJ: Rutgers University Press, 2011), chap. 5; Bérubé, *Coming Out under Fire*, 9–19.

15. For the dominance of psychiatrists in public debates, see D'Emilio, *Sexual Politics*, 16–17, 144; Terry, *An American Obsession*, 309–21, 265; Lewes, *Psychoanalysis and Male Homosexuality*, chap. 7; Minton, *Departing from Deviance*, 232–33; Ronald Bayer, *Homosexuality and American Psychiatry: The Politics of Diagnosis* (Princeton, NJ: Princeton University Press, 1987), chap. 1. For the range of opinions, see also Stephen D. Ford, "Homosexuals and the Law: Why the Status Quo?," *California Western Law Review* 5 (Spring 1969): 235–36.

16. Alfred C. Kinsey et al., *Sexual Behavior in the Human Male* (Philadelphia: W. B. Saunders, 1948). For enthusiastic reviews, see Albert Deutsch, "The Sex Habits of American Men," *Harper's*, December 1947, 495; James R. Newman, "The Proper Study of Mankind," *New Republic*, February 9, 1948, 26. For criticism, see Erdman Palmore, "Published Reactions to the Kinsey Report," *Social Forces*, December 1952, 165–70; Waldemar Kaempffert, "The Now Famous Kinsey Report Is Criticized on Statistical and Sociological Grounds," *NYT*, March 7, 1948, E9; Cuordileone, *Manhood and American Political Culture*, 83; James Howard Jones, *Alfred C. Kinsey: A Public/Private Life* (New York: Norton, 1997), 576. For Kinsey's prominence, see D'Emilio, *Sexual Politics*, 34; Miriam Reuman, *American Sexual Character: Sex, Gender, and National Identity in the Kinsey Reports* (Berkeley and Los Angeles: University of California Press, 2005), chap. 2; Albert Deutsch, "The Kinsey Report and Popular Culture," in *Sexual Behavior in American Society: An Appraisal of the First Two Kinsey Reports*, ed. Jerome Himelhoch and Sylvia Fleis Fava (New York: Norton, 1955), 384; Francis Sill Wickware, "Report on the Kinsey Report," *Life*, August 2, 1948, 87.

17. Kinsey et al., *Sexual Behavior in the Human Male*, 623 (37 percent, "city streets"), 637 (stereotypes). For the report's disruption of popular presumptions, see D'Emilio, *Sexual Politics*, 35–36; Craig M. Loftin, "Unacceptable Mannerisms: Gender Anxieties, Homosexual Activism, and Swish in the United States, 1945–1965," *Journal of Social History* 40 (Spring 2007): 579.

18. For the report's role, sometimes contested, in professionalizing the study of sexual-

ity, see Sarah E. Igo, *The Averaged American: Surveys, Citizens, and the Making of a Mass Public* (Cambridge, MA: Harvard University Press, 2007), chaps. 5–6; D'Emilio, *Sexual Politics*, 37. On conflicts between Kinsey and psychiatric authorities, see Dagmar Herzog, *Cold War Freud: Psychoanalysis in an Age of Catastrophes* (Cambridge: Cambridge University Press, 2017), chap. 2.

19. Freedman, "'Uncontrolled Desires'"; Robertson, *Crimes against Children*, chap. 10; Hurewitz, *Bohemian Los Angeles*, 132–34.

20. For de River's involvement, see Leon, *Sex Fiends*, 38–40. For state-commissioned studies and collaboration with psychiatrists, see Freedman, "'Uncontrolled Desires,'" 94–99; George, "Harmless Psychopath," 233–50; Robertson, *Crimes against Children*, 208–28; Leon, *Sex Fiends*, 25–53. For individual reports, see Joint State Government Commission, Pennsylvania General Assembly, "Sex Offenders: A Report of the Joint State Government Commission to the General Assembly of the Commonwealth of Pennsylvania" (Harrisburg, PA, 1951); Paul W. Tappan, "The Habitual Sex Offender: Report and Recommendations of the Commission on the Habitual Sex Offender, New Jersey" (Trenton, NJ, 1950); Bernard C. Glueck Jr., "Final Report: Research Project for the Study and Treatment of Persons Convicted of Crimes Involving Sexual Aberrations, June 1952 to June 1955" (Albany, NY, 1965). For Canty, see Alan Canty, "Sex Deviation and Crime!," *San Francisco Police and Peace Officer's Journal*, April–May 1957, 37.

21. Bertram Pollens, *The Sex Criminal* (New York: Macaulay, 1938), 39 (quoted). For the psychological prototype of the sexual psychopath and the scope of ensuing legislation, see Freedman, "'Uncontrolled Desires,'" 83–84, 90–92, 97–98; Robertson, *Crimes against Children*, 207–10, 218–23. For the funding of clinics specifically, see Philip Jenkins, *Moral Panic: Changing Concepts of the Child Molester in Modern America* (New Haven, CT: Yale University Press, 1998), 82–84; Canty, "Sex Deviation and Crime!," 37.

22. For psychiatrists welcoming their newfound influence, see Sheldon Glueck, "Sex Crimes and the Law," *The Nation*, September 25, 1937, 319–20; Pollens, *The Sex Criminal*, 13. For objections to the sexual psychopath laws, see Joint State Government Commission, "Sex Offenders," 5, 11; Frederick J. Hacker and Marcel Frym, "The Sexual Psychopath Act in Practice: A Critical Discussion," *California Law Review* 43 (1955): 767–76; Freedman, "'Uncontrolled Desires,'" 95, 98; Robertson, *Crimes against Children*, 207, 217, 222; George, "Harmless Psychopath," 231–33; Kunzel, "Sex Panic," 235–36.

23. *Stoumen*, Opening Brief for Appellant, 82–84, 97–100. On the Black Cat case generally, see Boyd, *Wide Open Town*, 145–46; Agee, *Streets of San Francisco*, 84–87.

24. *Stoumen*, Brief for Respondents, 89, 31e–31f; *Stoumen*, 222 P.2d at 683; *Stoumen*, 37 Cal. 2d at 717–18. For the 1956 dispute, see William Thomas, "Homosexual Rights in Bars Argued," *San Francisco Chronicle*, September 19, 1957, 11.

25. *Rutgers Cocktail Bar*, Bulletin 1133, no. 2, 1956, 4; *Murphy's Tavern*, Supreme Court, Appendix, 559a–561a, 563a, 570a, 573a; "Three Taverns Challenge ABC Homosexual Rulings," *Asbury Park Press*, August 27, 1967, 1, 63. Some defendants invoked expert opinions more peripherally in their briefs. *Paddock Bar*, Brief and Appendix for Appellant, 7; *Kerma Rest. Corp. v. State Liquor Auth.*, 21 N.Y.2d 111 (1967), Appellant's Brief, 31–32.

26. For Val's Bar, see *Val's Bar, Inc., v. Div. of Alcoholic Beverage Control*, Supreme Court of New Jersey, A-9, No. 5445 (1967), Appendix, 97a; *One Eleven Wines*, 50 N.J. at 334–35 (quoted). For Kaczka, see *N.Y. Bar*, Bulletin 1063, no. 1, 1955, 4–5.

27. *Kershaw*, Appellant's Brief, 36–38; *Kershaw*, Brief of Respondents, 4–5. For an analogous strategy in New Jersey, see *Zaro's Bar*, Bulletin 1150, no. 2, 1957, 4.

28. *Kershaw*, Appellant's Brief, 38. For First and Last Chance Bar, see *Vallerga v. Dep't of Alcoholic Beverage Control*, 343 P.2d 54 (Cal. Dist. Ct. App. 1959), Appellants' Opening Brief, 16; *Vallerga v. Dep't of Alcoholic Beverage Control*, 343 P.2d 54 (Cal. Dist. Ct. App. 1959), Brief of Morris Lowenthal et al. as Amici Curiae, v–vi, 39. For earlier cases invoking expert opinion to argue that homosexuality is not socially harmful, see *Stoumen*, Opening Brief for Appellant, 81–82; *Gloria*, Brief for Petitioner, 11.

29. *Kershaw*, Appellant's Brief, 38; *Nickola v. Munro*, 162 Cal. App. 2d 449 (1958), Appellant's Opening Brief, 12, 15–16.

30. *Morell v. Dep't of Alcoholic Beverage Control*, 204 Cal. App. 2d 504, 515–16 (1962); *Nickola*, Appellant's Opening Brief, 15–16; *Kershaw*, Appellant's Brief, 38; *Vallerga*, Brief of Morris Lowenthal et al., 17–41, 45–66; *Chez'l Cocktail Lounge*, Bulletin 1721, no. 1, 1967, 7.

31. *N.Y. Bar*, Bulletin 1063, no. 1, 1955, 5. For similar reasoning, see *Jack's Star Bar*, Bulletin 1667, no. 3, 1966, 9; *Murphy's Tavern*, Supreme Court, Appendix, 562–563a.

32. *Kershaw*, 155 Cal. App. 2d at 549. For similar dispositions, see *Stoumen*, 222 P.2d at 683; *Morell*, 204 Cal. App. 2d at 517–18.

33. *Val's Bar*, Bulletin 1685, no. 1, 1966, 6; *Murphy's Tavern*, Bulletin 1677, no. 1, 1966, 8; *Murphy's Tavern*, 70 N.J. Super. at 96.

34. *Murphy's Tavern*, Supreme Court, Appendix, 561a–562a; *Hoover's Tavern*, Bulletin 1521, no. 1, 1963, 7–8. The attorney general echoed the same argument. *Murphy's Tavern, Inc. v. Div. of Alcoholic Beverage Control*, Supreme Court of New Jersey, A-8, No. 5433 (1967), Brief for Respondents, 20–21.

35. *Rutgers Cocktail Bar*, Bulletin 1133, no. 2, 1956, 2, 4–5.

36. *N.Y. Bar*, Bulletin 1063, no. 1, 1955, 5; *Murphy's Tavern*, Supreme Court, Appendix, 575a. For Pomeroy, see *Val's Bar*, Bulletin 1685, no. 1, 1966, 4. For another example, see *Chez'l Cocktail Lounge*, Bulletin 1721, no. 1, 1967, 7.

37. *N.Y. Bar*, Bulletin 1063, no. 1, 1955, 5; *Murphy's Tavern*, Bulletin 1677, no. 1, 1966, 8. For another example, see *Val's Bar*, Bulletin 1685, no. 1, 1966, 6.

38. *Paddock Bar*, 46 N.J. Super. at 408–9 (Ct. App. Div. 1957); "Wilfred H. Jayne, Ex-Judge, 73, Dies," *NYT*, August 13, 1961, 89.

39. See chapter 3 below.

40. On the broader history of institutional pressures mediating the law's embrace of medical expertise, see James C. Mohr, *Doctors and the Law: Medical Jurisprudence in Nineteenth Century America* (New York: Oxford University Press, 1993).

41. *Murphy's Tavern*, 70 N.J. Super. 87, Appendix to Brief for Appellant, 85a–87a.

42. *Pine Brook Diner*, Bulletin 1406, no. 2, 1961, 4; *Helene's*, Bulletin 1405, no. 3, 1961, 12.

43. *Murphy's Tavern*, 70 N.J. Super. 87, Appendix to Brief for Appellant, 86a.

44. *Gloria*, Brief for Petitioner, 29 (quoted); *Gloria*, Record on Review, 279–93.

45. *Rutgers Cocktail Bar*, Bulletin 1133, no. 2, 1956, 4; *Paddock Inn*, Bulletin 1543, no. 3, 1964, 10–11. For additional examples, see *Hy and Sols Bar*, Bulletin 1356, no. 2, 1960, 5–6; *Helene's*, Bulletin 1405, no. 3, 1961, 12; *Hotel Penn*, Bulletin 1453, no. 2, 1962, 8; *Paddock Inn*, Bulletin 1342, no. 1, 1960, 2–3; *Herbie's Bar & Grill*, Bulletin 1087, no. 7, 1955, 9.

46. "Told How to Testify, Policeman Informs ABC," *WP*, November 10, 1948, 1.

47. *Hy and Sols Bar*, Bulletin 1356, no. 2, 1960, 5–6; *Herbie's Bar & Grill*, Bulletin 1087,

no. 7, 1955, 9. For examples of long-standing relationships, see also *Helene's*, Bulletin 1405, no. 3, 1961, 12.

48. *Hotel Penn*, Bulletin 1453, no. 2, 1962, 8. For similar examples, see *Paddock Inn*, Bulletin 1543, no. 3, 1964, 10–11. On graft, see chapter 1, n. 13, above.

49. *Tumulty*, Bulletin 1466, no. 1, 1962, 7. For cases raising similar defenses, see *Tollins' Bar*, Bulletin 1441, no. 5, 1962, 10; *Ally-Ally*, Bulletin 1757, no. 1, 1967, 7; *One Eleven Wines*, Bulletin 1656, no. 5, 1966, 8–9.

50. Lvovsky, "Judicial Presumption," 2003–36.

51. *Gloria*, Record on Review, 248; *Paddock Inn*, Bulletin 1543, no. 3, 1964, 10; *Val's Bar*, Bulletin 1747, no. 2, 1967, 6; *One Eleven Wines & Liquors, Inc. v. Div. of Alcoholic Beverage Control*, New Jersey Superior Court, Appellate Division, No. A-374-65 (1966), Appendix to Appellant's Brief, 37a, 40a (quoted), 52a–53a. For additional examples, see *Times Square*, Record on Review, 34, 40, 54; *Murphy's Tavern*, Supreme Court, Brief for Respondent, 20; *Loubor*, Record on Review, 95–97.

52. *Hoover's Tavern*, Bulletin 1521, no. 1, 1963, 7–8 ("substantial"); *One Eleven Wines*, Bulletin 1656, no. 5, 1966, 13; *Murphy's Tavern*, Bulletin 1677, no. 1, 1966, 8; *Murphy's Tavern*, 70 N.J. Super. 87, Brief for Respondent, 19–20.

53. *Paddock Bar*, Bulletin 1368, no. 5, 1960, 16.

54. On the appeal of diffusive legal regimes, see generally David Garland, "The Limits of the Sovereign State: Strategies of Crime Control in Contemporary Society," *British Journal of Criminology* 36 (Autumn 1996): 445–71.

CHAPTER THREE

1. *Peter Orsi*, Bulletin 326, no. 1, 1939, 1.

2. For accounts of police harassment, see *UCLA Law Review* Study, 718–19; Rosen, "Police Harassment," 162–65; Johnson, *Lavender Scare*, 59–61; D'Emilio, *Sexual Politics*, 30, 206–7; Faderman and Timmons, *Gay L.A.*, 77–86.

3. In this sense, this story aims to complicate scholarly accounts of the legal system's commitment to regulating same-sex conduct. Backer, "Constructing a 'Homosexual' for Constitutional Theory," 547; William N. Eskridge Jr., *Gaylaw: Challenging the Apartheid of the Closet* (Cambridge, MA: Harvard University Press, 1999), 43 (speculating that socially active men had "a good chance of spending time in jail" for misdemeanor convictions); Canaday, "Heterosexuality as a Legal Regime," 450. See generally introduction, n. 11, above.

4. For the history of plainclothes enforcement, see Cyrille Fijnaut and Gary T. Marx, introduction to *Undercover: Police Surveillance in Comparative Perspective*, ed. Cyrille Fijnaut and Gary T. Marx (Norwell: Kluwer Academic, 1995), 5, 11; Gary T. Marx, *Undercover: Police Surveillance in America* (Berkeley and Los Angeles: University of California Press, 1988), 24–30; Jennifer Fronc, *New York Undercover: Private Surveillance in the Progressive Era* (Chicago: University of Chicago Press, 2009). On the utility of decoys in vice enforcement, see Daniel L. Rotenberg, "The Police Detection Practice of Encouragement," *Virginia Law Review* 49 (June 1963): 873–74.

5. See generally chapter 1 above. For sexual advances, see *Gloria*, Record on Review, 69; *Times Square Garden*, Record on Review, 25–26; *Lynch's Builders*, 102 N.Y.S.2d at 607–8; *Giovatto*, Papers on Appeal, 27–41; *Stanwood*, 283 A.D. at 80–81; *Stanwood*, Record on Review, 82–83; *Casino*, Bulletin 1050, no. 1, 1955, 4. For failure to follow up on solicitations, see *Peter Orsi*, Bulletin 326, no. 1, 1939, 1; *Bader's Bar*, Bulletin 1073, no. 4, 1955, 6–8; *Entertainer's Club*, Bulletin 1088, no. 2, 1955, 4; *Zaro's Bar*,

Bulletin 1150, no. 2, 1957, 3–4. For agents pointedly presenting as heterosexuals, see *Paddock Inn*, Bulletin 1543, no. 3, 1964, 9; *Murphy's Tavern*, Bulletin 1677, no. 1, 1966, 3; *Gloria*, Record on Review, 321.

6. On the sexual psychopath laws and their effects on antigay enforcement, see Freedman, "'Uncontrolled Desires,'" 95; George Chauncey Jr., "The Postwar Sex Crime Panic," in *True Stories from the American Past*, ed. William Graebner (New York: McGraw-Hill, 1993), 160–78; Robertson, *Crimes against Children*, 216–17; Leon, *Sex Fiends*, 30–37. On police specialization, see Fogelson, *Big-City Police*, 177–79.

7. For San Francisco, see Agee, *The Streets of San Francisco*, 76; "New S.F. Police Details Begin Operating Today," *San Francisco Examiner*, November 11, 1948, 5; "Methods of Degenerates Are Studied," *Salinas Californian*, August 9, 1951, 4 (quoted); "Girl, 5, Dragged from Kidnap Car Outside Sunset School," *San Francisco Examiner*, November 10, 1949, 3. For DC, see Jean M. White, "Those Others IV: 49 States and the District Punish Overt Homosexual Acts as Crimes," *WP*, February 3, 1965, A19; *Guarro v. United States*, 237 F.2d 578 (D.C. Cir. 1956), Brief for Appellant, 2, box 5, RG276; Beemyn, *A Queer Capital*, 141. For Detroit, see John Warner and Herman Goldstein, "Progress Report on the Survey of the Detroit Police Department," November 20, 1956, 4, ABF; Field Report 11141, January 16, 1957, 2–3; Field Report 11037, November 17, 1956, 2–3. For Los Angeles, see *People v. Bentley*, 102 Cal. App. 2d 97 (1951), Reporter's Transcript on Appeal, 4; *People v. Sellers*, 103 Cal. App. 2d 830 (1951), Reporter's Transcript on Appeal, 5. For reliance on general detectives, see Fonzi, "Furtive Fraternity," 48–49 (Philadelphia); Field Report 10092, April 13, 1956, 3–4 (Wauwasota); Field Report 10247, July 24, 1956, 1 (Madison); *UCLA Law Review* Study, 694 n. 50.

8. For allegations of quotas, see Albert Deutsch, *The Trouble with Cops* (New York: Crown, 1968), 86; Cory and LeRoy, *The Homosexual and His Society*, 116–17; Levie, "Vice and Victim," 10–11; Dale Jennings, "To Be Accused, Is to Be Guilty," *ONE*, January 1953, 12. While generally denying strict quotas, vice officers admitted feeling pressured by superiors. Max K. Hurlbut to author, July 11, 2018.

9. Howard Whitman, "Terror in Our Cities," *Collier's*, November 19, 1949, 14–15. For a later example, see Gail Collins, "Flay SD Laws," *Metropolitan Citizen-News*, February 5, 1963, A1, A12. See also Frederick W. Egen, *Plainclothesman: A Handbook of Vice and Gambling Investigation* (New York: Arco, 1959), 107.

10. On the Lavender Scare, see Johnson, *Lavender Scare*, 2 (quoted), 85–87, 154, 174. For the report, see US Senate, *Employment of Homosexuals and Other Sex Perverts in Government* (Washington, DC: US Government Printing Office, 1950), 3, 5; William S. White, "Inquiry by Senators on Perverts Asked," *NYT*, May 20, 1950, 8; Richard Harness and Gladys Harkness, "How about Those Security Cases?," *Reader's Digest*, September 1955, 202–14.

11. For rising gay visibility fueling antihomosexual sentiment, see Chauncey, "The Postwar Sex Crime Panic," 169; Strub, "Clearly Obscene," 376–78; Ernest Lenn, "Sex Deviate Problem in S.F. Detailed," *San Francisco Examiner*, September 29, 1954, 1. For the return to normality, see Howard, *The Closet and the Cul-de-Sac*, 42–43. For discussions of so-called white flight, see Bryant Simon, *Boardwalk of Dreams: Atlantic City and the Fate of Urban America* (New York: Oxford University Press, 2004); Kevin M. Kruse, *White Flight: Atlanta and the Making of Modern Conservatism* (Princeton, NJ: Princeton University Press, 2005). For the emphasis on public nuisance, see Lawrence P. Tiffany, Donald M. McIntyre Jr., and Daniel L. Rotenberg, *The Detection of Crime* (Boston: Little, Brown, 1967), 238–39; Wayne R. LaFave, *Arrest: The Deci-*

sion to Take a Suspect into Custody (Little, Brown, 1965), 465; Robert W. Ferguson, *The Nature of Vice Control in the Administration of Justice* (St. Paul: West, 1974), 110, 117; Egen, *Plainclothesman*, 106. For department policies, see Max K. Hurlbut, *Vagabond Policeman* (n.p.: Max K. Hurlbut, 2013), 87 (Los Angeles); Agee, *Streets of San Francisco*, 75–76 (San Francisco). For the lack of interest in gay bars, see chapter 1, n. 13, above; Helmer, "New York's 'Middle Class' Homosexuals," 86; Fonzi, "Furtive Fraternity," 52.

12. For California, see *Sultan Turkish Bath, Inc. v. Bd. of Police Comm'rs*, 169 Cal. App. 2d 188, 197 (1959). For New York, see *People v. Humphrey*, 111 N.Y.S.2d 450, 452–53 (Co. Ct. 1952). For Michigan and Wisconsin, see Tiffany, McIntyre, and Rotenberg, *Detection of Crime*, 232–36. For DC, see *Bicksler v. United States*, 90 A.2d 233, 233 (D.C. July 25, 1952) (solicitation); *Dyson v. United States*, 97 A.2d 135, 136 (D.C. May 29, 1953) (assault). For an overview of misdemeanor laws generally, see *UCLA Law Review* Study, 663–67 and n. 57.

13. For police claims of reports and complaints by citizens, see Field Report 11178, January 19, 1957, 4; Field Report 11196, February 2, 1957, 3–4; "Arrests Total 43 in SM Crackdown on Sexual Deviates," *Santa Monica Outlook*, July 27, 1954, 1, 2; Max J. Hurlbut, "Presentation," 1; *UCLA Law Review* Study, 688 n. 17; "Screen 'Toughie' Dates Officers," *Los Angeles Daily News*, July 13, 1950. For the boilerplate, see Barry Copilow and Thomas Coleman, "Enforcement of Section 647(a) of the California Penal Code by the Los Angeles Police Department" (1972, typescript), 6, Thomas F. Coleman and Jay M. Kohorn Papers, Coll2014-031, ONE Archives. A study of midwestern policing reported that police "often" receive complaints from citizens who had been "accosted," but my review of the underlying field reports revealed only a single instance, involving a store owner soliciting two young men in Detroit. LaFave, *Arrest*, 465; Field Report 11174, January 21, 1957, 14. For the efficacy of decoys, see *UCLA Law Review* Study, 687 n. 8 ("minutes"); *Kelly v. United States*, 194 F.2d 150, 152 (D.C. Cir. 1952); Field Report 11196, February 2, 1957, 3–4 (Pontiac).

14. For the range of locations, see Harold Jacobs, "Decoy Enforcement of Homosexual Laws," *University of Pennsylvania Law Review* 112 (December 1963): 259; "Donaldson, Smith, Leighton and May v. City and County of San Francisco," 1, folder 11, box 46, Evander Smith Papers, Gay and Lesbian Center, San Francisco Public Library; *UCLA Law Review* Study, 691 n. 31; Roger S. Mitchell, *The Homosexual and the Law* (New York: Arco, 1969), 35; Field Report 11141, January 16, 1957, 6; Field Report 11172, January 25, 1957, 1. For the recruit lecture, see Hurlbut, "Presentation," 5 ("small plot"). For Griffith Park, see Max K. Hurlbut to author, October 12, 2017, item 18 ("notorious"). For the Lafayette wiretap, see "State Official Dismissed After Perversion Charge," *Atlanta Daily World*, November 22, 1947, 2; "Can't Even Trust Park Bench If It Is Wired for Sound," *WP*, November 11, 1947, 1, 6. On the role of Lafayette Park in the Lavender Scare, see "Senate Unit OK's Pervert Inquiry," *Baltimore Sun*, May 20, 1950, 1; George Tagge, "Dirksen Urges Moral Crusade for Campaign," *CDT*, June 13, 1950, 16 ("I know").

15. For the Committee's demands, see Joseph Goldstein, "Police Discretion Not to Invoke the Criminal Process: Low-Visibility Decisions in the Administration of Justice," *Yale Law Journal* 69 (March 1960): 594. For Blick's career and zeal, see "Roy Blick Promoted to Police Captaincy," *WP*, November 17, 1950, B1; "Roy Blick, Ex-Police Official, Dies at 72," *WP*, June 19, 1972, C4 (quoted); Phil Casey, "Safe Holding Vice, Sex Crimes Files Stays with Police Morals Division," *WP*, July 3, 1964, A3; Alfred E. Lewis and Harry Gabbett, "It's D.C.'s Sex File but Blick's Key," *WP*, Sep-

tember 29, 1963, E2; "Roy Blick to Retire, Recommends Moyer," *WP*, June 10, 1964, B5; "Morals in the Parks," *WP*, January 1, 1966, A6; Kaiser, *Gay Metropolis*, 71–72. For press coverage, see "Senator's Son Convicted on Morals Charge," *WP*, October 7, 1953, 11; "U.S. Employee Cleared in Morals Case," *WP*, May 19, 1954, 17; "Rule of Thumb Is Given with Morals Conviction," *WP*, April 2, 1954, B1; "Usefulness of Sex Squad Questioned by Kronheim," *WP*, June 5, 1954, 21; "Alexandrian Loses Appeal of Conviction," *WP*, February 17, 1951, B1.

16. For the defense attorney, see Levie, "Vice and Victim," 46–47. For Buscher, see "Maryland Official Arrested by Morals Squad Policeman," *WP*, February 16, 1954, 3. For Jenkins, see Tom Wicker, "Jenkins Cleared of Security Slip in F.B.I. Report," *NYT*, October 23, 1964, 1; Bart Barnes, "LBJ Aide Walter Jenkins Dies," *WP*, November 26, 1985, C4. For Lester Hunt Jr. and Sr., see "Senator's Son Convicted on Morals Charge," 11; Johnson, *Lavender Scare*, 140–41.

17. On inherited patterns of racist policing, see Anne Gray Fischer, "'Land of the White Hunter': Legal Liberalism and the Racial Politics of Morals Enforcement in Midcentury Los Angeles," *Journal of American History* 105 (March 2019): 870–71, 878–79; Strub, "Queerly Obscene," 377; Muhammad, *The Condemnation of Blackness*, chap. 6; Fogelson, *Big-City Police*, chap. 1.

18. For economic disparities, see Donald J. Newman, *Conviction: The Determination of Guilt or Innocence without Conviction* (Boston: Little, Brown, 1966), 168; Ronald A. Farrell, "Class Linkages of Legal Treatment of Homosexuals," *Criminology* 9, no. 1 (May 1971): 55; *UCLA Law Review* Study, 740–41. For the more insular practices of wealthier men, see Chauncey, *Gay New York*, 349–50; Johnson, *Lavender Scare*, 150. For the geography of cruising sites, see Hobson, "Policing Gay L.A.," 192–200; Timothy Retzloff, "City, Suburb, and the Changing Bounds of Lesbian and Gay Life and Politics in Metropolitan Detroit, 1945–1985" (PhD diss., Yale University, 2014), 26, 47, 76, 106–8; Laud Humphreys, *Tearoom Trade: Impersonal Sex in Public Places* (Chicago: Aldine, 1970), 7–8. For the focus on effeminate or flamboyant suspects, see Farrell, "Class Linkages," 56; Tiffany, McIntyre, and Rotenberg, *Detection of Crime*, 234; Max K. Hurlbut to author, October 16, 2017, item 17 (quoted). For class valences of effeminate conduct, see Maurice Leznoff, "Interviewing Homosexuals," *American Journal of Sociology* 62 (September 1956): 203.

19. LaFave, *Arrest*, 143 ("undo"); Field Report 11178, January 19, 1957, 5–6 ("all walks"); Field Report 11021, October 29, 1956, 6; Field Report 11171, January 23, 1957, 2. For the Greyhound arrest, see Field Report 21110, June 14, 1957, 3 ("messiest").

20. Field Report 11042, November 19, 1956, 6–7 ("rolling"); Field Report 11051, November 27, 1956, 8 ("razz"); Field Report 11056, November 28, 1956, 4 (jail). See also Field Report 31030, December 10, 1956, 2. For a general discussion of differential treatment, see LaFave, *Arrest*, 143 and nn. 68–69, 466–67, 469.

21. For the attractiveness of decoys, see Stearn, *Sixth Man*, 145; Michael Rumaker, *Robert Duncan in San Francisco* (San Francisco: City Lights, 2013), 16; "Tex or JR," interview by Len Evans, transcript, n.d., 24, Oral History Project, GLBTHS. For Pontiac, see Field Report 11196, February 2, 1957, 3. For Philadelphia, see Richard H. Elliott, "Control of Homosexual Activity by Philadelphia Police: A Study of Enforcement and the Enforcers" (University of Pennsylvania Law School, December 4, 1961, typescript), 4; Fonzi, "Furtive Fraternity," 49 (quoted).

22. For the utility of nonwhite decoys, see Williams, *Vice Control in California*, 30; Max K. Hurlbut to author, May 7, 2018, item 2. For successful defenses, see *Kelly*, 194 F.2d

at 151, 155–56; "Educator Goes Free on Morals Charge," *CDT*, November 11, 1955, 1 (quoted). For Wildeblood, see *Wildeblood v. United States*, 284 F.2d 592, 598 (D.C. Cir. 1960); *Wildeblood v. United States*, 284 F.2d 592 (D.C. Cir. 1960), Memorandum in Support of Petition for Leave to File Appeal, 4–5, box 87, RG276; *Wildeblood v. United States*, 284 F.2d 592 (D.C. Cir. 1960), Order, March 31, 1960, 3, box 87, RG276.

23. For Mary's First and Last Chance, see *Vallerga*, Respondent's Brief, 5. For policies against lesbian decoys, see *UCLA Law Review* Study, 693 n. 46 ("degrading"); Copilow and Coleman, "Enforcement of Section 647(a)," 4, 12; Karl M. Bowman and Bernice Engle, "A Psychiatric Evaluation of Laws of Homosexuality," *Temple Law Quarterly* 29 (Spring 1956): 280–81; "Vice Hunting in Los Angeles," 20 (quoting Souza). For the Tallahassee case, see *Florida League for Good Government Viewpoint*, January 1967, 1, MSP; James A. Schnur, "Closet Crusaders: The Johns Committee and Homophobia, 1956–1965," 146, in *Carryin' On in the Lesbian and Gay South*, ed. John Howard (New York: New York University Press, 1997).

24. For vice work as a career advancement, see Max K. Hurlbut to author, October 12, 2017, item 12. For police resentment, see Agee, *Streets of San Francisco*, 77 (quoting Cahill); Ferguson, *Nature of Vice Control*, 118.

25. For concerns about dirty work, see Deutsch, *Trouble with Cops*, 91 (quoted); Albert Deutsch, "Vice Squad," *Collier's*, May 28, 1954, 66; Agee, *Streets of San Francisco*, 80. For precautions, see Deutsch, *Trouble with Cops*, 90; Max K. Hurlbut to author, October 12, 2017, item 11. For teasing, see Herb Selwyn, interview by John D'Emilio, October 25, 1976, NYPL ("takes one"); Max K. Hurlbut to author, October 12, 2017, item 14 ("prefer"). For the rumors of gay officers, see "Tex or JR," interview by Len Evans, 24; Stearn, *Sixth Man*, 167; Levie, "Vice and Victim," 35. On the Naval investigation, see George Chauncey Jr., "Christian Brotherhood or Sexual Perversion? Homosexual Identities and the Construction of Sexual Boundaries in the World War One Era," *Journal of Social History* 19 (Winter 1985): 189–211.

26. For conservative views among the police, see Max K. Hurlbut to author, October 12, 2017, item 15, 11; Joseph Wambaugh, *The Onion Field* (New York: Delacorte, 1973), 31–33; *Florida League for Good Government Viewpoint*, February 1967, 3, MSP. For brutality against gay men, see Levie "Vice and Victim," 36; Thomas R. Brooks, "'New York's Finest,'" *Commentary*, August 1965, 29–36, 32; Stein, *City of Sisterly and Brotherly Loves*, 100. For preference for decoy work, see Max K. Hurlbut to author, October 12, 2017, item 12 (work in the field); Max K. Hurlbut to author, July 11, 2018 ("bath tub").

27. Field Report 21064, April 30, 1957, 9.

28. For minimal guidance, see Tiffany, McIntyre, and Rotenberg, *The Detection of Crime*, 235. For decoys in bars, see *Giovatto*, Papers on Appeal, 27–41; *Lynch's Builders*, 102 N.Y.S.2d at 607–8; *Stanwood*, 283 A.D. at 80–81; *Louise G. Mack*, Bulletin 1088, no. 2, 1955, 3–4; *People v. Pleasant*, 23 Misc. 2d 367, 368–69 (N.Y. Magis. Ct. 1953) (Diamond Jim's); *Ekim Broadway*, Papers on Appeal, 32. For parks and streets, see *People v. Humphrey*, 111 N.Y.S.2d 450, 452–53 (Co. Ct. 1952); *People v. Feliciano*, 10 Misc. 2d 836, 837 (N.Y. Magis. Ct. 1958); *Kelly*, 194 F.2d at 151; Elliott, "Control of Homosexual Activity by Philadelphia Police," 5–6; *Brenke v. United States*, 78 A.2d 677, 677–78 (D.C. February 16, 1951). For Wallace, see Beemyn, *A Queer Capital*, 142. I adopt the pseudonym "Ed Wallace" from Beemyn, who unearthed this material.

29. For tactics in bathrooms, see *Bicksler v. United States*, 90 A.2d 233, 234 (D.C. 1952); Jennings, "To Be Accused," 11–12; *Henderson v. United States*, 117 A.2d 456, 456

(D.C. 1955); *McDermett v. United States*, 98 A.2d 287, 289 (D.C. 1953); *Guarro v. United States*, 237 F.2d 578, 579 (D.C. Cir. 1956); *Dyson*, 97 A.2d at 136. For decoys exposing themselves or opening coats, see *Seitner v. United States*, 143 A.2d 101, 102 (D.C. 1958); *Guarro v. United States*, 116 A.2d 408, 409 (D.C. 1955); *McDermett*, 98 A.2d at 289; Field Report 11288, April 14, 1957, 2–3. For Bradlee, see Kaiser, *Gay Metropolis*, 71.

30. Donald Webster Cory, *The Homosexual in America: A Subjective Approach* (New York: Greenberg, 1951), 117. For liquor agents distancing themselves from gay men, see chapter 1, n. 40, above; *Murphy's Tavern*, 70 N.J. Super. 87, Appendix to Brief for Appellant, 40a. For Longo, see "Rule of Thumb Is Given with Morals Conviction," B1. Others similarly reported reading Longo as homosexual. "U.S. Employee Cleared in Morals Case," 17; "Former Court Clerk Freed in Sex Case," *WP*, May 21, 1954, 31.

31. Cory, *Homosexual in America*, 109. For early research, see Myles Vollmer, "Glossary of Homosexual Terms," folder 8, box 145, EWBP; Untitled List of Gay Slang, folder 3, box 98, EWBP; Gershon Legman, "The Language of Homosexuality," in George W. Henry, *Sex Variants: A Study of Homosexual Patterns* (New York: Paul B. Hoeber, 1941), 2:1149–79. For the military, see "David—Age Twenty-One," 12, folder 8, box 128, EWBP. For decoys, see *Kelly v. United States*, 194 F.2d 150 (D.C. Cir. 1952), Joint Appendix, 33, box 1390, RG276; "Usefulness of Sex Squad Questioned by Kronheim," 21; *Bicksler*, 90 A.2d at 234 (Costanzo); Beemyn, *A Queer Capital*, 142 (Wallace).

32. For Fochett's biography, see "Police Lt. Louis Fochett, Served in Morals Unit," *WP*, April 16, 1968, B8; "White House Screening," *WP*, October 18, 1964, E6. For "every night," see *Guarro*, Brief for Appellant, 2. For Fochett's tactics, see *Henderson*, 117 A.2d at 456; *Guarro*, 237 F.2d at 579; *Seitner v. United States*, 143 A.2d 101 (D.C. 1958), Brief for Appellant, 2, box 1890, RG276. For the Mattachine Society meeting, see Johnson, *Lavender Scare*, 183.

33. *Humphrey*, 111 N.Y.S.2d at 452–53.

34. Jennings, "To Be Accused," 11–13.

35. For dueling versions of Jennings's arrest and lingering skepticism, see C. Todd White, *Pre-Gay L.A.: A Social History of the Movement for Homosexual Rights* (Urbana: University of Illinois Press, 2009), 24–25. For a similar case, see "Case #1," box 1, folder 14, MSP. For the trial, see D'Emilio, *Sexual Politics*, 70–71; Douglas M. Charles, "From Subversion to Obscenity: The FBI's Investigations of the Early Homophile Movement in the United States, 1953–1958," *Journal of the History of Sexuality* 19 (May 2010): 265–67.

36. For Los Angeles, see Levie, "Vice and Victim," 96–97 (quote 97), 99. For DC, see Johnson, *Lavender Scare*, 176; *Dyson*, 97 A.2d at 138–39.

37. For private compassion, see Levie, "Vice and Victim," 100–101. For prosecutors reducing or dropping charges, see Frank W. Miller, *Prosecution: The Decision to Charge a Suspect with a Crime* (Boston: Little, Brown, 1969), 17 and n. 20, 209; R. W. Bowling, "The Sex Offender and Law Enforcement," *Federal Probation* 14 (September 1950): 13. For Wauwatosa, see Field Report 10085, April 4, 1956, 5.

38. For "collateral harm," see Miller, *Prosecution*, 209. For leniency with multiple categories of sex crimes, see Newman, *Conviction*, 106–7; Bowling, "The Sex Offender," 13. Officers also exercised leniency in deference to a suspect's reputation, particularly where youth or alcohol was involved. William A. Westley, "Violence and the Police," *American Journal of Sociology* 59 (July 1953): 37.

39. For factors guiding discretion, see Miller, *Prosecution*, 278–79; Newman, *Conviction*,

118 (quoted), 107, 168. For the businessman, see Newman, *Conviction*, 106–7. For the physician, see Field Report 21112, June 12, 1957, 2; Field Report 21110, June 14, 1957, 3. Friends of policemen or prosecutors also got special dispensation. Field Report 11178, January 19, 1957, 4–8.

40. For the range of justifications, see Newman, *Conviction*, 118; Miller, *Prosecution*, 279; Field Report 31089, April 16, 1957, 4; Field Report 31045, February 4, 1957, 8; Levie, "Vice and Victim," 53, 49–50, 87. On the broader use of prosecutorial and judicial discretion to privatize dependency, see Willrich, *City of Courts*, 163–67; Alison Lefkovitz, *Strange Bedfellows: Marriage in the Age of Women's Liberation* (Philadelphia: University of Pennsylvania Press, 2018).

41. For gay men's pessimistic views of judges, see Levie, "Vice and Victim," 46; Donald Webster Cory, *Homosexuality: A Cross Cultural Approach* (New York: Julian, 1956), 399. For early reticence around homosexual conduct, see Morris Ploscowe, *Sex and the Law* (New York: Prentice-Hall, 1951), 196–98. For midcentury expressions of antipathy, see *People v. Young*, 214 Cal. App. 2d 131, 135 (1963); *Pleasant*, 23 Misc. 2d at 370–71. For Rover, see "Rover Takes Oath as Appeals Judge," *WP*, April 11, 1956, 17.

42. For wasted resources, see Newman, *Conviction*, 192–93 (quoted); Stanley Mosk, foreword to *UCLA Law Review* Study, 645. For concerns with judges' time, see Miller, *Prosecution*, 17 n. 20. For excessive penalties, see Newman, *Conviction*, 174; Levie, "Vice and Victim," 120. For sensitivity to criminal punishment, see Stearn, *Sixth Man*, 169; *People v. Liebenthal*, 5 N.Y.2d 876 (1959), Record on Appeal, 101–2; "Female Impersonators Freed by Directed Verdict; Nothing Lewd in Women's Clothes, Judge's Stand," *Passaic Herald-News*, November 16, 1934, 17.

43. For partial liberalization following the Kinsey Report, see George, "Harmless Psychopath," 252–56; Ploscowe, *Sex and the Law*, 136; Egen, *Plainclothesman*, 8–9. One author noted liberalizing attitudes generally but found lawyers to be comparatively conservative. Ford, "Homosexuals and the Law," 239. For the legislative survey, see Fowler V. Harper, "Book Review: Sexual Behavior in the Human Female," *Yale Law Journal* 63 (April 1954): 899. For the American Law Institute, see American Law Institute, *Model Penal Code, Tentative Draft No. 4* (Philadelphia: American Law Institute, 1955), 276–91 (comments to sec. 207.5). In 1956, the influential Wolfenden Report in England proposed a similar measure. David Minto, "Perversion by Penumbras: Wolfenden, *Griswold*, and the Transatlantic Trajectory of Sexual Privacy," *American Historical Review* 123 (October 2018): 1106–9.

44. "Usefulness of Sex Squad Questioned by Kronheim," 21; Mosk, foreword to *UCLA Law Review* Study, 645. For judicial reservations, see also Tiffany, McIntyre, and Rotenberg, *Detection of Crime*, 237.

45. For Milwaukee, see Field Report 30009, February 14, 1956, 8. For Los Angeles judges, see Carol Collins, "Judges Explain SD 'Leniency,'" *Metropolitan Citizen-News*, February 7, 1963, A1–A2. Defense attorneys who represented gay men sometimes spoke in similar terms. Levie, "Vice and Victim," 11, 53.

46. For discussions of the draconian effects of the sexual psychopath laws on minor criminals like homosexuals, see Chauncey, "Postwar Sex Crime Panic," 166; Freedman, "'Uncontrolled Desires,'" 95–100; Fred Fejes, "Murder, Perversion, and Moral Panic: The 1954 Media Campaign against Miami's Homosexuals and the Discourse of Civic Betterment," *Journal of the History of Sexuality* 9 (July 2000): 318–19; Kunzel, "Sex Panic," 230–31, 237–39. For cases of commitment, see George, "Harmless Psychopath," 225–26, 246; Eskridge, *Gaylaw*, 61–62; Freedman, "'Uncontrolled

Desires,'" 102–3 n. 41; New Jersey Commission on the Habitual Sex Offender, *The Habitual Sex Offender* (Trenton, NJ, 1950), 29; Elias S. Cohen, "Administration of the Criminal Sexual Psychopath Statute in Indiana," *Indiana Law Journal* 32 (Summer 1957): 453–54; Neil Miller, *Sex-Crime Panic: A Journey to the Paranoid Heart of the 1950s* (Los Angeles: Alyson, 2002). Nonwhite and gender-nonconforming men may have been especially vulnerable. Retzloff, "City, Suburb," 92–93.

47. For the typical legislative focus on predatory crimes, see Field Report 40069, May 29, 1956, 2; George, "Harmless Psychopath," 243, 250. For extensive discussions of sexual psychopath cases focusing entirely on molestation or rape, see Field Report 40072, May 25, 1956; Field Report 40073, May 25, 1956; Field Report 40064, May 18, 1956; Field Report 40144, July 11, 1956; Field Report 21046, March 10, 1957; Field Report 41124, March 11, 1957. This focus on predatory crimes persisted even though judges and prosecutors expressly situated "confirmed homosexuals" within the category of sex deviates. Field Report 30575, September 29, 1956, 2. For hesitation to use the law, see Field Report 41124, March 11, 1957, 3 ("cautious"); Field Report 41045, December 7, 1956, 2 ("rough"); Field Report 41033, December 11, 1956, 3. In Detroit, the law was so rarely used that many probation officers did not know basic details of its application. Field Report 41033, December 11, 1956, 2–3; Field Report 41045, December 7, 1956, 2; Field Report 41049, January 2, 1957, 2, 5.

Studies in other states reported similarly few cases of consenting homosexual conduct processed under the laws by the 1950s. New Jersey Commission on the Habitual Sex Offender, *The Habitual Sex Offender*, 29; Domenico Caporale and Deryl F. Hamann, "Sexual Psychopathy—a Legal Labyrinth of Medicine, Morals and Mythology," *Nebraska Law Review* 36 (March 1957): 325. William Eskridge reads *The Habitual Sex Offender* as stating that nearly half of New Jersey's sexual psychopath dispositions involved homosexual offenders, but this reading assumes that "lewdness" charges involved homosexual conduct. See Eskridge, *Dishonorable Passions*, 95. Regardless, my emphasis is not the proportion of sexual psychopath cases that involved homosexuality-related offense but the proportion of homosexuality-related offenses processed under the law.

48. On the funding of clinics, see chapter 2, n. 21, above. For judicial reliance on professional evaluations, see Field Report 30514, May 16, 1956, 2–3; Field Report 30575, September 29, 1956, 4; Field Report 31104, June 24, 1957, 6–7; Field Report 40508, May 11, 1956, 2–3; Field Report 30052, March 30, 1956, 1; Field Report 41144, April 1, 1957, 5; The Administration of Criminal Justice in the United States, Pilot Project Report, vol. 6, 218, box 3, ABF. Others did question the helpfulness of local psychiatrists. See Field Report 20503, April 30, 1956, 10; Field Report 41024, November 27, 1956, 4; Field Report 41045, December 7, 1956, 7. For Kansas, see The Administration of Criminal Justice in the United States, Pilot Project Report, 218 (quoted); Field Report 40508, May 11, 1956, 2–5. For Ventura County, see *Sultan Turkish Bath, Inc. v. Bd. of Police Comm'rs*, 169 Cal. App. 2d 188 (1959), Appellant's Reply Brief, 2 n. 2.

49. For general observations of lenient sentencing, see Cory, *Homosexual in America*, 56; Edwin M. Schur, *Crimes without Victims: Deviant Behavior and Public Policy* (Englewood Cliffs, NJ: Prentice-Hall, 1965), 79. For New York, see Stearn, *Sixth Man*, 169; *Giovatto*, Papers on Appeal, 47; *Lynch Builder's*, Record on Appeal, 166–71; *People v. Lopez*, 7 N.Y.2d 825 (1959), Record on Appeal, 40. For DC, see "Usefulness of Sex Squad Questioned by Kronheim," 21; *Brenke*, 78 A.2d at 677; *Kelly*, 194 F.2d at 151;

"$100 Fine in Morals Case," *WP*, March 24, 1954, 17; "Andrews Sergeant Given Jail Term in Morals Case," *WP*, January 17, 1951, 8; "3 Convicted of Charges on Morals," *WP*, December 29, 1950, 14; John P. MacKenzie, "Court Divided on Appeal Case," *WP*, November 4, 1960, B7; *Thomas v. United States*, 129 A.2d 852, 852 (D.C. 1957) (promise not to repeat). For Los Angeles, see Collins, "Judges Explain SD 'Leniency,'" A1; Levie, "Vice and Victim," 25, 74–75 (seventh-time offender), 106–7.

50. For Los Angeles, "Case #1," box 1, folder 14, MSP. For Atlanta, see "Ex-Pastor Guilty of Indecency," *Atlanta Journal*, January 23, 1957. For Detroit, see Robert O. Dawson, *Sentencing: The Decision as to Type, Length, and Conditions of Sentence* (Boston: Little, Brown, 1969), 114 and n. 43; Field Report 41079, January 30, 1957, 7; Field Report 11171, January 23, 1957, 4; Newman, *Conviction*, 166–67 (bank vice president). For DC courts, "Judge Suspends Morals Sentence," *WP*, January 16, 1954, 3. Prosecutors imposed similar conditions on reduced or dismissed charges. Field Report 11178, January 19, 1957, 7–8; Field Report 21112, June 12, 1957, 2.

51. On the classed and racialized character of psychiatric discourse, see Fischer, "'Land of the White Hunter,'" 868–70, 872–74. For Milwaukee, see Field Report 40024, March 21, 1956, 4. For judicial sensitivities to poor defendants, see Levie, "Vice and Victim," 109; Dawson, *Sentencing*, 114 and n. 43.

52. For reductions, see Newman, *Conviction*, 106–7. For acquittals and dismissals, see ibid., 148; Levie, "Vice and Victim," 105. For Wayne County, see Field Report 21096, May 28, 1957, 2 (quoted); Field Report 21090, May 27, 1957, 2, 6; Field Report 21110, June 14, 1957, 6–7; Miller, *Prosecution*, 17 and n. 20.

53. Levie, "Vice and Victim," 77–78, 105; Carol Collins, "Jail for SDs," *Metropolitan Citizen-News*, February 6, 1963, A1 (quoted).

54. For the Detroit scandal, see Newman, *Conviction*, 148. For similar controversies over leniency toward homosexual offenders, see Field Report 30523, May 31, 1956, 6; Field Report 41146, April 3–4, 1957, 4; Dawson, *Sentencing*, 90 n. 61. Leniency toward other sex offenders also caused outrage. Field Report 30531, May 12, 1956, 3; "Writers Pour Wrath on Gillis for His Freeing of Sex Criminal," *Detroit Free Press*, June 20, 1950, 6. For reactions in Los Angeles, see Collins, "Jail for SDs," A2 ("coddl[ing]"); *UCLA Law Review* Study, 737 and n. 300; Carol Collins, "SD Law Probe," *Metropolitan Citizen-News*, February 8, 1963, A1, and "L.A. Judge, Public Back SD Crusade," *Metropolitan Citizen-News*, February 8, 1963, A1 ("more serious").

55. On racial disparities, see, in addition to the discussion above, Retzloff, "City, Suburb," 48–49. For the intrinsic harms of an arrest or a trial, see Cory, *Homosexual in America*, 56; Schur, *Crimes without Victims*, 79. For professional consequences, see Levie, "Vice and Victim," 47–54. For the negative repercussions of even reduced charges, see Frank C. Wood Jr., "The Homosexual and the Police," *ONE*, May 1963, 21–22. For comparatively stringent probation conditions, see Copilow and Coleman, "Enforcement of Section 647(a)," 16; Levie, "Vice and Victim," 69–72, 111.

56. Deutsch, *Trouble with Cops*, 87 (Murtagh); "Usefulness of Sex Squad Questioned by Kronheim," 21. For Miller, see Field Report 31045, February 4, 1957, 8. For private criticism, see Field Report 31075, March 22, 1957, 3 (Stewart); Tiffany, McIntyre, and Rotenberg, *Detection of Crime*, 237; Newman, *Conviction*, 174, 189–90. Because restrictions on the American Bar Foundation papers prohibit researchers from identifying interview subjects, I use pseudonyms to refer to the judges of the Recorder's Court.

57. For the effects of Prohibition, see Marilyn Johnson, *Street Justice: A History of Police Violence in New York City* (New York: Beacon, 2004), chap. 4; Wickersham Commis-

sion, *Report on Lawlessness in Law Enforcement* (Washington, DC: US Government Printing Office, 1931). For growing judicial attention to race and criminal justice, see Dan T. Carter, *Scottsboro: A Tragedy of the American South* (Baton Rouge: Louisiana State University Press, 1969), esp. chap. 8; Patricia Sullivan, *Lift Every Voice: The NAACP and the Making of the Civil Rights Movement* (New York: New Press, 2009), 398–99; Michael J. Klarman, "The Racial Origins of Modern Criminal Procedure," *Michigan Law Review* 99 (October 2000): 48–97. For growing challenges to police discretion, see Goluboff, *Vagrant Nation*, esp. chap. 4. For concerns with antidemocratic policing, see Sarah A. Seo, "Democratic Policing Before the Due Process Revolution," *Yale Law Journal* 128 (2019): 1283–90; chapter 6, nn. 33–34, below.

58. For Howard, see "Judge Frees 2, Rebukes Morals Squad Men," *WP*, May 7, 1953, 8; "Judge Howard Dies at 72," *WP*, April 21, 1969. For analogous scrutiny of prostitution arrests, see LaFave, *Arrest*, 458; Newman, *Conviction*, 191; Tiffany, McIntyre, and Rotenberg, *Detection of Crime*, 237. On the ACLU, see Marc Stein, *Sexual Injustice: Supreme Court Decisions from Griswold to Roe* (Chapel Hill: University of North Carolina Press, 2010), 158–62, 159 (quoted); Leigh Ann Wheeler, *How Sex Became a Civil Liberty* (New York: Oxford University Press, 2013), 108–19.

59. For Stewart (pseudonymous), see Field Report 31075, March 22, 1957, 4 ("poor souls"). For the director, see Field Report 11288, April 14, 1957, 2–3 (interviewer's paraphrase). See also Tiffany, McIntyre, and Rotenberg, *Detection of Crime*, 236–37.

60. For defense attorneys emphasizing clients' heterosexual personal lives, see Levie, "Vice and Victim," 53, 49–50, 87. For Jenkins, see Edelman, *Homographesis*, 149–50. For harsher treatment of "confirmed homosexuals," see Levie, "Vice and Victim," 94, 103; Field Report 30575, September 29, 1956, 2; Field Report 11141, January 16, 1957, 12. For discriminatory legal incentives toward marriage, see Canaday, "Heterosexuality as a Legal Regime," 460–61.

61. George Henry Mortenson, "To Be Accused Is to Be Guilty: Casual Death Sentence," *ONE*, May 1953, 12 (quoted); Jennings, "To Be Accused," 10–12. For pervasive concerns about entrapment, see also Rumaker, *Robert Duncan in San Francisco*, 16; James Melvin Reinhardt, *Sex Perversions and Sex Crimes* (Springfield, IL: Charles C. Thomas, 1957), 33; "Tex or JR," interview by Len Evans, 24; Samuel Steward, interview by Len Evans, July 2, 1983, 20–21, Oral History Project, GLBTHS.

62. On the development of entrapment law, see Michael A. DeFeo, "Entrapment as a Defense to Criminal Responsibility: Its History, Theory and Application," *University of San Francisco Law Review* 1 (April 1967): 244–52, 274 n. 171; "State Estopped to Prosecute Criminal Conduct Suggested by Police," *Harvard Law Review* 81 (June 1968), 895 n. 1. For the Supreme Court's high bar, see *Sorrells v. United States*, 287 U.S. 435, 451 (1932); *Sherman v. United States*, 356 U.S. 369, 372–73 (1958).

63. "The Law: A Discussion of Entrapment," *ONE*, April 1954, 8 (quoted). See also *UCLA Law Review* Study, 703; *State v. Trombley*, 3 Conn. Cir. Ct. 28, 32–33 (1964); *Willis v. United States*, 198 A.2d 751, 752 (D.C. 1964). For the Ross case, see "Rule of Thumb Is Given with Morals Conviction," B1.

64. Stearn, *Sixth Man*, 169; Irwin D. Strauss to Raul L. Lovett, September 10, 1965, folder 30, box 3, reel 10, MSC.

65. For Miller (pseudonymous), see Field Report 31094, May 9, 1957, 4. For Doyle (pseudonymous), see Field Report 31024, December 6, 1956, 7. For prosecutors' and police officers' remarks on pervasive and systematic dismissals, see Field Report 11178, January 19, 1957, 3; Field Report 31047, February 2, 1957, 2; Field Re-

port 21087, May 23, 1957, 4–5; Field Report 31087, April 12, 1957, 2; Field Report 31045, February 4, 1957, 1. Researchers similarly appraised these practices. Newman, *Conviction*, 152, 174, 180–90.

66. For the pseudonymous Stewart's reputation, see Field Report 21049, April 5, 1957, 7; Field Report 21087, May 23, 1957, 4; Field Report 31075, March 22, 1957, 5. For his courtroom procedures, see Field Report 31075, March 22, 1957, 2–5 (quoted). For the schoolteacher, see ibid., 6 (quoted).

67. Field Report 31089, April 16, 1957, 4–5 (quoting Doyle, pseudonymous); Tiffany, McIntyre, and Rotenberg, *Detection of Crime*, 232, 236.

68. For Wisconsin, see Tiffany, McIntyre, and Rotenberg, *Detection of Crime*, 232, 236. For the Cox case, see "U.S. Employee Cleared in Morals Case," 17. For similar judicial inquiries, see "Court Frees Vice Suspect; Hits Arrest," *WP*, November 27, 1956, B4; "Senator's Son Convicted on Morals Charge," 11.

69. For expansive interpretations, see *Pleasant*, 23 Misc. 2d at 371. For stricter reinterpretations, see *People v. Feliciano*, 10 Misc. 2d 836, 837–39 (N.Y. Magis. Ct. 1958) (quoted); *People v. Evans*, 19 Misc. 2d 1071, 1073 (N.Y. Sp. Sess. 1959); *People v. Strauss*, 114 N.Y.S.2d 322, 324 (N.Y. Magis. Ct. 1952). In 1959, the Court of Appeals seemed to reject this narrow reading in two summary affirmances. *People v. Liebenthal*, 5 N.Y.2d 876, 876 (1959); *People v. Lopez*, 7 N.Y.2d 825, 825–26 (1959).

70. For the Kuebler case, see "West Coast Educator Faces Court on Cop Morals Charge," One Subject Files Collection: "Entrapment," Coll1012.001, ONE Archives; "Prof. Insists He's Innocent in Sex Case," *CDT*, November 7, 1955, 1; "Educator Upheld in Morals Case," *NYT*, November 11, 1955, 54 ("homosexual"); "Educator Freed on Morals Charge," *New York Herald Tribune*, November 11, 1955, A1 ("public place"); "Educator Goes Free on Morals Charge," 1.

71. *Feliciano*, 10 Misc. 2d at 839 ("abhorrence"); *Strauss*, 114 N.Y.S.2d at 324 ("repulsive"); *Evans*, 19 Misc. 2d at 1073. For Solomon's amendment, see *Feliciano*, 10 Misc. 2d at 839.

72. For Bushel's reasoning, see "Educator Upheld in Morals Case," 54; *Humphrey*, 111 N.Y.S.2d at 454–55 (quoted).

73. For discretionary dismissals, see "Court Frees Vice Suspect; Hits Arrest," B4; "U.S. Employee Cleared in Morals Case," 17.

74. *Kelly*, 194 F.2d at 150–51; *Kelly*, Joint Appendix, 3–4, 33–35; *Kelly v. United States*, 194 F.2d 150 (D.C. Cir. 1952), Transcript of Record, 5–6, 31–35, 76, box 1832, RG276.

75. *Kelly*, Transcript of Record, 168–75.

76. Johnson, *Lavender Scare*, 175. For the testimony, see *Kelly*, Transcript of Record, 76–77 (quoted). For Manthos's prior arrests, see *Kelly v. United States*, 194 F.2d 150 (D.C. Cir. 1952), Brief for Appellant, 3, box 1390, RG276 ("one-man"); *Kelly*, Transcript of Record, 5; *Kelly*, 194 F.2d at 152.

77. *Kelly*, 194 F.2d at 153–56.

78. For Blick's reaction, see Don Olesen, "Court Cautions against Unsupported Word of Officer in Morals Case, Reverses Conviction," *WP*, January 11, 1952, 1. For declining conviction rates, see "Sex Case Convictions Show Sharp Decline," *WP*, February 24, 1952, M13. For trial judges invoking the rules, see "Single Witness Held Insufficient for Lewd Charge," *WP*, February 12, 1955, 24; "Former Court Clerk Freed in Sex Case," 31; "2 Acquittals Follow Court Morals Ruling," *WP*, January 13, 1952, M11; "Virginian Cleared in Morals Case," *WP*, February 4, 1956, 3. For Rover's interven-

tion, see "Instructing Judges," *WP*, April 1, 1954, A14; Philip Dawson, "Rover Sends Judges Views on Morals Cases," *WP*, May 7, 1954, 21. For Kronheim quotation, see J. Philip Dawson, "Controversy Flares over Morals Cases," *WP*, April 5, 1954, 17.

79. For assault prosecutions, see *Dyson*, 97 A.2d at 136; *McDermett*, 98 A.2d at 288–89; *Guarro*, 237 F.2d at 579; *Henderson*, 117 A.2d at 458. For the boost to anti-homosexual prosecutions, see Johnson, *Lavender Scare*, 176. For judges applying *Kelly* in assault cases, see "2 Acquittals Follow Court Morals Ruling," 11; *Guarro*, 237 F.2d at 579. For the trial with Judge Howard, see "Rover Asks Jury Trial for Buscher," *WP*, February 19, 1954, 31; "Buscher Acquitted of Assault," *WP*, February 24, 1954, 34; "Maryland Official Arrested by Morals Squad Policeman," 3.

80. *McDermett*, 98 A.2d at 288–90.

81. *Guarro*, 116 A.2d at 409–10; *Guarro*, 237 F.2d at 581–82.

82. For DC judges deferring to police testimony, see *Seitner*, Brief for Appellant, 2–3; Oleson, "Court Cautions against Unsupported Word of Officer," 1; *Wildeblood*, Memorandum in Support of Petition, 4. For deference in other states, see Council on Religion and the Homosexual, *The Challenge and Progress of Homosexual Law Reform* (San Francisco, 1968), 22; Branson, *Gay Bar*, 42. For convictions in New York, see *Robillard v. New York*, United States Supreme Court, No. 447 (1966), Petition for a Writ of Certiorari, 3–4; *Pleasant*, 23 Misc. 2d at 368–69. For the researcher, see Herman Goldstein, interview by author, May 9, 2018.

83. For Skousen, see W. Cleon Skousen, "Sex Deviates . . . What Can the Police Do about Them? Part III," *Law and Order*, June 1961, 19–20; Jim Boardman, "Right-Winger Emerges as Political Force in Utah," *LAT*, July 20, 1980, 2. For Detroit, see Field Report 11105, December 29, 1956, 7 (quoted). For other examples, see *UCLA Law Review* Study, 737; Newman, *Conviction*, 148; Field Report 11167, January 22, 1957, 2.

84. For judges' reticence to explain objections, see Newman, *Conviction*, 175, 189–90; Tiffany, McIntyre, and Rotenberg, *Detection of Crime*, 211, 237; R. E. L. Masters, *The Homosexual Revolution* (New York: Julian, 1962), 198.

85. For San Francisco, see Lenn, "Sex Deviate Problem in S.F. Detailed," 11. For Philadelphia, see Richard H. Elliott, "The Morals Squad," *DRUM*, September 1967, 11. For Detroit, see Field Report 11178, January 19, 1957, 2–3. For Pontiac, see Field Report 11226, February 26, 1957, 6.

86. Max K. Hurlbut to author, October 16, 2017, item 3; Field Report 11167, January 22, 1957, 2 ("complete lack"). For additional quibbles with the courts' legal reading, see Field Report 11174, January 21, 1957, 10.

87. For general discussion, see Newman, *Conviction*, 195–96. For adaptability to presiding judges, see Field Report 11178, January 19, 1957, 4. For investigation arrests, see Field Report 11109, January 3, 1957, 4; Field Report 11105, December 29, 1956, 7; Field Report 11167, January 22, 1957, 2. For judges' awareness of the program, see Field Report 31094, May 9, 1957, 4 (discussing Miller, pseudonymous).

88. For police abuse of gay men, see n. 26 above; Levie, "Vice and Victim," 36; Rosen, "Police Harassment," 165–66. For observations of police violence as a response to perceived leniency, see Council on Religion and the Homosexual, *The Challenge and Progress of Homosexual Law Reform*, 27; Westley, "Violence and the Police," 38. For broader patterns of police resorting to violence in response to perceived judicial leniency and procedural restrictions, see Herman Goldstein, *Policing a Free Society* (Cambridge, MA: Ballinger, 1977), 13, 15; Harlan Hahn, "A Profile of Urban Police," *Law and Contemporary Problems* 36 (Autumn 1971): 465; Jerome Skolnick, *Jus-*

tice without Trial: Law Enforcement in Democratic Society (New York: John Wiley & Sons, 1966), chap. 9 (discussing hostility toward policed groups).

89. For skepticism of police attention to trial outcomes, see Seth W. Stoughton, "Policing Facts," *Tulane Law Review* 88 (May 2014): 877–81; Oren Bar-Gill and Barry Friedman, "Taking Warrants Seriously," *Northwestern University Law Review* 106 (Fall 2012): 1625; Wayne R. LaFave and Frank J. Remington, "Controlling the Police: The Judge's Role in Making and Reviewing Enforcement Decisions," *Michigan Law Review* 65 (April 1965): 1005–6. Some have suggested that specialized units care more about trial outcomes than do patrolmen. Myron W. Orfield Jr., "Deterrence, Perjury, and the Heater Factor: An Exclusionary Rule in the Chicago Criminal Courts," *University of Colorado Law Review* 63, no. 1 (1992): 82, 85–90.

CHAPTER FOUR

1. Evelyn Hooker, "A Preliminary Analysis of Group Behavior of Homosexuals," *Journal of Psychology* 42 (1956): 221 (quoting Ernest W. Burgess). On Hooker's background and influence, see Minton, *Departing from Deviance*, 220–26, 229; D'Emilio, *Sexual Politics*, 141. For ethnographic studies of gay life, some as early as the mid-1950s, see Leznoff, "The Homosexual in Urban Society"; Maurice Leznoff and William A. Westley, "The Homosexual Community," *Social Problems* 3 (April 1956): 257–63; Evelyn Hooker, "The Homosexual Community," in *Sexual Deviance*, ed. John H. Gagnon and William Simon (New York: Harper & Row, 1967), 167–84; Masters, *Homosexual Revolution*; Sherri Cavan, "Interaction in Home Territories," *Berkeley Journal of Sociology* 8 (1963): 17–32; Nancy B. Achilles, "The Homosexual Bar" (MA thesis, University of Chicago, 1964); Hoffman, *The Gay World*; Mary McIntosh, "The Homosexual Role," *Social Problems* 16 (Fall 1968): 182–92; Albert J. Reiss Jr., "The Social Integration of Queers and Peers," *Social Problems* 9 (Fall 1961): 102–20; Michael Schofield, *Sociological Aspects of Homosexuality: A Comparative Study of Three Types of Homosexuals* (London: Longmans, 1965); Humphreys, *Tearoom Trade*; Barry M. Dank, "Coming Out in the Gay World," *Psychiatry* 34 (May 1971): 180–97.

2. For the difficulty of infiltrating the group, see Leznoff, "The Homosexual in Urban Society," 157 (quoted); Cory, *Homosexual in America*, 103; Humphreys, *Tearoom Trade*, 24; Donald J. Black and Maureen A. Mileski, "Passing as Deviant: Methodological Problems and Tactics," Center for Research on Social Organization Working Paper no. 36 (Ann Arbor: University of Michigan, Department of Sociology, November 1967), 5–6. The technique would find its most famous practitioner in Laud Humphreys, who emulated the "watchqueen" to blend into tearooms and eventually came out as gay himself. Humphreys, *Tearoom Trade*, 27; John F. Galliher, Wayne H. Brekhus, and David P. Keys, *Laud Humphreys: Prophet of Homosexuality and Sociology* (Madison: University of Wisconsin Press, 2004), 78–79.

3. On the sociological study of homosexuality as an ally in the cause of gay liberation, see D'Emilio, *Sexual Politics*, 109–8, 140–44; Heap, *Homosexuality in the City*, 34; Minton, *Departing from Deviance*, 239; George Chauncey, introduction to Heap, *Homosexuality in the City*, 7. For Burgess, see Chad Heap, "The City as a Sexual Laboratory: The Queer Heritage of the Chicago School," *Qualitative Sociology* 26 (December 2003): 465–67. Debates on whether ethnographic study can or should support particular political commitments are of course long-standing, as are concerns that ethnographic methods are inherently hierarchical. Karen Engle, "From Skepticism to Embrace: Human Rights and the American Anthropological Association from 1947–1999," *Human Rights Quarterly* 23 (2001): 536–599; Brian Hochman, *Sav-*

age Preservation: The Ethnographic Origins of Modern Media Technology (Minneapolis: University of Minnesota Press, 2014), xiii–xiv; Andrew D. Evans, *Anthropology at War: World War I and the Science of Race in Germany* (Chicago: University of Chicago Press, 2010), 3–4.

4. See introduction, n. 28 above.

5. For growing attention to entrapment, see chapter 3, n. 61, above.

6. For *ONE*, see Mortenson, "To Be Accused," 12–13; "The Law," *ONE*, January 1953, 21–22; "The Law: A Discussion of Entrapment," 7–8. For the card, see Vern L. Bullough, "Herb Selwyn," in *Before Stonewall: Activists for Gay and Lesbian Rights in Historical Context*, ed. Vern L. Bullough (New York: Harrington Park, 2002), 149. For physical confrontations, see "Morals Squad Detective Attacked Arresting a Suspect in Apartment," *WP*, January 25, 1957, A3; "Suspect Arrested on Morals Charge," *WP*, May 16, 1958, D2.

7. For the role of homophile societies, see D'Emilio, *Sexual Politics*, chap. 4; Boyd, *Wide Open Town*, chap. 4; Meeker, "Behind the Mask of Respectability." On homophile publications, see Martin Meeker, *Contacts Desired: Gay and Lesbian Communications and Community, 1940s–1970s* (Chicago: University of Chicago Press, 2006), pt. 1.

8. For limited participation in homophile societies, see D'Emilio, *Sexual Politics*, 175. For the growing cohesion and insularity of gay culture, see ibid., 32–33; Boyd, *Wide Open Town*, 125–26; Johnson, *Lavender Scare*, 150–51. For academic recognition, see Hooker, "A Preliminary Analysis of Group Behavior of Homosexuals," 221 (quoted).

9. Hooker, "The Homosexual Community," 172. For defensive mechanisms in bars, see Boyd, *Wide Open Town*, 126–27; *UCLA Law Review* Study, 689–90 n. 24; Branson, *Gay Bar*, 42–43; *Snug Harbor Inn*, Bulletin 1161, no. 3, 1957, 6–8; chapter 1, n. 20, above. For the San Francisco bar, see Cavan, "Interaction in Home Territories," 26–27.

10. Hooker, "The Homosexual Community," 179. See also Beemyn, *A Queer Capital*, 142.

11. For the expressive function of early signals, see Chauncey, *Gay New York*, 50–63.

12. For the popularity and significance of gay fashions, see Leznoff, "The Homosexual in Urban Society," 164 ("suspicions"); Hoffman, *The Gay World*, 55; Welch, "The 'Gay' World,'" 68. For observers noting the innocuous nature of gay fashion trends in the 1960s, see Helmer, "New York's 'Middle-Class' Homosexuals," 86 ("dashing"); Hoffman, *The Gay World*, 55. For the leather bar, see Welch, "The 'Gay' World,'" 68.

13. For the persistence of camp in some bars, see Boyd, *Wide Open Town*. For dancing and other affectionate displays, see Helmer, "New York's 'Middle-Class' Homosexuals," 86; chapter 1, n. 52, above.

14. For pressures against flamboyant conduct, see Helmer, "New York's 'Middle-Class' Homosexuals," 86. For cruising codes, see Hooker, "The Homosexual Community," 175–76; Black and Mileski, "Passing as Deviant," 7; Welch, "The 'Gay' World," 68.

15. Stearn, *Sixth Man*, 55.

16. For the Illinois decoy, see Ed Pound, "Alton Police Decoy Nabs Sex Deviates in Park," *Alton Evening Telegraph*, April 3, 1965, 1. For codes in bathrooms, see Humphreys, *Tearoom Trade*, 64–65; *UCLA Law Review* Study, 692 n. 37. On the inconspicuous nature of cruising, see Jacobs, "Decoy Enforcement of Homosexual Laws," 259 (quoted); Council on Religion and the Homosexual, *The Challenge and Progress*

of Homosexual Law Reform, 21; *UCLA Law Review* Study, 699 n. 84; Maureen Mileski and Donald J. Black, "The Social Organization of Homosexuality," *Urban Life and Culture* 1 (July 1972): 190–94; Hoffman, *The Gay World*, 47; Arthur C. Warner, "Non-Commercial Sexual Solicitation: The Case for Judicial Invalidation," *Sexual Law Reporter* 4, no. 1 (1978): 1, 10–20.

17. For the emergent framework, see David M. Halperin, *How to Do the History of Homosexuality* (Chicago: University of Chicago Press, 2002), 133–34; Chauncey, *Gay New York*, 96. For alternate accounts, see generally Bérubé, *Coming Out under Fire*; D'Emilio, *Sexual Politics* (demographic shifts); Meeker, *Contacts Desired*; Hurewitz, *Bohemian Los Angeles*; Stein, *City of Sisterly and Brotherly Loves* (homophile activism); D'Emilio, *Sexual Politics* (psychiatry).

18. See chapter 1, nn. 60–62, above, and the text at that point.

19. For the SFPD patrolman, see Agee, *Streets of San Francisco*, 77–78. For the investigation, see Memorandum, April 5, 1955, folder 3, box 1, Memorandum, July 31, 1956, folder 17, box 1, Memorandum to Front Office, March 15, 1956, folder 12, box 1, Memorandum to Front Office, March 25, 1956, folder 13, box 1, Report from X., October 16, 1956, folder 18, box 1, and Memorandum to Chief of Police Frank Ahern, January 20, 1958, folder 19, box 1, all in Thomas J. Cahill Papers, San Francisco Public Library.

20. Memorandum to Front Office, March 25, 1956, Memorandum, April 5, 1955, 8–9, folder 3, box 1, Memorandum to Front Office, December 27, 1955, folder 3, box 1, Memorandum to Front Office, March 15, 1956, and Memorandum, July 31, 1956, all in Thomas J. Cahill Papers, San Francisco Public Library.

21. For the project's funding and background, see Reinhardt, *Sex Perversions and Sex Crimes*, vii–viii, vii ("socio-cultural"). For discussions of homosexuality, see ibid., chaps. 2–4, esp. 36–43, 36 ("sociological study").

22. Reinhardt, *Sex Perversions and Sex Crimes*, 39–49 (quotations, in order, on 43, 45, 46, 45, 49).

23. For Pennsylvania, see Samuel Siegle, "Training Program for Morals Squad," *Police Chief*, January 1960, 16–18. For San Francisco, see Ernest Lenn, "Special Cops for 'Gay' Bars," *San Francisco Examiner*, October 12, 1961, 3. For the LAPD, see Hurlbut, "Presentation," 1–6, 18–19; Max K. Hurlbut to author, October 12, 2017, item 1. For contemporary reports of decoy training, see Masters, *Homosexual Revolution*, 168; Branson, *Gay Bar*, 42; Cory and LeRoy, *The Homosexual and His Society*, 116; Achilles, "The Homosexual Bar," 59; Loftin, ed., *Letters to ONE*, 104. The FBI also prepared training programs on homosexuality. Walter V. McLaughlin, "The Sex Offender," *Police Chief*, December 1962, 28–29.

24. Egen, *Plainclothesman*, 105–7, jacket; John B. Williams, *Vice Control in California* (Beverly Hills, CA: Glencoe, 1964), 27–34, 28–29 (quoted). For Williams's background and influence, see "Criminology Teacher Raps Vice Textbook at Forum," *The Advocate*, July 7–20, 1971, 17, 26. For the Florida pamphlet, see *Homosexuality and Citizenship in Florida: A Report of the Florida Legislative Investigation Committee* (Tallahassee: Florida Legislative Investigations Committee, 1964). For a history of the Johns Committee, see Braukman, *Communists and Perverts*, 169–73. For the pamphlet's use, see R. O. Mitchell, "Report of the Florida Legislative Investigation Committee" (Tallahassee, FL, 1965), 2–3. For the national handbook, see Denny F. Pace, *Handbook of Vice Control* (Englewood Cliffs, NJ: Prentice-Hall, 1971), 55.

25. For the rise of police training programs, see Lvovsky, "Judicial Presumption," 2006–8. For training as a mode of top-down control, see Josh Segal, "'All the Mysticism of

Police Expertise': Legalizing Stop-and-Frisk in New York, 1961–1968," *Harvard Civil Rights–Civil Liberties Law Review* 47 (Spring 2012): 573–616.

26. For Pontiac, see Field Report 11226, February 26, 1957, 6. For cautionary instructions, see Hurlbut, "Presentation," 12–13; "Vice Hunting in Los Angeles," 20; Williams, *Vice Control in California*, 29; Ferguson, *Nature of Vice Control*, 119. For specific references to entrapment as a concern, see Williams, *Vice Control in California*, 29; Pace, *Handbook of Vice Control*, 58; "Vice Hunting in Los Angeles," 20.

27. On the limitations of police training, see Lvovsky, "Judicial Presumption," 2012–15; Fogelson, *Big-City Police*, 235–36. For Hurlbut's process and outline, see Max K. Hurlbut to author, October 12, 2017, items 4, 6, 8; Max K. Hurlbut to author, October 16, 2017, items 1, 2; Hurlbut, "Presentation," 2–7, 18–19. For published manuals, see Pace, *Handbook of Vice Control*, 56–57; Williams, *Vice Control in California*, 28.

28. Williams, *Vice Control in California*, 28–29 ("normal"); Pace, *Handbook of Vice Control*, 56–57. For the dearth of decoy policing against gay women, see chapter 3, n. 23, above.

29. Max K. Hurlbut to author, October 12, 2017, item 21 (quoted); Max K. Hurlbut to author, October 16, 2017, item 17; Williams, *Vice Control in California*, 29; Egen, *Plainclothesman*, 108. For overviews of slang, see Williams, *Vice Control in California*, 31–34; *Homosexuality and Citizenship in Florida*, "Glossary of Homosexual Terms and Deviate Acts"; *Instructor's Manual, Law Enforcement Officer Training: Basic Course* (Columbus, OH: Ohio Trade and Industrial Education Service, 1971), app. 60. For the 1974 survey, see Ferguson, *Nature of Vice Control*, 117.

30. For reliance on the advice of older colleagues, see Max K. Hurlbut to author, October 12, 2017, items 7, 20; Levie, "Vice and Victim," 34. On the broader trend of policemen preferring informal advice over formal instruction, see Neal A. Milner, "Supreme Court Effectiveness and the Police Organization," *Law and Contemporary Problems* 36 (Autumn 1971): 472–73; Hahn, "A Profile of Urban Police," 455.

31. Council on Religion and the Homosexual, *The Challenge and Progress of Homosexual Law Reform*, 21. See also Nancy Achilles, "The Development of the Homosexual Bar as an Institution," in Gagnon and Simon, eds., *Sexual Deviance*, 233.

32. For nonstrategic clothes in the 1950s, see *Seitner v. United States*, 143 A.2d 101 (D.C. 1958), Joint Appendix, 5, box 1890, RG276. For the proliferation of collegiate fashions, see Rosen, "Police Harassment," 166; *UCLA Law Review* Study, 692 n. 37; Eric Pace, "Garelik Urges Public to Report Police Trapping of Homosexuals," *NYT*, April 2, 1966, 60; "Pablo Mojica—from Queens—Student at or from Columbia—Accent," folder 30, box 3, reel 10, MSC; Levie, "Vice and Victim," 33–34; *Loubor*, Respondent's Brief, 22. For Philadelphia, see Fonzi, "Furtive Fraternity," 22. For San Francisco, see Achilles, "Development of the Homosexual Bar," 234. For the LAPD, see Hurlbut, "Presentation," 13; *UCLA Law Review* Study, 692 n. 37; Welch, "The 'Gay' World," 72. For officers emphasizing strategic value, see *People v. Robillard*, Supreme Court of New York, Nos. C 9847–49/65 (1966), Defendants' Brief, 2 (quoted); Welch, "The 'Gay' World," 72.

33. For DC, see White, "Those Others IV," A19. For Los Angeles, see *UCLA Law Review* Study, 692 n. 37, 796. For additional accounts, see Masters, *Homosexual Revolution*, 167–68; Mitchell, *The Homosexual and the Law*, 35; Jacobs, "Decoy Enforcement of Homosexual Laws," 259–60. For the contrary policy, see Hurlbut, "Presentation," 12; *UCLA Law Review* Study, 692 n. 37.

34. For the Mattachine Society, see "The Right of Peaceable Assembly," folder 30, box 3,

reel 10, MSC. For additional remarks on the difficulty of distinguishing officers, see Stearn, *Sixth Man*, 55, 141. For Arscott, see "$2500 Bond Fixed for 5 in Assault on Policeman," *WP*, February 24, 1960, A3.

35. For well-established slang like *gay* and *straight*, see James F. Kearful, "The New Nazism," *ONE*, May 1963, 7–8; Jacobs, "Decoy Enforcement of Homosexual Laws," 260; Robert Veit Sherwin, "Sodomy," in *Sexual Behavior and the Law*, ed. Ralph Slovenko (Springfield, IL: Charles C. Thomas, 1965), 430; Wood, "The Homosexual and the Police," 21. For reliance on camp expression and diverse sources of knowledge, see Hurlbut, *Vagabond Policeman*, 90; Max K. Hurlbut to author, October 12, 2017, item 52; Max K. Hurlbut to author, October 16, 2017, items 3, 6; Williams, *Vice Control in California*, 31–34; *Homosexuality and Citizenship in Florida*, "Glossary of Homosexual Terms and Deviate Acts"; *Instructor's Manual, Law Enforcement Officer Training*, app. 60. On the value of slang, see Max K. Hurlbut to author, October 12, 2017, items 21, 52 ("at ease").

36. For "standard procedure," see *UCLA Law Review* Study, 695 n. 60; Herb Selwyn, interview by John D'Emilio. For similar techniques in other cities, see Achilles, "The Homosexual Bar," 59 (San Francisco); *Kerma*, Record on Review, 7, 43–44 (New York); Elliott, "Control of Homosexual Activity by Philadelphia Police," 6.

37. Welch, "The 'Gay' World," 72–73. The transcript is lightly edited for concision and repetition, though many ellipses appear in the original. For similar conversations leading to arrest, see Jim W., "The Fine Art of Entrapment," *The Advocate*, May 1968, Stuart Timmons Papers, ONE Archives; Levie, "Vice and Victim," 13–20, 25–33.

38. Max K. Hurlbut to author, October 12, 2017, item 20; Jim W., "The Fine Art of Entrapment"; Levie, "Vice and Victim," 30.

39. For tactics in theaters, see Levie, "Vice and Victim," 11–12, 91. For lingering glances, see Mitchell, *The Homosexual and the Law*, 35; *UCLA Law Review* Study, 692 n. 37. For officers sitting with their backs against the wall, see *People v. Mesa*, 265 Cal. App. 2d 746, 747–48 (1968).

40. For decoys loitering in bathrooms, see *UCLA Law Review* Study, 691–92; Mitchell, *The Homosexual and the Law*, 35–36; Stearn, *Sixth Man*, 169; Fonzi, "Furtive Fraternity," 50. For the strategic use of glances and eye contact, see Levie, "Vice and Victim," 12–13; Max K. Hurlbut to author, October 12, 2017, item 21; Mitchell, *The Homosexual and the Law*, 35; Elliott, "Control of Homosexual Activity by Philadelphia Police," 5–6 ("apparent"); *UCLA Law Review* Study, 691–92 n. 37 ("outright").

41. *Homosexuality and Citizenship in Florida*, "Why Be Concerned?"; Pace, *Handbook of Vice Control*, 55–57.

42. For glory holes, see Levie, "Vice and Victim," 39. I infer vice officers' use of jingling keys and change from the fact that the LAPD prohibited the practice as an "embarrassment" alongside common tactics like wearing tight pants and swishing. *UCLA Law Review* Study, 692 n. 37; Hurlbut, "Presentation," 12. For decoys tapping their feet, see Mitchell, *The Homosexual and the Law*, 35–36; *UCLA Law Review* Study, 692 n. 40, 706. For Ohio, see "Playboy Forum," *Playboy*, August 1966, 144–45.

43. For the YMCA, see Masters, *Homosexual Revolution*, 190. For Lafayette Park, see Leslie H. Whitten, "Well-Patrolled Park Leads to Police Fight," *WP*, November 13, 1960, A3; "Lafayette, Here We Come," *WP*, November 16, 1960, A16.

44. For the persistence of overtly sexual conduct, see *UCLA Law Review* Study, 706; Fonzi, "Furtive Fraternity," 49; Levie, "Vice and Victim," 39; "Pablo Mojica—from Queens." For vulgarities, see *Beard v. Stahr*, 200 F. Supp. 766, 768 (D.D.C 1961);

"Officer's Bad Discharge Upheld," *WP*, December 19, 1961, B7. For Leitsch, see Dick Leitsch, Letter to Editor, *Fire Island News*, August 23, 1966, 1, folder 7, box 6, reel 15, MSC.

45. For remarks on the effectiveness of police camouflage, see n. 34 above.

46. For Fochett, see *Seitner*, Brief for Appellant, 2–3. For the NYPD, see Doty, "Growth of Overt Homosexuality," 33.

47. Walter E. Kreutzer, "The Elusive Professionalization That Police Officers Seek," *Police Chief*, August 1968, 26 ("bond"); Arthur M. Thurston, "Scientific Training for Police," *Police Yearbook*, 1952, 137 ("specialist"). For a broader discussion of mid-century departments emphasizing police insight into crime, see Lvovsky, "Judicial Presumption," 2005–8.

48. Williams, *Vice Control in California*, 29, 27; Max K. Hurlbut to author, October 12, 2017, item 21; Hurlbut, "Presentation," 1; Pace, *Handbook of Vice Control*, 58. For another example, see "Vice Hunting in Los Angeles," 20.

49. Hurlbut, "Presentation," 3 (quoting J. Tudor Rees and Harley V. Usill, eds., *They Stand Apart: A Critical Survey of the Problems of Homosexuality* [New York: Macmillan, 1955], 28–29). For similar warnings, see Egen, *Plainclothesman*, 107–8; Williams, *Vice Control in California*, 27; *Homosexuality and Citizenship in Florida*, "Why Be Concerned?"

50. Williams, *Vice Control in California*, 27; *Homosexuality and Citizenship in Florida*, "Why Be Concerned?"; Hurlbut, "Presentation," 1–6, 17–18 ("information"), 21 ("complete destruction"). For the social conservatism of police officers, see Brooks, "'New York's Finest,'" 29; Skolnick, *Justice without Trial*, 42–65.

51. Williams, *Vice Control in California*, 29, 27. For another example, see Hurlbut, "Presentation," 1.

52. Pace, *Handbook of Vice Control*, 54. For some officers' long-standing distaste for decoy work, see chapter 3, nn. 24–25, above, and the text at that point.

53. For the study, see *UCLA Law Review* Study, 699 n. 84. For Hurlbut's comments, see Max K. Hurlbut to author, October 16, 2017, items 17, 6; Max K. Hurlbut to author, June 27, 2018, item 1; Max K. Hurlbut to author, October 12, 2017, item 15. For reports of police indifference to potentially gay officers beyond the vice squad, see Cory and Leroy, *The Homosexual and His Society*, 132–33.

54. *F & C Holding Corp. v. State Liquor Authority*, New York Supreme Court, Appellate Division, First Department, No. 7349 (1966), Record on Review, 45 (quoted), 46–49. For another example, see *Kifisia*, Record on Review, 57–58, 111. Judges at liquor proceedings voiced similar skepticism of "contrived" arrests. *Kerma*, Appellant's Brief, 21; *Clock Bar*, 85 Dauph. at 132

55. *Rittenour v. District of Columbia*, 163 A.2d 558, 559–60 (D.C. August 19, 1960).

56. *Wildeblood*, 284 F.2d at 598; *Wildeblood v. United States*, 284 F.2d 592 (D.C. Cir. 1960), Opposition to Petition for Leave to Prosecute Appeal in Forma Pauperis, 3, box 87, RG276; *Mesa*, 265 Cal. App. 2d at 747–48; Stearn, *Sixth Man*, 168. For other examples of allegedly spontaneous solicitations, see *Willis v. United States*, 198 A.2d 751, 751 (D.C. 1964); *People v. Greenberg*, Respondent's Brief, 1–2, folder 30, box 3, reel 10, MSC; *People v. Harold Bramson*, Trial Transcript, No. C-1660 (1966), 5–6, MssCol 18787, International Gay Information Center, NYPL.

57. Harold Bramson to Mimi Bowling, December 7, 1994, 3, MssCol 18787, International Gay Information Center, NYPL; *Bramson*, Trial Transcript, 14. One Los Angles study found that vice officers submitted dubiously consistent reports in solicitation cases. Copilow and Coleman, "Enforcement of Section 647(a)," 7.

58. *Mesa*, 265 Cal. App. 2d at 747. For tactics in public bathrooms, see Max K. Hurlbut to author, October 12, 2017, item 21; Elliott, "Control of Homosexual Activity by Philadelphia Police," 5 (quoted); Humphreys, *Tearoom Trade*, 64.

59. Humphreys, *Tearoom Trade*, 87; *UCLA Law Review* Study, 692 n. 37 ("tantamount"). For gay men's broader definitions of entrapment, see ibid., 704 n. 119 (quoted); Achilles, "Development of the Homosexual Bar," 233–34; Council on Religion and the Homosexual, *A Brief of Injustices* (Los Angeles: Pan-Graphic, 1965), reprinted in *ONE*, October 1965, 9.

60. For skepticism of police officers' claims of entirely spontaneous solicitations, see Jim W., "The Fine Art of Entrapment"; Levie, "Vice and Victim," 83–84, 101–2 (discussing juries); Field Report 31089, April 16, 1957, 4–5 (Doyle, pseudonymous). For DC, see *Seitner*, Joint Appendix, 17, 25–26. For California, see Herb Selwyn, interview by author, July 12, 2014; *Mesa*, 265 Cal. App. 2d at 748.

61. *Robillard*, Petition for a Writ of Certiorari, 3; *Robillard*, Defendants' Brief, 2–3; *Robillard v. New York*, United States Supreme Court, No. 447 (1966), Respondent's Brief in Opposition to Petition for Writ of Certiorari, 3–4; Lewis Merrifield, Memo on *Robillard v. New York*, 1966 Term, Docket No. 447, 1, box 1380, Papers of William O. Douglas, Library of Congress.

62. For the national ACLU's ambivalence and local chapters' involvement, see Stein, *Sexual Injustice*, 158–62; D'Emilio, *Sexual Politics*, 212, 155–57.

63. *Robillard*, Defendants' Brief, 2–3, 4; *Robillard*, Respondent's Brief in Opposition, 4–5; *Robillard*, Petition for a Writ of Certiorari, 5. For the statutory point, see *Robillard*, Defendants' Brief, 8–9.

64. For the convictions, see *Robillard*, Petition for a Writ of Certiorari, 4–5. For Fingerhood and di Suvero's arguments, see *Robillard*, Defendants' Brief, 19, 3.

65. *Robillard*, Petition for a Writ of Certiorari, 7–8, 10–11.

66. *Robillard*, Respondent's Brief in Opposition, 3, 9–12.

67. On Merrifield's view and background, see Lewis Merrifield, Memo on *Robillard*, 2 (quoted); Joyce Murdoch and Deb Price, *Courting Justice: Gay Men and Lesbians v. the Supreme Court* (New York: Basic, 2001), 137–41; Sklansky, "'One Train May Hide Another,'" 892–93, 928–29 (discussing Justice Douglas). See also Douglas Kranwinkle, Memo on *Robillard v. New York*, 1966 Term, Docket No. 447, 3–4, box 387, Papers of Earl Warren, Library of Congress (quoted); Daniel Levitt, Memo on *Robillard v. New York*, 1966 Term, No. 447, 2, box 23, series 1, MS 858, Abe Fortas Papers, Yale University Manuscripts and Archives (quoted); *Robillard v. New York*, 385 U.S. 928, 928 (1966).

CHAPTER FIVE

1. *People v. Bielicki*, Municipal Court of Long Beach Judicial District, Los Angeles County, Dept. 4, No. F-9393 (Oct. 18, 1961), Reporter's Transcript of Preliminary Examination, 2–3, 11–12, 16, 21, in *Bielicki v. Superior Court of Los Angeles County*, 57 Cal. 2d 602 (1962) Case File, CSA; Frank C. Wood, Jr., "The Right to Be Free from Unreasonable Search and Seizure," *ONE*, April 1963, 7.

2. Humphreys, *Tearoom Trade*, 24, 59–80, 11.

3. Chauncey, *Gay New York*, 196 and n. 60, 198. For the early history of public bathrooms, including their common use for sexual encounters, see Peter C. Baldwin, "Public Privacy: Restrooms in American Cities, 1869–1932," *Journal of Social History* 48 (Winter 2014): 278; Andrew Israel Ross, "Dirty Desire: The Uses and Misuses of Public Urinals in Nineteenth-Century Paris," *Berkeley Journal of Sociology* 53 (2009):

64; Maynard, "Through a Hole in the Lavatory Wall," 214 (Toronto). For the inspector, see "May 19, 1927, Miscellaneous, 6:15 P.M.," box 35, Committee of Fourteen Records, NYPL.

4. D'Emilio, *Sexual Politics*, chaps. 5–6; Meeker, "Behind the Mask of Respectability," 78–116; Johnson, *Lavender Scare*, chap. 8; Boyd, *Wide Open Town*, chaps. 3–4; Stein, *City of Sisterly and Brotherly Loves*, chap. 8.

5. Humphreys, *Tearoom Trade*, 105. See also Elliott, "The Morals Squad," 28.

6. For homophile publications, see Mortenson, "To Be Accused"; Del McIntire, "Tangents: News & Views," *ONE*, April–May 1956, 14, "Tangents: News & Views," *ONE*, February 1958, 15, 18, and "Tangents," *ONE*, December 1958, 12–13.

7. For the coded nature of cruising, see *UCLA Law Review* Study, 692 nn. 37 and 40; Humphreys, *Tearoom Trade*, 64–65; Cory, *Homosexual in America*, 117–18; Chauncey, *Gay New York*, 188. For cruising practices as an organized subculture, starting well before the mid-twentieth century, see Maynard, "Through a Hole in the Lavatory Wall," 220–21; John Howard, "The Library, the Park, and the Pervert: Public Space and the Homosexual Encounter in Post–World War II Atlanta," *Radical History Review* 62 (1995): 172.

8. For spatial safeguards, signals, and lookouts, see Humphreys, *Tearoom Trade*, 7–8, 27–28. For cruisers' care to cover up prior to a stranger's entry, see ibid., 70–71, 74–75, 78–80; Council on Religion and the Homosexual, *The Challenge and Progress of Homosexual Law Reform*, 21.

9. For citizens' complaints, see *Smayda v. United States*, 352 F.2d 251, 252 (9th Cir. 1965); *Bielicki v. Superior Court of Los Angeles County*, 57 Cal. 2d 602, 604 (1962); *People v. Strahan*, 153 Cal. App. 2d 100 (1957), Reporter's Transcript on Appeal, 6; *People v. Roberts*, 256 Cal. App. 2d 488 (1967), Reporter's Transcript on Appeal, 42–43; *Kroehler v. Scott*, 391 F. Supp. 1114 (E.D. Pa. 1975), Stipulation of Facts, 1; *Buchanan v. State*, 471 S.W.2d 401 (Tex. Crim. App. 1971), District Clerk's File, Case No. 14010, 101, 103, 113, Texas State Library. For media reports, see *People v. Maldonado*, 240 Cal. App. 2d 812 (1966), Reporter's Transcript, 327–28. On white flight, see chapter 3, n. 11, above. *People v. Mason*, 130 Cal. App. 2d 533 (1955), Reporter's Transcript on Appeal, 228 ("any man").

10. William F. McKee, "Evidentiary Problems—Camera Surveillance of Sex Deviates," *Law and Order*, August 1964, 72 ("results"). See also Clare W. Kyler, "Camera Surveillance of Sex Deviates," *Law and Order*, November 1963, 16 ("fruitless"). For the nature of citizens complaints, see *Smayda v. United States*, 352 F.2d 251 (9th Cir. 1965), Brief of the Appellee, 6–8. See also *Mason*, Reporter's Transcript, 229; Max K. Hurlbut to author, October 12, 2017, item 27; Reporter's Transcript of Preliminary Hearing, May 3, 1962, 5, in *People v. Young*, 214 Cal. App. 2d 131 (1963), Clerk's Transcript, CSA. On the rarity of unsolicited propositions, see Tiffany, McIntyre, and Rotenberg, *Detection of Crime*, 231–32; *UCLA Law Review* Study, 804, 688 n. 17. For police reporting that cruisers ceased activities before others could enter, see *Sellers*, Reporter's Transcript, 56; *Shaw v. Pitchess*, 324 F. Supp. 781, 782 (C.D. Cal. 1969); *Maldonado*, Reporter's Transcript, 216–17. After one person claimed to have witnessed an actual homosexual encounter, the prosecution itself cast doubt on his credibility. *Smayda*, Brief of the Appellee, 8–9 and n. 45.

11. *UCLA Law Review* Study, 708 n. 141; Kyler, "Camera Surveillance of Sex Deviates," 16.

12. For early surveillance campaigns, see Chauncey, *Gay New York*, 198 and n. 63. On the demands of surveillance, see *UCLA Law Review* Study, 687 n. 8, 716–17. For

warnings among cruisers, see *Mason*, Reporter's Transcript, 106–7; *Roberts*, Reporter's Transcript, 41.

13. *Strahan*, Reporter's Transcript, 16.

14. Max K. Hurlbut to author, October 12, 2017, item 26; Karl Wickstrom, "Suspension of Dade Officer Is Reviewed," *Miami Herald*, February 4, 1967, reprinted in *Florida League for Good Government Viewpoint*, February 1967, 1, MSP; Richard A. Inman, "Dear Reader," *Florida League for Good Government Viewpoint*, February 1967, 2, MSP (quoted).

15. For justifications, see Hurlbut, "Presentation," 3–4; Egen, *Plainclothesman*, 106–7; Stearn, *Sixth Man*, 172. For police aggression and derision, see *Maldonado*, Reporter's Transcript, 309; *Liebenthal*, Record on Appeal, 65, 68–69; *Mason*, Reporter's Transcript, 204; *Strahan*, Reporter's Transcript, 62–63, 74–75.

16. For the advantages of clandestine surveillance, see *UCLA Law Review* Study, 708 n. 141; Kyler, "Camera Surveillance of Sex Deviates," 16; Max K. Hurlbut to author, October 12, 2017, item 26. For arrest rates, see McIntire, "Tangents" (April–May 1956), 14, and "Tangents" (February 1958), 18; *UCLA Law Review* Study, 716 n. 192.

17. For evidentiary difficulties, see Eskridge, "Law and the Construction of the Closet," 1011–16. For policies and practices with regard to waiting for felonious conduct, see *UCLA Law Review* Study, 735–36; Hurlbut, "Presentation," 12; *Mason*, Reporter's Transcript, 83. For officers failing to fix glory holes or graffiti, see *State v. Bryant*, 287 Minn. 205 (1970), Appellant's Brief and Appendix, 4, Minnesota Historical Society; *Sellers*, Reporter's Transcript, 63–64; *Smayda*, Brief of the Appellee, 9. For 93 percent, see *UCLA Law Review* Study, 707 n. 133.

18. For the geographic range, see *People v. Sanabria*, 249 N.Y.S.2d 66, 67 (App. Term 1964) (New York); Fonzi, "Furtive Fraternity," 23 (Philadelphia); White, "Those Others IV," A19 (DC); *Bielicki*, 57 Cal. 2d at 604 (Long Beach); McIntire, "Tangents" (April–May 1956), 14 (Palo Alto); *Britt v. Superior Court of Santa Clara County*, 58 Cal. 2d 469, 470–71 (1962) (Santa Clara); McIntire, "Tangents" (February 1958), 18 (Oklahoma City, Kansas); *Johnson v. State*, 96 Ga. App. 682, 682 (1957) (Columbus); *Poore v. State of Ohio*, 243 F. Supp. 777, 779 (N.D. Ohio 1965) (Mansfield). For the types of property targeted, see *UCLA Law Review* Study, 707; *Sanabria*, 249 N.Y.S.2d at 67; *Kroehler v. Scott*, 391 F. Supp. 1114, 1119 (E.D. Pa. 1975); *State v. Coyle*, 181 So. 2d 671, 672 (Fla. Dist. Ct. App. 1966); *Britt*, 58 Cal. 2d at 470–71; *Bielicki*, 57 Cal. 2d at 604; *People v. Norton*, 209 Cal. App. 2d 173, 174 (1962); *Shaw*, 324 F. Supp. at 782; *Johnson*, 96 Ga. App. at 682. For the Pentagon, see Jim Hoagland, "Hidden Cameras Used in Pentagon Toilets," *WP*, December 17, 1966, C7.

19. *People v. Bentley*, 102 Cal. App. 2d 97, 98 (1951); *Johnson*, 96 Ga. App. at 682. For other examples, see *People v. Sellers*, 103 Cal. App. 2d 830, 831 (1951); *People v. Strahan*, 153 Cal. App. 2d 100, 101 (1957).

20. For Playa del Rey, see *People v. Mason*, 130 Cal. App. 2d 533, 534 (1955); *Mason*, Reporter's Transcript, 107–9, 116. For the Paris Theatre, see *Norton*, 209 Cal. App. 2d at 174–75 and n. 1. For additional examples, see *Kroehler*, 391 F. Supp. at 1115–16; *Sanabria*, 249 N.Y.S.2d at 67; McIntire, "Tangents" (December 1958), 13; "Senior Armed Forces Disciplinary Control Board Meeting Minutes," January 24, 1951, 9–10, CSA.

21. *Britt*, 58 Cal. 2d at 470–71; *People v. Maldonado*, 240 Cal. App. 2d 812, 813–14 (1966). For other examples, see *Young*, 214 Cal. App. 2d at 133; *People v. Hensel*, 233

Cal. App. 2d 834, 836 (1965); *State v. Bryant*, 287 Minn. 205, 206 (1970). Some departments used slatted or louvered doors. *Coyle*, 181 So. 2d at 672.

22. *Smayda*, 352 F.2d at 252–54, 258, 260; *Smayda v. United States*, 86 S. Ct. 555 (1966), Brief for the United States in Opposition to a Petition for a Writ of Certiorari, 2–5. For another example, see *Shaw*, 324 F. Supp. at 782.

23. For early photo technology, see Maynard, "Through a Hole in the Lavatory Wall," 222–29. For vice officers recording sex acts, see McKee, "Evidentiary Problems," 72–74; Fonzi, "Furtive Fraternity," 23; *Britt*, 58 Cal. 2d at 470–71; Hurlbut, "Presentation," 7. For the YMCA and other uses of closed-circuit television, see Fonzi, "Furtive Fraternity," 23; Humphreys, *Tearoom Trade*, 84–85.

24. Kyler, "Camera Surveillance of Sex Deviates," 16 ("beatings," "fruitless"); McKee, "Evidentiary Problems," 72 ("any use").

25. For an account of the planning, see Kyler, "Camera Surveillance of Sex Deviates," 16–20; Donn Gaynor, "Hidden Movie Camera Used by Police to Trap Sexual Deviates at Park Hangout," *MNJ*, August 22, 1962, 2. I credit Kyler's more specific account regarding the duration. For the video footage, see Mansfield Police Department, "Camera Surveillance" (videorecording) (1962), Kinsey Institute for Research in Sex, Gender, and Reproduction Library and Special Collections. For media coverage, see "4 Sentenced to Ohio Penitentiary," *MNJ*, March 4, 1963, 9; "Sent to Pen," *MNJ*, June 25, 1963, 11; "Found Guilty by Jury of 1962 Morals Charge," *MNJ*, March 31, 1965, 13; "Admits He Killed Girl," *MNJ*, January 4, 1966, 1. For Kyler's claims to the press, see Gaynor, "Hidden Movie Camera Used by Police," 1–2.

26. For an additional police concession of stealth, see Egen, *Plainclothesman*, 16.

27. *Smayda v. United States*, 86 S. Ct. 555 (1966), Petition for a Writ of Certiorari, 5; *Smayda*, Brief of the Appellee, 18.

28. For the range of authorized punishments, see Bowman and Engle, "A Psychiatric Evaluation of Laws of Homosexuality," 278–79; Schur, *Crimes without Victims*, 78; *UCLA Law Review* Study, 662–63 and nn. 36–42. Sodomy statutes also frequently differed in their treatment of oral sex. *UCLA Law Review* Study, 658–62.

29. For lenient sentencing practices, see Field Report 31045, February 4, 1957, 6; Dawson, *Sentencing*, 90; *State v. Coyle*, Circuit Court of the Sixth Judicial Circuit of the State of Florida in and for Pinellas County, No. 14,891, Order of Probation, December 20, 1966; *Bryant*, Appellant's Brief and Appendix, 2. For conditions of psychiatric treatment, see *Liebenthal*, Record on Appeal, 93; *Smayda*, Brief of the Appellee, 5 and n. 23; *People v. Hensel*, 233 Cal. App. 2d 834 (1965), Reporter's Transcript on Appeal, 28–29; *People v. Triggs*, 26 Cal. App. 3d 381 (1972), Reporter's Transcript on Appeal, 28. For Kansas, see Field Report 30575, September 29, 1956, 2. For St. Petersburg, see *Coyle*, Order of Probation. In Detroit, men apprehended for sodomy were often instead convicted of gross indecency. Field Report 31033, December 13, 1956, 3; Field Report 31045, February 4, 1957, 6. In New York, where sodomy was itself a misdemeanor, police officers typically just invoked the disorderly conduct law. George, "Harmless Psychopath," 239.

30. For California's legislative changes, see Eskridge, *Gaylaw*, 61; California Statutes, 1st Extr. Sess., chap. 56 (1950); *Bentley*, Reporter's Transcript, 79–80. For the study of judicial behavior, see Bowling, "The Sex Offender," 15. For the prevailing practice of reducing felony charges, see *UCLA Law Review* Study, 765 nn. 10–11, 770–71, 783; *Hensel*, Reporter's Transcript, 25–26; *People v. Heath*, 266 Cal. App. 2d 754 (1968), Reporter's Transcript on Appeal, 12, 15. For relatively mild sentences, see *Bentley*, Reporter's Transcript, 81; *Sellers*, Reporter's Transcript, 186; *Mason*, Reporter's Tran-

script, 259–61; *Strahan*, Reporter's Transcript, 98–99; *Hensel*, Reporter's Transcript, 27–28; *Maldonado*, Reporter's Transcript, 438–40; Mosk, foreword to *UCLA Law Review* Study, 645; *UCLA Law Review* Study, 736 n. 293; Levie, "Vice and Victim," 122–23. Judges also tried to avoid registration requirements. *Shaw v. Pitchess*, 440 F.2d 412 (9th Cir. 1971), Transmitted Record, 4, National Archives and Records Administration, Washington, DC; *UCLA Law Review* Study, 754–55.

31. *Johnson v. State*, 96 Ga. App. 682 (1957), Bill of Exceptions, 3, Georgia Archives; *Buchanan*, District Clerk's File, 5; "Sent to Pen," 11 (Ohio); *Perkins v. State*, 234 F. Supp. 333, 334 (W.D.N.C. 1964). For the Dallas judge, see *Buchanan*, District Clerk's File, 53 (quoted). For Maxine's case, see *Perkins*, 234 F. Supp. at 334, 337; Dwayne Walls, "'Maxine' Will Get New Trial Here in Vice Case," *Charlotte Observer*, December 10, 1964, 11. The sentence was overturned on other grounds.

32. For registration requirements, see *UCLA Law Review* Study, 736 n. 294. For military consequences, see *Bielicki v. Superior Court of Los Angeles County*, 57 Cal. 2d 602 (1962), Petition for Hearing before Supreme Court, 3. For immigration consequences, see *Maldonado*, Reporter's Transcript, 437; Canaday, *Straight State*, chap. 6. For newspaper coverage, see "Sent to Pen," 11; "Found Guilty by Jury of 1962 Morals Charge," 13; "18 Facing Trial Here Next Week," *Pennsylvania Simpson's Daily Leader-Times*, September 15, 1960, 1; "Sixth Sodomy Charge Filed in under Month," *Iowa City Press-Citizen*, August 21, 1968, 2; "Plea Is Changed on Sodomy Count," *Lincoln Star*, December 10, 1959, 17; "Sodomy Charge Pleas Conflict," *Lincoln Evening Journal and Nebraska State Journal*, December 7, 1959, 13; "Acquitted by Jury," *MNJ*, March 20, 1963, 10.

33. For the frequency of guilty pleas, see *UCLA Law Review* Study, 763–65, 805. For defendants' preference for bench trials, see ibid., 805; Levie, "Vice and Victim," 81.

34. *Commonwealth v. Cummings*, 273 Mass. 229, 231–32 (1930); "Petit Ballet Russe," *Boston Globe*, April 3, 1935, 19.

35. For lawyers specializing in civil rights and police abuses, see *Maldonado*, Reporter's Transcript, A-3; Elaine Woo, "L.A. Civil Rights Lawyers Fought for the Victims of Police Misconduct," *LAT*, June 18, 2009, A23; *Bielicki*, Reporter's Transcript, 1; Wood, "The Right to Be Free from Unreasonable Search and Seizure," 7. For the experiences of wealthier and poorer defendants, see the discussion below.

36. For statutory arguments, see *Liebenthal*, Record on Appeal, 53–55. For procedural errors, see *People v. Strahan*, 153 Cal. App. 2d 100 (1957), Appellant's Opening Brief, 9–10, 12–13; *Johnson*, Bill of Exceptions, 13–14; *People v. Roberts*, 256 Cal. App. 2d 488, 492 (1967); *Mason*, Reporter's Transcript, 256; *Maldonado*, 240 Cal. App. 2d at 816. For successful challenges, see *Maldonado* and *Roberts* above; Hoagland, "Hidden Cameras Used in Pentagon Toilets," C7.

37. *Bentley*, Reporter's Transcript, 11–14, 21–24; *Sellers*, Reporter's Transcript, 192; *Johnson*, Bill of Exceptions, 10–11; *Roberts*, Reporter's Transcript, 217–29. For the case against Owens, see *Mason*, 130 Cal. App. 2d at 534–35; *People v. Mason*, 130 Cal. App. 2d 533 (1955), Appellant's Opening Brief, 9–10.

38. *Roberts*, Reporter's Transcript, 217–29, 268. *Bentley*, Reporter's Transcript, 75–76.

39. *Liebenthal*, Record on Appeal, 59–64, 79–81; *Strahan*, Reporter's Transcript, 50, 57, 71. Defendants commonly claimed they had reached inside a neighboring stall for toilet paper. *Mason*, Reporter's Transcript, 196; *Bielicki*, Reporter's Transcript, 7–8; McIntire, "Tangents" (December 1958), 13.

40. *People v. Sellers*, 103 Cal. App. 2d 830 (1951), Appellant's Opening Brief, 13–14; *Shaw*, Transmitted Record, 17–18.

316 / Notes to Pages 200–204

41. *People v. Bentley*, 102 Cal. App. 2d 97 (1951), Appellant's Closing Brief, 3–4; *Sellers*, Reporter's Transcript, 57–58, 63–64; *Maldonado*, Reporter's Transcript, 323. For another example of defendants questioning vice officers' zeal, see *Roberts*, Reporter's Transcript, 22–23.

42. For Wood, see Reporter's Transcript of Preliminary Examination, 19, in *Byars v. Superior Court of Los Angeles County*, 57 Cal. 2d 869 (1962) Case File, CSA; *Bielicki*, Reporter's Transcript, 26–27. For Sellers, see *Sellers*, Reporter's Transcript, 143–46, 154.

43. For judges noting the gravity of the charges, see *Liebenthal*, Record on Appeal, 21 (quoted); *Bentley*, Reporter's Transcript, 61; *Bielicki*, Reporter's Transcript, 2. For judicial patience with extensions, witnesses, and cross-examination, see *Roberts*, Reporter's Transcript, 215–29, 242–64; *Bentley*, Reporter's Transcript, 75–76; *Liebenthal*, Record on Appeal, 21; *Mason*, Reporter's Transcript. For judges and jurors visiting restrooms, see *Bentley*, Reporter's Transcript, 78–79 (quoted), 61; *Mason*, Reporter's Transcript, 201–2, 234; "Court Here Clears Mayor of Oswego," *NYT*, October 17, 1958, 18. On Jefferson, see Myrna Oliver, "Pioneer Black Judge Edwin Jefferson Dies," *LAT*, August 22, 1989, A1. For cases of acquittal based on unreliable evidence, see McIntire, "Tangents" (December 1958), 12–13; "Who's Whose Boss in Oswego?," *Life*, January 20, 1958, 46; "Grand Jury Probe of Policeman's Testimony in Vice Case Ordered," *Los Angeles Daily News*, March 31, 1953, 3; Field Report 31089, April 16, 1957, 4. For prosecutors' and officers' caution, see *UCLA Law Review* Study, 748, 750–51; Hurlbut, "Presentation," 10.

44. *Maldonado*, Reporter's Transcript, 56–57.

45. *Strahan*, Reporter's Transcript, 37–45; *Sellers*, Reporter's Transcript, 148–58, 170. For Holman, see *Maldonado*, Reporter's Transcript, 325, 375–76; *People v. Maldonado*, 240 Cal. App. 2d 812 (1966), Reply Brief of Joseph Johnson Holman Jr. (moving for permission for late filing); *People v. Holman*, California District Court of Appeal, 2d Crim. 10258, Affidavit of Financial Ability, 1, in *People v. Maldonado*, 240 Cal. App. 2d 812 (1966) Case File, CSA. See also *Bentley*, Reporter's Transcript, 32–34, 56–59.

46. *Strahan*, Reporter's Transcript, 40.

47. *Sellers*, Reporter's Transcript, 141–42; *Bentley*, Reporter's Transcript, 37–38. For other examples, see *Strahan*, Reporter's Transcript 68, 53; *Sanabria*, 249 N.Y.S.2d at 67; Field Report 31089, April 16, 1957, 4.

48. *Sellers*, Reporter's Transcript, 133–36, 135 (quoted); *Maldonado*, Reporter's Transcript, 331–32, 334–35, 338; *People v. Maldonado*, 240 Cal. App. 2d 812 (1966), Clerk's Transcript, 37. Men lacking the resources to hire psychiatrists tried calling personal physicians or family friends. *Liebenthal*, Record on Appeal, 82–87.

49. *Maldonado*, Reporter's Transcript, 334 (Briehl), 339; *Sellers*, Appellant's Opening Brief, 18; *Sellers*, Reporter's Transcript, 135–36. For defense attorneys' invoking marital status as mitigating circumstances, see chapter 3, n. 60, above.

50. For a classic account of medicalization recasting homosexuality as an identity, see Freedman, "'Uncontrolled Desires.'" In later years, that precise duality would help conservative courts defend the validity of sodomy laws, allowing them to switch strategically between the two accounts. Janet E. Halley, "Reasoning about Sodomy: Act and Identity in and After *Bowers v. Hardwick*," *Virginia Law Review* 79 (1993): 1747–48.

51. *Sellers*, Reporter's Transcript, 135–36; *People v. Sellers*, 103 Cal. App. 2d 830 (1951), Respondent's Brief, 16.

52. *Bentley*, Reporter's Transcript, 49–50; *Strahan*, Reporter's Transcript, 9–10, 53. For

defendants emphasizing sexual unavailability, see also *Sellers*, Reporter's Transcript, 92, 166.

53. *Sellers*, Reporter's Transcript, 136–37 (quoted); *Sellers*, 103 Cal. App. 2d at 831; *People v. Jones*, 42 Cal. 2d 219, 225 (1954) ("nonperformance"). For another court rejecting psychiatric evidence as irrelevant, see *State v. Sinnott*, 24 N.J. 408, 428–29 (1957).

54. *Sellers*, Reporter's Transcript, 147–70. For long-standing concerns that expert witnesses elicit undue deference from juries, see Neil Vidmar and Shari Seidman Diamond, "Juries and Expert Evidence," *Brooklyn Law Review* 66 (2001): 1121–25; Jennifer Mnookin, "Idealizing Science and Demonizing Experts: An Intellectual History of Expert Evidence," *Villanova Law Review* 52 (2007): 763–802.

55. *Strahan*, Reporter's Transcript, 49; "W. A. Strahans to Honeymoon in Acapulco," *LAT*, April 3, 1950, B2; *State v. Coyle*, Circuit Court for the Sixth Judicial Circuit of the State of Florida in and for Pinellas County, No. 14,891, Alice G. Coyle to Judge Joseph P. McNulty, February 15, 1968.

56. *Maldonado*, Reporter's Transcript, 438–40; *Liebenthal*, Record on Appeal, 99–102.

57. *Coyle*, Order of Probation; *Strahan*, Reporter's Transcript, 99.

58. For the rarity of constitutional challenges, see Del McIntire, "Tangents," *ONE*, June 1962, 17. For the young attorney, see Levie, "Vice and Victim," 48. California adopted an exclusionary rule in 1955. *People v. Cahan*, 44 Cal. 2d 434 (1955).

59. *Mapp v. Ohio*, 367 U.S. 643, 654–55 (1961). For concerns about surveillance, see Deborah Nelson, *Pursuing Privacy in Cold War America* (New York: Columbia University Press, 2002), 9–11; Sarah E. Igo, *The Known Citizen: A History of Privacy in Modern America* (Cambridge, MA: Harvard University Press, 2018), 114–16; "The Miniature Tools of the Eavesdropper's Trade," *Life*, May 20, 1966, 41 (quoted). For the switch to protecting privacy, see *Katz v. United States*, 389 U.S. 347 (1967); *Smayda*, 352 F.2d 251; *Bielicki*, 57 Cal. 2d 602. Many state court decisions dealt not with the federal Fourth Amendment but comparable state-level provisions. For simplicity's sake, I use the term *Fourth Amendment* to encompass these analogous provisions.

60. For police objections, see William W. Turner, *The Police Establishment* (New York: G. P. Putnam's Sons, 1968), 239–43, 251. For concerns about street crime and the conservative backlash, see Johnson, *Street Justice*, 229–51; Tracy Maclin, "*Terry v. Ohio*'s Fourth Amendment Legacy: Black Men and Police Discretion," *Saint John's Law Review* 72 (1998): 1317–18; Michael W. Flamm, *Law and Order: Street Crime, Civil Unrest, and the Crisis of Liberalism in the 1960s* (New York: Columbia University Press, 2005).

61. *Bielicki*, 57 Cal. 2d at 604–5; *Britt*, 58 Cal. 2d at 470–71. For Wood's background, see Wood, "The Right to Be Free from Unreasonable Search and Seizure," and "The Homosexual and the Police," 21–23. For Wood's argument, see Petition for Writ of Prohibition in the District Court of Appeal, 22, in *Bielicki v. Superior Court of Los Angeles County*, 57 Cal. 2d 602 (1962) Case File, CSA (quoted). See also Memorandum of Points and Authorities in Support of Petition for Writ of Prohibition in the District Court of Appeal, 4, in *Britt v. Superior Court of Santa Clara County*, 58 Cal. 2d 469 (1962) Case File, CSA.

62. *Bielicki*, 57 Cal. 2d at 605–7, 609; *Britt*, 58 Cal. 2d at 472–73. For the court's liberal character, see chapter 1, n. 45, above, and the text at that point.

63. For effects in California, see *UCLA Law Review* Study, 714 and n. 176, 716 and n. 189. For the impact outside California, see *Bryant*, 287 Minn. at 206; *Kroehler*

v. Scott, 391 F. Supp. 1114 (E.D. Pa. 1975), Plaintiffs' Brief for Relief, 2, 5–6 (Pennsylvania); *Brown v. State,* 3 Md. App. 90, 94 (1968) (involving narcotics). For the Mansfield case, see *Poore,* 243 F. Supp. at 782–84 (quoted); McKee, "Evidentiary Problems," 72–73.

64. For police reactions, see *UCLA Law Review* Study, 687 n. 10, 714 and n. 176. For Walker, see *People v. Young,* 214 Cal. App. 2d 131 (1963), Reporter's Transcript on Appeal, 18.

65. *People v. Norton,* 209 Cal. App. 2d at 174–76; *People v. Norton,* 209 Cal. App. 2d 173 (1962), Reporter's Transcript on Appeal, 14, 4.

66. For police interpretations, see *UCLA Law Review* Study, 714, 715 n. 181; Hurlbut, "Presentation," 9.

67. For Pinellas County, see *State v. Coyle,* Circuit Court for the Sixth Judicial Circuit of the State of Florida in and for Pinellas County, No. 14,891, Order, February 12, 1965, 2–3. For Cooke, see *Maldonado,* Clerk's Transcript, 2–3; *People v. Maldonado,* 240 Cal. App. 2d 812 (1966), Appellant's Opening Brief, Appendix A, D (quoted). For additional cases, see *Hensel,* Reporter's Transcript, 15, 18–19.

68. *Coyle,* 181 So. 2d at 675; *Smayda,* 352 F.2d at 252, 254–57, 260; *Smayda,* Brief in Opposition, 2–5.

69. *Smayda,* 352 F.2d at 257. For other judges and legal commentators similarly balancing equities, see also *Kroehler,* 391 F. Supp. at 1119; *Bryant,* 287 Minn. at 211, 212–13; Roger M. Fritts and Favor R. Smith, "Deviate Sexual Behavior: The Desirability of Legislative Proscription," *Albany Law Review* 30 (1966): 294–95; "Clandestine Police Surveillance of Public Toilet Booth Held to Be Unreasonable Search," *Columbia Law Review* 63 (May 1964): 960–61.

70. *Bielicki,* 57 Cal. 2d at 609.

71. *Young,* 214 Cal. App. 2d at 135; Oliver, "Pioneer Black Judge Edwin Jefferson Dies," A1.

72. For citations to *Young,* see *Smayda,* 352 F.2d at 254–55; *Poore,* 243 F. Supp. at 784–85; *People v. Maldonado,* 240 Cal. App. 2d 812 (1966), Respondent's Brief, 19–20; *People v. Roberts,* 256 Cal. App. 2d 488 (1967), Respondent's Brief, 11–12; *Kroehler v. Scott,* 391 F. Supp. 1114 (E.D. Pa. 1975), Defendants' Brief in Opposition to Injunctive and Declaratory Relief, 13–15; *State v. Bryant,* 287 Minn. 205 (1970), Brief of Respondent, 6. For Coyle, see *Coyle,* Order, February 12, 1965, 2–3; *Coyle,* 181 So. 2d at 672, 674–75.

73. *Smayda,* Brief of the Appellee, 21–22.

74. For the California cases, see n. 30 above. In *Young* itself, the rare state case to yield a jail sentence, the judge ascribed that sentence to Young's probation violation on an unrelated felony. *Young,* Reporter's Transcript, 26–28. For Coyle, see *Coyle,* Order of Probation. For Creel, see *Liebenthal,* Record on Appeal, 95, 93.

75. *Strahan,* Reporter's Transcript, 97–98. For greater tolerance among judges than the general public, see also chapter 3, n. 54, above. For Judge MacBride's background, see "Biographical Summary" in Julie Shearer, "Oral History Interview with Hon. Thomas J. MacBride," April 21, May 14, 1987, ii, State Government Oral History Project, CSA.

76. For early examples of demonizing rhetoric, see *Bielicki v. Superior Court of Los Angeles County,* 57 Cal. 2d 602 (1962), Return and Answer and Additional Points and Authorities, 7–8; *Strahan,* Reporter's Transcript, 57. For insinuations about danger to children, see *Maldonado,* Reporter's Transcript, A-19, A-23, 211–12; *Buchanan,* District Clerk's File, 89–90, 103–105, 122–23. For prosecutors' briefs, see *Maldonado,*

Respondent's Brief, 19–20; *Roberts*, Respondent's Brief, 12; *Bryant*, Brief of Respondent, 5–7; *Kroehler*, Defendants' Brief in Opposition, 13–15, 23–24 (quoted).

77. *Townsend v. State of Ohio*, 366 F.2d 33 (6th Cir. 1966), Appellant's Brief, 12, 15–16.

78. For the ACLU's continuing ambivalence, see Stein, *Sexual Injustice*, 161–62. For the cases, see *People v. Roberts*, 256 Cal. App. 2d 488 (1967), Amicus Brief on Behalf of the ACLU, 8; *People v. Triggs*, 8 Cal. 3d 884 (1973), Amicus Brief on Behalf of the ACLU, 10. For academic critics similarly emphasizing the harmlessness of gay culture, see Fritts and Smith, "Deviate Sexual Behavior," 294.

79. *Roberts*, Respondent's Brief, 11–12; *People v. Triggs*, 8 Cal. 3d 884 (1973), Supplemental Points and Authorities in Response, 5–6.

80. For the new law, see *People v. Metcalf*, 22 Cal. App. 3d 20, 23 (1971). For growing outcries against the police, see chapter 6, n. 32, below. For rising gay activism, see D'Emilio, *Sexual Politics*, chap. 12; Lillian Faderman, *The Gay Revolution: The Story of the Struggle* (New York: Simon & Schuster, 2015), pt. 4. On media accounts, see chapter 6 below.

81. *People v. Triggs*, 8 Cal. 3d 884, 889–93, 894 n. 7 (1973).

CHAPTER SIX

1. Helmer, "New York's 'Middle-Class' Homosexuals," 86.

2. Doty, "Growth of Overt Homosexuality," 33 ("obtrusive"); Stearn, *Sixth Man*, 39 ("masculine-looking").

3. For histories identifying 1960s media coverage as a step toward public acceptance, see D'Emilio, *Sexual Politics*, 138–40; Boyd, *Wide Open Town*, 200–202; Faderman and Timmons, *Gay L.A.*, 136–37. For histories emphasizing the utility of sociological studies of homosexuality to liberation efforts, see chapter 4, n. 3, above.

4. For the Hays Code, see Eugene Archer, "Code Amended to Allow Films to Deal with Homosexuality," *NYT*, October 4, 1961, 41. For homophile publications, see Bob Whearley, "'Militant Minority' Poses Serious Problem for Society," *Denver Post*, February 14, 1965, 25; Meeker, "Behind the Mask of Respectability," 100–105; Boyd, *Wide Open Town*, 172; Stein, *Sexual Injustice*, 57. For contemporary books on homosexuality, see Edmund Bergler, *Homosexuality: Disease or Way of Life?* (New York: Hill & Wang, 1956); A. M. Krich, ed., *The Homosexuals: As Seen by Themselves and Thirty Authorities* (New York: Citadel, 1954); Rees and Usill, eds., *They Stand Apart*; Charles Berg and Clifford Allen, *The Problem of Homosexuality* (New York: Citadel, 1958); Alfred Gross, *Strangers in Our Midst: Problems of the Homosexual in American Society* (Washington, DC: Public Affairs Press, 1962); Donald James West, *The Other Man: A Study of the Social, Legal and Clinical Aspects of Homosexuality* (London: W. H. Allen, 1955); Douglas Plummer, *Queer People: The Truth about Homosexuals* (New York: Citadel, 1963). For city life, see Doty, "Growth of Overt Homosexuality," 33 (New York); Fonzi, "Furtive Fraternity," 20–23, 48–65; Stein, *City of Sisterly and Brotherly Loves*, 212 (Philadelphia); Welch, "The 'Gay' World," 68 (Chicago, San Francisco, Los Angeles); Whearley, "'Militant Minority,'" 25 (Denver). For homophile initiatives, see Welch, "The 'Gay' World," 71 (quoted); Helmer, "New York's 'Middle-Class' Homosexuals," 91–92; Lois Wille, "Chicago's Twilight World: The Homosexuals—a Growing Problem," *CDN*, June 20, 1966, 4; Faderman and Timmons, *Gay L.A.*, 120–21; Fonzi, "Furtive Fraternity," 53–54; Stein, *City of Sisterly and Brotherly Loves*, 207–11; Edward Alwood, *Straight News: Gays, Lesbians, and the News Media* (New York: Columbia University Press, 1996), 45–47.

5. Stearn, *Sixth Man*, 13; Sherry, *Gay Artists*, 105; Fonzi, "Furtive Fraternity," 20–23,

48–65; Stein, *City of Sisterly and Brotherly Loves*, 215–19; Helmer, "New York's 'Middle-Class' Homosexuals," 85–92. In February 1963, the conservative Los Angeles newspaper *Metropolitan Citizen-News* also ran a multipart series on homosexuals, derogatorily dubbed *sexual deviates*, though its focus was on decrying judicial leniency rather than surveying contemporary gay life. See chapter 3, n. 54, above.

6. Doty, "Growth of Overt Homosexuality," 33. See also Alwood, *Straight News*, 44–50; Kaiser, *Gay Metropolis*, 156–57.

7. For coverage of Doty's article, see "City Side," *Newsweek*, December 30, 1963, 42. For *Life*, see Welch, "The 'Gay' World"; Ernest Havemann, "Why?," *Life*, June 26, 1964, 76. For the reception in gay communities, see Alwood, *Straight News*, 49–50. For the Brooklynite, see Arthur E. Demeritt, "Letters to the Editors: Homosexuality," *Life*, July 17, 1964, 28. For positive reader responses, see generally "Letters to the Editor: Homosexuality," *Life*, July 17, 1964, 28.

8. For initial newspaper installments, see Jean M. White, "Those Others I: A Report on Homosexuality," *WP*, January 31, 1965, E1, E3; Whearley, "'Militant Minority,'" *Denver Post*, 25; Dick Hebert, "They Meet without Fear in 'Gay' Bars around the City," *Atlanta Constitution*, January 3, 1966, 1; Wille, "Chicago's Twilight World," 3. For periodicals, see "The Homosexual in America," *Time*, January 21, 1966, 40–41; Star, "The Sad 'Gay' Life," 30–33. For *Playboy*, see Hugh M. Hefner, "The Playboy Philosophy," *Playboy*, September 1964, 71–74, 161–68; "Playboy Forum," *Playboy*, October 1964, 63–64; "Playboy Forum," *Playboy*, February 1965, 38–39, 140; "Playboy Forum," *Playboy*, January 1967, 55–56; "Playboy Forum," *Playboy*, April 1967, 51–54, 170. For *Time*, see "Homosexual in America," 40.

9. "Homosexuality in America," *Life*, June 26, 1964, 66 ("furtive"); Doty, "Growth of Overt Homosexuality," 33 ("shadows"); Whearley, "'Militant Minority,'" 25 ("obvious"); Wille, "Chicago's Twilight World," 3 ("emerging"); White, "Those Others I," E1 ("more visible").

10. Jean M. White, "Those Others III: Homosexuals Are in All Kinds of Jobs," *WP*, February 2, 1965, A1; Helmer, "New York's 'Middle-Class' Homosexuals," 86; Irving Bieber, "Speaking Frankly on a Once Taboo Subject," *NYT Sunday Magazine*, August 23, 1964, 75. On gay men's inconspicuous appearance, see also Star, "The Sad 'Gay' Life," 31; Havemann, "Why?," 77; Wille, "Chicago's Twilight World," 4; Whearley, "'Militant Minority,'" 25; Henry J. Taylor, "Government Security Practices Are Strict but Very Necessary," *LAT*, October 30, 1964, A5; Nate Haseltine, "One City's Homosexuals Called Disease Carriers," *WP*, September 6, 1962, A3; Stearn, *Sixth Man*, 39.

11. Chapter 1, n. 32, above (the Chicagoan); Doty, "Growth of Overt Homosexuality," 33; Playboy Forum," *Playboy*, September 1967, 81, 184; Havemann, "Why?," 77. For other remarks on misguided public confidence, see Alfred A. Gross, foreword to Stearn, *Sixth Man*, 6; White, "Those Others III," A1; Taylor, "Government Security Practices," A5; Star, "The Sad 'Gay' Life," 31.

12. For the threat to children, see "Homosexuality in America," 66 (quoted); Helmer, "New York's 'Middle-Class' Homosexuals," 88; Whearley, "'Militant Minority,'" 25; Star, "The Sad 'Gay' Life," 32. For public health, see Whearley, "'Militant Minority,'" 25; White, "Those Others III," A12; Stearn, *Sixth Man*, 15. For rhetoric echoing national security concerns, see Fonzi, "Furtive Fraternity," 21.

13. Doty, "Growth of Overt Homosexuality," 33; Welch, "The 'Gay' World," 68; "Homosexual in America," 40. For additional discussion, see White, "Those Others I," E1. On the idealization of domesticity during the Cold War, see May, *Homeward Bound*.

14. Reinhardt, *Sex Perversions and Sex Crimes*, 47; White, "Those Others III," A1; Doty, "Growth of Overt Homosexuality," 33; Advertisement in *Life*, June 26, 1964, 6. For another example, see Lois Wille, "Homosexual Clergyman Tells of His Bizarre Double Life," *CDN*, June 21, 1966, 3.

15. "Homosexuality in America," 66. For similar rhetoric, see Whearley, "'Militant Minority,'" 26; Gross, foreword, 6.

16. For the high status of medical professionals, see chapter 2, n. 15, above, and the text at that point. For media references, see Doty, "Growth of Overt Homosexuality," 33; Helmer, "New York's 'Middle-Class' Homosexuals," 89; Jean M. White, "Those Others II: Scientists Disagree on Basic Nature of Homosexuality, Chance of Cure," *WP*, February 1, 1965, A1, A16; Havemann, "Why?," 76. For other examples, see Lois Wille, "Is Homosexuality a Sickness? The Deviates Maintain It Isn't," *CDN*, June 23, 1966, 4; Dick Hebert, "They're Insecure, Unhappy and Emotionally Immature," *Atlanta Constitution*, January 7, 1966, 1, 9; Star, "The Sad 'Gay' Life," 31.

17. Stearn, *Sixth Man*, 16. See also Helmer, "New York's 'Middle-Class' Homosexuals," 85.

18. For academic studies of gay communities, see chapter 4, n. 1, above. For *Newsweek*, see "City Side," 42. For journalistic references to academics, see "Homosexual in America," 40; Stearn, *Sixth Man*, 16; Fonzi, "Furtive Fraternity," 21. For references to Hooker, see Helmer, "New York's 'Middle-Class' Homosexuals," 89–90; Havemann, "Why?," 78–79; White, "Those Others II," A16; "Homosexual in America," 40; Star, "The Sad 'Gay' Life," 31.

19. Alwood, *Straight News*, 47–48, 51–52.

20. For discussions of homosexuality-related cases within broader reporting on sexual predation, see Ralph H. Major Jr., "New Moral Menace to Our Youth," *Coronet*, September 1950, 101–8; Whitman, "Terror in Our Cities," 14–15; J. Edgar Hoover, "How Safe Is Your Youngster?" *American Magazine*, March 1955, 101–2. For local coverage of police operations, see chapter 5, nn. 25 and 32, above.

21. Stearn, *Sixth Man*, 147, 146, 152; Bob Whearley, "Clientele Feels Safer in 'Gay Bars,'" *Denver Post*, February 16, 1965, 15; Elliott, "Control of Homosexual Activity by Philadelphia Police," 3 ("parlance"). Several phrases in Fonzi's piece seem lifted directly from Elliott. Fonzi, "Furtive Fraternity," 23, 50; Elliott, "Control of Homosexual Activity by Philadelphia Police," 5, 7–8. For reporters consulting policemen for insight, see also Lois Wille, "Police Watch Homosexuals' Hangouts Here," *CDN*, June 22, 1966, 1, 4.

22. For gay men's neighborhoods, see Stearn, *Sixth Man*, 51–53; Doty, "Growth of Overt Homosexuality," 33; Fonzi, "Furtive Fraternity," 23; Welch, "The 'Gay' World," 68; Whearley, "'Militant Minority,'" 25. On Fire Island, see Helmer, "New York's 'Middle-Class' Homosexuals," 86; Doty, "Growth of Overt Homosexuality," 33; Stearn, *Sixth Man*, 65–75. For professions, see Welch, "The 'Gay' World," 68; Helmer, "New York's 'Middle-Class' Homosexuals," 90; White, "Those Others III," A1, A12; Fonzi, "Furtive Fraternity," 21. For slang, see Helmer, "New York's 'Middle-Class' Homosexuals," 85–88; Doty, "Growth of Overt Homosexuality," 33; Welch, "The 'Gay' World," 68; White, "Those Others I"; "Homosexual in America," 40–41; Star, "The Sad 'Gay' Life," 31–33.

23. For surveys of bars, see Hebert, "They Meet without Fear," 1, 10; Fonzi, "Furtive Fraternity," 20, 52–53; Helmer, "New York's 'Middle-Class' Homosexuals," 86; Welch, "The 'Gay' World," 68; Wille, "Chicago's Twilight World," 3–4; "Homosexual in

America," 40; Whearley, "Clientele Feels Safer," 15. For *Time*, see "Homosexual in America," 40–41. For scientized depictions, see Welch, "The 'Gay' World," 68; Fonzi, "Furtive Fraternity," 21.

24. For attempts to disclaim the centrality of bars, see Fonzi, "Furtive Fraternity," 53; Helmer, "New York's 'Middle-Class' Homosexuals," 85. See also Bob Whearley, "Minority on Increase Affects All Citizens," *Denver Post*, February 19, 1963, 12. For reports emphasizing bar pickup culture, see Doty, "Growth of Overt Homosexuality," 33; White, "Those Others III," A12; Welch, "The 'Gay' World," 68, 71; Hebert, "They Meet without Fear," 10; Dick Hebert, "2 in a 'Straight' Society Lead a Quiet Double Life," *Atlanta Constitution*, January 6, 1966, 15 (quoted).

25. Scholars have suggested that journalists' performatively scientific tone camouflaged their underlying antipathy to homosexuality or that their reductive focus on the body betrayed the limits of their supposedly scientific project. Mark Caldwell, *New York Night: The Mystique and Its History* (New York: Scribner, 2005), 317; Edelman, *Homographesis*, 155. I argue that these features were neither a smokescreen nor an internal contradiction but themselves central to the media's project of reasserting some sense of mastery over gay life.

26. Helmer, "New York's 'Middle-Class' Homosexuals," 86 ("dashing"). See also Hoffman, *The Gay World*, 55. For surveys of common gay fashions, see Doty, "Growth of Overt Homosexuality," 33; Welch, "The 'Gay' World," 68–74; Fonzi, "Furtive Fraternity," 21; Helmer, "New York's 'Middle-Class' Homosexuals," 86.

27. White, "Those Others I," E1; Hebert, "They Meet without Fear," 10; Pace, "Garelik Urges Public to Report," 60. The *Wall Street Journal* summarized the NYCLU's claim as charging the city with sending "effeminately dressed New York police" to gay bars. Norman Sklarewitz, "Caught in the Act: Police Don Disguises to Capture Criminals," *Wall Street Journal*, April 18, 1967, 1. For other reporters invoking common fashions, see Whearley, "'Militant Minority,'" 25; Wille, "Chicago's Twilight World," 3–4.

28. For broader discussions of media coverage in the 1960s as serving to elevate the visibility and familiarity of urban gay life, see Edelman, *Homographesis*, 152; Sherry, *Gay Artists*, 108, 118.

29. Doty, "Growth of Overt Homosexuality," 33; Lois Wille, "Police Watch Homosexuals' Hangouts," 4. For an additional example, see Dick Hebert, "Detectives Watch Hangouts and Curb Some of Activity," *Atlanta Constitution*, January 4, 1966, 1, 6.

30. Welch, "The 'Gay' World," 72–73.

31. Wille, "Police Watch Homosexuals' Hangouts," 4. See also Stewart-Winter, *Queer Clout*, 35–36. For the acknowledgment of civil libertarian critiques, see White, "Those Others IV," A19.

32. On the early history of police violence, see Johnson, *Street Justice*, chaps. 1–4. For growing criticism at midcentury, see "Civil Rights Commission Lashes at Police Brutality," *New York Herald Tribune*, November 17, 1961, 10; Leonard M. Moore, *Black Rage in New Orleans: Police Brutality and African American Activism from World War II to Hurricane Katrina* (Baton Rouge: Louisiana State University Press, 2010); Simon Balto, "'Occupied Territory': Police Repression and Black Resistance in Postwar Milwaukee, 1950–1968," *Journal of African American History* 98 (Spring 2013): 241–47; Johnson, *Street Justice*, 248–49, 255–66; Heather Ann Thompson, *Whose Detroit? Politics, Labor, and Race in a Modern American City* (Ithaca, NY: Cornell University Press, 2001), 90–94. For police resentment, see Brooks, "'New York's Finest,'" 30; Herbert L. Packer, "The Courts, the Police, and the Rest of Us," *Journal of Criminal*

Law and Criminology 57 (September 1966): 240; "Support for Police Seen at Low Point," *NYT*, February 4, 1966, 38.

33. For concerns with fascism, see Christopher Vials, *Haunted by Hitler: Liberals, the Left, and the Fight against Fascism in the United States* (Amherst: University of Massachusetts Press, 2014); Seo, "Democratic Policing Before the Due Process Revolution." On wiretaps, see Don Whitehead, "Wiretapping: Is It Menace or Safeguard for Liberties," *Austin Statesman*, February 11, 1954, B6; Louis B. Schwartz, "On Current Proposals to Legalize Wire Tapping," *University of Pennsylvania Law Review* 103 (November 1954): 157–67; Victor Riesel, "Civil Liberties Being Infringed," *LAT*, July 15, 1964, A5. On critiques extending to clandestine surveillance, see *Osborn v. United States*, 385 U.S. 323, 342 (1966) (Douglas, J., dissenting). See also Fritts and Smith, "Deviate Sexual Behavior," 295–97. For concerns about surveillance generally, see chapter 5, n. 59, above.

34. For media criticism of entrapment, see "Creating Crime," *WP*, September 18, 1960, E4 ("ugly business"); "Vice Squad Having Rough Time; Court Upholds Entrapment Charge," *HC*, July 17, 1958, 2; "Supt. Wilson Orders End of Entrapment," *CDT*, September 5, 1962, 16. For invocations, see "Snoopers for Hire," *Cleveland Call and Post*, June 16, 1962, 2C ("Communist"); "Candidate Blasts State Police for Use of Unmarked Cruisers," *WP*, October 6, 1953, 9 ("Gestapo"); "Doubtful, Maybe, but Not Entrapment," *HC*, January 23, 1962, 12 ("Gestapo"). For Hartford, see "Pinching 'Cute' Policemen Is Legal, If Not Very Nice," *HC*, February 28, 1960, 9B2 (quoted).

35. For coverage of rebukes, see Morrey Dunie, "Court Warns Police on Methods of Getting Evidence in Morals Cases," *WP*, September 28, 1956, 32; "Morals Detective Rebuked, Assault Conviction Reversed," *WP*, July 15, 1953, 21; chapter 3, nn. 44 and 58, above. For criticism in the press, see "Letters to the Editor: Entrapment," *WP*, November 26, 1948, 12; "Morality and Crime," *WP*, August 28, 1960, E4.

36. "Letters to the Editors," *Life*, July 17, 1964, 28. For similar criticism, see James A. Wechsler, "Entrapment Inc.," *New York Post*, March 7, 1966, 26; "Justice for Homosexuals," *The Nation*, November 8, 1965, 318–19; Carol Jameson, "Law, Human Sexuality Topic for Speaker at YC Workshop," *Yuba City Appeal-Democrat*, April 23, 1969, 5; Scott Thurber, "The City's Homosexuals—and Police," *San Francisco Chronicle*, September 25, 1965, 1, 4; Sanford H. Kadish, "The Crisis of Overcriminalization," *American Criminal Law Quarterly* 7 (1968): 17–34, 22; Schur, *Crimes without Victims*, 82. For the *Post*'s disagreement, see Editorial Board, "Homosexuals in Denver," *Denver Post*, February 25, 1965, 18.

37. "The Law and the Homosexual Problem," *Life*, June 11, 1965, 4. For the ACLU's complex history with gay rights litigation, see chapters 3–5 above. On the Council on Religion and the Homosexual, see Boyd, *Wide Open Town*, 231–36; Thurber, "The City's Homosexuals," 4 (quoting *Brief of Injustices*). For similar critiques, see also Kadish, "The Crisis of Overcriminalization," 21–22; Gene Blake, "Easing of Law against Homosexual Act Urged," *LAT*, April 28, 1966, 21; Herbert L. Packer, *The Limits of the Criminal Sanction* (Stanford, CA: Stanford University Press, 1968), 305–6.

38. Saul Bellow, *Herzog* (New York: Viking, 1964), 227. See also Allen Drury, *Advise and Consent* (New York: Doubleday, 1959). For similar concerns in individual editorials, see "Letters to the Editor: Entrapment," 12.

39. Brooks, "'New York's Finest,'" 31; Robert H. Williams, "Sex, Tallahassee," *New Republic*, May 23, 1964, 5; Alexander M. Bickel, "Homosexuality as Crime in North Carolina," *New Republic*, December 12, 1964, 5–6; James Ridgeway, "Snooping in the

Park," *New Republic,* January 16, 1965, 9–10, and "The Cops & the Kids," *New Republic,* September 7, 1968, 11–14; Ronald Goldfarb, "The High Price of Civil Rights Protest," *New Republic,* October 16, 1965, 11–12; Robert A. Levin, "Gang-Busting in Chicago," *New Republic,* June 1, 1968, 16–18. Civil liberties groups like the NYCLU similarly intermixed their criticisms. Eric Pace, "Times Sq. Cleanup Brings a Protest," *NYT,* March 18, 1966, 42.

40. Lenn, "Special Cops for 'Gay' Bars," 3; H.T.K., "Letter to the Editor," *News-Call Bulletin,* reprinted in *Mattachine Review,* November 1961, 6; "Playboy Forum," *Playboy,* August 1966, 145.

41. Thurber, "The City's Homosexuals," 4 (quoting Council on Religion and the Homosexual, *Brief of Injustices*).

42. *Homosexuality and Citizenship in Florida,* preface. For public support, see Braukman, *Communists and Perverts,* 176–77. For the history of the committee generally, see chapter 4, n. 24, above.

43. *Homosexuality and Citizenship in Florida,* "Why Be Concerned?," and "Glossary of Homosexual Terms and Deviate Acts." The illustrations are unpaginated. For the Guild Press republication, see Thomas Waugh, *Hard to Imagine: Gay Male Eroticism in Photography and Film from Their Beginnings to Stonewall* (New York: Columbia University Press, 1996), 375.

44. "Uproar Follows Report on Deviates in Florida," *HC,* March 19, 1964, 20; "Still Another List," *The Nation,* June 22, 1964, 615; Williams, "Sex, Tallahassee," 5. For additional criticism, see Welch, "The 'Gay' World," 74. For aspersions against politicians leading the Lavender Scare, see Johnson, *Lavender Scare,* 106–7. For the Johns Committee's disintegration, see Braukman, *Communists and Perverts,* 191.

45. Wechsler, "Entrapment Inc." (March 7, 1966), 26.

46. Stearn, *Sixth Man,* 168; Hebert, "Detectives Watch Hangouts," 1; "Playboy Forum," *Playboy,* August 1966, 144–45; "Playboy Forum," January 1967, 56.

47. Rumaker, *Robert Duncan in San Francisco,* 16; "Tex or JR," interview by Len Evans, 24; Stearn, *Sixth Man,* 167.

48. Cory, *Homosexual in America,* 80; Doty, "Growth of Overt Homosexuality," 33; Stearn, *Sixth Man,* 55.

49. George W. Henry and Alfred A. Gross, "Social Factors in the Case Histories of One Hundred Under-Privileged Homosexuals," *Mental Hygiene* 22 (October 1938): 608; Abram Kardiner, *Sex and Morality* (Indianapolis: Bobbs-Merrill, 1954), 161; Bieber, "Speaking Frankly," 75; Abrahamsen, *Crime and the Human Mind,* 119; David Abrahamsen, *Psychology of Crime* (New York: Columbia University Press, 1960), 169.

50. For psychiatrists' efforts to cement their professional status in the 1950s, see chapter 2 above.

51. "Ann Landers Talks to Teen-Agers: Why Do Some People Prefer Their Own Sex?" *Detroit Free Press,* January 19, 1964, 29; Stearn, *Sixth Man,* 149–50.

52. Wille, "Police Watch Homosexuals' Hangouts," 4; Webster Schott, "Civil Rights and the Homosexual: A 4-Million Minority Asks for Equal Rights," *NYT,* November 12, 1967, 47; Fonzi, "Furtive Fraternity," 63; "Playboy Forum," reprinted in *Florida League for Good Government Viewpoint,* September 1967, 4, MSP. For analogous concerns about squalid vice squad tactics among more academic circles, see Sklansky, "'One Train May Hide Another,'" 915–16.

53. Herb Selwyn, interview by John D'Emilio; Max K. Hurlbut to author, October 12, 2017, item 14; Stearn, *Sixth Man,* 167. For additional examples of policemen's dis-

comfort at being placed in a "compromising position" by their antihomosexual assignments, see Agee, *Streets of San Francisco*, 77–78.

54. White, "Those Others IV," A19; Wille, "Police Watch Homosexuals' Hangouts," 4.

55. Francis X. Clines, "L.I. Homosexuals to Get Legal Aid," *NYT*, July 24, 1967, 19; Pace, "Garelik Urges Public to Report," 60; "Playboy Forum," *Playboy*, December 1967, 84.

56. For the LAPD's policies, see Hurlbut, "Presentation," 11–12; *UCLA Law Review* Study, 694 and n. 53, 704 n. 119 (both quoting). For the contemporary study, see *UCLA Law Review* Study, 706 n. 127 ("society").

57. For the LAPD's reactions, see Max K. Hurlbut to author, October 12, 2017, items 43, 45–47; Hurlbut, *Vagabond Policeman*, 86–87. For denials of the pamphlet, see "Playboy Forum," *Playboy*, February 1965, 37–38.

58. "Roy Blick to Retire, Recommends Moyer"; White, "Those Others IV," A19; "Morals in the Parks."

59. For the NYCLU, see Pace, "Garelik Urges Public to Report," 60; chapter 4, nn. 62–65, above. For the *Post*'s growing support, see Alwood, *Straight News*, 58–59; Wechsler, "Entrapment Inc." (March 7, 1966), 26.

60. Pace, "Garelik Urges Public to Report," 60. The announcement was widely reported. "Chief Asks Reports on Trapping," *Arizona Daily Star*, April 3, 1966, 30; "NY Police Official Decries Homosexual 'Entrapment,'" *Fresno Bee Republican*, April 5, 1966, 3; "Police Aide Asks Report of Homosexual Entrapment," *Dayton Daily News*, April 3, 1966, 46.

61. For the ensuing criticism, see Wechsler, "Entrapment Inc.," *New York Post*, April 5, 1966; Eric Pace, "Policemen Forbidden to Entrap Homosexuals to Make Arrests," *NYT*, May 11, 1966, 36. For Leary's capitulation, see Pace, "Policemen Forbidden to Entrap Homosexuals," 36; "Police Policies and Sex Deviates," *HC*, May 27, 1966, 20; Gregory Battock, "Police as Decoys," *NYT*, January 8, 1968, 38. For the effectiveness of the change, see Sklarewitz, "Caught in the Act," 1; "The Problem Society Won't Discuss," *Detroit Free Press*, October 5, 1969, 1969, 23; D'Emilio, *Sexual Politics*, 207.

62. Deutsch, *Trouble with Cops*, 86 ("rats"). For continuing prosecutions in New York, see Harold Bramson to Mimi Bowling, December 7, 1994, 1; Schott, "Civil Rights and the Homosexual," 47. For continuing enticement in California, see Don Jackson, "How the Vice Squad Works," *Los Angeles Free Press*, August 27, 1971, 6; "S.I.R. Sues to Halt Police East Bay 'Decoy' Squads," *Vector*, August 1969, 8.

63. White, "Those Others IV," A19.

64. For criticism of the Kinsey investigators, see Cuordileone, *Manhood and American Political Culture*, 83–85; Jones, *Alfred C. Kinsey*, 576.

65. Niles, *Strange Brother*, 55.

EPILOGUE

1. *One Eleven Wines*, 50 N.J. at 340; "Three Taverns Challenge ABC Homosexual Rulings," 1, 63; chapter 2 above.

2. Charles K. Sergis, "State Rated Toughest in Liquor Control," *Hackensack Record*, November 25, 1966, 18; *One Eleven Wines*, 50 N.J. at 334–36, 342; *Becker v. New York State Liquor Auth.*, 21 N.Y.2d 289, 292 (1967).

3. For New York and DC, see chapter 6 above. For San Francisco, see Agee, *Streets of San Francisco*, 193–97, 104–7; Boyd, *Wide Open Town*, 233–36; D'Emilio, *Sexual Politics*,

202–3. For Los Angeles, see Faderman and Timmons, *Gay L.A.*, 147–48, 156–65; D'Emilio, *Sexual Politics*, 149, 227; Self, *All in the Family*, 89–90. For judicial limits on surveillance, see, in addition to chapter 5 above, *Buchanan v. State*, 471 S.W.2d 401, 404 (Tex. Crim. App. 1971); *Bryant*, 287 Minn. at 211; *Brown*, 3 Md. App. at 93–94; *Kroehler*, 391 F. Supp. at 1117; *State v. Jarrell*, 24 N.C. App. 610, 613 (1975).

4. For harassment, see D'Emilio, *Sexual Politics*, 200–201; Stein, *City of Sisterly and Brotherly Loves*, 99–100. For plainclothes arrests, see "Vice Hunting in Los Angeles," 1, 20; "S.I.R. Sues to Halt Police East Boy 'Decoy' Squads," 8; "Coming to Terms," *Time*, October 24, 1969, 88. For surveillance, see *People v. Dezek*, 107 Mich. App. 78, 85 (1981). Departments still intermittently engage in undercover stings in public bathrooms and raid gay bars for legal violations, though on a dramatically lesser scale. Mogul, Ritchie, and Whitlock, *Queer (In)Justice*, 54–56; J. Kelly Strader and Lindsey Hay, "Lewd Stings: Extending *Lawrence v. Texas* to Discriminatory Enforcement," *American Criminal Law Review* 56 (Spring 2009): 465–510.

5. On the Stonewall riots, see Martin Duberman, *Stonewall: The Definitive Story of the LGBTQ Rights Uprising that Changed America* (New York: Dutton, 1993); Kaiser, *Gay Metropolis*, 198–201; Larry Gross, *Up from Invisibility: Lesbians, Gay Men, and the Media in America* (New York: Columbia University Press, 2001), chap. 3. On the redistribution of policing, see Timothy Stewart-Winter, "Queer Law and Order: Sex, Criminality, and Policing in the Late Twentieth-Century United States," *Journal of American History* 102 (2015): 61–72; Christina B. Hanhardt, *Safe Spaces: Gay Neighborhood History and the Politics of Violence* (Durham, NC: Duke University Press, 2013).

6. On activists' critiques, see chapter 6 above; Jared Leighton, "'All of Us Are Unapprehended Felons': Gay Liberation, the Black Panther Party, and Intercommunal Efforts against Police Brutality in the Bay Area," *Journal of Social History* 52 (Spring 2019): 860–85; Stewart-Winter, *Queer Clout*. On privacy, see Minto, "Penumbras of Privacy"; Sklansky, "'One Train May Hide Another,'" 914–15. On the counterculture, see Self, *All in the Family*, 87.

7. Kathleen E. Hull, "The Role of Social Science Expertise in Same-Sex Marriage Litigation," *Annual Review of Law and Social Science* 13 (2017), 474–75, 477–85.

8. On the contingencies of expertise, see introduction, n. 20, above.

9. For a review of controversies over police expertise, see Lvovsky, "Judicial Presumption," 1997–98 and nn. 3–8. For sensitivities to relative competence, see Andrew E. Taslitz, "Stories of Fourth Amendment Disrespect: From Elian to the Internment," *Fordham Law Review* 70 (2002): 2271; Craig S. Lerner, "Reasonable Suspicion and Mere Hunches," *Vanderbilt Law Review* 59 (2006): 472–73; Debra Livingston, "Police Discretion and the Quality of Life in Public Places," *Columbia Law Review* 97 (1997): 594–95. For political considerations, see Maclin, "*Terry v. Ohio*'s Fourth Amendment Legacy," 1317–18; Albert W. Alschuler, "Bright Line Fever and the Fourth Amendment," *University of Pittsburgh Law Review* 45 (1984): 233–34; Stephanos Bibas, "Transparency and Participation in Criminal Procedure," *New York University Law Review* 81 (2006): 912–13.

INDEX

Page numbers in italics refer to illustrations.

CPSIA information can be obtained
at www.ICGtesting.com
Printed in the USA
LVHW111959130722
723217LV00005B/173